CAXTON
SPANISH
DICTIONARY

CAXTON EDITIONS

First published in Great Britain by
CAXTON EDITIONS
an imprint of
the Caxton Publishing Group
20 Bloomsbury Street
London
WCIB 3JH
This edition copyright
©1999 CAXTON EDITIONS
Reprint 2002
Prepared and designed
for Caxton Editions by
Superlaunch Limited
PO Box 207
Abingdon
Oxfordshire OX13 6TA

Consultant editor M. Dolores Lledó Barrena

ISBN 1 84067 066 5

A copy of the CIP data for this book is available from
the British Library upon request

Printed and bound in India

ESPAÑOL INGLÉS
SPANISH ENGLISH

Abbreviations

abbr	abbreviation
acc	accusative
adj	adjective
adv	adverb
art	article
aux	auxiliary
conj	conjunction
def	definite
dem	demonstrative
etc	et cetera
excl	exclamation
f	feminine
fam	familiar
fig	figurative
fpl	feminine plural
gr	grammar
indef	indefinite
interj	interjection
inv	invariable
m	masculine
mpl	masculine plural
n	noun
npl	noun plural
num	number
pej	pejorative
pl	plural
poss	possessive
prep	preposition
pron	pronoun
sl	slang
vi	intransitive verb
vr	reflexive verb
vt	transitive verb
vulg	vulgar

A

a *prep* to, in, at, according to, on, by, for, of.
abadía *f* abbey.
abajo *adv* under, underneath, below.
abalanzarse *vr* to rush forward.
abandonado(a) *adj* abandoned, derelict, neglected.
abandonar *vt* to abandon, to leave; * ~se a *vr* to give oneself up to.
abarrotado(a) *adj* packed.
abarrotar *vt* to tie down, (marine) to stow.
abastecer *vt* to supply.
abatido(a) *adj* dejected, depressed, low-spirited, abject.
abatimiento *m* low spirits *pl*, depression.
abatir *vt* to shoot down, to humble.
abdicar *vt* to abdicate.
abdomen *m* abdomen.
abdominal *adj* abdominal.
abecedario *m* alphabet, spelling book, primer.
abeja *f* bee.
aberración *f* aberration.
abertura *f* aperture, chink, opening.
abeto *m* fir tree.
abierto(a) *adj* open, sincere, frank.
abismal *adj* abysmal.
abismo *m* abyss, gulf, hell.
ablandar *vt, vi* to soften.
abnegado(a) *adj* selfless.
abogacía *f* legal profession.
abogado(a) *m(f)* lawyer, barrister.
abogar *vi* to intercede; ~ por to advocate.
abolir *vt* to abolish.
abollar *vt* to dent.
abonado(a) *adj* paid-up; * *m(f)* subscriber.

abonar *vt* to settle, to fertilise.
abono *m* payment, subscription, dung, manure.
aborrecer *vt* to hate, abhor.
abortar *vi* to miscarry, to have an abortion.
aborto *m* abortion, monster.
abotonar *vt* to button.
abovedado(a) *adj* vaulted.
abrasar *vt* to burn, to parch; * ~se *vr* to burn oneself.
abrazar *vt* to embrace, to surround, to contain.
abrazo *m* embrace, hug.
abrebotellas *m invar* bottle opener.
abrelatas *m invar* can opener.
abreviar *vt* to abridge, to be quick.
abridor *m* opener.
abrigar *vt* to shelter, to protect.
abrigo *m* coat, shelter, protection.
abril *m* April.
abrillantar *vt* to polish.
abrir *vt* to open, to unlock.
abrochar *vt* to button, to do up.
abrumar *vt* to overwhelm.
absolución *f* forgiveness, absolution.
absoluto(a) *adj* absolute.
absorber *vt* to absorb.
absorción *f* absorption, takeover.
absorto *adj* engrossed.
abstemio *adj* teetotal.
abstracción *f* abstraction.
abstracto(a) *adj* abstract.
abstraer *vt* to abstract; * ~se *vr* to be absorbed.
absuelto(a) *adj* absolved.
absurdo(a) *adj* absurd.
abuela *f* grandmother.
abuelo *m* grandfather.
abulia *f* lack of willpower.
abultado(a) *adj* bulky, large, massive.
abultar *vt* to increase,

enlarge; * *vi* to be bulky.

abundante *adj* abundant, copious.

aburrido(a) *adj* boring, bored.

aburrir *vt* to bore, weary.

abusar *vt* to abuse.

acá *adv* here.

acabado(a) *adj* finished, perfect, accomplished, old.

acabar *vt* to finish, to complete, to achieve; * ~se *vr* to finish, expire.

academia *f* academy, literary society.

acaecer *vi* to happen.

acallar *vt* to quiet, to hush, to soften, to appease.

acalorado(a) *adj* heated.

acampar *vt* (military) to encamp.

acanalado(a) *adj* grooved, fluted.

acaparar *vt* to monopolise, to hoard.

acariciar *vt* to fondle, caress.

acarrear *vt* to transport, to occasion.

acaso *m* chance; * *adv* perhaps.

acatarrarse *vr* to catch cold.

acceder *vi* to agree; ~ a to have access to.

accesible *adj* attainable, accessible.

acceso *m* access, fit.

accidentado(a) *adj* uneven, hilly, eventful.

accidental *adj* accidental, casual.

accidente *m* accident.

acción *f* action, operation, share.

accionar *vt* to work.

accionista *m* or *f* shareholder.

acebo *m* (botany) holly.

acechar *vt* to lie in ambush for, to spy on.

aceite *m* oil.

aceituna *f* olive.

aceitunado(a) *adj* olive-green.

aceleración *f* acceleration.

aceleradamente *adv* swiftly, hastily.

acelerar *vt* to accelerate, to hurry.

acento *m* accent.

aceptar *vt* to accept, to admit.

acera *f* pavement.

acerca *prep* about, relating to.

acercar *vt* to move nearer; * ~se a *vr* to approach.

acero *m* steel.

acertar *vt* to hit, to guess right.

acertijo *m* riddle.

achacar *vt* to impute.

achaque *m* ailment, excuse, subject, matter.

achicar *vt* to diminish, to humiliate, to bale (out).

achicharrar *vt* to scorch, to overheat.

aciago(a) *adj* unlucky, ominous.

ácido *m* acid; * ~a *adj* acid, sour.

acierto *m* success, solution, dexterity.

aclamar *vt* to applaud, to acclaim.

aclaración *f* clarification.

aclarar *vt* to clear, to brighten, to explain, to clarify.

acobardar *vt* to intimidate.

acodarse *vr* to lean.

acoger *vt* to receive, to welcome, to harbour; * ~se *vr* to take refuge.

acogida *f* reception, asylum.

acometida *f* attack, assault.

acomodar *vt* to accommodate, to arrange; * ~se *vr* to comply.

acompañar *vt* to accompany, to join, (music) to accompany.

acompasado(a) *adj* measured, well-proportioned.

acondicionar *vt* to arrange, to condition.

acongojar *vt* to distress.

aconsejar *vt* to advise; * ~se *vr* to take advice.

acontecer *vi* to happen.

acontecimiento *m* event,

incident.

acoplar *vt* to couple, to fit, to connect.

acordar *vt* to agree, to remind; * ~se *vr* to agree, to remember.

acorde *adj* harmonious; * *m* chord.

acordeón *m* accordion.

acorralar *vt* to round up, to intimidate.

acortar *vt* to abridge, to shorten; * ~se *vr* to become shorter.

acostar *vt* to put to bed, to lay down; * ~se *vr* to go to bed, to lie down.

acostumbrar *vi* to be in the habit; * ~ a *vt* to accustom, to get someone used to something; * ~se (a) *vr* to get used to.

acotar *vt* to set bounds to, to annotate.

ácrata *m* or *f* anarchist.

acreditar *vt* to guarantee, to assure, to authorise.

acreedor(a) *m(f)* creditor.

acribillar *vt* to riddle with bullets, to molest, torment.

acta *f* act; ~s *fpl* records *pl*.

actitud *f* attitude, posture.

actividad *f* activity, liveliness.

activo(a) *adj* active, diligent.

acto *m* act, action, act of a play, ceremony.

actor *m* actor.

actriz *f* actress.

actuación *f* action, behaviour, proceedings *pl*.

actual *adj* actual, present.

actualizar *vt* to update.

actuar *vt* to work, to operate; * *vi* to work, to act.

acuarela *f* watercolour.

acudir *vi* to go to, to attend, to assist.

acuerdo *m* agreement: — de ~ OK.

acumular *vt* to accumulate, to

collect.

acurrucarse *vr* to squat, to huddle up.

adelantado(a) *adj* advanced, fast.

adelantar *vt*, *vi* to advance, to accelerate, to pass.

adelante *adv* forward(s): — ¡~! *excl* come in!

adelanto *m* advance, progress, improvement.

adelgazar *vt* to make thin or slender.

además *adv* moreover, besides; ~ de besides.

adentro *adv* in, inside.

aderezar *vt* to dress, to adorn, to prepare, to season.

adeudar *vt* to owe; * ~se *vr* to run into debt.

adherir *vi*; ~ a to adhere to, to espouse.

adiestrar *vt* to guide, to teach, instruct.

adiós *excl* goodbye.

adivinar *vt* to foretell, to guess.

admirar *vt* to admire, to surprise; * ~se *vr* to be surprised.

admitir *vt* to admit, to let in, to concede, to permit.

admonición *f* warning.

adobar *vt* to dress, to season.

adobe *m* adobe, sun-dried brick.

adobo *m* dressing, pickle sauce.

adolecer *vi* to suffer from.

adolescencia *f* adolescence.

adónde *adv* where.

adoptar *vt* to adopt.

adoquín *m* paving stone.

adorar *vt* to adore, to love.

adormecer *vt* to put to sleep; * ~se *vr* to fall asleep.

adornar *vt* to embellish, to adorn.

adosado(a) *adj* semi-detached.

adquirir *vt* to acquire.

adrede *adv* on purpose.

aduana *f* customs *pl*.

adueñarse *vr*; ~ de to take

possession of.

adular *vt* to flatter.

adulterio *m* adultery.

adulto(a) *adj*, *m(f)* adult, grown-up.

advenedizo *m* upstart.

advenimiento *m* arrival, accession.

adversidad *f* adversity, setback.

advertencia *f* warning, preface, foreword.

advertir *vt* to notice, to warn.

aerodeslizador *m* hovercraft.

aeronave *f* spaceship.

aeropuerto *m* airport.

afán *m* hard work, desire.

afanar *vt* to harass, (*sl*) to pinch; ~se *vr* to strive.

afear *vt* to deform, to misshape.

afección *f* affection, fondness, attachment, disease.

afectar *vt* to affect, feign.

afectuoso(a) *adj* affectionate, moving, tender.

afeitar *vt*; * ~se *vr* to shave.

aferrar *vt* to grapple, to grasp, to seize.

afianzar *vt* to strengthen, to prop up.

aficionado(a) *adj* keen; lover, devotee, amateur.

afilado *adj* sharp.

afilar *vt* to sharpen, to grind.

afín *adj* related, similar.

afinar *vt* to tune, to refine.

afincarse *vr* to settle.

afirmar *vt* to secure, to fasten, to affirm, to assure.

aflicción *f* affliction, grief.

aflictivo(a) *adj* distressing.

aflojar *vt* to loosen, to slacken, to relax.

aflorar *vi* to emerge.

afluente *adj* flowing; * *m* tributary.

afónico(a) *adj* hoarse, voiceless.

afortunado(a) *adj* fortunate, lucky.

afrenta *f* outrage, insult.

afrontar *vt* to confront, to bring face to face.

afuera *adv* out, outside.

agacharse *vr* to stoop, to squat.

agarradero *m* handle.

agarrar *vt* to grasp, seize; * ~se *vr* to hold on tightly.

agasajar *vt* to receive and treat kindly, to regale.

agenciarse *vr* to obtain.

agenda *f* diary.

agente *m* agent, policeman.

ágil *adj* agile.

agilidad *f* agility, nimbleness.

agitar *vt* to wave, to move; * ~se *vr* to become excited, to become worried.

aglomeración *f* crowd, jam.

agobiar *vt* to weigh down, to oppress, to burden.

agolparse *vr* to assemble in crowds.

agonía *f* agony.

agostar *vt* to parch.

agosto *m* August.

agotado(a) *adj* exhausted, finished, sold out.

agotar *vt* to exhaust, to drain, to misspend.

agradable *adj* pleasant, lovely.

agradar *vt* to please, to gratify.

agradecer *vt* to be grateful for, to thank.

agradecido(a) *adj* thankful.

agrandar *vt* to enlarge, to exaggerate.

agrario(a) *adj* agrarian, agricultural.

agravante *f* further difficulty.

agraviar *vt* to wrong, to offend; * ~se *vr* to be aggrieved, to be piqued.

agredir *vt* to attack.

agregar *vt* to aggregate, to heap together, to collate, to appoint.

agreste *adj* rustic, rural.

agrícola *adj* farming (in compounds).

agricultor(a) *m(f)* farmer.
agrietarse *vr* to crack.
agrimensor *m* surveyor.
agrio(a) *adj* sour, acrid, rough, craggy, sharp, rude, unpleasant.
agrupar *vt* to group, to cluster, to crowd.
agua *f* water.
aguacate *m* avocado pear.
aguacero *m* cloudburst, downpour.
aguado(a) *adj* watery.
aguafuerte *m* etching.
aguamarina *f* aquamarine (precious stone).
aguanieve *f* sleet.
aguantar *vt* to bear, to suffer, to hold up.
aguardar *vt* to wait for.
aguarrás *f* turpentine.
agudo(a) *adj* sharp, keen-edged, smart, fine, acute, witty, brisk.
aguijón *m* sting (of a bee, wasp, etc); stimulation.
águila *f* eagle.
aguileño(a) *adj* aquiline, sharp-featured.
aguja *f* needle, spire, hand (of watch), magnetic needle, (railway) points *pl*.
agujerear *vt* to pierce, to bore.
agujero *m* hole.
ahí *adv* there.
ahijada *f* god-daughter.
ahijado *m* godson.
ahínco *m* earnestness, eagerness.
ahogar *vt* to smother, to drown, to suffocate, to oppress, to quench.
ahora *adv* now, at present, just now.
ahorrar *vt* to save, to avoid.
ahumar *vt* to smoke, to cure (in smoke); * ~se *vr* to fill with smoke.
ahuyentar *vt* to drive off, to dispel.

aire *m* air, wind, aspect, musical composition.
aislar *vt* to insulate, to isolate.
ajardinado(a) *adj* landscaped.
ajedrez *m* chess.
ajedrezado(a) *adj* chequered.
ajeno(a) *adj* someone else's, foreign, improper.
ajetreo *m* activity, bustling.
ajo *m* garlic.
ajustar *vt* to regulate, adjust, to settle (a balance), to fit.
al = a el.
ala *f* wing, aisle, row, brim, winger.
alabar *vt* to praise, to applaud.
alacena *f* cupboard.
alacrán *m* scorpion.
alambre *m* wire.
alameda *f* avenue, poplar grove.
álamo *m* aspen, poplar.
alargar *vt* to lengthen, to extend.
alarido *m* outcry, shout:
— dar ~s to howl.
alarma *f* alarm.
alba *f* dawn.
albañil *m* mason, bricklayer.
albarán *m* invoice.
albaricoque *m* apricot.
albedrío *m* free will.
albergue *m* shelter;
~ de juventud youth hostel.
albóndiga *f* meatball.
albornoz *m* burnous, bath robe.
alboroto *m* noise, disturbance, riot.
alborozo *m* joy.
albricias *fpl* good news.
albufera *f* lagoon.
álbum *m* album.
alcachofa *f* artichoke.
alcalde *m* mayor.
alcaldesa *f* mayoress.
alcantarilla *m* sewer, gutter.
alcanzar *vt* to reach, to get, obtain, to hit.
alcaparra *f* caper.
alcayata *f* hook.
alcázar *m* castle, fortress.

alcornoque *m* cork tree.

aldea *f* village.

aleatorio(a) *adj* random.

aleccionar *vt* to instruct, to train.

alegar *vt* to allege, to quote.

alegrar *vt* to cheer, to poke, to liven up; * ~se *vr* to get merry.

alegre *adj* happy, merry, joyful, content.

alegría *f* happiness, merriment.

alejar *vt* to remove, to estrange; * ~se *vr* to go away.

alemán(ana) *adj*, *m(f)* German; * *m* German language.

alentar *vt* to encourage.

alergia *f* allergy.

alero *m* gable-end, eaves *pl*.

alertar *vt* to alert.

aleta *f* fin, wing, flipper.

alfabeto *m* alphabet.

alfarería *f* pottery.

alféizar *m* windowsill.

alfiler *m* pin, clip, clothespeg.

alfombra *f* carpet, rug.

alga *f* (botany) seaweed.

algo *pron* something, anything; *adv* somewhat.

algodón *m* cotton, cotton plant, cottonwool.

alguien *pron* someone, somebody, anyone, anybody.

alguno(a) *adj* some, any; * *pron* someone, somebody.

alhaja *f* jewel.

aliado(a) *adj* allied.

alianza *f* alliance, wedding ring.

alicates *mpl* pincers *pl*, nippers *pl*.

aliciente *m* attraction, incitement.

aliento *m* breath, respiration.

aligerar *vt* to lighten, to alleviate, to hasten, to ease.

alijo *m* lightening of a ship, alleviation, cache.

alimentar *vt* to feed, to nourish; * ~se *vr* to feed.

alinear *vt* to arrange in line; * ~se *vr* to line up.

aliñar *vt* to adorn, to season.

alisar *vt* to plane, to polish, to smooth.

aliviar *vt* to lighten, to ease, to relieve, to mollify.

allá *adv* there, over there.

allanar *vt* to level, to flatten, to subdue, to burgle.

allí *adv* there, in that place.

alma *f* soul, human being.

almacén *m* warehouse, store, magazine.

almacenar *vt* to store (up).

almeja *f* claim.

almena *f* battlement.

almendra *f* almond.

almíbar *m* syrup.

almizcle *m* musk.

almohada *f* pillow, cushion.

almorranas *fpl* haemorrhoids *pl*.

almuerzo *m* lunch.

alocado(a) *adj* crazy, foolish, inconsiderate.

alojamiento *m* lodging, housing.

alpargata *f* rope-soled shoe.

alpinismo *m* mountaineering.

alquilar *vt* to let, to rent, to hire.

alquitrán *m* tar, liquid pitch.

alrededor *adv* around.

alta *f* (military) discharge from hospital.

altanero(a) *adj* haughty, arrogant, vain, proud.

altavoz *m* loudspeaker, amplifier.

alterar *vt* to alter, to change, to disturb.

altercado *m* altercation, controversy, quarrel.

alterno(a) *adj* alternate, alternating.

Alteza *f* Highness (title).

altibajos *mpl* ups and downs *pl*.

altitud *f* height, altitude.

altivo(a) *adj* haughty, proud, high-flown.

alto(a) *adj* high, tall; * *m*
height; storey; highland;
(music) alto; (military) halt;
* ¡~!, ¡~ ahí! *interj* stop!

altura *f* height, depth,
mountain summit, altitude.

alubia *f* kidney bean.

alucinar *vt* to blind, to
deceive; * *vi* to hallucinate.

alumbrado *m* lighting,
illumination.

alumbrar *vt* to light; * *vi* to
give birth.

alumno(a) *m(f)* student, pupil.

alza *f* rise, sight.

alzar *vt* to raise, to lift up;
* ~se *vr* to get up, to rise in
rebellion.

ama *f* mistress, owner,
housewife, foster mother.

amable *adj* kind, pleasant.

amagar *vt* to threaten, to
shake one's fist at; * *vi* to
feint.

amamantar *vt* to suckle.

amanecer *vi* to dawn:
— al ~ at daybreak.

amanerado(a) *adj* affected.

amansar *vt* to tame, to soften,
to subdue; * ~se *vr* to calm
down.

amante *m* or *f* lover.

amapola *f* (botany) poppy.

amar *vt* to love.

amargo(a) *adj* bitter, acrid,
painful; * *m* bitterness.

amarillo(a) *adj* yellow;
* *m* yellow.

amarrar *vt* to moor, to tie, to
fasten.

amasar *vt* to knead, (*fig*) to
arrange, to settle, to prepare.

ámbar *m* amber.

ambiente *m* atmosphere,
environment.

ambiguo(a) *adj* ambiguous,
doubtful, equivocal.

ámbito *m* circuit,
circumference, field, scope.

ambos(as) *adj, pron* both.

ambulante *adj* travelling.

ambulatorio *m* state-run clinic.

amenazar *vt* to threaten.

ameno(a) *adj* pleasant,
delicious, flowery (of
language).

América *f* America; ~ del Norte
(Sur) North (South) America.

amianto *m* asbestos.

amigo(a) *m(f)* friend;
* *adj* friendly.

aminorar *vt* to diminish, to
reduce.

amistad *f* friendship.

amistoso(a) *adj* friendly,
cordial.

amo *m* owner, boss.

amoldar *vt* to mould, to adapt;
* ~se *vr* to adapt oneself.

amor *m* love, fancy, lover;
~ mío my love: — por ~ de
Dios for God's sake; ~ propio
self-respect.

amortiguador *m* shock
absorber.

amortizar *vt* to redeem, to
pay, to liquidate, to
discharge (a debt).

amperio *m* amp.

ampliar *vt* to amplify, to
enlarge, to extend, to expand.

amplificador *m* amplifier.

amplio(a) *adj* ample, extensive.

ampolla *f* blister, ampoule.

amueblar *vt* to furnish.

anacoreta *m* anchorite, hermit.

anacronisino *m* anachronism.

analfabeto(a) *adj* illiterate.

analgésico *m* painkiller.

análisis *m* analysis.

anaranjado(a) *adj* orange-
coloured.

anarquía *f* anarchy.

ancho(a) *adj* broad, wide,
large; * *m* breadth, width.

anchoa *f* anchovy.

anchura *f* width, breadth.

anciano(a) *adj* old; * *m(f)* old
man or woman.

ancla *f* anchor.

anclaje *m* anchorage.

andamiaje *m* scaffolding.

andar *vi* to go, to walk, to fare, to act, to proceed.

andén *m* platform, pavement, hard shoulder.

andrajo *m* rag.

anegar *vt* to inundate, to submerge.

anexión *f* annexation.

anfibio(a) *adj* amphibious.

anfitrión(ona) *m(f)* host(ess).

ángel *m* angel.

angosto(a) *adj* narrow, close.

anguila *f* eel.

angula *f* elver.

angular *adj* angular: — **piedra** ~ *f* cornerstone.

ángulo *m* angle, corner.

angustia *f* anguish, heartache.

anhelar *vi* to gasp; * *vt* to long for.

anidar *vi* to nestle, to make a nest, to dwell, to inhabit.

anillo *m* ring.

ánima *f* soul.

animación *f* liveliness, activity.

animado(a) *adj* lively.

animal *adj*, *m* animal.

animar *vt* to animate, to liven up, to comfort, to revive; * ~se *vr* to cheer up.

ánimo *m* soul, courage, mind, intention; * ¡~! *excl* come on!

anís *m* aniseed, anisette.

aniversario *m* anniversary.

ano *m* anus.

anoche *adv* last night.

anochecer *vi* to grow dark; * *m* nightfall.

anónimo(a) *adj* anonymous.

anormal *adj* abnormal.

anotar *vt* to comment, to note.

anquilosamiento *m* paralysis.

ánsar *m* goose.

ansiar *vt* to desire.

ansiedad *f* anxiety.

antagónico(a) *adj* antagonistic, opposed.

antaño *adv* formerly.

ante *m* suède; * *prep* before, in the presence of, faced with.

anteanoche *adv* the night before last.

anteayer *adv* the day before yesterday.

antebrazo *m* forearm.

antelación *f*: — **con** ~ in advance.

antemano *adv*: — **de** ~ beforehand.

antena *f* feeler, antenna, aerial.

antepasado(a) *adj* passed, elapsed; * ~s *mpl* ancestors *pl*.

anterior *adj* preceding, former.

antes *prep*, *adv* before; * *conj* before.

antibiótico *m* antibiotic.

anticiclón *m* anticyclone.

anticipar *vt* to anticipate, to forestall, to advance.

anticonceptivo *m* contraceptive.

anticongelante *m* antifreeze.

anticuado(a) *adj* antiquated.

anticuerpo *m* antibody.

antiestético(a) *adj* unsightly.

antifaz *m* mask.

antiguamente *adv* in ancient times, of old.

antiguo(a) *adj* antique, old, ancient.

antipático(a) *adj* unpleasant.

antojo *m* whim, fancy, longing.

antorcha *f* torch, taper.

antro *m* (poetical) cavern, den, grotto.

antropófago(a) *m(f)* cannibal.

antropología *f* anthropology.

anual *adj* annual.

anudar *vt* to knot, to join; * ~se *vr* to get into knots.

anular *vt* to annul, to revoke, to cancel; * *adj* annular.

anunciar *vt* to announce, to advertise.

anuncio *m* advertisement.

anzuelo *m* hook, allurement.

añadir *vt* to add.

añejo(a) *adj* old, stale, musty.

añil *m* indigo plant, indigo.

año *m* year.

añoranza *f* longing.

apacible *adj* affable, gentle, placid, quiet.

apaciguar *vt* to appease, to pacify, to calm.

apagar *vt* to put out, to turn off, to quench, extinguish.

apañar *vt* to grasp, to pick up, to patch; * ~se *vr* to manage.

aparador *m* sideboard, store window.

aparato *m* apparatus, machine, ostentation.

aparcamiento *m* car park.

aparcar *vt*, *vi* to park.

aparecer *vi* to appear; * ~se *vr* to appear.

aparentar *vt* to look, to pretend, to deceive.

apariencia *f* outward appearance.

apartamento *m* flat, apartment.

apartar *vt* to separate, to divide, to remove, to sort.

aparte *m* aside, new paragraph; * *adv* apart, separately, besides.

apasionado(a) *adj* passionate, devoted, fond, biased.

apeadero *m* halt, stopping place, station.

apearse *vr* to dismount, to get down, out or off.

apechugar *vt* to face up to.

apego *m* attachment, fondness.

apelar *vi* (law) to appeal; ~ a to have recourse to.

apellido *m* surname, family name.

apenar *vt* to grieve, to embarrass; * ~se *vr* to grieve.

apenas *adv* scarcely, hardly; * *conj* as soon as.

apéndice *m* appendix, supplement.

apercibirse *vr* to notice.

aperitivo *m* aperitif, appetiser.

apero *m* agricultural implement.

apesadumbrar *vt* to sadden.

apestar *vt* to infect; * ~ a *vi* to stink of.

apetito *m* appetite.

apiadarse *vr* to take pity.

apilar *vt* to pile up; * ~se *vr* to pile up.

apiñado(a) *adj* crowded; pyramidal, pine-shaped.

apio *m* (botany) celery.

apisonadora *f* steamroller.

aplacar *vt* to appease, to pacify; * ~se *vr* to calm down.

aplastar *vt* to flatten, to crush.

aplatanarse *vr* to get weary.

aplaudir *vt* to applaud, to extol.

aplauso *m* applause, approbation, praise.

aplazar *vt* to postpone.

aplicado(a) *adj* studious, industrious.

aplicar *vt* to apply, to clasp, to attribute; * ~se a *vr* to devote oneself to.

aplique *m* wall light.

aplomo *m* self-assurance.

apocado(a) *adj* timid.

apoderado(a) *adj* powerful; * *m* proxy, attorney, agent.

apodo *m* nickname.

apogeo *m* peak.

apósito *m* (medical) external dressing.

aposta *adv* on purpose.

apostar *vt* to bet, to wager, to post (soldiers); * *vi* to bet.

apóstol *m* apostle.

apoteosis *f* apotheosis.

apoyar *vt* to rest, to favour, to patronise, to support; * ~se *vr* to lean.

apreciar *vt* to appreciate, to estimate, to value.

aprecio *m* appreciation, esteem.

apremiante *adj* urgent.

aprender *vt* to learn; ~ de memoria to learn by heart.

aprensión *f* apprehension.

apresar *vt* to seize, to grasp.

apresurar *vt* to accelerate, to hasten, to expedite;
* ~se *vr* to hurry.

apretar *vt* to compress, to tighten, to constrain; * *vi* to be too tight.

aprisa *adv* quickly, swiftly, promptly.

aprobar *vt* to approve, to pass;
* *vi* to pass.

apropiado(a) *adj* appropriate.

aprovechar *vt* to use, to exploit, to profit from;
* *vi* to be useful, to progress;
* ~se de *vr* to use, to take advantage of.

aproximar *vt* to approach;
* ~se *vr* to approach.

aptitud *f* aptitude, fitness, ability.

apto(a) *adj* apt, fit, able, clever.

apuesta *f* bet, wager.

apuntar *vt* to aim, to level, to point at, to mark; * *vi* to begin to appear or show itself, to prompt (theatre);
* ~se *vr* to score, to enrol.

apuñalar *vt* to stab.

apurado(a) *adj* poor, destitute of means, exhausted, hurried.

aquél, aquella *pron* that (one);
~llos, ~llas *pl* those (ones);
* aquel, aquella *adj* that;
~llos, ~llas *pl* those.

aquello *pron* that, that business.

aquí *adv* here, now.

árabe *adj*, *m(f)* (language) Arab, Arabic.

arado *m* plough.

arancel *m* tariff.

arandela *f* washer.

araña *f* spider, chandelier.

arañar *vt* to scratch, to scrape, to corrode.

arar *vt* to plough.

árbitro *m* arbitrator, referee, umpire.

árbol *m* tree, (marine) mast, shaft.

arbolado(a) *adj* forested, wooded; * *m* woodland.

arbusto *m* shrub.

arca *f* chest, wooden box.

arcada *f* arch, arcade:
~s *fpl* retching.

arce *m* maple tree.

archivar *vt* to file.

arcilla *f* clay.

arco *m* arc, arch, fiddle bow, hoop; ~ iris rainbow.

arder *vi* to burn, to blaze.

ardilla *f* squirrel.

área *f* area.

arena *f* sand, grit, arena.

arenque *m* herring; ~ ahumado red herring.

argolla *f* large ring.

argucia *f* subtlety.

argumentar *vt*, *vi* to argue, to dispute, to conclude.

árido(a) *adj* dry, barren.

arisco(a) *adj* fierce, rude, intractable.

arlequín *m* harlequin, buffoon.

arma *f* weapon, arms.

armado(a) *adj* armed, reinforced.

armador *m* shipowner, privateer, jacket, jerkin.

armar *vt* to man, to arm, to fit; ~la to start a row.

armario *m* wardrobe, cupboard.

armazón *f* chassis, skeleton, frame.

armonía *f* harmony.

armonizar *vt* to harmonise, to reconcile.

arnés *m* harness; ~eses *mpl* gear, trappings *pl*.

aro *m* ring, earring.

aroma *m* aroma, fragrance.

arpa *f* harp.

arpía *f* (poetical) harpy, shrew.

arpillera *f* sackcloth.

arpón *m* harpoon.

arqueado(a) *adj* arched, vaulted.

arquero *m* archer.

arquitectónico(a) *adj* architectural.

arrabal *m* suburb, slum.

arraigado *adj* deep-rooted, established.

arraigar *vi* to root, to establish; * *vt* to establish.

arrancar *vt* to pull up by the roots, to pull out; * *vi* to start, to move.

arrasar *vt* to demolish, to destroy.

arrastrar *vt* to drag; * *vi* to creep, to crawl, to lead a trump at cards; * ~se *vr* to crawl, to grovel.

arrebatar *vt* to carry off, to snatch, to enrapture.

arrebato *m* fury, rapture.

arrecife *m* reef.

arreglar *vt* to regulate, to tidy, to adjust; * ~se *vr* to come to an understanding.

arrellanarse *vr* to sit at ease, to make oneself comfortable.

arrendar *vt* to rent, to let out, to lease.

arrendatario(a) *m(f)* tenant.

arrepentirse *vr* to repent.

arrestar *vt* to arrest, to imprison.

arriate *m* flowerbed, causeway.

arriba *adv* above, over, up, high, on high, overhead, aloft.

arribista *m* or *f* upstart.

arriendo *m* lease, farm rent.

arriesgar *vt* to risk, to hazard, to expose to danger; * ~se *vr* to take a chance.

arrimar *vt* to approach, to draw near, (marine) to stow (cargo); * ~se *vr* to sidle up, to lean.

arrinconar *vt* to put in a corner, to lay aside.

arrodillarse *vr* to kneel down.

arrogante *adj* arrogant, haughty, proud, stout.

arrojar *vt* to throw, to fling,

to dash, to emit, to shoot, to sprout; * ~se *vr* to hurl oneself.

arrollar *vt* to run over, to defeat heavily.

arropar *vt* to clothe, to dress; * ~se *vr* to wrap up.

arroyo *m* stream, gutter.

arroz *m* rice.

arrozal *m* rice field.

arrugar *vt* to wrinkle, to rumple, to fold; ~ la frente to frown; * ~se *vr* to shrivel.

arruinar *vt* to demolish, to ruin; * ~se *vr* to go bankrupt.

arrullar *vt* to lull; * *vi* to coo.

artesanía *f* craftsmanship.

ártico(a) *adj* arctic, northern; * el Á~ *m* the Arctic.

articular *vt* to articulate, to joint.

artículo *m* article, clause, point, (*gr*) article, condition.

artífice *m* artisan, artist.

artificio *m* workmanship, craft, artifice, cunning trick.

artimaña *f* trap, cunning.

artista *m* or *f* artist, craftsman.

arzobispo *m* archbishop.

asa *f* handle, lever.

asado *m* roast meat, barbecue.

asaltar *vt* to assault, to storm (a position), to assail.

asamblea *f* assembly, meeting.

asar *vt* to roast.

ascender *vi* to be promoted, to rise; * *vt* to promote.

ascenso *m* promotion, ascent.

ascensor *m* elevator.

asco *m* nausea, loathing.

ascua *f* red-hot coal.

asear *vt* to clean, to tidy.

asedio *m* siege.

asegurar *vt* to secure, to insure, to affirm, to bail; * ~se *vr* to make sure.

asentar *vt* to sit down, to affirm, to assure, to note; * *vi* to suit.

asentir *vi* to acquiesce, to concede.

aseo *m* cleanliness, neatness;
~s *mpl* toilets *pl*.

aséptico(a) *adj* germ-free.

asequible *adj* attainable,
obtainable.

aserrar *vt* to saw.

aserrín *m* sawdust.

asesinar *vt* to assassinate, to
murder.

asesorar *vt* to advise, to act as
consultant; * ~se *vr* to
consult.

asfalto *m* asphalt.

asfixiar *vt* to suffocate;
* ~se *vr* to suffocate.

así *adv* so, thus, in this
manner, like this, therefore,
so that, also; ~ que so that,
therefore; así, así so-so,
middling.

asiento *m* chair, bench, stool,
seat, contract, entry,
residence.

asignar *vt* to assign, to
attribute.

asignatura *f* subject, course.

asilo *m* asylum, refuge.

asimismo *adv* similarly, in
the same manner.

asir *vt* to grasp, to seize, to
hold, grip; * *vi* to take root.

asistencia *f* audience,
presence, assistance, help.

asistir *vi* to be present, to
assist; * *vt* to help.

asma *f* asthma.

asno *m* ass.

asociación *f* association,
partnership.

asolear *vt* to expose to the
sun; * ~se *vr* to sunbathe.

asomar *vi* to appear;
* ~se *vr* to appear, to show up.

asombrar *vt* to amaze, to
astonish; * ~se *vr* to be
amazed, to get a fright.

aspa *f* cross, sail.

aspecto *m* appearance, aspect.

áspero(a) *adj* rough, rugged;
harsh, hard, severe.

aspiración *f* breath, pause.

asqueroso(a) *adj* disgusting.

asta *f* lance, horn, handle.

astilla *f* chip (of wood),
splinter.

astillero *m* dockyard.

astral *adj* astral.

astro *m* star.

astrología *m* astrology.

astronomía *f* astronomy.

astucia *f* cunning, slyness.

astuto(a) *adj* cunning, sly,
astute.

asumir *vt* to assume.

asunto *m* subject, matter,
affair, business.

asustar *vt* to frighten;
* ~se *vr* to be frightened.

atacar *vt* to attack.

atajo *m* short cut.

atañer *vi*; ~ a to concern.

atar *vt* to tie, to fasten.

atardecer *vi* to get dark;
* *m* dusk, evening.

atascar *vt* to jam, to hinder;
* ~se *vr* to become bogged
down.

ataúd *m* coffin.

atemorizar *vt* to frighten;
* ~se *vr* to become scared.

atención *f* attention,
heedfulness, civility,
observance, consideration.

atender *vi* to be attentive;
* *vt* to attend to, to heed, to
expect, to look at.

atenerse *vr*; ~ a to adhere to.

atentamente *adv*: — le saluda
~ yours faithfully.

atento(a) *adj* attentive,
heedful, observing, mindful,
polite, courteous, mannerly.

atenuar *vt* to diminish, to
lessen.

ateo(a) *adj*, *m(f)* atheist.

aterciopelado(a) *adj* velvety.

aterrar *vt* to terrify;
* ~se *vr* to be terrified.

aterrizar *vi* to land.

aterrorizar *vt* to frighten, to

terrify.

atesorar *vt* to treasure or hoard up (riches).

atestado(a) *adj* packed; * *m* affidavit.

atestiguar *vt* to witness, to attest.

atiborrar *vt* to stuff; * ~se *vr* to stuff oneself.

ático *m* attic.

atinado(a) *adj* wise, correct.

atizar *vt* to stir (the fire) with a poker, to stir up.

atlántico(a) *adj* Atlantic.

atleta *m* or *f* athlete.

atletismo *m* athletics.

atomizador *m* spray.

átomo *m* atom.

atónito(a) *adj* astonished, amazed.

atontado(a) *adj* stunned, silly.

atornillar *vt* to screw on, to screw down.

atosigar *vt* to poison, to harass, to oppress.

atracar *vt* to moor, to rob; * ~se (de) *vr* to stuff oneself (with).

atractivo(a) *adj* attractive, magnetic; * *m* charm.

atraer *vt* to attract.

atragantarse *vr* to stick in the throat, to choke.

atrapar *vt* to trap, to nab, to deceive.

atrás *adv* backward(s), behind, previously: — hacia ~ backward(s).

atrasar *vi* to be slow; * *vt* to postpone; ~ el reloj to put back a watch; * ~se *vr* to stay behind, to be late.

atravesado(a) *adj* oblique, cross, perverse, mongrel, degenerate.

atravesar *vt* to cross, to pass over, to pierce, to go through; * ~se *vr* to get in the way, to meddle.

atreverse *vr* to dare, to

venture.

atribuir *vt* to attribute, to ascribe, to impute.

atril *m* lectern, bookrest.

atrio *m* porch, portico.

atrocidad *f* atrocity.

atropellar *vt* to trample, to run down, to hurry, to insult; * ~se *vr* to hurry.

atroz *adj* atrocious, heinous, cruel.

atuendo *m* attire.

atún *m* tuna (fish).

aturdir *vt* to stun, to confuse, to stupefy.

audaz *adj* audacious, bold.

audiencia *f* audience.

auge *m* boom, climax.

augurio *m* omen.

aula *f* lecture room.

aullar *vi* to howl.

aumentar *vt* to augment, to increase, to magnify, to put up; * *vi* to increase, to grow larger.

aún *adv* even; ~ así even so.

aunque *adv* though, although.

auricular *m* receiver; ~es *mpl* headphones *pl*.

aurora *f* dawn.

ausencia *f* absence.

ausente *adj* absent.

auspicio *m* auspice, prediction, protection.

austero(a) *adj* austere, severe.

auténtico(a) *adj* authentic.

autoadhesivo(a) *adj* self-adhesive.

autobús *m* bus, coach.

autocar *m* bus, coach

autóctono(a) *adj* native.

autodefensa *f* self-defence.

autodeterminación *f* self-determination.

autoescuela *f* driving school.

automovilismo *m* motoring, motor racing.

autónomo(a) *adj* autonomous.

autopista *f* motorway.

autopsia *f* post-mortem,

autopsy.

autor(a) m(f) author, maker, writer.

autoridad f authority.

autorizar vt to authorise.

autorretrato m self-portrait.

autoservicio m self-service store or restaurant.

autostop m hitch-hiking.

autosuficiencia f self-sufficiency.

autovía f state highway.

auxiliar vt to aid, to help, to assist, to attend; * adj auxiliary.

aval m guarantee, guarantor.

avanzar vt, vi to advance.

avaricia f avarice.

avaro(a) adj miserly; * m(f) miser.

ave f bird, fowl.

avecinarse vr to approach.

avellana f hazelnut.

avena f oats pl.

avenida f avenue.

aventajar vt to surpass, to excel.

aventura f adventure, event, incident.

avergonzar vt to shame, to abash; * ~se vr to be ashamed.

avería f breakdown.

averiado(a) adj broken down, out of order.

averiguar vt to find out, to inquire into, to investigate.

avestruz m ostrich.

aviación f aviation, air force.

avicultura f poultry farming.

avidez f covetousness.

avinagrado(a) adj sour.

avión m aeroplane.

avioneta f light aircraft.

avisar vt to inform, to warn, to advise.

aviso m notice, warning, hint.

avispa f wasp.

avispado(a) adj lively, brisk, vivacious.

¡ay! excl alas!, ow!: — ¡~ de mí!

alas! poor me!

ayer adv yesterday.

ayuda f help, aid, support; * m deputy, assistant.

ayudar vt to help, to assist, to further.

ayunar vi to fast, to abstain from food.

ayuntamiento m town or city hall.

azabache m jet.

azafata f air hostess, stewardess.

azafrán m saffron.

azahar m orange or lemon blossom.

azar m fate: — por ~ by chance: — al ~ at random.

azotar vt to whip, to lash.

azotea f flat roof of a house.

azúcar m or f sugar.

azufre m sulphur, brimstone.

azul adj blue; ~ celeste sky blue.

azulejo m tile.

B

baba f dribble, spittle.

babero m bib.

babia f: — estar en ~ to be absent, minded or dreaming.

baca f (car) roof rack.

bacalao m cod.

bache m pothole.

bachillerato m secondary school course.

bahía f bay.

bailar vi to dance.

bailarín(rina) m(f) dancer.

baile m dance.

baja f fall; casualty.

bajada f descent; inclination; slope.

bajamar f low tide.

bajar vt to lower, to let down; to lessen; to humble; to go or come down.

bajo(a) adj low; abject,

despicable; common; humble;
* *prep* under, underneath,
below; * *adv* softly; quietly;
* *m* (music) bass; low place.

bajón *m* decline, fall: — **dar un**
~ to fall away sharply.

bala *f* bullet.

balance *m* hesitation; balance
sheet; balance; rolling (of a
ship).

balanza *f* scale; balance;
judgment.

balar *vi* to bleat.

balcón *m* balcony.

balde *m* bucket;
* **de** ~ *adv* gratis, for nothing:
— **en** ~ in vain.

baldío(a) *adj* waste;
uncultivated.

baldosa *f* floor tile; flagstone.

ballena *f* whale; whalebone.

balneario *m* spa.

balón *m* ball.

baloncesto *m* basketball.

balonmano *m* handball.

balonvolea *m* volleyball.

balsa *f* balsa wood; pool; raft,
float; ferry.

banal *adj* trivial; superficial.

bancarrota *f* bankruptcy.

banco *m* bench; work bench;
bank.

banda *f* band; sash; ribbon;
troop; party; gang;
touchline.

bandada *f* flock; shoal.

bandeja *f* tray, salver.

bandera *f* banner, standard;
flag.

bando *m* faction; edict.

bandolero *m* bandit.

banqueta *f* three-legged stool;
pavement, sidewalk.

banquete *m* banquet, formal
dinner.

banquillo *m* dock.

bañador *m* swimsuit.

bañar *vi* to bathe; to dip; to
coat (with varnish);
* ~**se** *vr* to bathe; to swim.

bañera *f* bath (tub).

baño *m* bath; dip; bathtub;
varnish; crust of sugar;
coating.

bar *m* bar.

baraja *f* pack of cards.

barandilla *f* small balustrade
or railing.

barato(a) *adj* cheap; * *m*
cheapness; bargain sale.

barba *f* chin; beard.

barbaridad *f* barbarity,
barbarism; outrage.

bárbaro(a) *adj* barbarous;
cruel; rude; rough.

barbecho *m* first ploughing,
fallow land.

barbero *m* barber.

barbilampiño(a) *adj* clean-
shaven; (*fig*) inexperienced.

barbilla *f* chin.

barca *f* boat.

barco *m* boat; ship.

barniz *m* varnish; glaze.

barómetro *m* barometer.

barquillo *m* wafer; cornet, cone.

barra *f* bar; rod; lever;
French loaf; sandbank.

barraca *f* hut.

barranco *m* gully, ravine; (*fig*)
great difficulty.

barrenar *vt* to drill, to bore;
(*fig*) to frustrate.

barrendero *m* street sweeper.

barreño *m* washing up bowl.

barrer *vt* to sweep.

barrera *f* barrier; turnpike,
claypit.

barriga *f* abdomen; belly.

barril *m* barrel; cask.

barrio *m* area, district.

barro *m* clay, mud.

barrote *m* ironwork of doors,
windows, tables; crosspiece.

barruntar *vt* to guess; to
foresee; to conjecture.

bártulos *mpl* gear, belongings *pl*.

barullo *m* uproar.

basar *vt* to base; * ~**se en** *vr* to
be based on.

báscula f scales pl.
base f base, basis.
básico(a) adj basic.
bastante adj sufficient, enough; * adv quite.
bastar vi to be sufficient, to be enough.
bastidor m embroidery frame; ~es mpl scenery (on stage).
basto(a) adj coarse, rude, unpolished.
bastón m cane, stick; truncheon; (fig) command.
bastos mpl clubs pl (one of the four suits at cards).
basura f rubbish; trash.
bata f dressing gown; overall; laboratory coat.
batalla f battle, combat; fight.
batata f sweet potato.
batería m battery; percussion; set.
batir vt to beat; to whisk; to dash; to demolish; to defeat.
baúl m trunk.
bautizar vt to baptise, to christen.
baza f card-trick.
bazo m spleen.
baya f berry.
beato(a) adj blessed; devout; * m lay brother: — m(f) pious person.
bebé m or f baby.
beber vt to drink.
bebida f drink, beverage.
beca f fellowship; grant, bursary, scholarship; sash; hood.
bedel m head porter; uniformed employee.
belén m nativity scene.
bélico(a) adj warlike, martial.
belladona f (botany) deadly nightshade.
belleza f beauty.
bello(a) adj beautiful; handsome; lovely.
bellota f acorn.
bemol m (music) flat.

bendecir vt to bless; to consecrate; to praise.
bendito(a) adj saintly; blessed; simple; happy.
beneficiar vt to benefit; to be of benefit to.
beneficio m benefit, advantage; profit; benefit night.
beneficioso(a) adj beneficial.
beneplácito m consent, approbation,
benévolo(a) adj benevolent, kind-hearted.
benigno(a) adj benign; kind; mild.
berberecho m cockle.
berenjena f aubergine, eggplant.
bergantín m (marine) brig.
berrear vi to low, to bellow.
berrinche m anger, rage, tantrum (applied to children).
berro m watercress.
berza f cabbage.
besar vt to kiss; * ~se vr to kiss.
bestia f beast, animal; idiot.
bestial adj bestial; terrific; (sl) marvellous, super.
besugo m sea bream.
betún m shoe polish.
biberón m feeding bottle.
bibliófilo(a) m(f) book-lover, bookworm.
bibliografía f bibliography.
biblioteca f library.
bicarbonato m bicarbonate.
bicho m small animal; bug: —mal ~ (fig) villain.
bici f (sl) bike.
bicicleta f bicycle.
bidé m bidet.
bien m good, benefit; profit: ~es mpl goods pl, property; wealth; * adv well, right; very; willingly; easily; * ~ que conj although: — muy ~ very well.
bienestar m well-being.
bienhechor(a) m(f) benefactor.
bienvenido(a) adj welcome;

~os a bordo welcome on
board; * f welcome.
bifurcación f fork.
bigote m moustache; whiskers pl.
bilingüe adj bilingual.
bilis f bile.
billar m billiards pl.
billete m note, banknote;
ticket; (railway) ticket;
~ sencillo single ticket;
~ de ida y vuelta return ticket.
billetero(a) m(f) wallet,
notecase.
biografía f biography.
biología f biology.
biombo m screen.
birlar vt to knock down at one
blow; to pinch (sl).
bis excl encore; twice.
bisabuela f great-grandmother.
bisabuelo m great-grandfather.
bisagra f hinge.
bisiesto adj: — año ~ leap year.
bisnieto m great-grandson.
bisnieta f great-grand-
daughter.
bistec m steak.
bisturí f m scalpel.
bisutería f costume jewellery.
bizco(a) adj cross-eyed.
bizcocho m sponge cake;
biscuit; ship's biscuit.
blanco(a) adj white, blank;
* m whiteness; a white
person; blank space; target.
blando(a) adj soft, smooth;
mild, gentle; (sl) cowardly.
blanquear vt to bleach; to
whitewash; to launder
(money).
blasfemar vi to blaspheme.
bledo m: — (no) me importa un
~ I don't give a damn (sl).
blindado(a) adj armour-plated;
bullet-proof.
bloc m writing pad.
bloque m block.
bloquear vi to block; to
blockade.
blusa f blouse.

bobada f folly, foolishness.
bobina f bobbin.
bobo(a) m(f) idiot, fool; clown,
funny man; * adj stupid,
silly.
bobada f silly thing, stupid
thing.
boca f mouth; entrance,
opening; mouth of a river;
* en ~ adv by word of mouth:
— a pedir de ~ to one's
heart's content.
bocacalle f entrance to a
street.
bocadillo m sandwich, roll.
bocado m mouthful.
bocazas m invar bigmouth.
boceto m sketch.
bochorno m sultry weather,
scorching heat; blush.
boda f wedding.
bodega f wine cellar;
warehouse; bar.
bofetada f slap (in the face).
boina f beret.
boj m (botany) box, box tree.
bola f ball; marble; globe; (sl)
lie, fib.
bolera f bowling alley.
bolero m bolero jacket or
dance.
boletín m bulletin; journal,
review.
boleto m ticket.
boliche m jack at bowls; bowls,
bowling alley; dragnet.
bolígrafo m (ballpoint) pen.
bollo m bread roll; lump.
bolsa f handbag; bag; pocket;
sac; stock exchange.
bolsillo m pocket; purse.
bomba f pump; bomb; surprise:
— dar a la ~ to pump;
~ de gasolina petrol pump;
(sl) pasarlo ~ to have a great
time.
bombero m fireman.
bombilla f light bulb.
bombo m large drum.
bombón m chocolate.

bondad *f* goodness, kindness; courtesy.
bondadoso(a) *adj* good, kind.
bonito *adj* pretty, nice-looking; pretty good, passable; * *m* tuna (fish).
boñiga *f* cowpat.
boquerón *m* anchovy; large hole.
boquilla *f* mouthpiece of a musical instrument; nozzle.
borde *m* border; margin; (marine) board.
bordear *vi* (marine) to tack; * *vt* to go along the edge of; to flank.
bordillo *m* kerb.
bordo *m* (marine) aboard.
boreal *adj* boreal, northern.
borracho(a) *adj* drunk, intoxicated; blind with passion; * *m(f)* drunk, drunkard.
borrador *m* first draft; scribbling pad; eraser.
borrar *vt* to erase, to rub out; to blur; to obscure.
borrasca *f* storm; violent squall of wind; hazard; danger.
borrico(a) *m(f)* donkey, ass; blockhead.
borrón *m* blot, blur.
bosque *m* forest; wood.
bosquejo *m* sketch (of a painting); unfinished work.
bostezar *vi* to yawn; to gape.
bota *f* leather wine-bag; boot.
botánica *f* botany.
bote *m* bounce; thrust; tin, can; boat.
botella *f* bottle.
botijo *m* earthenware jug.
botín *m* high boot, half-boot; gaiter; booty.
botiquín *m* medicine chest.
botón *m* button; knob (of a radio etc); (bar) bud.
bóveda *f* arch, vault.
boxeo *m* boxing.

boya *f* (marine) buoy.
boyante *adj* buoyant, floating; (*fig*) fortunate, successful.
bozo *m* down (on the upper lip or chin); headstall (of a horse).
braga *f* sling, rope; nappy; ~s *fpl* breeches *pl*; panties *pl*.
bragueta *f* fly, flies *pl* (of trousers).
brasa *f* live coal: —estar hecho una ~ to be very flushed.
bravío(a) *adj* ferocious, savage, wild; coarse.
bravo(a) *adj* brave, valiant; bullying; savage, fierce; rough; sumptuous; excellent, fine; * ¡~! *m excl* well done!
braza *f* fathom.
brazo *m* arm; branch (of a tree); enterprise; courage: —luchar a ~ partido to fight hand-to-hand.
brea *f* pitch; tar.
brebaje *m* potion.
brecha *f* (military) breach; gap, opening.
breva *f* early fig.
breve *adj* brief, short: —en ~ shortly; * *f* (music) breve.
brezo *m* (botany) heather.
bribón(ona) *adj* dishonest, rascally.
bricolaje *m* do-it-yourself.
brida *f* bridle; clamp, flange.
brigada *f* brigade; squad, gang.
brillante *adj* brilliant; bright, shining; * *m* diamond.
brillar *vi* to shine; to sparkle, to glisten; to shine, to be outstanding.
brincar *vi* to skip; to leap, to jump; to gambol; to fly into a passion.
brindis *m invar* toast.
brío *m* spirit, dash.
brisca *f* card game.
broca *f* reel; drill; shoemaker's tack.

brocado *m* gold or silver brocade; * ~(a) *adj* embroidered, like brocade.

brocha *f* large brush; ~ de afeitar shaving brush.

broche *m* clasp; brooch; cufflink.

broma *f* joke.

bromear *vi* to joke.

bronca *f* row.

bronceado(a) *adj* tanned; * *m* bronzing, suntan.

bronceador *m* suntan lotion.

brotar *vi* (botany) to bud, to germinate; to gush, to rush out; (medical) to break out.

bruces *adv*; de ~ face downward(s).

bruja *f* witch.

brújula *f* compass.

bruma *f* mist; (marine) sea mist.

bruñir *vt* to polish; to put rouge on.

brusco(a) *adj* rude; sudden; brusque.

brutal *adj* brutal, brutish; * *m* brute.

bruto *m* brute, beast; * ~(a) *adj* stupid; gross; brutish.

bucal *adj* oral.

bucear *vi* to dive.

bucle *m* curl.

buen *adj* (before *m* nouns) good.

bueno(a) *adj* good, perfect; fair; fit, proper; good-looking: — ¡buenos días! good morning! — ¡~! right!

buey *m* ox, bullock.

bufanda *f* scarf.

bufete *m* desk, writing-table; lawyer's office.

bufo(a) *adj* comic: — opera ~a *f* comic opera.

buhardilla *f* attic.

búho *m* owl.

buitre *m* vulture.

bujía *f* candle; spark plug.

bulbo *m* (botany) bulb.

bullicio *m* bustle; uproar.

bulto *m* bulk; tumour, swelling; bust, statue; baggage.

buñuelo *m* doughnut; fritter.

buque *m* vessel, ship, tonnage, (marine) capacity or hull.

burbuja *f* bubble.

burdel *m* brothel.

burguesía *f* bourgeoisie.

burlar *vt* to hoax; to defeat; to play tricks on, to deceive; to frustrate; * ~se *vr* to joke, to laugh at.

burro(a) *m(f)* ass, donkey; idiot; saw-horse.

bursátil *adj* stock exchange (in compounds).

buscar *vt* to seek, to search for; to look for; to hunt after; * *vi* to look, to search, to seek.

busto *m* (anatomy) bust.

butaca *f* armchair; seat.

butano *m* butane.

butifarra *f* Catalan sausage.

buzo *m* diver.

buzón *m* malbox; conduit, canal; cover of a jar.

C

cabalgar *vi* to ride, to go riding.

cabalgata *f* procession.

caballa *f* mackerel.

caballería *f* mount, steed; cavalry; cavalry horse; chivalry; knighthood.

caballero *m* knight; gentleman; rider, horseman.

caballete *m* ridge of a roof, painter's easel; trestle; bridge (of the nose).

caballo *m* horse; (at chess) knight; (in cards) queen : — a ~ on horseback.

cabaña *f* hut, cabin.

cabecera *f* headboard; head; far end; pillow; headline; vignette.

cabecilla *m* ringleader.
cabello *m* hair.
caber *vi* to fit.
cabeza *f* head; chief, leader;
main town, chief centre.
cabezota *adj* obstinate
cabida *f* room, capacity.
cabina *f* cabin; telephone
booth.
cabizbajo(a) *adj* crestfallen;
pensive, thoughtful.
cable *m* cable, lead, wire:
— echar un ~ a uno to give
someone a helping hand.
cabo *m* end, extremity; cape,
headland; (marine) cable, rope.
cabra *f* goat.
cabrón *m* cuckold; ¡~! (*sl*)
bastard!
caca *f* (*sl*) shit.
cacao *m* (botany) cacao tree;
cocoa.
cacarear *vi* to crow; to brag,
boast.
cacerola *f* pan, saucepan;
casserole.
caco *m* pickpocket; coward.
cachalote *m* sperm whale.
cacharro *m* pot.
cachear *vt* to search, to frisk.
cachivache *m* pot; piece of junk.
cachondo(a) *adj* randy; funny.
cachorro(a) *m(f)* puppy; cub
(of any animal).
cada *adj invar* each; every.
cadáver *m* corpse, cadaver.
cadena *f* chain; series, link;
radio or TV channel.
cadera *f* hip.
caducar *vi* to become senile;
to expire, to lapse; to
deteriorate.
caer *vi* to fall; to tumble down;
to lapse; to happen; to die;
* ~se *vr* to fall down.
café *m* coffee; café, coffee
house.
cafetera *f* coffee pot.
cagar *vi* (*sl*) to have a shit.

caimán *m* caiman, alligator.
caja *f* box, case; casket;
cashbox; cash desk;
supermarket checkout;
~ de ahorros savings bank;
~ de cambios gearbox.
cajero(a) *m(f)* cashier;
~ automático cash dispenser.
cajón *m* chest of drawers;
locker.
cal *f* lime; ~ viva quicklime.
cala *f* cove, inlet.
calabacín *m* small marrow,
courgette.
calabaza *f* pumpkin, squash.
calamar *m* squid.
calar *vt* to soak, to drench; to
penetrate, to pierce; to see
through; to lower; * ~se *vr* to
stall (of a car).
calavera *f* skull; madcap.
calcar *vt* to trace, to copy.
calcetín *m* sock.
calcio *m* calcium.
calcomanía *f* transfer.
calculadora *f* calculator.
calcular *vt* to calculate, to
reckon; to compute.
caldear *vt* to weld; to warm, to
heat up.
caldera *f* boiler.
calderada *f* stew.
calderilla *f* small change.
caldo *m* stock; broth.
calefacción *f* heating.
calendario *m* calendar.
calentar *vt* to warm up, to
heat up; * ~ se *vr* to grow hot;
to dispute.
calidad *f* grade, quality,
condition; kind.
cálido(a) *adj* hot; (*fig*) warm.
caliente *adj* hot; fiery:
— en ~ in the heat of the
moment.
callado(a) *adj* silent, quiet.
callar *vi*; * ~se *vr* to be silent,
to keep quiet.
calle *f* street; road.
callejear *vi* to loiter about the

streets.
callejero *m* street map.
callejón *m* alley.
callo *m* corn; callus: ~s *mpl*
tripe.
calmante *m* (medical)
sedative, tranquilliser.
calmar *vt* to calm, to quiet, to
pacify; * *vi* to become calm.
calor *m* heat, warmth; ardour,
passion.
calumnia *f* calumny, slander.
caluroso(a) *adj* warm, hot;
enthusiastic.
calvo(a) *adj* bald; bare, barren.
calzado *m* footwear.
calzoncillos *mpl* underpants,
shorts *pl.*
cama *f* bed: — hacer la ~ to
make the bed.
cámara *f* hall; chamber; room;
camera; cine-camera.
camarada *m* or *f* comrade,
companion.
camarero(a) *m(f)* waiter,
waitress.
camarón *m* shrimp, prawn.
camarote *m* berth, cabin.
cambalache *m* exchange, swap.
cambiar *vt* to exchange; to
change; * *vi* to change, to
alter; * ~se *vr* to move house.
cambio *m* change, exchange;
rate of exchange; bureau de
change.
camelar *vt* to flirt with.
camello *m* camel; drug dealer.
camilla *f* couch; cot; stretcher.
caminar *vi* to travel; to walk,
to go.
caminata *f* long walk.
camino *m* road; way.
camión *m* truck.
camisa *f* shirt; chemise.
camiseta *f* T-shirt; vest.
camisón *m* nightgown.
campamento *m* (military)
encampment, camp.
campana *f* bell.
campanario *m* belfry.

campeón(ona) *m(f)* champion.
campesino(a) *adj* rural;
* *n* country man or woman.
campestre *adj* rural.
campo *m* country; field; camp;
ground; pitch.
canal *m* channel, canal.
canalla *f* mob, rabble.
canas *fpl* grey hair:
— peinar ~ to grow old.
cancelar *vt* to cancel; to write
off.
cancha *f* (tennis) court.
canción *f* song.
candado *m* padlock.
candilejas *fpl* footlights *pl.*
canela *f* cinnamon.
cangrejo *m* crab; crayfish.
canguro *m* kangaroo; baby
sitter.
canica *f* marble.
canilla *f* shinbone; arm-bone;
tap of a cask; spool.
canjear *vt* to exchange.
cano(a) *adj* grey-haired;
white-haired.
canoso(a) *adj* grey-haired;
white-haired.
cansancio *m* tiredness, fatigue.
cansar *vt* to tire, to tire out;
to bore; * ~se *vr* to get tired,
to grow weary.
cantante *m* or *f* singer.
cantar *m* song; * *vt* to sing; to
chant; * *vi* to sing; to chirp.
cántaro *m* pitcher; jug:
— llover a ~s to rain heavily,
pour.
cantera *f* quarry.
cantidad *f* quantity, amount;
number.
cantina *f* buffet, refreshment
room; canteen; cellar; snack
bar; bar.
canto *m* stone; singing; song;
edge.
canuto *m* (*sl*) joint, spliff,
marijuana cigarette.
caña *f* cane, reed; stalk;
shinbone; glass of beer;

~ dulce sugar cane.

cañada f gully; ravine; sheep path.

cáñamo m hemp.

cañaveral m reed-bed.

caño m tube, pipe; sewer.

cañón m tube, pipe; barrel; gun; canyon.

caoba f mahogany.

caos m chaos; confusion.

capa f cloak; cape; layer, stratum; cover; pretext.

capacidad f capacity; extent; talent.

capataz m foreman, overseer.

capaz adj capable; capacious, spacious, roomy.

capeo m using a cloak to attract the attention of a bull.

caperuza f hood.

capilla f chapel.

capirote m hood.

capital m capital; capital sum; * n, f capital, capital city; * adj capital; principal.

capítulo m chapter of a cathedral; chapter (of a book).

capó m (car) bonnet.

capote m greatcoat; bullfighter's cloak.

capricho m caprice, whim, fancy.

captar vt to captivate; to understand; (radio) to tune in to, to receive.

capturar vt to capture.

capucha f cap, cowl, hood of a cloak.

capullo m cocoon of a silkworm; rosebud.

cara f face; appearance; ~ a ~ face to face.

caracol m snail; seashell; spiral.

carácter m character; quality; condition; handwriting.

característico(a) adj characteristic.

caradura m or f: — es un(a) ~ (s)he's got a nerve.

¡caramba! excl well!

carámbano m icicle.

carambola f cannon (at billiards); trick.

caramelo m sweet; caramel.

caravana f caravan; tailback (of traffic).

carbón m coal; charcoal; carbon; carbon paper.

carboncillo m charcoal.

carbono m (chemistry) carbon.

carburador m carburettor.

carcajada f (loud) laugh.

cárcel f prison; jail.

carcoma f deathwatch beetle; woodworm; anxious concern.

cardenal m cardinal; cardinal bird; (medical) bruise, weal.

cardo m thistle.

carecer vi; ~ de to want, to lack.

cargar vt to load, to burden; to charge; * vi to charge; to load (up); to lean.

cargo m burden, loading; employment, post; office; charge, care; obligation; accusation.

carguero m freighter.

caricia f caress.

caridad f charity.

caries f (medical) tooth decay, caries.

cariño m fondness, tenderness; love.

cariñoso(a) adj affectionate.

carmesí adj, m crimson.

carmín m carmine; rouge; lipstick.

carne f flesh; meat; pulp (of fruit).

carné, carnet m driving licence; ~ de identidad identity card.

carnicería f butcher's shop; carnage, slaughter.

caro(a) adj dear; affectionate; expensive; * adv dearly.

carpa f carp (fish), goldfish; tent.

carpeta f table cover; folder, file, portfolio.

carpintero m carpenter.

carraca *f* carrack (ship); rattle.
carrera *f* career; course; race;
run, running; route; journey:
— a ~ abierta at full speed.
carrete *m* reel, spool, bobbin.
carretera *f* highway.
carril *m* lane (of highway);
furrow.
carrillo *m* cheek; pulley.
carro *m* cart; car.
carrocería *f* bodywork,
coachwork.
carta *f* letter; map; document;
playing card; menu; ~ blanca
carte blanche; ~ credencial
credentials *pl*; ~ certificada
registered letter; ~ de
crédito credit card; ~ verde
green card.
cartabón *m* square (tool).
cartel *m* placard; poster; wall
chart; cartel.
cartera *f* satchel; handbag;
briefcase.
carterista *m* or *f* pickpocket.
cartero *m* postman.
cartón *m* cardboard,
pasteboard; cartoon.
casa *f* house; home; firm,
company; ~ de campo
country house; ~ de moneda
mint; ~ de huéspedes
boarding house.
casar *vt* to marry; to couple;
to abrogate; to annul; * ~se
vr to marry, to get married.
cascabel *m* small bell;
rattlesnake.
cascada *f* cascade, waterfall.
cascanueces *m invar*
nutcracker.
cascar *vt* to crack, to break
into pieces; (*sl*) to beat;
* ~se *vr* to be broken open.
cáscara *f* rind, peel; husk,
shell; bark.
casco *m* skull; helmet;
fragment; shard; (marine)
hulk; crown (of a hat); hoof;
empty bottle, returnable

bottle.
cascote *m* rubble, fragment of
material used in building.
caserío *m* country house;
hamlet.
casero *m* landlord; janitor;
* ~(a) *adj* domestic; household
(*in compounds*); homemade.
caset(t)e *m* cassette;
* *n, f* cassette-player.
casi *adv* almost, nearly;
~ nada next to nothing;
~ nunca hardly ever, almost
never.
caso *m* case; occurrence,
event; occasion; (medical)
case: — en ~ que in case.
caspa *f* dandruff; scurf.
castaño *m* chestnut tree;
* ~(a) *adj* chestnut
(coloured), brown.
castañuela *f* castanet.
castellano(a) *m(f)* Castilian,
Spanish.
castigar *vt* to castigate, to
punish; to afflict.
castillo *m* castle.
castizo(a) *adj* pure,
thoroughbred.
casto(a) *adj* pure, chaste.
castor *m* beaver.
castrar *vt* to geld, castrate.
casualidad *f* chance, accident.
cataplasma *f* poultice.
catar *vt* to taste; to inspect,
to examine; to look at; to
esteem.
catarata *f* (medical) cataract;
waterfall.
catarro *m* catarrh; cold.
cátedra *f* professor's chair.
catedral *f* cathedral.
categoría *f* category; rank.
católico(a) *adj*, *m(f)* catholic.
catorce *adj*, *m* fourteen.
catre *m* cot.
cauce *m* riverbed; (*fig*) channel.
caucho *m* rubber; tyre.
caudal *m* volume, flow;
property, wealth; plenty.

causa *f* cause; motive, reason; lawsuit: — a ~ de considering, because of.

causar *vt* to cause; to produce; to occasion.

cautela *f* caution, cautiousness.

cautivar *vt* to take prisoner in war; to captivate, charm.

cauto(a) *adj* cautious, wary.

cavar *vt* to dig up, excavate; * *vi* to dig, delve; to think profoundly.

caverna *f* cavern, cave.

cavidad *f* cavity, hollow.

cavilar *vt* to ponder, to consider carefully.

cazador(a) *m(f)* hunter; *m* huntsman: ~ furtivo poacher.

cazar *vt* to chase, to hunt; to catch.

cazo *m* saucepan; ladle.

cazuela *f* casserole; pan.

cebada *f* barley.

cebar *vt* to feed (animals), to fatten.

cebo *m* feed, food; bait, lure; priming.

cebolla *f* onion; bulb.

cebra *f* zebra.

cedazo *m* sieve, strainer.

ceder *vt* to hand over; to transfer; to yield; * *vi* to submit, to comply; to diminish.

cedro *m* (botany) cedar.

cédula *f* certificate; document; slip of paper; bill; ~ de cambio bill of exchange.

cegar *vi* to grow blind; * *vt* to blind; to block up.

ceja *f* eyebrow.

cejar *vi* to go backward(s); to slacken, to give in.

celebrar *vt* to celebrate; to praise; ~ misa to say mass.

célebre *adj* famous, renowned; witty, funny.

celeste *adj* heavenly; sky-blue.

celestial *adj* heavenly; delightful.

celo *m* zeal; rut (in animals); ~s *mpl* jealousy.

celoso(a) *adj* zealous; jealous.

célula *f* cell.

cementerio *m* graveyard.

cena *f* supper, dinner.

cenar *vt* to have for dinner; * *vi* to have supper, to have dinner.

cenegal *m* quagmire.

cenicero *m* ashtray.

ceniza *f* ashes *pl*: — miércoles de ~ Ash Wednesday.

censo *m* census; tax; ground rent; ~ electoral electoral roll.

censurar *vt* to review, to criticise; to censure, to blame.

centella *f* lightning; spark.

centenar *m* hundred.

centeno *m* rye.

centésimo(a) *adj* hundredth; * *m* hundredth.

centígrado *m* centigrade.

centímetro *m* centimetre.

céntimo *m* cent.

centinela *m* or *f* sentry, guard.

centollo(a) *m(f)* large crab.

central *adj* central; * *f* head office, headquarters; (telephone) exchange.

centro *m* centre; ~ comercial shopping centre.

centuplicar *vt* to increase a hundredfold.

ceñido(a) *adj* tight-fitting; sparing, frugal.

ceñudo(a) *adj* frowning, grim.

cepa *f* stock (of a vine); origin (of a family).

cepillo *m* brush; plane (tool).

cepo *m* branch, bough; trap; snare; poorbox.

cera *f* wax; ~s *fpl* honeycomb.

cerámica *f* pottery.

cerca *f* enclosure; fence; * *adv* near, at hand, close by; ~ de close, near.

cercanía *f* nearness: — tren de ~s local train.

cercano(a) *adj* near, close by; neighbouring, adjoining.

cerciorar *vt* to assure, to ascertain, to affirm; * ~se *vr* to find out.

cerdo *m* pig.

cerebro *m* brain.

cereza *f* cherry.

cerilla *f* wax taper; ear wax; ~s *fpl* matches, safety matches *pl*.

cero *m* nothing, zero.

cerrado(a) *adj* closed, shut; locked; overcast, cloudy; broad (of accent).

cerrajero *m* locksmith.

cerrar *vt* to close, to shut; to block up; to lock; ~ la cuenta to close an account; * ~se *vr* to close; to heal; to cloud over; * *vi* to close, to shut; to lock.

cerro *m* hill; neck (of an animal); backbone; combed flax or hemp: — en ~ bareback.

cerrojo *m* bolt (of a door).

certamen *m* competition, contest.

certero *adj* accurate; well-aimed.

certeza, certidumbre *f* certainty.

certificado *m* certificate; * ~(a) *adj* registered (of a letter).

cerveza *m* beer.

cesar *vt* to cease, to stop; to fire (*sl*); to remove from office; * *vi* to cease, to stop; to retire.

cese *m* suspension; dismissal.

cesión *f* session; transfer.

césped *m* grass; lawn.

cesta *f* basket, pannier.

chabola *f* shack.

chal *m* shawl.

chalado(a) *adj* crazy.

chaleco *m* waistcoat.

chalet *m* detached house.

champán *m* champagne.

champiñón *m* mushroom.

champú *m* shampoo.

chamuscar *vt* to singe, to scorch.

chantaje *m* blackmail.

chapa *f* metal plate; panel; (car) numberplate.

chaparrón *m* heavy shower (of rain).

chapuza *f* badly done job.

chaqueta *f* jacket.

chaquetón *m* three-quarter-length coat.

charco *m* pool, puddle.

charcutería *f* shop selling pork meat products.

charlar *vi* to chat.

charlatán(ana) *m(f)* chatterbox.

charol *m* varnish; patent leather.

chasco *m* disappointment; joke, jest.

chasis *m invar* (car) chassis.

chasquido *m* crack; click.

chatarra *f* scrap.

chato(a) *adj* flat, flattish; snub-nosed.

chaval(a) *m(f)* lad or lass.

chicle *m* chewing gum.

chico(a) *adj* little, small; * *m(f)* boy or girl.

chiflado(a) *adj* crazy.

chile *m* chilli pepper.

chillar *vi* to scream, to shriek; to howl; to creak.

chimenea *f* chimney; fireplace.

chincheta *f* drawing pin, thumb tack.

chino(a) *adj*, *m(f)* Chinese: — *m* Chinese language.

chiquillo(a) *m(f)* kid, child.

chirriar *vi* to hiss; to creak; to chirp.

chisme *m* tale; gizmo.

chispa *f* spark; sparkle; wit; drop (of rain); drunkenness.

chispear *vi* to spark, to drizzle.

chiste *m* funny story, joke.

chivo(a) *m(f)* billy (nanny) goat.

chocar *vi* to strike, to knock; to crash; * *vt* to shock.

chochear *vi* to dodder, to be senile; to dote.

chocolate *m* chocolate.

chófer *m* driver.

chopo *m* (botany) black poplar.

chorizo *m* pork sausage.

chorro *m* gush; jet; stream: — a ~s abundantly.

chuchería *f* trinket.

chulear *vi* to brag.

chuleta *f* chop.

chulo *m* rascal; pip.

chupar *vt* to suck; to absorb.

chupete *m* dummy.

churro *m* fritter.

ciática *f* sciatica.

cicatriz *f* scar.

cicatrizar *vt* to heal.

ciclista *m* or *f* cyclist.

ciclo *m* cycle.

cicuta *f* (botany) hemlock.

ciego(a) *adj* blind.

cielo *m* sky, heaven; atmosphere.

ciempiés *m invar* centipede.

cien *adj*, *m* a hundred.

ciénaga *f* swamp.

ciencia *f* science: — saber algo a ~ cierta to know something for certain.

cieno *m* mud; mire.

cierto(a) *adj* certain, sure; right, correct: — por ~ certainly.

ciervo *m* deer, hart, stag: ~ volante stag beetle.

cierzo *m* cold northerly wind.

cifra *f* number, numeral; quantity; cipher; abbreviation.

cigarra *f* cicada.

cigarro *m* cigar; cigarette.

cigüeña *f* stork.

cilindro *m* cylinder.

cima *f* summit; peak; top.

cimiento *m* foundation, groundwork; basis, origin.

cinc *m* zinc.

cincelar *vt* to chisel, to engrave.

cinco *adj*, *m* five.

cincuenta *adj*, *m* fifty.

cine *m* cinema.

cínico(a) *adj* cynical.

cinta *f* band, ribbon; reel.

cintura *f* waist.

cinturón *m* belt, girdle; (*fig*) zone; ~ de seguridad seatbelt.

ciprés *m* (botany) cypress tree.

circo *m* circus.

circuito *m* circuit; circumference.

circular *adj* circular; circulatory; * *vt* to circulate; * *vi* (car) to drive.

círculo *m* circle; (*fig*) scope, compass.

circunspecto(a) *adj* circumspect, cautious.

circunstancia *f* circumstance.

circunvalacion *f*: — carretera de ~ bypass.

cirio *m* wax candle.

ciruela *f* plum: ~ pasa prune.

cirugía *f* surgery.

cisne *m* swan.

cita *f* appointment, meeting, date.

citar *vt* to make an appointment with; to quote; (law) to summon.

ciudad *f* city; town.

ciudadano(a) *m(f)* citizen; * *adj* civic.

clamor in clamour, outcry; peal of bells.

clandestino(a) *adj* clandestine, secret, concealed.

clara *f* egg-white.

claraboya *f* skylight.

clarear *vi* to dawn; * ~se *vr* to be transparent.

clarín *m* bugle; bugler.

clarinete *m* clarinet; * *m* or *f* clarinettist.

claro(a) *adj* clear, bright; evident, manifest; * *m* opening; clearing (in a wood).

clase *f* class; rank; order.

clasificar *vt* to classify.

claudicar *vi* to limp; to act

deceitfully; to back down.
claustro *m* cloister; faculty (of a university).
cláusula *f* clause.
clavar *vt* to nail.
clave *f* key; (music) clef; * *m* harpsichord.
clavel *m* (botany) carnation.
clavicordio *m* clavichord.
clavícula *f* clavicle, collar bone.
clavija *f* pin, peg.
clavo *m* nail; corn (on the feet); clove.
clemente *adj* clement, merciful.
clérigo *m* priest; clergyman.
cliente *m* or *f* client.
clima *m* climate.
climatizado(a) *adj* air-conditioned.
clínica *f* clinic; private hospital.
clip *m* paperclip.
cloaca *f* sewer.
coacción *f* coercion, compulsion.
coagular *vt*; * ~se *vr* to coagulate; to curdle.
coartada *f* (law) alibi.
coartar *vt* to limit, to restrict, to restrain.
cobalto *m* cobalt.
cobarde *adj* cowardly, timid.
cobaya *f* guinea pig.
cobertizo *in* small shed; shelter.
cobijar *vt* to cover; to shelter.
cobrar *vt* to recover; * ~se *vr* (medical) to come to.
cobre *m* copper; kitchen utensils *pl*; (music) brss.
cocear *vt* to kick; (*fig*) to resist.
cocer *vt* to boil; to bake (bricks); * *vi* to boil; to ferment; * ~se *vr* to suffer intense pain.
cochambroso(a) *adj* nasty; filthy, stinking.
coche *m* car; coach, carriage; pram, baby carriage: — (railway) ~ cama sleeping car: ~ restaurante restaurant car.
cochino(a) *adj* dirty, filthy; nasty; * *m* pig.

cocina *f* kitchen; cooker; cookery.
cocinero(a) *m(f)* cook.
coco *m* coconut; bogeyman.
cocodrilo *m* crocodile.
codazo *m* a blow of the elbow.
codear *vt*, *vi* to elbow; * ~se *vr* ~se con to rub shoulders with.
codiciar *vt* to covet, to desire.
código *in* code; law; set of rules.
codillo *m* knee of a four-legged animal; angle; (technical) elbow joint.
codo *m* elbow.
codorniz *f* quail.
coetáneo(a) *adj* contemporary.
coexistir *vi* to co-exist.
cofia *f* (nurse's) cap.
cofradía *f* brotherhood, fraternity.
cofre *m* trunk.
coger *vt* to catch, to take hold of; to occupy, to take up; * ~se *vr* to catch.
cogollo *m* heart of a lettuce or cabbage; shoot of a plant.
cogote *m* nape of the neck.
cohecho *m* bribery.
coherencia *f* coherence.
cohete *m* rocket.
cohibido(a) *adj* shy.
coincidir *vi* to coincide.
coito *m* intercourse, coitus.
cojear *vi* to limp, to hobble; (*fig*) to go astray.
cojín *m* cushion.
cojo(a) *adj* lame, crippled.
col *f* cabbage.
cola *f* tail; queue; last place; glue.
colaborar *vi* to collaborate.
colada *f* wash, washing; (chemistry) bleach; sheep run.
colador *m* sieve.
colar *vt* to strain, to filter; * *vi* to ooze; * ~se en *vr* to get into without paying.
colcha *f* bedspread, counterpane.
colchón *m* mattress.

coleccionar *vt* to collect.

colecta *f* collection (for charity).

colectivo(a) *adj* collective.

colega *m* or *f* colleague.

colegial(a) *m(f)* schoolboy, schoolgirl.

colegio *m* college; school.

cólera *f* anger; fury, rage; (medical) cholera.

coleta *f* pigtail.

colgar *vt* to hang; to suspend; to decorate with tapestry; * *vi* to be suspended.

colibrí *m* hummingbird.

coliflor *m* cauliflower.

colina *f* hill.

colisión *f* collision; friction.

colmar *vt* to heap up; * *vi* to fulfill, to realise.

colmena *f* hive, beehive.

colmillo *m* eye-tooth; tusk.

colmo *m* height, summit; extreme: — ¡es el ~! it's the limit!

colocar *vt* to arrange; to place; to provide with a job; * ~se *vr* to get a job.

collar *m* necklace; (dog) collar.

colono *m* colonist; farmer.

coloquio *m* conversation; conference.

color *m* colour, hue; dye; rouge; suit of cards.

colorado(a) *adj* ruddy; red.

colorete *m* rouge.

columna *f* column.

columpio *m* swing, seesaw.

colza *f* (botany) rape; rapeseed.

coma *f* comma; * *m* (medical) coma.

comadreja *f* weasel.

comandante *m* commander.

comarca *f* territory, district.

combatir *vt* to combat, to fight; to attack; * *vi* to fight.

combinar *vi* to combine.

combustible *adj* combustible; * *m* fuel.

comedia *f* comedy; play, drama.

comedido(a) *adj* moderate, restrained.

comedor(a) *m(f)* glutton; * *m* dining room.

comentar *vt* to comment on, to expound.

comentario *m* comment, remark; commentary.

comenzar *vi* to commence, to begin.

comer *vt* to eat; to take (a piece at chess); *vi* to have lunch.

comercial *adj* commercial.

comercio *m* trade, commerce; business.

comestible *adj* eatable: — *mpl* ~s food, foodstuffs *pl*.

cometa *m* comet; * *f* kite.

cometer *vt* to commit, to charge; to entrust.

cómico(a) *adj* comic, comical.

comida *f* food; eating; meal; lunch.

comillas *fpl* quotation marks *pl*.

comino *m* cumin (plant or seed).

comisaría *f* police station; commissariat.

como *adv* as; like; such as.

cómo *adv* how? why? * *excl* what?

cómoda *f* chest of drawers.

cómodo(a) *adj* convenient; comfortable.

compacto(a) *adj* compact; close, dense.

compadecer *vt* to pity; * ~se *vr* to agree with each other.

compaginar *vt* to arrange, to put in order; * ~se *vr* to tally.

compañero(a) *m(f)* companion, friend; comrade; partner.

compañía *f* company.

comparar *vt* to compare.

compartimento *m* compartment.

compartir *vt* to share.

compás *m* compass; pair of compasses; (music) measure, beat.

compatible *adj*: ~ con compatible with, consistent

with.

compensar *vt* to compensate; to recompense.

competencia *f* competition, rivalry; competence.

competente *adj* competent; adequate.

compilar *vt* to compile.

compinche *m* pal, mate (*sl*).

complacencia *f* pleasure; indulgence.

complacer *vt* to please; * ~se *vr* to be pleased with.

complejo *m* complex; * ~(a) *adj* complex.

complementario(a) *adj* complementary.

complemento *m* complement.

completar *vt* to complete.

completo(a) *adj* complete; perfect.

complicar *vt* to complicate.

cómplice *m* or *f* accomplice.

complot *m* plot.

componer *vt* to compose; to constitute; to mend, to repair; to calm; * ~se *vr* ~se de to consist of.

comportamiento *m* behaviour.

compostura *f* composition, composure; mending; discretion; modesty.

compota *f* stewed fruit.

comprar *vt* to buy, to purchase.

comprender *vt* to include, to contain; to comprehend, to understand.

compresa *f* sanitary towel.

comprimido *m* pill.

comprimir *vt* to compress; to repress, to restrain.

comprobar *vt* to verify, to confirm; to prove.

comprometer *vt* to compromise; to embarrass; to implicate; to put in danger; * ~se *vr* to compromise oneself.

compuerta *f* hatch; sluice.

compuesto *m* compound; * ~(a) *adj* composed; made up of.

compulsar *vt* to collate, to compare; to make an authentic copy.

compungirse *vr* to feel remorseful.

comulgar *vt* to administer communion to; * *vi* to receive communion.

común *adj* common, usual, general; * *m* community; public: — en ~ in common.

comunicar *vt* to communicate; * ~se *vr* to communicate (with each other).

comunidad *f* community.

con *prep* with; by; ~ que so then, providing that.

cóncavo(a) *adj* concave.

concebir *vt* to conceive; * *vi* to become pregnant.

conceder *vt* to give; to grant; to concede, to allow.

concejal(a) *m(f)* member of a council.

concentrar *vt*; * ~se *vr* to concentrate.

concepto *m* conceit, thought; judgement, opinion.

concerniente *adj* concerning, relatng to.

concertar *vt* to co-ordinate; to settle; to adjust; to agree; to arrange, to fix up; * *vi* (music) to harmonise, to be in tune.

concesión *f* concession.

concha *f* shell; tortoise-shell.

conciencia *f* conscience.

concienciar *vt* to make aware; * ~se *vr* to become aware.

concierto *m* concert; agreement; concerto: — de ~ in agreement, in concert.

conciliar *vt* to reconcile; ~ el sueño to get to sleep; * *adj* (religious) of a council.

conciso(a) *adj* concise, brief.

concluir *vt* to conclude, to end, to complete; to infer, to deduce; * ~se *vr* to conclude.

concordar *vt* to reconcile, to make agree; * *vi* to agree, to correspond.

concordia *f* conformity, agreement.

concretar *vt* to make concrete; to specify.

concubina *f* concubine.

concurrido(a) *adj* busy.

concursante *m or f* competitor.

concurso *m* crowd; competition; help, co-operation.

conde *m* earl, count.

condenable *adj* culpable.

condenar *vt* to condemn; to find guilty; * ~se *vr* to blame oneself, to confess guilt.

condensar *vt* to condense.

condescender *vi* to acquiesce, to comply.

condición *f* condition, state; quality; status; rank; stipulation.

condicional *adj* conditional.

condimentar *vt* to flavour, to season.

condolerse *vr* to sympathise.

condón *m* condom.

conducir *vt* to convey, to conduct; to manage; * *vi* to drive; * ~se *vr* to conduct oneself.

conducta *f* conduct, behaviour; management.

conducto *m* conduit, pipe; drain; (*fig*) channel.

conductor(a) *m(f)* conductor, guide; (railway) guard; driver.

conectar *vt* to connect.

conejo *m* rabbit.

conexión *f* connection; plug; relationship.

confección *f* preparation; clothing industry.

conferencia *f* conference; telephone call.

confesar *vt* to confess; to admit.

confianza *f* trust; confidence; conceit; familiarity:
— en ~ confidential.

confiar *vt* to confide, to entrust; * *vi* to trust.

confidencial *adj* confidential.

configurar *vt* to shape, to form.

confinar *vt* to confine.

confirmar *vt* to confirm; to corroborate.

confiscar *vt* to confiscate.

confitería *f* sweet shop.

confitura *f* preserve; jam.

conflicto *m* conflict.

conformar *vt* to shape; to adjust, to adapt; * *vi* to agree; * ~se *vr* to conform; to resign oneself.

conforme *adj* alike, similar; agreed; * *prep* according to.

confortar *vt* to comfort; to strengthen; to console.

confundir *vt* to confound, to jumble; to confuse; * ~se *vr* to make a mistake.

confusión *f* confusion.

congelado(a) *adj* frozen; * *mpl* ~s frozen food.

congelar *vt* to freeze; * ~se *vr* to congeal.

congeniar *vi* to get on well.

congoja *f* anguish, distress, grief.

congraciarse *vr* to ingratiate oneself.

congregar(se) *vt* (*vr*) to assemble, to meet, to collect.

conjetura *f* conjecture, guess.

conjugar *vt* (medical) to conjugate; to combine.

conjunto(a) *adj* united, joint; * *m* whole; (music) ensemble, band; team.

conjurar *vt* to exorcise; * *vi* to conspire, to plot.

conmemorar *vt* to commemorate.

conmigo *pron* with me.

conmover *vt* to move; to disturb.

conmutador *m* switch.

conmutar *vt* (law) to commute; to exchange.

connotar *vt* to imply.

cono *m* cone.

conocer *vt* to know, to understand; * ~se *vr* to know one another.

conocimiento *m* knowledge, understanding; (medical) consciousness; acquaintance; (marine) bill of lading.

conquistar *vt* to conquer.

consabido(a) *adj* well-known; above-mentioned.

consagrar *vt* to consecrate.

consanguíneo(a) *adj* blood relation.

consecuencia *f* consequence; conclusion; consistency.

consecuente *adj* consistent.

conseguir *vt* to attain; to get, to obtain.

consejo *m* advice; council.

consentir *vt* to consent to; to allow; to admit; to spoil (a child).

conserje *m* doorman; janitor.

conservar *vt* to conserve; to keep; to preserve (fruit).

conservas *fpl* canned food.

conservatorio *m* (music) conservatoire.

consideración *f* consideration; respect.

considerar *vt* to consider.

consigna, *f* (military) watchword; order, instruction; (railway) left-luggage office.

consignar *vt* to consign, dispatch; to assign; to record, register.

consigo *pron* (*m*) with him, (*f*) her, you; (*refl*) with oneself.

consiguiente *adj* consequent.

consistente *adj* consistent; firm, solid.

consistir *vi*; ~ en to consist of; to be due to.

consola *f* control panel.

consolar *vt* to console, comfort, cheer.

consolidar *vt* to consolidate.

consonante *m* rhyme;

* *f* (medical) consonant;

* *adj* consonant, harmonious.

consorcio *m* partnership.

consorte *m* or *f* consort, companion, partner; accomplice.

conspirar *vi* to conspire, plot.

constante *adj* constant; firm.

constar *vi* to be evident, be certain; to be composed of, to consist of.

constatar *vt* to note; to check.

consternar *vt* to dismay; to shock.

constipado(a) *adj*: — estar ~ to have a cold.

constituir *vt* to constitute; to establish; to appoint.

construir *vt* to form; to build, to construct; to construe.

consuegro(a) *m*(*f*) father-in-law or mother-in-law of one's son or daughter.

consuelo *m* consolation, comfort.

cónsul *m* consul.

consultar *vt* to consult, ask for advice.

consultor(a) *m*(*f*) adviser, consultant.

consultorio *m* (medical) surgery.

consumar *vt* to consummate, to finish; to carry out.

consumir *vt* to consume; to burn, to use; to waste, to exhaust; * ~se *vr* to waste away, to be consumed.

contabilidad *f* accounting; bookkeeping.

contacto *m* contact; (car) ignition.

contado(a) *adj*; ~s scarce, few; * *m* pagar al ~ to pay (in) cash.

contador *m* meter; counter in a café; * ~(a) *m*(*f*) accountant.

contagiar *vt* to infect; * ~se *vr* to get infected.

contaminar *vt* to contaminate;

to pollute; to corrupt.

contar *vt* to count, to reckon; to tell; * *vi* to count: ~ con to rely upon.

contemplar *vt* to look at; to contemplate, consider; to meditate.

contemporáneo(a) *adj* contemporary.

contenedor *m* container.

contener *vt* to contain, to hold; to hold back; to repress; * ~se *vr* to control oneself.

contentar *vt* to content, to satisfy; to please; * ~se *vr* to be pleased or satisfied.

contento(a) *adj* glad; pleased; content; * *m* contentment; (law) release.

contestador *m*; ~ automático answering machine.

contestar *vt* to answer, to reply; to prove, to corroborate.

contienda *f* contest, dispute.

contigo *pron* with you.

contiguo(a) *adj* contiguous, close.

continente *m* continent, mainland; * *adj* continent.

contingencia *f* risk; contingency.

continuar *vt*, *vi* to continue.

continuo(a) *adj* continuous.

contorno *m* environs *pl*; contour, outline: — en ~ round about.

contra *prep* against; contrary to; opposite.

contrabajo *m* (music) double bass; bass guitar; low bass.

contrabando *m* contraband; smuggling.

contrachapado *m* plywood.

contradecir *vt* to contradict.

contraer *vt* to contract, to shrink; to make (a bargain); * ~se *vr* to shrink, to contract.

contrahecho(a) *adj* deformed; hunchbacked; counterfeit, fake, false.

contralto *m* (music) contralto.

contrapartida *f* (commercial) balancing entry.

contrapelo *adv*: — a ~ against the grain.

contrapeso *m* counterpoise; counterweight.

contraproducente *adj* counterproductive.

contrariar *vt* to contradict, to oppose; to vex.

contrariedad *f* opposition; setback; annoyance.

contrario(a) *m(f)* opponent; * *adj* contrary, opposite: — por el ~ on the contrary.

contrarrestar *vt* to return a ball; (*fig*) to counteract.

contrasentido *m* contradiction.

contraseña *f* countersign; (military) password.

contrastar *vt* to resist; to contradict; to assay (metals); to verify (measures and weights); * *vi* to contrast.

contratar *vt* to contract; to hire, to engage.

contratiempo *m* setback; accident.

contrato *m* contract, agreement.

contravenir *vi* to contravene, to transgress; to violate.

contraventana *f* shutter.

contribución *f* contribution; tax.

contribuir *vt*, *vi* to contribute.

contrincante *m* competitor.

controlar *vt* to control; to check.

contumaz *adj* obstinate, stubborn; (law) guilty of contempt of court.

contundente *adj* overwhelming; blunt.

contusión *f* bruise.

convalecer *vi* to recover from sickness, to convalesce.

convencer *vt* to convince.

conveniencia *f* suitability; usefulness; agreement:

~s *fpl* property.

convenir *vi* to agree, to suit.

convento *m* convent, nunnery; monastery.

conversar *vi* to talk, to converse.

convicto(a) *adj* convicted (found guilty).

convidar *vt* to invite.

convocar *vt* to convoke, to assemble.

convocatoria *f* summons; notice of a meeting.

conyugal *adj* conjugal, married.

cónyuge *m* or *f* spouse, husband, partner.

coñac *m* brandy, cognac.

cooperar *vi* to co-operate.

coordinar *vt* to arrange, co-ordinate.

copa *f* cup; glass; top of a tree; crown of a hat; ~s *fpl* hearts *pl* (at cards).

copiar *vt* to copy; to imitate.

copla *f* verse; (music) popular song, folksong.

copo *m* small bundle; flake of snow.

coquetear *vi* to flirt.

coraje *m* courage; anger, passion.

coral *m* coral; choir; ** adj* choral.

corazón *m* heart; core: — de ~ willingly.

corazonada *f* inspiration; quick decision; presentiment.

corbata *f* tic.

corchete *m* clasp; hook and eye.

corcho *m* cork; float (for fishing); cork bark.

cordel *m* cord, rope; (marine) line.

cordero *m* lamb; lambskin; meek, gentle person.

cordial *adj* cordial, affectionate; ** m* cordial.

cordillera *f* range of mountains.

cordón *m* cord, string; lace; cordon.

cornada *f* thrust with a bull's horn.

coro *m* choir; chorus.

corona *f* crown; coronet; top of the head; crown (of a tooth); tonsure; halo.

coronilla *f* crown of the head.

corpiño *m* bodice.

corporal *adj* corporal.

corpulento(a) *adj* corpulent, bulky.

corral *m* yard; farmyard; corral; playpen.

correa *f* leather strap, thong; flexibility.

correcto(a) *adj* exact, correct

corregir *vt* to correct, to amend; to reprehend; ** ~se vr* to reform.

correo *m* post, mail; courier; postman: — a vuelta de ~ by return of post; ~s *mpl* post office; ~ electrónico electronic mail, email.

correr *vt* to run; to flow; to travel over; to draw a curtain; ** vi* to run, to rush; to flow; to blow (applied to the wind); ** ~se vr* to be ashamed; to slide, to move; to run (of colours).

correspondencia *f* correspondence; communication; agreement.

corresponder *vi* to correspond; to answer; to be suitable; to belong; to concern; ** ~se vr* to love one another.

corresponsal *m* or *f* correspondent.

corriente *f* current; course, progression; (electric) current; ** adj* current; common, ordinary, general; fluent; flowing, running.

corro *m* circle of people.

corroer *vt* to corrode, to erode.

corromper *vt* to corrupt; to rot; to turn bad; to seduce; to bribe; ** ~se vr* to rot; to become corrupted; ** vi* to stink.

corrosivo(a) *adj* corrosive.

corrupción *f* rot; corruption.

cortacesped *m* lawn mower.

cortado *m* coffee with a little milk; * ~(a) *adj* cut; sour; embarrassed.

cortar *vt* to cut; to cut off, to curtail; to intersect; to carve; to chop; to cut (at cards); to interrupt; * ~se *vr* to be ashamed or embarrassed; to curdle.

corte *m* cutting; cut; section; length (of cloth); style; * *f* (royal) court; capital (city): —C~s *fpl* Spanish Parliament.

cortejo *m* entourage; courtship; procession; lover.

cortés *adj* courteous, polite.

cortesía *f* courtesy, good manners *pl*.

corteza *f* bark; peel; crust; (*fig*) outward appearance.

cortina *f* curtain.

corto(a) *adj* short; scanty, small; stupid; bashful: — a la ~a or a la larga sooner or later; *m* ~ circuito short-circuit.

corzo(a) *m(f)* roe deer, fallow deer.

cosa *f* thing; matter, affair: — no hay tal ~ nothing of the sort!

cosecha *f* harvest; harvest time: — de su ~ of one's own invention.

coser *vt* to sew; to join.

cosquillas *fpl* tickling; (*fig*) agitation.

costa *f* cost, price; charge, expense; coast, shore: — a toda ~ at all events.

costado *m* side; (military) flank; side of a ship.

costal *m* sack, large bag.

costar *vt* to cost; to need.

coste *m* cost, expense.

costero(a) *adj* coastal; (marine) coasting.

costilla *f* rib; cutlet; ~s *fpl* back, shoulders *pl*.

costra *f* crust; (medical) scab.

costumbre *f* custom, habit.

cotejar *vt* to compare.

cotidiano(a) *adj* daily.

cotilla *m* or *f* gossip.

cotizar *vt* to quote; * ~se *vr* ~ a to sell at; to be quoted at.

coto *m* enclosure; reserve; boundary stone.

cotorra *f* small parrot; (*sl*) chatterbox.

covacha *f* small cave, grotto.

coyuntura *f* joint, articulation; juncture.

coz *f* kick; recoil (of a gun); ebbing (of a flood); (*fig*) insult.

cráneo *m* skull.

crear *vt* to create, to make; to establish.

crecer *vi* to grow, increase; to rise.

crecida *f* swell (of rivers).

creciente *f* crescent (moon); (marine) flood tide; * *adj* growing; crescent.

crecimiento *m* increase; growth.

crédito *m* credit; belief, faith; reputation.

creer *vt, vi* to believe; to think; to consider.

crema *f* cream; custard.

cremallera *f* zip.

crepúsculo *m* twilight.

cresta *f* crest (of birds).

creyente *m* or *f* believer.

cría *f* breeding; young.

criadero *m* nursery; breeding place.

criadilla *f* testicle; small loaf, truffle.

crianza *f* breeding, rearing.

criar *vt* to create, to produce; to breed; to breast-feed; to bring up.

criatura *f* creature; child.

crimen *m* crime.

criminal *adj, m* or *f* criminal.

crin *f* mane; horsehair.

crío(a) *m(f)* (*sl*) kid.

cripta *f* crypt.

crisis *f invar* crisis.
crisol *m* crucible; melting pot.
crispar *vt* to set on edge; to tense up.
cristal *m* crystal; glass; pane; lens.
cristalino(a) *adj* crystalline.
cristalizar *vt* to crystallise.
cristiano(a) *adj*, *m(f)* Christian.
criterio *m* criterion.
crítica *m* or *f* criticism.
criticar *vt* to criticise.
croar *vi* to croak.
cromo *m* chrome.
crónica *f* chronicle; news report; feature.
crónico(a) *adj* chronic.
cronista *m* or *f* chronicler; reporter, columnist.
cronómetro *m* stop-watch.
cruce *m* crossing; crossroads.
crucero *m* cruiser; cruise; transept; crossing.
crucifijo *m* crucifix.
crucigrama *m* crossword.
crudo(a) *adj* raw; green, unripe; crude; cruel; hard to digest.
cruel *adj* cruel.
crueldad *f* cruelty.
crujiente *adj* crunchy.
crujir *vi* to crackle; to rustle.
cruz *f* cross: — **C~ Roja** Red Cross
crustáceo *m* crustacean.
cruz *f* cross; tails (of a coin).
cruzar *vt* to cross; (marine) to cruise; * **~se** *vr* to cross; to pass each other.
cuaderno *m* notebook; exercise book; logbook.
cuadra *f* block; stable.
cuadrado *adj*, *m* square.
cuadrante *m* quadrant; dial.
cuadrar *vt*, *vi* to square; to fit, to suit, to correspond.
cuadrilátero *adj*, *m* quadrilateral.
cuadrilla *f* party, group; gang, crew.
cuadro *m* square; picture, painting; window frame; scene; chart.
cuadrúpedo(a) *adj* quadruped.
cuajar *vt* to coagulate; to thicken; to adorn; to set; * **~se** *vr* to coagulate, to curdle; to set; to fill up.
cual *pron* which; who; whom; * *adv* as; like; * *adj* such as.
cuál *pron* which (one).
cualidad *f* quality.
cualquier *adj* any.
cualquiera *adj* anyone, anybody; someone, somebody; whoever; whichever.
cuando *adv* when; if; even; * *conj* since: — **de vez en ~** from time to time; **~ más**, **~ mucho** at most, at best; **~ menos** at least.
cuándo *adv* when: — **¿de ~ acá?** since when?
cuánto *adj* what a lot of; how much?: — **¿~s?** how many?; * *pron*, *adv* how; how much; how many.
cuanto(a) *adj* as many as; as much as; all; whatever; * *adv* **en ~** as soon as: — **en ~ a** as regards; **~ más** moreover, the more as.
cuarenta *adj*, *m* forty.
cuaresma *f* Lent.
cuarto *m* fourth part; quarter; room, apartment; span; **~s** *mpl* cash, money; * **~(a)** *adj* fourth.
cuarzo *m* quartz.
cuatro *adj*, *m* four.
cuatrocientos(as) *adj* four hundred.
cuba *f* cask; tub; (*fig*) drunkard.
cubierta *f* cover; deck of a ship; (car) bonnet; tyre; pretext.
cubierto *m* cover; shelter; place at table; meal at a fixed charge; **~s** *mpl* cutlery.
cubo *m* cube; bucket.
cubrir *vt* to cover; to disguise; to protect; to roof a building;

* ~se *vr* to become overcast.
cucaracha *f* cockroach.
cuchara *f* spoon.
cucharada *f* spoonful; ladleful.
cucharadita *f* teaspoonful.
cuchichear *vi* to whisper.
cuchillo *m* knife.
cuclillas *adv*: —en ~ squatting.
cuello *m* neck; collar.
cuenca *m* bowl, deep valley;
hollow; socket of the eye.
cuenta *f* calculation; account;
bill (in a restaurant); count,
counting; bead; importance.
cuento *m* tale, story, narrative.
cuerda *f* rope; string; spring.
cuerdo(a) *adj* sane; prudent,
judicious.
cuerno *m* horn.
cuero *m* hide, skin, leather.
cuerpo *m* body; cadaver, corpse.
cuesta *f* slope, hill; incline:
— ir ~ abajo to go downhill;
~ arriba uphill.
cuestión *f* question, matter;
dispute; quarrel; problem.
cueva *f* cave; cellar.
cuidado *m* care, worry,
concern; charge: — ¡~!
careful! look out!
cuidar *vt* to care for; to mind,
to look after.
culebra *f* snake.
culo *m* backside; (*sl*) bum;
bottom.
culpa *f* fault, blame; guilt.
culpable *adj* culpable; guilty;
* *m* or *f* culprit.
culpar *vt* to blame; to accuse.
cultivar *vt* to cultivate.
culto(a) *adj* cultivated,
cultured; refined, civilised;
* *m* culture; worship.
cumbre *f* top, summit.
cumplir *vt* to carry out, to
fulfil; to serve (a prison
sentence); to carry out
(death penalty); to attain, to
reach (a certain age);
* ~se *vr* to be fulfilled; to

expire, to be up.
cuna *f* cradle.
cuña *f* wedge.
cuñado(a) *m(f)* brother or
sister-in-law.
cura *m* priest; * *f* cure;
treatment.
curar *vt* to cure; to treat,
dress (a wound); to salt; to
dress; to tan.
curioso(a) *adj* curious;
* *m(f)* bystander.
currar *vi* (*sl*) to work.
curso *m* course, direction;
year (at university); subject.
curtir *vt* to tan leather;
* ~se *vr* to become sunburned;
to become inured.
curva *f* curve, bend.
custodia *f* custody,
safekeeping, care; monstrance.
cutis *m* skin.
cutre *adj* (*sl*) mean, grotty.
cuyo(a) *pron* whose, of which,
of whom.

D

dado *m* die (*pl* dice).
daga *f* dagger.
dama *f* lady, gentlewoman;
mistress; queen; actress of
principal parts.
damnificar *vt* to hurt, injure,
damage.
danza *f* dance.
dañar *vt* to hurt, to injure; to
damage.
dañino(a) *adj* harmful;
noxious; mischievous.
dar *vt* to give; to supply, to
administer, to afford; to
deliver.
dátil *m* (botany) date.
dato *m* fact.
de *prep* of; from; for; by; on;
to; with.
debajo *adv* under, underneath,
below.

debatir *vt* to debate, to argue, to discuss.

debe *m* (commerce) debit; ~ y haber debit and credit.

deber *m* obligation, duty; debt; * *vt* to owe; to be obliged to; * *vi* ~ (de) it must, it should.

debidamente *adv* justly, duly; exactly, perfectly.

débil *adj* feeble, weak; sickly; frail.

debilitar *vt* to debilitate, to weaken.

década *f* decade.

decadencia *f* decay, decline.

decaído(a): —estar ~ to be down.

decena *f* (about) ten, tens.

decencia *f* decency.

decenio *f* decade.

decente *adj* proper, respectable.

decepción *f* disappointment.

decidir *vt* to decide, to determine.

décimo(a) *adj*, *m* tenth.

decir *vt* to say; to tell; to speak; to name.

decisión *f* decision; determination, resolution; sentence.

declamar *vi* to declaim; to harangue.

declarar *vt* to declare; to manifest; to expound; to explain; (law) to decide; * ~se *vr* to declare one's opinion; * *vi* to testify.

declinar *vi* to decline; to decay, to degenerate; * *vt* (medical) to decline.

declive *m* slope; decline.

decorar *vt* to decorate, to adorn; to illustrate.

decorado *m* scenery.

decrecer *vi* to decrease.

decrépito(a) *adj* decrepit, worn out with age.

decretar *vt* to decree, to determine.

dedal *m* thimble; very small drinking glass.

dedicar *vt* to dedicate, to devote; to consecrate; * ~se *vr* to apply oneself to.

dedo *m* finger; toe; small bit; ~ meñique little finger: — pulgar thumb; ~ corazón middle finger; ~ anular ring finger.

deducir *vt* to deduce, to infer; to allege in pleading; to subtract.

defecto *m* defect; defectiveness.

defectuoso(a) *adj* defective, imperfect, faulty.

defender *vt* to defend, to protect; to justify, to assert; to resist, to oppose.

defensor(a) *m(f)* defender, protector; lawyer, defence counsel.

deferir *vi* to defer; to yield (to another's opinion); * *vt* to communicate.

deficiente *adj* defective.

déficit *m* deficit.

definir *vt* to define, to describe, to explain; to decide.

definitivo(a) *adj* definitive; positive.

deformar *vt* to deform; * ~se *vr* to become deformed.

deforme *adj* deformed; ugly.

defraudar *vt* to defraud, to cheat; to usurp; to disturb.

defunción *f* death; funeral.

degenerar *vi* to degenerate.

degollar *vt* to behead; to destroy, to ruin.

degradar *vt* to degrade; * ~se *vr* to degrade or demean oneself.

degustar *vt* to taste.

dehesa *f* pasture.

dejadez *f* slovenliness, neglect.

dejar *vt* to leave, to quit; to omit; to let; to permit, to allow; to forsake; to bequeath; to pardon; ~ de to stop; to fail to;

* ~se *vr* to abandon oneself.

del = de el

delantal *m* apron.

delante *adv* in front; opposite; ahead: ~ de in front of; before.

delantero(a) *adj* front; * *m* forward.

delegar *vt* to delegate; to substitute.

deleitar *vt* to delight.

deletrear *vt* to spell; to examine; to conjecture.

delfín *m* dolphin; dauphin.

delgado(a) *adj* thin; delicate, fine; light; slender, lean.

deliberadamente *adv* deliberately.

deliberar *vi* to consider, to deliberate; * *vt* to debate; to consult.

delicado(a) *adj* delicate, tender; faint; exquisite; delicious, dainty; slender, subtle.

delicia *f* delight.

delicioso(a) *adj* delicious; delightful.

delincuencia *f* delinquency.

delineante *m* or *f* draftsman or woman.

delirar *vi* to rave; to talk nonsense.

delito *m* offence; crime.

demacrado(a) *adj* pale and drawn.

demandar *vt* to demand; to ask; to claim; to sue.

demarcar *vt* to mark out (limits).

demás *adj* other; remaining; * *pron* los or las ~ the others, the rest.

demasiado(a) *adj* too; excessive; * *adv* too, too much.

demencia *f* madness.

demoler *vt* to demolish; to destroy.

demonio *m* demon, devil.

demorar *vt* to delay; * ~se *vr* to be delayed;

* *vi* to linger.

demostrar *vt* to prove, to demonstrate; to manifest.

denegar *vt* to deny; to refuse.

denigrar *vt* to blacken; to insult.

denominar *vt* to name; to designate.

denominación *f* denomination; ~ de origen award given to designate products from prestigious regions (e.g. Manchego, Rioja)

denotar *vt* to denote; to express.

denso(a) *adj* dense, thick; compact.

dentado(a) *adj* dentated, toothed; indented.

dentadura *f* set of teeth; ~ postiza false teeth.

dentífrico *m* toothpaste.

dentista *m* or *f* dentist.

dentro *adv* within; * *pron* ~ de in, inside.

denunciar *vt* to advise; to denonce; to report.

depender *vi*; ~ de to depend on, to be dependent on.

dependiente *m* or *f* shop assistant; * *adj* dependent.

depilatorio *m* hair remover.

deponer *vt* to depose; to declare; to displace; to deposit.

deportar *vt* to deport.

deporte *m* sport.

deportista *m* or *f* sportsman or woman.

depositar *vt* to deposit; to confide; to put away for safekeeping.

depravación *f* depravity.

depresión *f* depression.

deprimir *vt* to depress; * ~se *vr* to become depressed.

deprisa *adv* quickly.

depurar *vt* to cleanse; to purify; to filter.

derecho(a) *adj* right; straight; just; perfect; certain; * *m* right, justice; law; just

claim; tax, duty; fee;
* *adv* straight.
derivar *vt*, *vi* to derive;
(marine) to drift.
derogar *vt* to derogate, to
abolish; to reform.
derramar *vt* to drain off
(water); to spread; to spill, to
scatter; to waste, to shed;
* ~se *vr* to pour out.
derretir *vt* to melt; to consume;
to thaw; * ~se *vr* to melt.
derribar *vt* to demolish; to
flatten.
derrochar *vt* to dissipate; to
squander.
derrotar *vt* to destroy; to
defeat.
derruir *vt* to demolish.
derrumbar *vt* to throw down;
* ~se *vr* to collapse.
desabrido(a) *adj* tasteless,
insipid; rude; unpleasant.
desacato *m* disrespect,
incivility.
desacertado(a) *adj* mistaken;
unwise; inconsiderate.
desaconsejar *vt* to advise
against.
desacostumbrado(a) *adj*
unusual.
desacuerdo *m* blunder;
disagreement; forgetfulness.
desafiar *vt* to challenge; to defy.
desafinar *vi* to be out of tune.
desafuero *m* outrage; excess.
desagradable *adj*
disagreeable, unpleasant.
desagradecido(a) *adj*
ungrateful.
desagüe *m* channel, drain;
drainpipe; drainage.
desahogar *vt* to ease; to vent;
* ~se *vr* to recover; to relax.
desahuciar *vt* to cause to
despair; to give up; to evict.
desajustar *vt* to make uneven;
to unbalance; * ~se *vr* to get
out of order.
desalentar *vt* to put out of

breath; to discourage.
desaliño *m* slovenliness;
carelessness.
desalmado(a) *adj* cruel,
inhuman.
desalojar *vt* to eject; to move
out; * *vi* to move out.
desamparar *vt* to forsake, to
abandon; to relinquish.
desangrar *vt* to bleed; to drain
(a pond); (*fig*) to exhaust
(one's means); * ~se *vr* to lose
a lot of blood.
desanimar *vt* to discourage;
* ~se *vr* to lose heart.
desaparecer *vi* to disappear.
desapercibido(a) *adj* unnoticed.
desaprobar *vt* to disapprove;
to condemn; to reject.
desaprovechado(a) *adj* useless;
unprofitable; backward; slack.
desaprovechar *vt* to waste, to
turn to a bad use.
desarmar *vt* to disarm; to
disband (troops); to
dismantle; (*fig*) to pacify.
desarraigar *vt* to uproot; to
root out; to extirpate.
desarrollar *vt* to develop; to
unroll; to unfold; * ~se *vr* to
develop; to be unfolded; to
open.
desasosiego *m* restlessness;
anxiety.
desastre *m* disaster; misfortune.
desatar *vt* to untie, to loose; to
separate; to solve; * ~se *vr* to
come undone; to break.
desatascar *vt* to unblock; to
clear.
desatender *vt* to pay no
attention to; to disregard.
desatinar *vi* to talk nonsense;
to reel, to stagger.
desatornillar *vt* to unscrew.
desayunar *vt* to have for
breakfast; * ~se *vr* to breakfast;
* *vi* to have breakfast.
desazón *f* disgust; uneasiness;
annoyance.

desbariar *vi* to talk rubbish.

desbordar *vt* to exceed;
* ~se *vr* to overflow.

descalabrado(a) *adj* wounded on the head; imprudent.

descalificar *vt* to disqualify; to discredit.

descalzo(a) *adj* barefooted; (*fig*) destitute.

descaminado(a) *adj* (*fig*) misguided.

descansar *vt* to rest; * *vi* to rest; to lie down.

descansillo *m* landing.

descapotable *m* convertible.

descarado(a) *adj* cheeky, barefaced.

descargar *vt* to unload, to discharge; * ~se *vr* to unburden oneself.

descarriar *vt* to lead astray; to misdirect; * ~se *vr* to lose one's way; to stray; to err.

descarrilar *vi* (railway) to leave or run off the rails.

descartar *vt* to discard; to dismiss; to rule out.

descendencia *f* descent, offspring.

descender *vt* to take down;
* *vi* to descend, to walk down; to flow; to fall; ~ de to be derived from.

descenso *m* descent; drop.

descifrar *vt* to decipher; to unravel.

descollar *vi* to excel.

descolorido(a) *adj* pale, colourless.

descomunal *adj* uncommon; huge.

desconcertar *vt* to disturb; to confound; to disconcert;
* ~se *vr* to be bewildered; to be upset.

desconectar *vt* to disconnect.

desconfiar *vi*: ~ de to mistrust, to suspect.

descongelar *vt* to defrost.

desconocer *vt* to disown, to disavow; to be totally ignorant of something; not to know someone; not to acknowledge a favour received.

desconsuelo *m* distress; trouble; despair.

descontar *vt* to discount; to deduct.

descontento *m* dissatisfaction; disgust.

descortés *adj* impolite, rude.

descoser *vt* to unseam; to separate; * ~se *vr* to come apart at the seams.

descreído(a) *adj* incredulous.

descremado(a) *adj* skimmed.

describir *vt* to describe.

descuartizar *vt* to quarter; to carve.

descubrir *vt* to discover, to disclose; to uncover; to reveal; to show; * ~se *vr* to reveal oneself; to take off one's hat; to confess.

descuento *m* discount; decrease.

descuidado(a) *adj* careless, negligent.

descuidar *vt* to neglect;
* *vi* ~se *vr* to be careless.

descuido *m* carelessness; negligence.

desde *prep* since; after; from;
~ luego of course; ~ entonces since then.

desdén *m* disdain, scorn.

desdentado(a) *adj* toothless.

desdeñar *vt* to disdain, to scorn;
* ~se *vr* to be disdainful.

desdicha *f* misfortune, calamity; great poverty.

desdoblar *vt* to unfold, to spread open.

desear *vt* to desire, to wish; to require, to demand.

desecar *vt* to dry up.

desechar *vt* to depreciate; to reject; to refuse; to throw away.

desecho *m* residue;

~s *mpl* rubbish.

desembarcar *vt* to unload, to disembark; * *vi* to disembark, to land.

desembolsar *vt* to pay out.

desempatar *vi* to hold a play-off.

desempeñar *vt* to redeem; to extricate from debt; to fulfil (any duty or promise); to acquit; * ~se *vr* to get out of debt.

desempleo *m* unemployment.

desencadenar *vt* to unchain; * ~se *vr* to break loose; to burst.

desencajar *vt* to disjoint; to dislocate; to disconnect.

desencanto *m* disenchantment.

desenchufar *vt* to unplug.

desenfado *m* ease; facility; calmness, relaxation.

desenfocado(a) *adj* out of focus.

desenfreno *m* wildness; lack of self-control.

desengañar *vt* to disillusion; * ~se *vr* to become disillusioned.

desenganchar *vt* to unhook; to uncouple.

desengrasar *vt* to take the grease from.

desenlace *m* climax; outcome.

desenredar *vt* to disentangle.

desenroscar to untwist; to unroll.

desentenderse *vr* to feign not to understand; to pass by without noticing.

desenterrar *vt* to exhume; to dig up.

desentonar *vi* to be out of tune; to clash.

desenvolver *vt* to unfold; to unroll; to decipher, to unravel; tô develop; * ~se *vr* to develop; to cope.

deseo *m* desire, wish.

desequilibrado(a) *adj* unbalanced.

desertar *vt* to desert; (law) to abandon (a cause).

desesperar *vi*, ~se *vr* to despair; * *vt* to make desperate.

desestabilizar *vt* to destabilise.

desfachatez *f* impudence.

desfalco *m* embezzlement.

desfallecer *vi* to get weak; to faint.

desfasado(a) *adj* old-fashioned.

desfavorable *adj* unfavorable.

desfiladero *m* gorge.

desfilar *vi* (military) to parade.

desfogarse *vr* to give vent to one's passion or anger.

desgana *f* disgust; loss of appetite; aversion, reluctance.

desgañitarse *vr* to scream, bawl.

desgarrar *vt* to tear; to shatter.

desgaste *m* wear and tear.

desgracia *f* misfortune; disgrace; accident; setback.

desgreñado(a) *adj* dishevelled.

deshabitado(a) *adj* deserted, uninbabited; desolate.

deshacer *vt* to undo, to destroy; to cancel, to efface; * ~se *vr* to melt; to come apart.

deshelar *vi* to thaw; * ~se *vr* to thaw, to melt.

desheredar *vt* to disinherit.

deshidratar *vt* to dehydrate.

deshinchar *vt* to deflate; * ~se *vr* to go flat, to go down.

deshonesto(a) *adj* indecent.

deshonrar *vt* to affront, to insult, to defame; to dishonour.

deshuesar *vt* to rid of bones; to stone.

desidia *f* idleness, indolence.

desierto(a) *adj* deserted; solitary; * *m* desert; wilderness.

designar *vt* to design; to intend; to appoint; to express, to name.

desigual *adj* unequal, unlike; uneven, craggy.

desilusionar *vt* to disappoint; * ~se *vr* to become

disillusioned.

desinfectar *vt* to disinfect.

desinflar *vt* to deflate.

desinteresado(a) *adj* disinterested; unselfish.

desistir *vi* to desist, to cease.

desleal *adj* disloyal; unfair.

desleír *vt* to dilute; to dissolve.

deslenguado(a) *adj* foul-mouthed.

deslizar *vt* to slip, to slide; to let slip (a comment); * ~se *vr* to slip; to skid; to flow softly; to creep in.

deslumbrar *vt* to dazzle; to puzzle.

desmayar *vi* to be dispirited or faint-hearted; * ~se *vr* to faint.

desmedido(a) *adj* disproportionate.

desmemoriado(a) *adj* forgetful.

desmentir *vt* to give the lie to; * ~se *vr* to contradict oneself.

desmenuzar *vt* to crumble; to chip at; to fritter away; to examine minutely.

desmesurado(a) *adj* excessive; huge; immeasurable.

desmoralizar *vt* to demoralise.

desnatado(a) *adj* skimmed.

desnivel *m* unevenness of the ground.

desnudar *vt* to undress; to strip; to discover, to reveal; * ~se *vr* to undress.

desnutrido(a) *adj* undernourished.

desobedecer *vt, vi* to disobey.

desocupar *vt* to vacate; to empty; * ~se *vr* to retire from a business; to withdraw from an arrangement.

desodorante *m* deodorant.

desolado(a) *adj* desolate, disconsolate.

desodenar *vt* to disorder; to untidy; * ~se *vr* to get out of order.

desorganizar *vt* to disorganise.

desorientar *vt* to mislead; to confuse; * ~se *vr* to lose one's way.

desovar *vi* to spawn.

despabilado(a) *adj* watchful, vigilant; wide-awake.

despacho *m* dispatch, expedition; cabinet; office; commission; warrant; patent; expedient; smart answer.

despachurrar *vt* to squash, to crush; to mangle.

despacio *adv* slowly, leisurely; little by little — ¡~! softly!, gently!

desparramar *vt* to disseminate, to spread; to spill; to squander, to lavish; * ~se *vr* to be dissipated.

despavorido *adj* frightened.

despecho *m* indignation; displeasure; spite; dismay, despair; deceit; derision, scorn: — a ~ de in spite of.

despectivo(a) *adj* pejorative, derogatory.

despedir *vt* to discharge; to dismiss (from office); to see off; * ~se *vr* ~ de to say goodbye to.

despegar *vt* to unglue; to take off; * ~se *vr* to come loose.

despegue *m* take-off.

despeinar *vt* to ruffle.

despejado(a) *adj* sprightly, quick; clear.

despellejar *vt* to skin.

despensa *f* pantry, larder; provisions *pl*.

desperdiciar *vi* to squander.

desperdigar *vt* to separate; to scatter.

desperfecto *m* slight damage; flaw.

despertador *m* alarm clock.

despertar *vt* to wake up, to rouse from sleep; to excite; * *vi* to wake up; to grow lively or sprightly; * ~se *vr* to wake up.

despiadado(a) *adj* heartless;

merciless.

despido *m* dismissal.

despierto(a) *adj* awake; vigilant; fierce; brisk, sprightly.

despistar *vt* to mislead; to throw off the track; * ~se *vr* to take the wrong way; to become confused.

desplazar *vt* to move; to scroll; * ~se *vr* to travel.

desplegar *vt* to unfold, to display; to explain, to elucidate; (marine) to unfurl; * ~se *vr* to open out; to travel.

desplomarse *vr* to fall to the ground; to collapse.

despoblar *vt* to depopulate; to desolate; * ~se *vr* to become depopulated.

despojar *vt*; * ~ (de) to strip (of); to deprive (of); * ~se *vr* to undress.

desposar *vt* to marry, to betroth; * ~se *vr* to be betrothed or married.

desposeer *vt* to dispossess.

déspota *m* despot.

despreciar *vt* to offend; to despise.

desprender *vt* to unfasten, to loosen; to separate; * ~se *vr* to give way; to fall down; to extricate oneself.

despreocupado(a) *adj* careless; unworried.

desprevenido(a) *adj* unawares, unprepared.

desproporcionado(a) *adj* disproportionate.

desprovisto(a) *adj* unprovided.

después *adv* after, afterwards; next.

despuntar *vt* to blunt; * *vi* to sprout; to dawn: — al ~ del día at break of day.

desquiciar *vt* to upset; to discompose; to disorder.

desquite *m* recovery of a loss; revenge, retaliation.

destacamento *m* (military) detachment.

destacar *vt* to emphasise; (military) to detach (a body of troops); * ~se *vr* to stand out.

destajo *m* piecework.

destapar *vt* to uncover; to open; * ~se *vr* to be uncovered.

destartalado(a) *adj* untidy.

destello *m* signal light; sparkle.

desternillarse *vr*; ~ de risa to roar with laughter.

desteñir *vt* to discolour; * ~se *vr* to fade.

desterrar *vt* to banish; to expel, to drive away.

destetar *vt* to wean.

destilar *vt*, *vi* to distil.

destinar *vt* to destine for, to intend for.

destinatario(a) *m(f)* addressee.

destino *m* destiny; fat, doom; destination; office.

destornillador *m* screwdriver.

destreza *f* dexterity, cleverness, cunning, expertness, skill.

destrozar *vt* to destroy, to break into pieces; (military) to defeat.

destruir *vt* to destroy.

desvalido(a) *adj* helpless; destitute.

desvalijar *vt* to rob; to burgle.

desván *m* garret.

desvanecer *vt* to dispel; * ~se *vr* to grow vapid, become insipid; to vanish; to be affected with giddiness.

desvarío *m* delirium; giddiness; inconstancy, caprice; extravagance.

desvelar *vt* to keep awake; * ~se *vr* to stay awake.

desventaja *f* disadvantage; damage.

desventura *f* misfortune; calamity.

desvergüenza *f* impudence; shamelessness.

desvestir *vt*; * ~se *vr* to undress.

desviar *vt* to divert; to dissuade; to parry (at fencing); * ~se *vr* to go off course.

detallar *vt* to detail, to relate minutely.

detener *vt* to stop, to detain; to arrest; to keep back; to reserve; to withhold; * ~se *vr* to stop; to stay.

detenidamente *adv* carefully.

detergente *m* detergent.

deteriorar *vt* to damage.

determinar *vt* to determine; * ~se *vr* to decide.

detestar *vt* to detest, abhor.

detonar *vi* to detonate.

detrás *adv* behind; at the back, in the back.

deuda *f* debt; fault; offence.

devanar *vt* to reel; to wrap up.

devastar *vt* to devastate.

devengar *vt* to accrue.

devoción *f* devotion, piety; strong affection; ardent love.

devolver *vt* to return; to send back; to refund; * *vi* to be sick.

devorar *vt* to devour, to swallow up.

día *m* day.

diablo *m* devil.

diablura *f* prank.

diana *f* (military) reveille; bull's-eye.

diapositiva *f* slide.

diario *m* journal, diary; daily newspaper; * ~(a) *adj* daily.

diarrea *f* diarrhoea.

dibujar *vt* to draw, to design.

diccionario *m* dictionary.

dicha *f* happiness, good fortune.

diciembre *m* December.

dictamen *m* opinion, notion; suggestion; judgment.

dictar *vt* to dictate.

diecinueve *adj*, *m* nineteen.

dieciocho *adj*, *m* eighteen.

dieciséis *adj*, *m* sixteen.

diecisiete *adj*, *m* seventeen.

diente *m* tooth; fang; tusk.

diestro(a) *adj* right; dexterous, skilful, clever; sagacious, prudent; sly, cunning; * *m* skilful fencer; halter; bridle; bullfighter.

dieta *f* diet, regimen; diet, assembly; daily salary of judges.

diez *adj*, *m* ten.

diezmar *vt* to decimate.

difamar *vt* to defame, to libel.

diferencia *f* difference.

diferenciar *vt* to differentiate, to distinguish; * ~se *vr* to differ, to distinguish oneself.

diferente *adj* different, unlike.

diferido(a) *adj* recorded.

difícil *adj* difficult.

dificultad *f* difficulty.

difundir *vt* to diffuse, to spread; to divulge; * ~se *vr* to spread (out).

difunto(a) *adj* dead, deceased.

digerir *vi* to digest; to bear with patience; to adjust, to arrange; (chemistry) to digest.

dignarse *vr* to condescend, to deign.

digno(a) *adj* worthy; suitable.

dilatado(a) *adj* large; numerous; prolix; spacious, extensive.

dilatar *vt* to dilate, to expand; to spread out; to defer, to protract.

dilema *m* dilemma.

diligencia *f* diligence; affair, business; call of nature.

dilucidar *vt* to elucidate, to explain.

diluir *vt* to dilute.

diluviar *vi* to rain in torrents.

diminutivo *m* diminutive.

diminuto(a) *adj* minute, small.

dimitir *vt* to give up, to abdicate; * *vi* to resign.

dinamita *f* dynamite.

dínamo, dinamo *f* dynamo.

dineral *m* large sum of money.

dinero *m* money.

dios *m* god.

diosa *f* goddess.

diplomado(a) *adj* qualified.

diputado(a) *m(f)* member of parliament.

dique *m* dam.

dirección *f* direction, guidance; administration; steering.

directo(a) *adj* direct, straight; apparent, evident; live.

director(a) *m(f)* director; conductor; president; manager.

dirigir *vt* to direct; to conduct; to regulate, to govern; * ~se *vr* to go towards; to address oneself to.

discernir *vt* to discern, to distinguish.

discípulo(a) *m(f)* disciple; scholar.

disco *m* disc; record; discus; light; face (of the sun or moon); lens (of a telescope).

díscolo(a) *adj* ungovernable; peevish.

discordante *adj* dissonant, discordant.

discreción *f* discretion; acuteness of mind.

discrepar *vi* to differ.

discreto(a) *adj* discreet; ingenious; witty, eloquent.

disculpar *vt* to exculpate, to excuse; to acquit, absolve; * ~se *vr* to apologise; to excuse oneself.

discurrir *vi* to ramble about; to discourse (on a subject); * *vt* to invent, to contrive; to meditate.

discurso *m* speech; conversation; dissertation; space of time.

discutir *vt*, *vi* to discuss; to argue about.

disecar *vt* to dissect; to stuff.

diseminar *vt* to scatter; to disseminate, to propagate.

diseñar *vt* to draw; to design.

disentir *vi* to dissent, to disagree.

disfrazar *vt* to disguise, to conceal; to cloak, to dissemble; * ~se *vr* to disguise oneself as.

disfrutar *vt* to enjoy; * ~se *vr* to enjoy oneself.

disgustar *vt* to disgust; to offend; * ~se *vr* to be displeased; to fall out.

disidente *adj* dissident; * *m* or *f* dissident, dissenter.

disimular *vt* to hide; to tolerate.

disipar *vt* to dissipate, to disperse, to scatter; to lavish.

dislocarse *vr* to be dislocated or out of joint.

disminuir *vt* to diminish; to decrease.

disolver *vt* to loosen, to untie; to dissolve; to disunite; to melt, to liquefy; to interrupt.

disparar *vt* to shoot, to discharge, to fire; to let off, to throw with violence; * *vi* to shoot, to fire.

disparate *m* nonsense, absurdity, extravagance.

displicencia *f* displeasure; dislike.

disponer *vt* to arrange, to prepare; to dispose.

disponible *adj* available; disposable.

dispositivo *m* device.

disputar *vt* to dispute, to controvert, to question; * *vi* to debate, to argue.

disquete *m* floppy disk.

distancia *f* distance; interval; difference.

distante *adj* distant, far off.

distinguido(a) *adj* distinguished, conspicuous.

distinguir *vt* to distinguish; to discern; * ~se *vr* to distinguish oneself.

distinto(a) *adj* distinct, different; clear.

distraer *vt* to distract; * ~se *vr* to be absent-minded, to be inattentive.

distraído(a) *adj* absent-minded, inattentive.

distribuir *vt* to distribute.

distrito *m* district; territory.

disturbio *m* riot; disturbance, interruption.

disuadir *vt* to dissuade.

diurno(a) *adj* daily.

diva *f* prima donna.

divagar *vt* to digress.

divergencia *f* divergence.

diversidad *f* diversity; variety of things.

diversificar *vt* to diversify; to vary.

diversión *f* diversion; sport; amusement; (military) diversion.

divertir *vt* to divert (the attention); to amuse, to entertain; (military) to draw off; * ~se *vr* to amuse oneself.

dividir *vi* to divide; to separate; to share out.

divino(a) *adj* divine, heavenly; excellent.

divorcio *m* divorce; separation, disunion.

divulgar *vt* to publish, to divulge.

dobladillo *m* hem; turn-up.

doblar *vt* to double; to fold; to bend; * *vi* to turn; to roll; * ~se *vr* to bend, to bow.

doble *adj* double; dual; deceitful: —al ~ doubly; * *m* double.

doblegar *vt* to bend; * ~se *vr* to yield.

doblez *m* crease; fold; turn-up; * *f* duplicity.

doce *adj*, *m* twelve.

docena *f* dozen.

dócil *adj* docile, tractable.

doctor(a) *m(f)* doctor.

documento *m* document; record.

dogma *m* dogma.

dólar *m* dollar.

doler *vt*, *vi* to feel pain; to ache; * ~se *vr* to feel for the sufferings of others; to complain.

dolor *m* pain; aching, ache; affliction.

domar *vt* to tame; to subdue, to master.

domesticar *vt* to domesticate.

domicilio *m* domicile; home, abode.

dominar *vt* to dominate; to be fluent in; * ~se *vr* to moderate one's passions.

domingo *m* Sunday; Christian Sabbath.

donar *vt* to donate; to bestow.

donativo *m* contribution.

doncella *f* virgin, maiden; lady's maid.

donde *relative adv* where.

dondequiera *adv* wherever.

dorado(a) *adj* golden; * *m* gilding.

dormir *vi* to sleep; * ~se *vr* to fall asleep.

dos *adj*, *m* two.

doscientos(as) *adj*, *pl* two hundred.

dosis *f invar* dose.

dotado(a) *adj* gifted.

drama *m* drama.

dramatizar *vt* to dramatise.

droga *f* drug; stratagem; artifice, deceit.

droguería *f* hardware store.

ducha *f* shower; (medical) douche.

ducho(a) *adj* skilled, experienced.

dudar *vt* to doubt.

duelo *m* grief, affliction; mourning.

duende *m* elf, hobgoblin.

dueño(a) *m(f)* owner; landlord or lady; employer.

dulce *adj* sweet; mild, gentle, meek; soft; *m* sweet, candy.

dúo *m* (music) duo, duet.

duodécimo(a) *adj* twelfth.

duplicar *vt* to duplicate, to double; to repeat.

duradero(a) *adj* lasting, durable.

durante *adv* during.

durar *vi* to last, to continue.

durazno *m* peach; peach tree.

dureza *f* hardness; harshness; ~ de oído hardness of hearing.

duro(a) *adj* hard; cruel; harsh, rough; *m* five-peseta coin; *adv* hard.

E

e *conj* and (before words starting with i or hi).

ébano *m* ebony.

ebrio(a) *adj* drunk.

ebullición *f* boiling.

echar *vt* to throw; to add; to pour out; to mail; *~se *vr* to lie down.

eco *m* echo.

económico(a) *adj* economic; cheap; thrifty; financial; avaricious.

ecuánime *adj* level-headed.

ecuménico(a) *adj* ecumenical; universal.

edad *f* age.

edición *f* edition; publication.

edificar *vt* to build, to construct; to edify.

edificio *m* building; structure.

editar *vt* to edit; to publish.

educación *f* education; upbringing; (good) manners *pl*.

educar *vt* to educate, to instruct; to bring up.

educado(a) *adj* well-mannered: — mal~ ill-mannered.

efectivamente *adv* exactly; really; in fact.

efecto *m* effect; consequence; purpose; ~s *mpl* effects *pl*,

goods *pl*: — en ~ in fact, really.

efectuar *vt* to effect, to carry out.

eficaz *adj* efficient; effective.

eficiente *adj* efficient.

egoísta *m* or *f* self-seeker; *adj* selfish.

eje *m* axle; axis.

ejecutar *vt* to execute, to perform; to put to death; (law) to distrain, to seize.

ejecutivo(a) *adj* exceutive; *m(f)* executive.

ejemplar *m* specimen; copy; example; *adj* exemplary.

ejemplo *m* example: — por ~ for example, for instance.

ejercer *vt* to exercise; *vi* to apply oneself to the functions of an office.

ejercicio *m* exercise; fiscal or financial year.

ejercitar *vt* to exercise.

ejército *m* army.

el *art*, *m* the.

él *pron* he, it.

elaborar *vt* to elaborate.

elástico(a) *adj* elastic.

elección *f* election; choice.

eléctrico(a) *adj* electric, electrical.

electrocutar *vt* to electrocute.

electrodomesticos *mpl* (electrical) household appliances *pl*.

elefante *m* elephant.

elegante *adj* elegant, fine.

elegir *vt* to choose, to elect.

elemental *adj* elementary, fundamental.

elemento *m* element; ~s *mpl* elements, rudiments, first principles *pl*.

elevar *vt* to raise; to elevate; *~se *vr* to rise; to be enraptured; to be conceited.

eliminar *vt* to eliminate, to remove.

eliminatoria *f* preliminary

(round).

ella *pron* she; it.

ello *pron* it.

elogiar *vt* to praise, to eulogise.

eludir *vt* to elude, to escape.

emanar *vi* to emanate.

embadurnar *vt* to smear, to bedaub.

embalaje *m* packing, package.

embalar *vt* to parcel, to wrap.

embaldosar *vt* to pave with tiles.

embalse *m* water reservoir.

embarazada *f* pregnant woman; * *adj* pregnant.

embarazoso(a) *adj* difficult; intricate, entangled.

embarcación *f* embarkation; any vessel or ship.

embarcar *vt* to embark; * ~se *vr* to go on board; (*fig*) to get involved (in a matter).

embargo *m* embargo: — sin ~ still, however.

embarque *m* embarkation.

embaucar *vt* to deceive; to trick.

embeber *vt* to soak; to saturate; * *vi* to shrink; * ~se *vr* to be enraptured; to be absorbed.

embeleso *m* amazement, enchantment.

embellecer *vt* to embellish, to beautify.

embestir *vt* to assault, to attack.

emblanquecer *vt* to whiten; * ~se *vr* to grow white; to bleach.

emblema *m* emblem.

embobado(a) *adj* amazed; fascinated.

émbolo *m* plunger; piston.

embolsar *vt* to put money into (a purse); to pocket.

emborrachar *vt* to intoxicate, to inebriate; * ~se *vr* to get drunk.

emboscada *f* (military) ambush.

embotar *vt* to blunt; * ~se *vr* to go numb.

embotellamiento *m* traffic jam.

embotellar *vt* to bottle (wine).

embrague *m* clutch.

embriagar *vt* to intoxicate, to inebriate; to transport, to enrapture.

embrión *m* embryo.

embrollo *m* muddle.

embromar *vt* to tease; to cajole, to wheedle.

embrujar *vt* to bewitch.

embrutecer *vt* to brutalise; * ~se *vr* to become depraved.

embudo *m* funnel.

embustero(a) *m(f)* impostor, cheat; liar; * *adj* deceitful.

embutido *m* sausage; inlay.

emerger *vi* to emerge, to appear.

emigrar *vi* to emigrate.

emigrado(a) *m(f)* emigrant.

eminente *adj* eminent, high; excellent, conspicuous.

emisión *f* emission.

emisora *f* broadcasting station.

emitir *vt* to emit, to send forth; to issue; to broadcast.

emoción *f* emotion; feeling; excitement.

emocionar *vt* to excite.

emotivo(a) *adj* emotional.

empacho *m* (medical) indigestion.

empalagoso(a) *adj* cloying; tiresome.

empalmar *vt* to join.

empanada *f* (meat) pie.

empanar *vt* to cover with breadcrumbs.

empantanarse *vr* to get swamped; to get bogged down.

empañarse *vr* to get misty, to steam up.

empapar *vt* to soak; to soak up; * ~se *vr* to soak.

empapelar *vt* to paper.

empaquetar *vt* to pack, to parcel up.

emparedado *m* sandwich.

emparrado *m* vine arbor.

empastar *vt* to paste; (medical) to fill (a tooth).

empatar *vi* to draw.

empedernido(a) *adj* inveterate; heartless.

empedrado *m* paving.

empeine *m* instep.

empellón *m* push; heavy blow.

empeñar *vt* to pawn, to pledge;
* ~se *vr* to pledge oneself to pay debts; to get into debt;
* ~se en algo to insist on something.

empeño *m* determination:
— casa de ~s pawnshop.

empeorar *vt* to make worse;
* *vi* ~se *vr* to grow worse.

empequeñecer *vt* to dwarf; (*fig*) to belittle.

empezar *vt* to begin, to start.

emplazamiento *m* summons; location.

empleado(a) *m(f)* official; employee.

emplear *vt* to employ; to occupy; to commission.

empobrecer *vt* to reduce to poverty; * *vi* to become poor.

empollar *vt* to incubate; to hatch; (*sl*) to swot (up).

empolvar *vt* to powder; to sprinkle powder upon.

empotrado(a) *adj* built-in.

emprender *vt* to embark on; to tackle; to undertake.

empresa *f* (commerce) company; enterprise, undertaking.

empujar *vt* to push; to press forward.

empujón *m* push; impulse:
— a ~ones in fits and starts.

emular *vt* to emulate, to rival.

en *prep* in; for; on, upon.

enaguas *fpl* petticoat.

enamorado(a) *adj* in love, lovesick.

enamorar *vt* to inspire love in;
* ~se *vr* to fall in love.

enano(a) *adj* dwarfish;
* *m* dwarf.

enardecer *vt* to fire with passion, inflame.

enarenar *vt* to fill with sand.

encabezar *vt* to head; to put a heading to; to lead.

encadenar *vt* to chain, to link together; to connect, to unite.

encajar *vt* to insert; to drive in; to encase; to intrude;
* *vi* to fit (well).

encaje *m* lace.

encalar *vt* to whitewash.

encallar *vi* (marine) to run aground.

encaminar *vt* to guide, to show the way; * ~se a *vr* to take the road to.

encandilar *vt* to dazzle.

encanecer *vi* to grow grey; to grow old.

encantado(a) *adj* bewitched; delighted; pleased.

encantador(a) *adj* charming;
* *m(f)* magician.

encantar *vt* to enchant, to charm; (*fig*) to delight.

encarcelar *vt* to imprison.

encarecimiento *m* price increase: — con ~ insistently.

encargado(a) *adj* in charge;
* *m(f)* representative; person in charge.

encargar *vt* to charge; to commission.

encariñarse *vr*; ~ con to grow fond of.

encarnar *vt* to embody, to personify.

encasillar *vt* to pigeonhole; to typecast.

encastillarse *vr* to refuse to yield.

encauzar *vt* to channel.

encebollado *m* casseroled spiced beef or lamb and

onions.

encenagado(a) *adj* muddy, mud-stained.

encendedor *m* lighter.

encender *vt* to kindle, to light, to set on fire; to inflame, to incite; to switch on, turn on; * ~se *vr* to catch fire; to flare up.

encerado *m* blackboard.

encerar *vt* to wax; to polish.

encerrar *vt* to shut up, to confine; to contain; * ~se *vr* to withdraw from the world.

enchufar *vt* to plug in; to connect.

enchufe *m* plug; socket; connection; (*sl*) contact, connection.

encía *f* gum (of the mouth).

encierro *m* confinement; enclosure; prison; bull-pen; penning (of bulls).

encima *adv* above; over; at the top; besides; * ~ de *prep* above; over; at the top of; besides.

encina *f* evergreen oak.

encinta *adj* pregnant.

enclenque *adj* weak, sickly; * *m* weakling.

encoger *vt* to contract, to shorten; to shrink; to discourage; * ~se *vr* to shrink; (*fig*) to cringe.

encolar *vt* to glue.

encolerizar *vt* to provoke, to irritate; * ~se *vr* to get angry.

encomendar *vt* to recommend; to entrust; * ~se a *vr* to entrust oneself to; to put one's trust in.

encontrar *vt* to meet, to encounter; * ~se con *vr* to run into; * *vi* to assemble, come together.

encrucijada *f* crossroads; junction.

encuadernar *vt* to bind (books).

encubierto(a) *adj* hidden, concealed.

encubrir *vt* to hide, to conceal.

encuesta *f* inquiry; opinion poll.

encurtir *vt* to pickle.

endeble *adj* feeble, weak.

endemoniado(a) *adj* possessed with the devil; devilish.

enderezar *vt* to straighten out; to set right; * ~se *vr* to stand upright.

endeudarse *vr* to get into debt.

endivia *f* (botany) endive.

endosar *vt* to endorse.

endrino *m* blackthorn, sloe.

endulzar *vt* to sweeten; to soften.

endurecer *vt* to harden, to toughen; * ~se *vr* to become cruel; to grow hard.

enebro *m* (botany) juniper.

enemigo(a) *m(f)* enemy, hostile.

enemistar *vt* to make an enemy; * ~se *vr* to become enemies; to fall out.

energía *f* energy, power, drive; strength of will.

energúmeno(a) *m(f)* (*sl*) mad man or woman.

enero *m* January.

enfadar *vt* to anger, to irritate; to trouble; * ~se *vr* to become angry.

énfasis *m* emphasis.

enfermar *vi* to fall ill; * *vt* to make sick; to weaken.

enfermedad *f* illness.

enfermero(a) *m(f)* nurse.

enfermo(a) *adj* sick, ill; * *m(f)* invalid, sick person; patient.

enfocar *vt* to focus; to consider (a problem).

enfoque *m* focus.

enfrentar *vt* to confront; to put face to face; * ~se *vr* to face each other; to meet (two teams).

enfrente *adv* over against, opposite; in front.

enfriar *vt* to cool; to refrigerate; * ~se *vr* to cool down; (medical) to catch a cold.

enfurecer *vt* to madden, to enrage; * ~se *vr* to get rough (of the weather); to become furious or enraged.

enfurruñarse *vr* to get sulky; to frown.

engañar *vt* to deceive, to cheat; * ~se *vr* to be deceived; to be wrong.

enganchar *vt* to hook, to hang up; to hitch up; to couple, to connect; to recruit into military service; * ~se *vr* (military) to enlist.

engañoso(a) *adj* deceitful, artful, false.

engatusar *vt* to coax.

engendrar *vt* to beget, to engender; to produce.

englobar *vt* to include.

engordar *vt* to fatten; * *vi* to grow fat; to put on weight.

engorroso(a) *adj* troublesome, cumbersome.

engranaje *m* gear; gearing.

engrasar *vt* to grease, to lubricate.

engreído(a) *adj* conceited, vain.

engullir *vt* to swallow; to gobble, to devour.

enharinar *vt* to cover or sprinkle with flour.

enhebrar *vt* to thread.

enhorabuena *f* congratulations *pl.*

enhoramala *interj* good riddance!

enjambre *m* swarm of bees; crowd, multitude.

enjuagar *vt* to rinse out; to wash out.

enjuiciar *vt* to prosecute, to try; to pass judgment on, judge.

enlace *m* connection, link; relationship.

enladrillar *vt* to pave with bricks.

enlazar *vt* to join, to unite; to tie.

enlodar *vt* to cover in mud; (*fig*) to stain.

enloquecer *vt* to madden, to drive crazy; * *vi* to go mad.

enmarañar *vt* to entangle; to complicate; to confuse; * ~se *vr* to become entangled; to get confused.

enmarcar *vt* to frame.

enmendar *vt* to correct; to reform; to repair; to compensate for; to amend; * ~se *vr* to mend one's ways.

enmohecer *vt* to make mouldy; to rust; * ~se *vr* to grow mouldy or musty; to rust.

enmudecer *vt* to silence; * ~se *vr* to grow dumb; to be silent.

ennegrecer *vt* to blacken; to darken; to obscure.

enojar *vt* to irritate, to make angry; to annoy; to upset; to offend; * ~se *vr* to get angry.

enorgullecerse *vr*; ~ (de) to be proud (of).

enorme *adj* enormous, vast, huge; horrible.

enredadera *f* climbing plant; bindweed.

enredar *vt* to entangle, to ensnare, to confound, to perplex; to puzzle; to sow discord among; * ~se *vr* to get entangled; to get complicated; to get embroiled.

enrejado *m* trelliswork.

enrevesado(a) *adj* complicated.

enriquecer *vt* to enrich; to adorn; * ~se *vr* to grow rich.

enrojecer *vt* to redden; * *vi* to blush.

enrolar *vt* to recruit; * ~se *vr* (military) to join up.

enrollar *vt* to roll (up).

enroscar *vt* to twist; * ~se *vr* to curl or roll up.

ensalada *f* salad.

ensalmo *m* enchantment, spell.

ensalzar *vt* to exalt, to aggrandise; to exaggerate.

ensamblar *vt* to assemble.

ensanchar *vt* to widen; to extend; to enlarge; * ~se *vr* to expand; to assume an air of importance.

ensangrentar *vt* to stain with blood.

ensañar *vt* to irritate, to enrage; * ~se con *vr* to treat brutally.

ensartar *vt* to string (beads, etc).

ensayar *vt* to test; to rehearse.

ensayo *m* test, trial; rehearsal of a play; essay.

enseguida *adv* at once, right away.

enseñar *vt* to teach, to instruct; to show.

ensimismar *vr*; ~se to be or become lost in thought.

ensordecer *vt* to deafen; * *vi* to grow deaf.

ensuciar *vt* to stain, to soil; to defile; * ~se *vr* to wet oneself; to dirty oneself.

ensueño *m* fantasy; daydream; illusion.

entablar *vt* to board (up); to strike up (conversation).

entabillar *vt* (medical) to put in a splint.

entallar *vi* to tailor (a suit); * *vi* to fit.

ente *m* organisation; entity, being; (*sl*) odd character.

entender *vt*, *vi* to understand, to comprehend; to remark, to take notice (of); to reason, to think; * a mi ~ *m* in my opinion; * ~se *vr* to understand each other.

enterar *vt* to inform; to instruct; * ~se *vr* to find out.

enternecer *vt* to soften; to move (to pity); * ~se *vr* to be moved (to pity).

entero(a) *adj* entire, complete; perfect; honest; resolute:
— por ~ entirely, completely.

enterrar *vt* to inter, to bury.

entidad *f* entity; company; body; society.

entierro *m* burial; funeral.

entonar *vt* to tune, to intonate; to intone; to tone; * *vi* to be in tune; * ~se *vr* to give oneself airs.

entonces *adv* then, at that time.

entornar *vt* to half-close.

entorpecer *vt* to dull; to make lethargic; to hinder; to delay.

entrada *f* entrance, entry; gate; (commerce) receipts *pl*; entree; ticket (for cinema, theatre, etc): — prohibida la ~ no entry.

entrampar *vt* to trap, to snare to mess up; to burden with debts; * ~se *vr* get into debt.

entrañable *adj* intimate; affectionate.

entrañas *fpl* entrails *pl*, intestines *pl*.

entrar *vi* to enter, to go in; to commence.

entre *prep* between, amongst, in; ~ manos in hand.

entrecejo *m* space between the eyebrows; frown.

entredicho *m* (law) injunction:
— estar en ~ to be banned:
— poner en ~ to cast doubt on.

entrega *f* delivery; ~ a domicilio door to door service.

entregar *vt* to deliver; to hand over; * ~se *vr* to surrender; to devote oneself.

entremeses *mpl* hors d'oeuvres.

entrenarse *vr* to train.

entrepierna *f* crotch.

entresuelo *m* entresol; mezzanine.

entretanto *adv* meanwhile.

entretejer *vt* to interweave.

entretela *f* interfacing, stiffening, interlining.

entretener *vt* to amuse; to entertain, to divert; to hold up; to maintain; * ~se *vr* to amuse oneself; to linger.

entrever *vt* to have a glimpse of.

entrevistar *vt* to interview; * ~se *vr* to have an interview.

entristecer *vt* to sadden.

entrometer *vt* to put (one thing) between (others); * ~se *vr* to interfere, to meddle.

entumecido(a) *adj* numb, stiff.

enturbiar *vt* to make cloudy; to obscure, to confound; * ~se *vr* to become cloudy; (*fig*) to get confused.

entusiasmar *vt* to excite, to fill with enthusiasm; to delight.

enumerar *vt* to enumerate.

envalentonar *vt* to give courage to; * ~se *vr* to boast.

envanecer *vt* to make vain; to swell with pride; * ~se *vr* to become proud.

envaramiento *m* stiffness; numbness.

envasar *vt* to pack; to bottle; to can.

envase *m* packing; bottling; canning; container; package; bottle; can.

envejecer *vt* to make old; * *vi*, ~se *vr* to grow old.

envenenar *vt* to poison; to embitter.

envés *m* back, wrong side (of material).

enviar *vt* to send, to transmit, to convey, to dispatch.

enviciar *vt* to vitiate, to corrupt; * ~se *vr* to get corrupted.

envidia *f* envy; jealousy.

envidiar *vt* to envy; to grudge; to be jealous of.

envilecer *vt* to vilify, to debase; * ~se *vr* to degrade oneself.

envío *m* (commerce) dispatch, remittance of goods; consignment.

enviudar *vi* to become a widower or widow.

envolver *vt* to involve; to wrap up.

enyesar *vt* to plaster; (medical) to put in a plaster cast.

enzarzarse *vr* to get involved in a dispute; to get oneself into trouble.

épico(a) *adj* epic.

epígrafe *f* epigraph, inscription; motto; headline.

episodio *m* episode, instalment.

época *f* epoch; period, time.

epopeya *f* epic.

equidad *f* equity, honesty; impartiality, justice.

equilibrar *vt* to balance; to poise.

equilibrio *m* balance, equilibrium.

equipaje *m* luggage; equipment.

equipar *vt* to fit out, to equip, to furnish.

equipararse *vt*; ~ con to be on a level with.

equipo *m* equipment; team; shift.

equitación *f* horsemanship; riding.

equitativo(a) *adj* equitable; just.

equivaler *vi* to be of equal value.

equivocación *f* mistake, error; misunderstanding.

equivocar *vt* to mistake; * ~se *vr* to make a mistake, to be wrong.

equivoco(a) *adj* equivocal, ambiguous; * *m* equivocation; quibble.

era *f* era, age; threshing floor.

erario *m* treasury, public funds *pl*.

erguir *vt* to erect, to raise up straight; * ~se *vr* to straighten up.

erial *m* fallow land.

erigir *vt* to erect, to raise, to build; to establish.

erizarse *vr* to bristle; to stand on end.

erizo *m* hedgehog; ~ de mar sea urchin.

ermita *f* hermitage.

erotismo *m* eroticism.

errar *vi* to be mistaken; to wander.

errata *f* misprint.

erre: — ~ que ~ *adv* obstinately.

error *m* error, mistake, fault.

eructar *vi* to belch, to burp.

esa, esas *adj*, *see* ese.

ésa, ésas *pron*, *see* ése.

esbelto(a) *adj* slim, slender.

esbirro *m* bailiff; henchman; killer.

esbozo *m* outline.

escabeche *m* pickle; pickled fish.

escabroso(a) *adj* rough, uneven; craggy; rude, risqué, blue.

escabullirse *vr* to escape, to evade; to slip through one's fingers.

escafandra *f* diving suit; space suit.

escala *f* ladder; (music) scale; stopover.

escalar *vt* to climb.

escalera *f* staircase; ladder; ~ mecánica escalator; ~ de incendios fire escape.

escalfar *vt* to poach (eggs).

escalofriante *adj* chilling.

escalón *m* step of a stair; rung.

escama *f* (fish) scale.

escamar *vt* to scale, to take off scales; * ~se *vr* to flake off, to become suspicious.

escamotear *vt* to swipe; to make disappear.

escampar *vi* to stop raining.

escándalo *m* scandal; uproar.

escaño *m* bench with a back; seat (parliament).

escapar *vi* to escape;

* ~se *vr* to get away; to leak.

escaparate *m* shop window; wardrobe.

escape *m* escape, flight; leak; — tubo de ~ exhaust (car).

escarabajo *m* beetle.

escaramuza *f* skirmish; dispute, quarrel.

escarbar *vt* to scratch (the earth as hens do); to inquire into.

escarcha *f* white frost.

escarlata *adj* scarlet.

escarlatina *f* scarlet fever.

escarmentar *vi* to learn one's lesson; * *vt* to punish severely.

escarola *f* (botany) endive.

escarpado(a) *adj* sloped; craggy.

escaso(a) *adj* small, short, little; sparing; scarce; scanty.

escenario *m* stage; set.

escéptico(a) *adj* sceptic, sceptical.

esclarecer *vt* to lighten; to illuminate; to illustrate; to shed light on (problem, etc).

esclavo(a) *m(f)* slave; captive.

esclusa *f* sluice, floodgate.

escoba *f* broom, brush.

escocer *vt* to sting; to burn; * ~se *vr* to chafe.

escocés(a) *m(f)* Scots; Scotch whisky.

Escocia *f* Scotland.

escoger *vt* to choose, to select.

escolar *m* or *f* schoolboy or girl; * *adj* scholastic.

escollo *m* reef, rock.

escoltar *vt* to escort.

escombros *mpl* rubbish; debris.

esconder *vt* to hide, to conceal; * ~se *vr* to be hidden.

escondite *m* hiding place: — juego del ~ hide-and-seek.

escoplo *m* chisel.

escorbuto *m* scurvy.

escote *m* low neck (of a dress).

escribir *vi* to write; to spell.

escrito *m* document; manuscript, text.

escritor(a) *m(f)* writer, author.

escritorio *m* writing desk, office, study.

escrúpulo *m* doubt, scruple, scrupulousness.

escuchar *vt* to listen to, to heed, to listen.

escudilla *f* bowl.

escudo *m* shield.

escudriñar *vt* to search, to examine; to pry into.

escuela *f* school.

esculpir *vt* to sculpt.

escupir *vt* to spit.

escurreplatos *m invar* plate rack.

escurrir *vt* to drain; to drip; * ~se *vr* to slip away; to slip, to slide; * *vi* to wring out.

ese, **esa** *adj* that: — **esos**, **esas** *pl* those.

ése, **ésa** *pron* that (one): — **ésos**, **ésas** *pl* those (ones).

esencial *adj* essential; principal.

esfera *f* sphere; globe.

esforzarse *vr* to exert oneself, to make an effort.

esfuerzo *m* effort.

esfumarse *vr* to fade away.

esgrima *f* fencing.

esguince *m* (medical) sprain.

eslabón *m* link of a chain; steel; shackle.

esmalte *m* enamel; ~ de uñas nail varnish.

esmerado(a) *adj* careful, neat.

esmeralda *m* emerald.

esmero *m* careful attention, great care.

eso *pron* that.

esos, **ésos** *pl* of **esa**, **ésa**; *see* **ese**, **ése**.

espabilar *vt* to wake up; * ~se *vr* to wake up; (*fig*) to get a move on.

espaciar *vt* to spread out; to space (out).

espacio *m* space; (radio or TV) programme.

espada *f* sword; ace of spades.

espalda *f* back; (swimming) backstroke; ~s *fpl* shoulders *pl*.

espantajo *m* scarecrow; bogeyman.

espantar *vt* to frighten; to chase or drive away.

España *f* Spain.

español(a) *adj* Spanish; * *m(f)* Spaniard; * *pron* Spanish language.

esparadrapo *m* adhesive tape.

esparcir *vt* to scatter; to divulge; * ~se *vr* to amuse oneself.

espárrago *m* asparagus.

espátula *f* spatula.

especia *f* spice.

especial *adj* special; particular: — en ~ especially.

especie *f* species; kind, sort; matter.

especificar *vt* to specify.

espectáculo *m* spectacle; show.

espectador(a) *m(f)* spectator.

especular *vt* to speculate.

espejismo *m* mirage.

espejo *m* mirror.

espeluznante *adj* horrifying.

esperanza *f* hope.

esperar *vt* to hope; to expect, to wait for.

esperma *f* sperm.

espeso(a) *adj* thick, dense.

espesor *m* thickness.

espía *m* or *f* spy.

espiga *f* ear (of corn).

espigón *m* ear of corn; sting; (marine) breakwater.

espina *f* thorn; fishbone.

espinaca *f* (botany) spinach.

espinilla *f* shinbone.

espino *m* hawthorn.

espiral *adj*, *f* spiral.

espirar *vt* to exhale.

espíritu *m* spirit, soul; mind; intelligence: — el E~ Santo the Holy Ghost; ~s *pl* demons, hobgoblins *pl*.

espléndido(a) *adj* splendid.

espliego *m* (botany) lavender.

espolón *m* spur (of a cock); spur (of a mountain range); sea wall; jetty; (marine) buttress.

espolvorear *vt* to sprinkle.

esponja *f* sponge.

espontáneo(a) *adj* spontaneous.

esposa *f* wife.

esposas *fpl* handcuffs *pl*.

esposo *m* husband.

espuma *f* froth, foam.

espumar *vt* to skim, to take the scum off.

espumoso(a) *adj* frothy, foamy; sparkling (wine).

esputo *m* spit, saliva.

esqueje *m* cutting (of plant).

esquela *f* note, slip of paper, announcement.

esqueleto *m* skeleton.

esquema *m* scheme; diagram; plan.

esquí *m* ski; skiing; ~ acuático water-skiing.

esquina *f* corner, angle.

esquirol *m* blackleg; (*sl*) strikebreaker.

esquivar *vt* to shun, to avoid, to evade.

esta *adj f* this; ~s *pl* these.

ésta *pron f* this; ~s *pl* these.

estable *adj* stable.

establecer *vt* to establish.

establo *m* stable.

estaca *f* stake; stick; post.

estación *f* season (of the year); station; railway station, terminus; ~ de autobuses bus station; ~ de servicio service station.

estacionar *vt* to park; (military) to station.

estadio *m* phase; stadium.

estado *m* state, condition.

Estados Unidos *mpl* United States (of America).

estafar *vt* to deceive, to defraud.

estallar *vi* to crack; to burst; to break out.

estambre *m* (botany) stamen.

estamento *m* estate; body; layer; class.

estampa *f* print; engraving; appearance.

estampar *vt* to print.

estancar *vt* to check (a current); to monopolise; to prohibit, to suspend; * ~se *vr* to stagnate.

estancia *f* stay; bedroom; ranch; (poetical) stanza.

estanco *m* tobacconist's (shop).

estándar *adj*, *m* standard.

estaño *m* tin.

estanque *m* pond, pool; reservoir.

estante *m* rack, stand; bookcase; shelf.

estantería *f* shelves *pl*, shelving.

estar *vi* to be.

estatua *f* statue.

este *m* east.

este, **esta** *adj* this; **estos**, **estas** *pl* these.

éste, **ésta** *pron* this one; **éstos**, **éstas** *pl* these ones.

estera *f* mat.

estéreo *m* stereo.

estereotipo *m* stereotype.

estéril *adj* sterile, infertile.

esterlina *adj*: — libra ~ pound sterling.

estético(a) *adj* aesthetic; * *f* aesthetics.

estiércol *m* dung; manure.

estilo *m* style; fashion; stroke (swimming).

estima *f* esteem.

estimar *vi* to estimate, to value; to esteem; to judge; to think.

estimular *vt* to stimulate, to excite; to goad.

estío *m* summer.

estipular *vt* to stipulate.

estirar *vt* to stretch out.

esto *pron* this.

estofado *m* stew.

estómago *m* stomach.

estopa *f* tow.

estorbar *vt* to hinder; (*fig*) to bother; * *vi* to be in the way.

estornudar *vi* to sneeze.

estos, estas *pl* of este.

éstos, éstas *pl* of éste.

estrado *m* drawing room; stage, platform.

estrafalario(a) *adj* slovenly; eccentric.

estrago *m* ruin, destruction; havoc.

estrangular *vt* to strangle; (medical) to strangulate.

estraperlo *m* black market.

estratagema *f* stratagem, trick.

estrato *m* stratum, layer.

estraza *f* rag: — papel de ~ brown paper.

estrechar *vt* to tighten; to contract, to constrain; to compress; * ~se *vr* to grow narrow; to embrace; ~ la mano to shake hands.

estrecho *m* straits; channel *pl*; * ~(a) *adj* narrow, close; tight; intimate; rigid, austere; short (of money).

estrella *f* star.

estrellar *vt* to dash to pieces; * ~se *vr* to smash; to crash; to fail.

estremecer *vt* to shake, to make tremble; * ~se *vr* to shake, to tremble.

estrenar *vt* to wear for the first time; to move into (a house); to show (a film) for the first time; * ~se *vr* to make one's début.

estreñido(a) *adj* constipated.

estrépito *m* noise, racket; fuss.

estribillo *m* chorus.

estribo *m* buttress; stirrup; running board: — perder los ~s to fly off the handle (*sl*).

estribor *m* (marine) starboard.

estricto(a) *adj* strict; severe.

estrofa *f* (poetical) verse, strophe.

estropajo *m* scourer.

estropear *vt* to spoil; to damage; * ~se *vr* to get damaged.

estructura *f* structure.

estruendo *m* clamour, noise; confusion, uproar; pomp, ostentation.

estuche *m* case (for e.g. scissors); sheath.

estudiar *vt* to study.

estudio *m* study, research.

estufa *f* heater, fire.

estupefaciente *m* narcotic.

estupefacto(a) *adj* speechless; thunderstruck.

estupendo(a) *adj* terrific, marvellous.

estúpido(a) *adj* stupid.

etapa *f* stage; stopping place; (*fig*) phase.

etcétera *adv* etcetera, and so on.

eterno(a) *adj* eternal.

ético(a) *adj* ethical, moral.

etiqueta *f* etiquette; label.

evacuar *vt* to evacuate, to empty.

evadir *vt* to evade, to escape.

evaluar *vt* to evaluate.

evaporar *vt* to evaporate; * ~se *vr* to vanish.

eventual *adj* possible; temporary, casual (worker).

evidente *adj* evident, clear.

evitar *vt* to avoid.

evolucionar *vi* to evolve.

ex *adj* ex.

ex profeso *adv* on purpose.

exacerbar *vt* to exacerbate; to irritate.

exacto(a) *adj* exact; punctual; accurate.

exagerar *vt* to exaggerate.

exaltar *vt* to exalt, to elevate; to praise, to extol; * ~se *vr* to get excited.

examen *m* exam, examination, test, inquiry.

examinar *vt* to examine.

exasperar *vt* to exasperate, to irritate.

excavar *vt* to excavate, to dig out.

exceder *vt* to exceed, to surpass, to excel, to outdo.

excelente *adj* excellent.

excéntrico(a) *adj* eccentric.

excepto *adv* excepting, except (for).

excesivo(a) *adj* excessive, unreasonable.

exceso *m* excess.

excitar *vt* to excite; * ~se *vr* to get excited.

exclamar *vt* to exclaim, to cry out.

excluir *vt* to exclude.

excremento *m* excrement.

excursión *f* excursion, trip.

excusa *f* excuse, apology.

excusado *m* toilet.

excusar *vt* to excuse; to avoid; ~ de to exempt from; * ~se *vr* to apologise.

exento(a) *adj* exempt, free.

exhalar *vt* to exhale; to give off, to heave (a sigh).

exhausto(a) *adj* exhausted.

exhibir *vt* to exhibit.

exhortar *vt* to exhort.

exhumar *vt* to disinter, to exhume.

exigir *vt* to demand, to require.

exiliado(a) *adj* exiled; * *m(f)* exile.

existir *vi* to exist, to be.

éxito *m* outcome; success; (music, *sl*) hit: — tener ~ to be successful.

exorbitante *adj* exhorbitant, excessive.

exótico(a) *adj* exotic.

expandir *vt* to expand.

expatriarse *vr* to emigrate; to go into exile.

expectativa *f* expectation; prospect.

expedición *f* expedition.

expediente *m* expedient; means; (law) proceedings *pl*; dossier, file.

expedir *vt* to send, to forward, to dispatch.

expensas *fpl*: — a ~ de at the expense of.

experimentar *vt* to experience; * *vi* ~ con to experiment with.

experto(a) *adj* expert; experienced.

expiar *vt* to atone for; to purify.

expirar *vi* to expire.

explayarse *vr* to speak at length.

explicar *vt* to explain, to expound; * ~se *vr* to explain oneself.

explorar *vt* to explore.

explotar *vt* to exploit; to run; * *vi* to explode.

exponer *vt* to expose; to explain.

exportar *vt* to export.

exposición *f* exposure; exhibition; explanation; account.

expresar *vt* to express.

expreso(a) *adj* express, clear, specific; fast (train).

exprimir *vt* to squeeze out.

expropriar *vt* to expropriate.

expulsar *vt* to expel, to drive out.

éxtasis *m* ecstasy, enthusiasm.

extender *vt* to extend, stretch out; * ~se *vr* to extend; to spread.

extenso(a) *adj* extensive.

extenuar *vt* to exhaust, to debilitate.

exterior *adj* exterior, external; * *m* exterior, outward appearance.

exterminar *vt* to exterminate.

externo(a) *adj* external, outer; * *m(f)* day pupil.

extinguir *vt* to wipe out; to extinguish.

extintor *m* (fire) extinguisher.
extra *adj invar* extra; good
quality; * *m* or *f* extra:
— *m* bonus.
extraer *vt* to extract.
extranjero(a) *m(f)* stranger;
foreigner; *adj* foreign, alien.
extrañar *vt* to find strange; to
miss; * ~se *vr* to be surprised;
to grow apart.
extraño(a) *adj* foreign; rare;
singular, strange, odd.
extraviar *vt* to mislead;
* ~se *vr* to lose one's way.
extremidad *f* extremity; brim;
tip; ~es *fpl* extremities *pl*.
extremo(a) *adj* extreme, last;
* *m* extreme, highest degree:
— en ~, por ~ extremely.
extrovertido(a) *adj*, *m(f)*
extrovert.
exuberencia *f* exuberance;
luxuriance.

F

fabada *f* bean and sausage stew.
fábrica *f* factory.
fabricación *f* manufacture:
— de ~ casera home made.
fabricar *vt* to build, to
construct; to manufacture;
(*fig*) to fabricate.
fábula *f* fable; fiction;
rumour, common talk.
fabuloso(a) *adj* fabulous,
fictitious.
facción *f* (political) faction;
feature.
fachada *f* façade, face, front.
facial *adj* facial.
fácil *adj* facile, easy.
facilidad *f* ease; simplicity;
~ de pago credit facilities.
facilitar *vt* to facilitate.
fácilmente *adv* easily.
factor *m* (maths) factor;
(commerce) factor, agent.
factura *f* invoice.

facultativo(a) *adj* optional;
* *m(f)* doctor, practitioner.
faena *f* task, job; hard work.
faisán *m* pheasant.
fajo *m* bundle; wad.
falaz *adj* deceitful, fraudulent;
fallacious.
falda *f* skirt; lap; flap; train;
slope, hillside.
fallar *vt* (law) to pronounce
sentence on, judge; * *vi* to fail.
fallecer *vi* to die.
fallo *m* verdict, ruling;
decision; failure.
falso(a) *adj* false, untrue;
deceitful; fake.
falta *f* fault, defect; want;
flaw, mistake; (sport) foul.
faltar *vi* to fail; not to fulfil
one's promise; to need; to be
missing.
fama *f* fame; reputation, name.
familia *f* family.
familiar *adj* familiar; homely,
domestic; * *m* or *f* relative,
relation.
famoso(a) *adj* famous.
fanático(a) *adj* fanatical,
fanatic.
fanfarrón *m* bully, braggart.
fango *m* mire, mud.
fantasía *f* fancy; fantasy;
caprice; presumption.
fantasma *f* phantom, ghost.
fantástico(a) *adj* fantastic.
fardo *m* bale, parcel.
farmacia *f* pharmacy.
faro *m* (marine) lighthouse;
(car) headlamp; floodlight.
farola *f* street light.
fascículo *m* part, instalment.
fascinante *adj* fascinating.
fascinar *vt* to fascinate; to
enchant.
fase *f* phase.
fastidiar *vt* to annoy; to
offend; to spoil.
fatal *adj* fatal; mortal; awful.
fatiga *f* weariness, fatigue.
fatuo(a) *adj* fatuous, stupid,

foolish; conceited.

fauces *fpl* jaws *pl*, gullet.

favor *m* favour; protection; good turn: — **por** ~ please.

favorecer *vt* to favour, to protect.

fax *m* fax.

faz *f* face.

fe *f* faith, belief.

febrero *m* February.

fecha *f* date (of a letter etc).

fecundar *vt* to fertilise.

felicitar *vt* to congratulate.

feliz *adj* happy, fortunate.

felpa *f* plush; towelling.

felpudo *m* doormat.

femenino(a) *adj* feminine; female.

feo(a) *adj* ugly; bad, nasty.

feria *f* fair, rest day; village market.

fermentar *vi* to ferment.

feroz *adj* ferocious, savage; cruel.

ferretería *f* ironmonger's shop.

ferrocarril *m* railway.

ferroviario(a) *adj* rail, railway; railway workers.

fértil *adj* fertile, fruitful.

festejo *m* courtship; feast.

festivo(a) *adj* festive, merry; witty: — **día** ~ bank holiday.

eto *m* foetus.

fiable *adj* trustworthy; reliable.

fiambre *m* cold meat; (*sl*) cadaver.

fiambrera *f* lunch box.

fianza *f* (law) surety: —**libertad bajo** ~ release on bail.

fiar *vt* to entrust, to confide; to bail; to sell on credit; * ~**se** *vr* to trust.

fibra *f* fibre.

ficha *f* token, counter (at games); (index) card.

fidelidad *f* fidelity; loyalty.

fideos *mpl* noodles *pl*.

fiebre *f* fever.

fiel *adj* faithful, loyal; * *mpl* **los** ~**es** the faithful *pl*.

fieltro *m* felt.

fiera *f* wild beast.

fiero(a) *adj* fierce, ferocious.

fiesta *f* party; festivity; ~**s** *fpl* holidays *pl*, vacations *pl*.

figura *f* figure, shape.

figurar *vt* to figure; * ~**se** *vr* to fancy, to imagine.

fijar *vt* to fix, to fasten; * ~**se** *vr* to become fixed; ~**se en** to notice.

fijo(a) *adj* fixed, firm; settled, permanent.

fila *f* row, line; (military) rank: — **en** ~ in a line, in a row.

filete *m* fillet; fillet steak.

filmar *vt* to film.

filo *m* edge, blade.

filosofía *f* philosophy.

filtro *m* filter.

fin *m* end; termination, conclusion; aim, purpose: — **al** ~ at last; * **en** ~ (*fig*) well then: — **por** ~ finally, lastly.

final *adj* end, conclusion.

finalmente *adv* finally, at last.

financiar *vt* to finance.

finca *f* land, property; country house; farm.

fingir *vt* to feign, to fake; * ~**se** *vr* to pretend to be; * *vi* to pretend.

fino(a) *adj* fine, pure; slender; polite; acute; dry (sherry).

firma *f* signature; (commerce) company.

firmamento *m* firmament, sky, heaven.

firme *adj* firm, stable, strong, secure; constant; resolute; * *m* road surface.

fiscal *adj* fiscal; * *m* or *f* district attorney.

fisco *m* treasury, exchequer.

fisgar *vt* to pry into.

física *f* physics.

flaco(a) *adj* lean, skinny; feeble.

flan *m* crème caramel.

flauta *f* (music) flute.

flecha *f* arrow.
fleco *m* fringe.
flequillo *m* fringe (of hair).
flete *m* (marine) freight;
charter.
flexible *adj* flexible;
compliant; docile.
flojo(a) *adj* loose; flexible; lax,
slack; lazy.
flor *f* flower.
florecer *vi* to blossom.
florero *m* vase.
flotador *m* float; rubber ring.
flotar *vi* to float.
fluctuar *vi* to fluctuate; to
waver.
fluido(a) *adj* fluid, fluent.
fluir *vi* to flow.
flujo *m* flow; swing.
fluvial *adj* fluvial, riverine.
folio *m* leaf, paper.
foca *f* seal.
foco *m* focus; centre; source;
floodlight; (light)bulb.
fogón *m* stove; hearth.
fogoso(a) *adj* fiery; ardent,
fervent; impetuous,
boisterous.
folleto *m* pamphlet; folder,
brochure.
follón *m* (*sl*) mess; fuss.
fomentar *vt* to encourage; to
promote.
fondo *m* bottom; back;
background; space;
~s *mpl* stock, funds *pl*, capital:
— a ~ perfectly, completely.
fontanero(a) *m(f)* plumber.
forjar *vt* to forge; to frame; to
invent.
forma *f* form, shape; pattern;
(medical) fitness; (sport) form;
means, method: — de ~ que in
such a manner that.
formación *f* formation; form,
figure; education; training.
formar *vt* to form, to shape.
fornido(a) *adj* well-built.
forro *m* lining; book jacket.
fortuna *f* fortune; wealth.

forzar *vt* to force.
forzoso(a) *adj* indispensable,
necessary.
fosa *f* grave; pit.
fósforo *m* phosphorus;
— ~s *mpl* matches *pl*.
fotocopia *f* photocopy.
foto *m* photo; sacar una ~ to
take a photo.
fotografía *f* photography;
photograph.
fotomatón *m* photo booth.
fracasar *vi* to fail.
frágil *adj* fragile, frail.
fraguar *vt* to forge; to contrive;
* *vi* to solidify, to harden.
fraile *m* friar, monk.
frambuesa *f* raspberry.
francés(a) *adj* French;
* *m* French language;
m(f) French man or woman.
Francia *m* France.
frasco *m* flask.
frase *f* phrase.
fraternal *adj* fraternal,
brotherly.
fraude *m* fraud, deceit; cheat.
frecuencia *f* frequency.
fregar *vt* to scrub; to wash up.
freír *vt* to fry.
freído(a) *adj* fried.
frenar *vt* to brake; (*fig*) to check.
frenesí *m* frenzy.
freno *m* bit; brake; (*fig*) check.
frente *f* front; face; ~ a ~ face to
face: — en~ opposite; (military)
front; * *m* forehead.
fresa *f* strawberry.
fresco(a) *adj* fresh; cool; new;
ruddy; * *m* fresh air: — *m(f)* (*sl*)
shameless or impudent person.
fresno *m* ash tree.
frigorífico *m* fridge.
frío(a) *adj* cold; indifferent;
* *m* cold; indifference.
frito(a) *adj* fried.
frívolo(a) *adj* frivolous.
frondoso(a) *adj* leafy.
frontera *f* frontier.
frontón *m* (sport) pelota court.

frotar *vt* to rub.
fructificar *vi* to bear fruit; to come to fruition.
frugal *adj* frugal, sparing.
fruncir *vt* to pleat; to knit; to contract; ~ las cejas, ~ el ceño to knit the eyebrows.
frustrar *vt* to frustrate.
fruta *f* fruit; ~ del tiempo seasonal fruit.
frutal *m* fruit tree.
frutería *f* fruit shop.
fuego *m* fire.
fuente *f* fountain; spring; source; large dish.
fuera *adv* out(side); away; * ~ de *prep* outside: — ¡~! out of the way!
fuerte *m* (military) fortification, fort; forte; * *adj* vigorous, tough; strong; loud; heavy; * *adv* strongly; hard.
fuerza *f* force, strength; (electricity) power; violence: — a ~ de by dint of; ~s *mpl* troops *pl*.
fugarse *vr* to escape, to flee.
fugaz *adj* fleeting.
fumar *vt, vi* to smoke.
función *f* function; duties *pl*; show, performance.
funcionar *vi* to function; to work (of a machine).
funcionario(a) *m(f)* official; civil servant.
funda *f* case, cover, sheath; ~ de almohada pillowcase.
fundar *vt* to found; to establish; to ground.
fundir *vt* to fuse; to melt; to smelt; (commerce) to merge; to bankrupt; (electricity) to fuse, blow.
fúnebre *adj* mournful, sad; funereal.
furgoneta *f* pick-up (truck).
furioso(a) *adj* furious.
furtivo(a) *adj* furtive.
fusible *m* fuse.

fusión *f* fusion; (commerce) merger.
fútbol *m* football.
futuro(a) *adj, m* future.

G

gabardina *f* gabardine; raincoat.
gabinete *m* (politics) cabinet, study; office (eg of solicitors).
gafas *fpl* glasses *pl*, spectacles *pl*.
gafe *m* jinx.
gajo *m* segment (of orange).
galápago *m* tortoise.
galardón *m* reward, prize.
galera *f* (marine) galley; wagon.
galería *f* gallery.
galgo *m* greyhound.
gallardo(a) *adj* graceful, elegant; brave, daring.
galleta *f* biscuit.
gallina *f* hen: — *m* or *f* (*fig*) coward.
gallo *m* cock.
gama *f* (music) scale; (*fig*) range, gamut; doe.
gamba *f* prawn.
gamberro(a) *m(f)* hooligan.
gamuza *f* chamois.
gana *f* desire, wish; appetite; will, longing: — de buena ~ with pleasure, voluntarily: — de mala ~ unwillingly, with reluctance.
ganado *m* livestock, cattle *pl*: ~ mayor horses and mules *pl*: ~ menor sheep, goats and pigs *pl*.
ganador(a) *adj* winning; winner.
ganar *vt* to gain; to win; to earn; * *vi* to win.
gancho *m* hook; crook.
gandul *adj, m* or *f* layabout.
ganga *f* bargain.
ganso(a) *m(f)* gander; goose; (*sl*) idiot.

garaje *m* garage.
garantía *f* warranty,
  guarantee.
garbanzo *m* chickpea.
garbo *m* gracefulness, elegance;
  stylishness; generosity.
garganta *f* throat, gullet;
  instep; neck (of a bottle);
  narrow pass between
  mountains or rivers.
gárgara *f* gargling, gargle.
garra *f* claw; talon; paw.
garrafa *f* carafe; (gas)
  cylinder.
garrafal *adj* great, vast, huge.
garrapata *f* (zoology) tick.
garrucha *f* pulley.
garza *f* heron.
gasa *f* gauze.
gaseoso(a) *adj* fizzy;
  * *f* lemonade.
gasoil *m* diesel (oil).
gasolina *f* petrol.
gasolinera *f* petrol station.
gastar *vt* to spend; to expend;
  to waste; to wear away; to
  use up; * ~se *vr* to wear out;
  to waste.
gata *f* she-cat: — a ~s on all
  fours.
gato *m* cat; jack.
gavilán *m* sparrowhawk.
gavilla *f* sheaf of corn.
gaviota *f* seagull.
gazpacho *m* chilled soup of
  tomatoes or almonds.
gelatina *f* jelly; gelatine.
gemelo(a) *m(f)* twin.
gemir *vi* to groan, to moan.
generación *f* generation;
  progeny, race.
general *m* general; * *adj* general:
  — en ~ generally, in general.
género *m* genus; kind, type;
  gender; cloth, material;
  ~s *mpl* goods,
  commodities *pl*.
generoso(a) *adj* noble,
  generous.
genial *adj* brilliant; genial.

genio *m* nature, character;
  genius.
genital *adj* genital;
  * *mpl* ~es genitals *pl*.
gente *f* people; nation; family.
gentileza *f* grace; charm;
  politeness.
genuino(a) *adj* genuine; pure.
geografía *f* geography.
geología *f* geology.
geometría *f* geometry.
geranio *m* (botany) geranium.
gerente *m* or *f* manager;
  director.
germinar *vi* to germinate, to
  bud.
gestión *f* management;
  negotiation.
gesticular *vi* to gesture; to
  make faces.
gesto *m* face; grimace; gesture.
gigante *m* giant; * *adj* gigantic.
gilipollas *adj invar* (*sl*) stupid.
gimnasia *f* gymnastics.
ginebra *f* gin.
ginecólogo(a) *m(f)* gynecologist.
gira *f* trip, tour.
girar *vt* to turn around; to
  swivel; * *vi* to go round, to
  revolve.
girasol *m* (botany) sunflower.
gitano(a) *m(f)* gipsy.
glacial *adj* icy.
glándula *f* gland.
globo *m* globe; sphere; orb;
  balloon; ~ aerostático air
  balloon.
glorieta *f* bower, arbour;
  roundabout.
glotón(a) *m(f)* glutton.
gobierno *m* government.
goce *m* enjoyment.
gol *m* goal.
golondrina *f* swallow.
golosina *f* dainty, titbit; sweet.
golpe *m* blow, stroke, hit;
  knock; clash; coup:
  — de ~ suddenly.
goma *f* gum; rubber; elastic;
  (*sl*) condom.

gordo(a) *adj* fat, plump, big-bellied; first, main; (*sl*) enormous.

gorjear *vi* to twitter, to chirp.

gorrión *m* sparrow.

gorro *m* cap; bonnet.

gorrón(ona) *m(f)* scrounger.

gota *f* drop; (medical) gout.

gotera *f* leak.

gozar *vt* to enjoy, to have, to possess; * ~se *vr* to enjoy oneself, rejoice.

gozne *m* hinge.

gozo *m* joy, pleasure.

grabado *m* engraving.

grabar *vt* to engrave; to record.

gracia *f* grace, gracefulness; wit: — ¡(muchas) ~s! thanks (very much): — tener ~ to be funny.

gracioso(a) *adj* graceful; beautiful; funny; pleasing.

grada *f* step of a staircase; tier, row: ~s *fpl* seats *pl*.

grado *m* step; degree: — de buen ~ willingly.

gráfico(a) *adj* graphic; * *m* diagram: — *f* graph.

grajo *m* rook.

gramo *m* gram(me).

gran *adj* = grande.

granada *f* pomegranate.

granate *m* garnet (precious stone).

grande *adj* great; big; tall; grand; * *m* or *f* adult.

grandioso(a) *adj* grand, magnificent.

granel *adv*: — a ~ in bulk.

granizado *m* iced drink.

granizo *m* hail.

granja *f* farm.

grano *m* grain; seed.

granuja *m* or *f* rogue; urchin.

grapa *f* staple; clamp.

grasa *f* suet, fat; grease.

gratis *adj* free.

grato(a) *adj* pleasant, agreeable.

grave *adj* weighty, heavy; grave, important; serious.

gravilla *f* gravel.

gravoso(a) *adj* onerous, burdensome; costly.

graznar *vi* to croak; to cackle; to quack.

gremio *m* union, guild; society; company, corporation.

greña *f* tangle; shock of hair.

gresca *f* clatter; outcry; confusion; wrangle, quarrel.

grieta *f* crevice, crack, chink.

grifo *m* tap, faucet; petrol station.

grillo *m* cricket; bud, shoot.

gripe *f* flu, influenza.

gris *adj* grey.

gritar *vi* to cry out, to shout, to yell.

grosella *f* redcurrant; ~ negra blackcurrant.

grosero(a) *adj* coarse; rude, bad mannered.

grosor *m* thickness.

grúa *f* crane (machine); derrick.

grueso(a) *adj* thick; bulky; large; coarse; * *m* bulk.

grulla *f* crane (bird).

gruñir *vi* to grunt; to grumble; to creak (of hinges etc).

grupo *m* group.

gruta *f* grotto.

guadaña *f* scythe.

guagua *f* bus.

guante *m* glove.

guapo(a) *adj* good-looking; handsome; smart.

guardabosque *m* gamekeeper; ranger.

guardacostas *m invar* coastguard vessel.

guardaespaldas *m* or *f invar* bodyguard.

guardar *vt* to keep, to preserve; to save (money); to guard; * ~se *vr* to be on one's guard; ~se de to avoid, to abstain from.

guardarropa *f* wardrobe;

cloakroom.

guardia *f* guard; (marine) watch; care, custody: — *m* or *f* guard; policeman or woman: — *m* (military) guardsman.

guarecer *vt* to protect; to shelter; * ~se *vr* to take refuge.

guarnecer *vt* to provide, to equip; to reinforce; to garnish, to set (in gold, etc); to adorn.

guarnición *f* garnish.

guasa *f* joke.

gubernamental *adj* governmental.

guía *m* or *f* guide: — *f* guidebook.

guiar *vt* to guide; (car) to steer.

guijarro *m* pebble.

guiñar *vt* to wink.

guinda *f* cherry.

guindilla *f* chilli pepper.

guión *m* hyphen (in writing); script (of film).

guisante *m* (botany) pea.

guisar *vt* to cook.

guitarra *f* guitar.

gula *f* gluttony.

gusano *m* maggot, worm.

gustar *vt* to taste; to sample; * *vi* to please, be pleasing: — me gusta … I like …

H

haba *f* bean.

haber *vt* to get one's hands on; to occur; * *v imp* hay there is, there are; * *v aux* to have.

hábil *adj* able, clever, skilful, dexterous, apt.

habitación *f* dwelling, residence; room, bedroom.

habitar *vt* to inhabit, to live in.

hábito *m* dress; habit, custom.

habitual *adj* habitual, customary.

hablar *vt*, *vi* to speak; to talk.

hacendoso(a) *adj* industrious.

hacer *vt* to make; to do; (maths) to amount to, to make; * *vi* to act, to behave; * ~se *vr* to become.

hacha *f* torch; axe, hatchet.

hacia *adv* toward(s); about; ~ arriba or ~ abajo up(wards) or down(wards).

hada *f* fairy.

halagar *vt* to cajole, to flatter.

halcón *m* falcon.

hallar *vt* to find; to meet with; to discover; * ~se *vr* to find oneself, to be.

hambre *f* hunger; famine; longing.

harina *f* flour.

harto(a) *adj* full; fed up; * *adv* enough.

hasta *prep* up to; down to; until, as far as; * *adv* even.

haya *f* (botany) beech tree.

hazaña *f* exploit, achievement.

hebilla *f* buckle.

hebra *f* thread.

hebreo(a) *m*(*f*) Hebrew; Israeli: — *m* Hebrew language; * *adj* Hebrew; Israeli.

hechizar *vt* to bewitch, to enchant; to charm.

hecho(a) *adj* made; done; mature; ready-to-wear; cooked; * *m* action; act; fact; matter; event.

hectárea *f* hectare.

helado(a) *adj* frozen; icy; astonished; * *m* ice cream.

helar *vt* to freeze; to congeal; to astonish, * ~se *vr* to be frozen; to turn into ice; to congeal; * *vi* to freeze; to congeal.

helecho *m* (botany) fern.

hélice *f* helix; propeller.

hembra *f* female.

heno *m* hay.

heredar *vt* to inherit.

hereje *m* or *f* heretic.

herencia *f* inheritance;

heredity.

herir *vi* to wound, to hurt; to beat, to strike; to offend.

hermano(a) *m(f)* brother, sister.

hermético(a) *adj* hermetic, airtight.

hermoso(a) *adj* beautiful, handsome, lovely; large, robust.

héroe *m* hero.

heroína *f* heroine; heroin.

herradura *f* horse-shoe.

herrero *m* smith.

hervir *vt* to boil; to cook; * *vi* to boil; to bubble; to seethe.

hez *f* dregs **heces** *pl*.

hiedra *f* (botany) ivy.

hiel *f* gall, bile.

hielo *m* frost; ice.

hierba *f* grass; herb.

hierro *m* iron.

hígado *m* liver; (*fig*) courage, pluck.

higiene *f* hygiene.

higo *m* (botany) fig.

hijo(a) *m(f)* son or daughter; child; offspring.

hilera *f* row, line, file.

hilo *m* thread; wire.

himno *m* hymn; ~ **nacional** national anthem.

hincar *vt* to thrust in, to drive in.

hinchar *vt* to swell; to inflate; (*fig*) to exaggerate; * ~**se** *vr* to swell; to become vain.

hinojo *m* (botany) fennel.

hipo *m* hiccups *pl*.

hipócrita *adj* hypocritical; * *m* or *f* hypocrite.

hipódromo *m* racetrack.

hipoteca *f* mortgage.

historia *f* history; tale, story.

historieta *f* short story; short novel; comic strip.

hocico *m* snout: — **meter el ~ en todo** to meddle in everything.

hogar *m* hearth, fireplace; (*fig*) house, home; family life.

hogareño(a) *adj* home-loving.

hogaza *f* large loaf of bread.

hoguera *f* bonfire; blaze.

hoj *f* leaf; petal; sheet of paper; blade.

hojalata *f* tin (plate).

hojaldre *f* puff pastry.

hojear *vt* to turn the pages of.

hola *excl* hello!

holgado(a) *adj* loose, wide, baggy; at leisure; idle, unoccupied, well-to-do; well-off.

hollín *m* soot.

hombre *m* man; human being.

hombro *m* shoulder.

homenaje *m* homage.

homicidio *m* murder.

hondo(a) *adj* deep, profound.

honesto(a) *adj* honest; modest.

hongo *m* (botany) fungus.

honor *m* honour.

honorario(a) *adj* honorary; * ~**s** *mpl* fees *pl*.

honra *f* honour, reverence; self-esteem; reputation; integrity; ~**s funebres** *pl* funeral honours *pl*.

hora *f* hour; time.

horario(a) *adj* hourly, hour (*in compounds*); * *m* timetable.

horchata *f* tiger-nut milk.

horma *f* mould, form.

hormiga *f* ant.

hormigón *m* concrete.

horno *m* oven; furnace.

horquilla *f* pitchfork; hairpin.

hórreo *m* granary.

horrible *adj* horrid, horrible.

horror *m* horror, fright; atrocity.

hortaliza *f* vegetable.

hospedar *vt* to put up, to lodge; to entertain.

hospicio *m* orphanage; hospice.

hospital *m* hospital.

hostal *m* small hotel.

hostelería *f* hotel business or trade.

hostia *f* host; wafer; (*sl*) whack (*sl*), punch.

hostil *adj* hostile; adverse.

hotel *m* hotel.

hoy *adv* today; now, nowadays: — de ~ en adelante from now on, henceforward.

hoyo *m* hole, pit; excavation.

hoz *f* sickle; gorge.

hucha *f* money-box.

hueco(a) *adj* hollow, concave; empty; vain, ostentatious; * *m* interval; gap, hole; vacancy.

huelga *f* strike.

huella *f* track, footstep.

huérfano(a) *adj*, *m(f)* orphan.

huerta *f* market garden; irrigated region.

huerto *m* kitchen garden.

hueso *m* bone; stone, core.

huésped *m* or *f* guest, lodger; innkeeper.

huevo *m* egg.

huir *vi* to flee, to escape.

humano(a) *adj* human; humane, kind.

húmedo(a) *adj* humid; wet; damp.

humilde *adj* humble.

humillar *vt* to humble; to subdue; * ~se *vr* to humble oneself.

humo *m* smoke; fumes *pl*.

humor *m* mood, temper; humour: — de buen(mal) ~ in a good(bad) mood.

hundir *vt* to submerge; to sink; to ruin; * ~se *vr* to sink, to go to the bottom; to collapse; to be ruined.

huraño(a) *adj* shy; unsociable.

hurtadillas *adv*: — a ~ by stealth.

hurtar *vt* to steal, rob.

husmear *vt* to scent; to pry into.

I

ictericia *f* jaundice.

ida *f* departure, going: — (viaje de) ~ outward journey; ~ y vuelta round trip; ~s y venidas comings and goings *pl*.

idea *f* idea; scheme.

ideal *adj* ideal.

idear *vt* to think up; to invent; to plan.

idem *pron* ditto.

idéntico(a) *adj* identical.

idioma *m* language.

idiota *m* or *f* idiot.

idóneo(a) *adj* suitable, fit.

iglesia *f* church.

ignorar *vt* to be ignorant of, not to know.

igual *adj* equal; similar; the same: — al ~ equally.

ilegal *adj* illegal, unlawful.

ileso(a) *adj* unhurt.

ilimitado(a) *adj* unlimited.

iluminar *vt* to illumine, to illuminate, to enlighten.

ilusión *f* illusion; hope: — hacerse ~ones to build up one's hopes.

ilustre *adj* illustrious, famous.

imagen *f* image.

imaginar *vt* to imagine; to think up; * *vi* ~se *vr* to imagine.

imán *m* magnet.

imitar *vt* to imitate, to copy; to counterfeit.

impaciente *adj* impatient.

impar *adj* odd.

imparcial *adj* impartial.

impedir *vt* to impede, to hinder; to prevent.

impeler *vt* to drive, to propel; to impel; to incite.

impenetrable *adj* impenetrable, impervious; incomprehensible.

imperdible *m* safety pin.

imperdonable *adj* unforgivable.

imperfecto(a) *adj* imperfect.

impermeable *adj* waterproof; * *m* raincoat.

imperturbable *adj* imperturbable; unruffled.

implacable *adj* implacable,

inexorable.

implicar *vt* to implicate, to involve.

imponer *vt* to impose; to command; * ~se *vr* to assert oneself; to prevail.

impopular *adj* unpopular.

importante *adj* important, considerable.

importar *vi* to be important, to matter; * *vt* to import; to be worth.

importe *m* amount, cost.

importunar *vt* to bother, to pester.

imposible *adj* impossible; extremely difficult; slovenly.

impostor(a) *m(f)* impostor, fraud.

impotencia *f* impotence.

impracticable *adj* impracticable, unworkable.

impreciso(a) *adj* imprecise, vague.

imprenta *f* printing; press; printing office.

impregnar *vt* to impregnate.

imprescindible *adj* essential.

impresión *f* impression; stamp; print; edition.

impresionar *vt* to move; to impress; * ~se *vr* to be impressed; to be moved.

imprevisto(a) *adj* unforeseen, unexpected.

imprimir *vt* to print; to imprint; to stamp.

improbable *adj* improbable, unlikely.

improvisar *vt* to extemporise; to improvise.

improviso(a) *adj*:
— de ~ unexpectedly.

imprudente *adj* imprudent; indiscreet; unwise.

impúdico(a) *adj* shameless; lecherous.

impuesto(a) *adj* imposed;
* *m* tax, duty.

impulso *m* impulse; thrust; (*fig*) impulse.

impune *adj* unpunished.

impuro(a) *adj* impure; foul.

inaccesible *adj* inaccessible.

inadvertido(a) *adj* unnoticed.

inagotable *adj* inexhaustible.

inaguantable *adj* unbearable, intolerable.

inalterable *adj* unalterable.

inapreciable *adj* imperceptible; invaluable.

inaudito(a) *adj* unheard-of.

inaugurar *vt* to inaugurate.

incalculable *adj* incalculable.

incansable *adj* untiring, tireless.

incapaz *adj* incapable, unable.

incauto(a) *adj* incautious, unwary.

incendio *m* fire.

incentivo *m* incentive.

incertidumbre *f* doubt, uncertainty.

incierto(a) *adj* uncertain, doubtful.

incineración *f* incineration; cremation.

incitar *vt* to incite.

inclemencia *f* inclemency, severity; inclemency (of the weather).

inclinar *vt* to incline; to nod, to bow (the head); * ~se *vr* to bow; to stoop.

incluir *vt* to include, to comprise; to incorporate; to enclose.

incluído(a) *adj* included

incluso *adj* included;
* *adv* inclusively; even.

incógnito(a) *adj* unknown:
— de ~ incognito.

incombustible *adj* incombustible, fireproof.

incómodo(a) *adj* uncomfortable; annoying; inconvenient.

incomparable *adj* incomparable, matchless.

incompleto(a) *adj* incomplete.

incomunicado(a) *adj* isolated, cut off, in solitary confinement.

inconcebible *adj* inconceivable.

incondicional *adj* unconditional; whole-hearted; staunch.

inconfundible *adj* unmistakable.

inconsciente *adj* unconscious; thoughtless.

inconstante *adj* inconstant, variable, fickle.

incorporar *vt* to incorporate; * ~se *vr* to sit up; to join (an organisation), to become incorporated.

incorrecto(a) *adj* incorrect.

incrédulo(a) *adj* incredulous.

increíble *adj* incredible.

incremento *m* increment, increase; growth; rise.

inculcar *vt* to inculcate.

inculto(a) *adj* uncultivated; uneducated; uncouth.

incumbencia *f* obligation; duty.

incurable *adj* incurable; irremediable.

indagar *vt* to inquire into.

indebido(a) *adj* undue; illegal, unlawful.

indeciso(a) *adj* hesitant; undecided.

indefenso(a) *adj* defenceless.

indemnizar *vt* to indemnify, to compensate.

independiente *adj* independent.

indeterminado(a) *adj* indeterminate; indefinite.

indicador *m* indicator; gauge.

indicar *vt* to indicate.

índice *m* ratio, rate; index; table of contents; catalogue; forefinger, index finger.

indicio *m* indication, mark; sign, token; clue.

indiferencia *f* indifference, apathy.

indígena *adj* indigenous, native; * *m* or *f* native.

indignar *vt* to irritate; to provoke, to tease;

* ~se *vr* ~ por to get indignant about.

indigno(a) *adj* unworthy, contemptible, low.

indirecta *f* innuendo, hint.

indiscreción *f* indiscretion, tactlessness; gaffe.

individual *adj* individual; single (of a room); * *m* (sport) singles.

individuo *m* individual.

índole *f* disposition, nature, character; soft, kind.

indolente *adj* indolent, lazy.

indómito(a) *adj* untamed, ungoverned.

inducir *vt* to induce, to persuade.

indudable *adj* undoubted; unquestionable.

indultar *vt* to pardon; to exempt.

industria *f* industry; skill.

inédito(a) *adj* unpublished; (*fig*) new.

ineficaz *adj* ineffective; inefficient.

inepto(a) *adj* inept, unfit, useless.

inercia *f* inertia, inactivity.

inerte *adj* inert; dull; sluggish, motionless.

inesperado(a) *adj* unexpected, unforeseen.

inevitable *adj* unavoidable.

inexacto(a) *adj* inaccurate, untrue.

inexperto(a) *adj* inexperienced.

infame *adj* infamous.

infancia *f* infancy, childhood.

infantil *adj* infantile; childlike; children's.

infarto *m* heart attack.

infatigable *adj* tireless, untiring.

infectar *vt* to infect.

infeliz *adj* unhappy, unfortunate.

inferior *adj* inferior.

infernal *adj* infernal, hellish.

infiel *adj* unfaithful; disloyal; inaccurate.

infierno *m* hell.

infiltrarse *vr* to infiltrate.

ínfimo(a) *adj* lowest; of very poor quality.

infinidad *f* infinity; immensity.

infinito(a) *adj* infinite; immense.

inflamable *adj* inflammable.

inflar *vt* to inflate, to blow up; (*fig*) to exaggerate.

inflexible *adj* inflexible.

influir *vt* to influence.

información *f* information; news; (military) intelligence; investigation, judicial inquiry.

informal *adj* irregular, incorrect; untrustworthy; informal.

informar *vt* to inform; to reveal, to make known; * ~se *vr* to find out; * *vi* to report; (law) to plead; to inform.

informática *f* computer science, information technology.

informe *m* report, statement; piece of information, account; * *adj* shapeless, formless.

infortunio *m* misfortune, ill luck.

infracción *f* infraction; breach, infringement.

infructuoso(a) *adj* fruitless, unproductive, unprofitable.

infundado(a) *adj* groundless.

ingeniero(a) *m(f)* enginer.

ingenio *m* talent; wit; ingenuity; engine.

ingenuo(a) *adj* naive.

ingerir *vt* to ingest; to swallow; to consume.

Inglaterra *m* England.

ingle *f* groin.

inglés(a) *adj* English; * *m* English language;

m(f) English man or woman.

ingrato(a) *adj* ungrateful, thankless; disagreeable.

ingresar *vt* to deposit; * *vi* to come in.

inhabilitar *vt* to disqualify, to disable.

inhabitable *adj* uninhabitable.

inhibir *vt* to inhibit; to restrain.

iniciar *vt* to initiate; to begin.

ininteligible *adj* unintelligible.

injertar *vt* to graft.

injuriar *vt* to insult, to wrong.

injusto(a) *adj* unjust.

inmediaciones *fpl* neighbourhood.

inmediatamente *adv* immediately, at once.

inmobiliario(a) *adj* property; * *f* estate agency.

inmortal *adj* immortal.

inmóvil *adj* immovable, still.

inmueble *m* property; * *adj* bienes ~ s real estate.

inmundo(a) *adj* filthy, dirty; nasty.

inmune *adj* (medical) immune; free, exempt.

innato(a) *adj* inborn, innate.

innecesario(a) *adj* unnecessary.

innegable *adj* undeniable.

innumerable *adj* innumerable, countless.

inocente *adj* innocent.

inodoro *m* toilet.

inofensivo(a) *adj* harmless.

inolvidable *adj* unforgettable.

inoxidable *adj*: — acero ~ stainless steel.

inquietar *vt* to worry, disturb; * ~se *vr* to worry, to get worried.

inquilino(a) *m(f)* tenant; lodger.

inquirir *vt* to inquire into, to investigate.

inscribir *vt* to inscribe; to list, to register.

insecto *m* insect.

insensato(a) *adj* senseless,

stupid; mad.

insensible *adj* insensitive; imperceptible; numb.

inseparable *adj* inseparable.

insertar *vt* to insert.

inservible *adj* useless.

insignia *f* badge; ~s *fpl* insignia *pl*.

insinuar *vt* to insinuate; * ~se *vr* ~ en to worm one's way into.

insipido(a) *adj* insipid.

insistir *vi* to insist, to persist.

insolación *f* (medical) sunstroke.

insolencia *f* insolence, rudeness, effrontery.

insólito(a) *adj* unusual.

insolvente *adj* insolvent.

insomnio *m* insomnia.

insondable *adj* unfathomable; inscrutable.

insoportable *adj* unbearable.

inspeccionar *vt* to inspect; to supervise.

inspector(a) *m(f)* inspector; superintendent.

inspirar *vt* to inspire; (medical) to inhale.

instalar *vt* to install.

instantáneo(a) *adj* instantaneous; * *f* snap(shot): — café ~ instant coffee.

instante *m* instant: — al ~ immediately, instantly.

instigar *vt* to instigate.

instinto *m* instinct.

instructivo(a) *adj* instructive; educational.

instrumento *m* instrument; tool, implement.

insuficiente *adj* insufficient, inadequate.

insulso(a) *adj* insipid; dull.

insultar *vt* to insult.

insuperable *adj* insuperable, insurmountable.

intacto(a) *adj* untouched; entire; intact.

integral *adj* integral, whole:

— pan ~ wholemeal bread.

íntegro(a) *adj* whole, entire; honest.

intelectual *adj* intellectual.

inteligencia *f* intelligence; ability.

intemperie *f*: — a la ~ out in the open.

intencionado(a) *adj* meaningful; deliberate.

intenso(a) *adj* intense, strong; deep.

intentar *vt* to try, to attempt.

intercalar *vt* to insert.

intercambio *m* exchange, swap.

interés *m* interest; share part; concern, advantage; profit.

interesar *vt* to be of interest to, to interest; * ~se *vr* ~ en or por to take an interest in; * *vi* to be of interest.

interferir *vt* to interfere with; to jam (radio); * *vi* to interfere.

interfono *m* intercom.

interino(a) *adj* provisional, temporary; * *m(f)* holder of a post; stand-in.

interior *adj* interior, internal; * *m* interior, inside.

intermedio(a) *adj* intermediate; * *m* interval.

interminable *adj* interminable, endless.

intermitente *adj* intermittent; *m* (car) indicator.

internado *m* boarding school.

interno(a) *adj* interior, internal; * *m(f)* boarder.

interpretar *vt* to interpret, to explain; (feat) to perform; to translate.

interrogación *f* interrogation; question mark.

interrogatorio *m* questioning; (law) examination; questionnaire.

interrumpir *vt* to interrupt.

interruptor *m* switch.

intervenir *vt* to control, to supervise; (commerce) to

audit; (medical) to operate on; * vi to participate; to intervene.

intestino m intestine.

íntimo(a) adj internal, innermost; intimate, private.

intranquilo(a) adj worried.

intransitable adj impassable.

intrépido(a) adj intrepid, daring.

intrigar vt, vi to intrigue.

introducir vt to introduce; to insert.

introvertido(a) adj, m(f) introvert.

intruso(a) adj intrusive; * m(f) intruder.

inundar vt to inundate, to overflow; to flood.

inusitado(a) adj unusual.

inútil adj useless.

inválido(a) adj invalid, null and void; * m(f) invalid.

invencible adj invincible.

invernadero m greenhouse.

inverosímil adj unlikely, improbable.

inverso(a) adj inverse; inverted; contrary.

invertir vt (commerce) to invest; to invert.

investigar vt to investigate; to do research into.

invierno m winter.

invitar vt to invite; to entice; to pay for.

invocar vt to invoke.

ir vi to go; to walk; to travel; * ~se vr to go away, to depart.

ira f anger, wrath.

iris m iris (of eye): — arco ~ rainbow.

ironía f irony.

irracional adj irrational.

irreal adj unreal.

irreflexión f rashness, thoughtlessness.

irregular adj irregular; abnormal.

irremediable adj irremediable; incurable.

irresistible adj irresistible.

irreverente adj irreverent; disrespectful.

irrisorio(a) adj derisory, ridiculous.

irritación f irritation.

irritar vt to irritate, to exasperate; to stir up; to inflame.

isla f island, isle.

istmo m isthmus.

Italia f Italy.

italiano(a) adj Italian; * m Italian language: — m(j) Italian.

itinerario m itinerary.

IVA m abbr VAT.

izquierdo(a) adj left; * f left; left (wing).

J

jabalí m wild boar.

jabón m soap.

jaca f pony.

jacinto m (botany) hyacinth.

jadear vi to pant.

jaleo m racket, uproar.

jamás adv never: — para siempre ~ for ever.

jamón m ham; ~ de York cooked ham; ~ serrano cured ham.

jaque m check (at game of chess); ~mate checkmate.

jaqueca f migraine.

jarabe m syrup.

jardín m garden.

jardinería f gardening.

jardinero(a) m(f) gardener.

jarra f jug, jar, pitcher: — brazos en ~s with hands to the sides.

jaula f cage; cell.

jazmín m (botany) jasmine.

jefe m chief, head, leader.

jerarquía f hierarchy.

jeringa f syringe.

jeroglífico(a) adj hieroglyphic;

*m hieroglyph, hieroglyphic.
jersey m sweater, pullover.
jilguero m goldfinch.
jinete(a) m(f) horseman or woman, rider.
jirón m rag, shred.
jornada f journey; day's journey; working day.
jornal m day's wage.
jornalero m (day) labourer.
joroba f hump: — f hunchback.
jota f jot, iota; Spanish dance.
joven adj young;
* m or f youth; young woman.
jovial adj jovial, cheerful.
joya f jewel; ~s fpl jewellery.
juanete m (medical) bunion.
jubilar vt to pension off, to superannuate; to discard;
* ~se vr to retire.
júbilo m joy, rejoicing.
judía f bean; ~ verde French bean.
judicial adj judicial.
judío(a) adj Jewish;
* m(f) Jewish man or woman.
juego m play; amusement; sport; game; gambling.
jueves m invar Thursday.
juez m or f judge.
jugar vt, vi to play, to sport, to gamble.
jugo m sap, juice.
juguete m toy, plaything.
juicio m judgement, reason; sanity; opinion.
julio m July.
junco m (botany) rush; junk (small Chinese ship).
junio m June.
junta f meeting; assembly; congress; council.
juntar vt to join; to unite;
* ~se vr to meet, to assemble; to draw closer.
junto(a) adj joined; united; near; adjacent; ~s together;
* adv todo ~ all at once.
jurado m jury.
jurar vt, vi to swear.

jurídico(a) adj lawful, legal; juridical.
justicia f justice; equity.
justificante m voucher; receipt.
justo(a) adj just; fair, right; exact, correct; tight;
* adv exactly, precisely; just in time.
juventud f youthfulness, youth; young people pl.
juzgado m tribunal; court.

K

kilogramo m kilogramme.
kilómetro m kilometre.
kiosco m kiosk.

L

la art f the; * pron her; you; it.
labio m lip; edge.
labor f labour, task; needlework; farm work; ploughing.
laborioso(a) adj laborious; hardworking.
labrar vt to work; to carve; to farm; (fig) to bring about.
laca f lacquer; hairspray.
lacio(a) adj faded, withered; languid; lank (hair).
lacrar vt to seal (with sealing wax).
lactancia f lactation; breast-feeding.
lácteo(a) adj milky, lactic:
— productos ~s dairy products.
ladera f slope.
ladino(a) adj cunning, crafty.
lado m side; faction, party; (military) flank.
ladrar vt to bark.
ladrillo m brick.
ladrón(ona) m(f) thief, robber.
lagar m wine press.
lagartija f (small) lizard.

lagarto *m* lizard.
lago *m* lake.
lágrima *f* tear.
laguna *f* lake; lagoon; gap.
laico(a) *adj* lay.
lamentar *vt* to be sorry about;
to lament, to regret; * *vi* ~se
vr to complain; to mourn.
lamer *vt* to lick, to lap.
lámina *f* plate, sheet of metal;
engraving.
lámpara *f* lamp.
lamparón *m* large grease spot.
lana *f* wool.
lancha *f* barge, lighter; launch.
langosta *f* locust; lobster.
lanzar *vt* to throw; (sport) to
bowl, to pitch; to launch, to
fling; (law) to evict.
lápida *f* flat stone, tablet.
lápiz *m* pencil; propelling
pencil.
largamente *adv* for a long time.
largo(a) *adj* long; lengthy,
generous; copious: — a la ~a
in the end, eventually.
las *art fpl* the; * *pron* them; you.
lascivo(a) *adj* lascivious; lewd.
láser *m* laser.
lástima *f* compassion, pity;
shame.
lastimar *vt* to hurt; to wound;
to feel pity for; * ~se *vr* to
hurt oneself.
lastre *m* ballast.
lata *f* tin; tin can; (*sl*)
nuisance.
latido *m* (heart)beat.
latifundio *m* large estate.
latir *vi* to beat, to palpitate.
latitud *f* latitude.
latón *m* brass.
latoso(a) *adj* annoying; boring.
laúd *f* flute (musical instrument).
laudable *adj* laudable,
praiseworthy.
laurel *m* (botany) laurel;
reward.
lavable *adj* washable.
lavabo *m* washbasin;

washroom.
lavadora *f* washing machine.
lavanda *f* (botany) lavender.
lavandería *f* laundry;
launderette.
lavaplatos *m* dishwasher.
lavar *vt* to wash; to wipe away;
* ~se *vr* to wash oneself.
lavavajillas *m* dishwasher.
laxante *m* (medical) laxative.
lazarillo *m*: — perro ~ guide dog.
lazo *m* knot; bow; snare; bond.
le *pron* him; you; (*dative*) to
him; to her; to it; to you.
leal *adj* loyal; faithful.
lección *f* reading; lesson;
lecture; class.
leche *f* milk.
lecho *m* bed; layer.
lechón *m* sucking pig.
lechuga *f* lettuce.
lechuza *f* owl.
lector(a) *m(f)* reader.
leer *vt*, *vi* to read.
legado *m* bequest, legacy;
legate.
legal *adj* legal; trustworthy.
legaña *f* sleep (in eyes).
legible *adj* legible.
legislar *vt* to legislate.
legítimo(a) *adj* legitimate,
lawful; authentic.
legumbres *fpl* pulses *pl*.
lejano(a) *adj* distant, remote.
lejía *f* bleach.
lejos *adv* at a great distance.
lelo(a) *adj* stupid, ignorant;
* *m(f)* idiot.
lema *m* motto; slogan.
lencería *f* linen, drapery;
lingerie.
lengua *f* tongue; language.
lenguado *m* sole.
lenguaje *m* language.
lente *m* or *f* lens.
lenteja *f* lentil.
lentilla *f* contact lens.
lento(a) *adj* slow.
leña *f* wood, timber.
león *m* lion.

leopardo *m* leopard.
leotardos *mpl* tights.
lesión *f* wound; injury; damage.
letal *adj* mortal, deadly.
letanía *f* litany.
letargo *m* lethargy.
letra *f* letter; handwriting; printing type; draft of a song; bill, draft.
letrero *m* sign; label.
leucemia *f* leukaemia.
levadura *f* yeast.
levantar *vt* to raise, to lift up; to build; * ~se *vr* to get up; to stand up.
levante *m* Levant; east; east wind.
leve *adj* light; trivial.
léxico *m* vocabulary.
ley *f* law; standard (for metal).
leyenda *f* legend.
liar *vt* to tie, to bind; to confuse.
libélula *f* dragonfly.
liberal *adj* liberal, generous; * *m* or *f* liberal.
libertad *f* liberty, freedom.
libra *f* pound; ~ esterlina pound sterling.
libre *adj* free; exempt; vacant.
librería *f* bookshop.
libreta *f* notebook; ~ de ahorros savings book.
libro *m* book.
licencia *f* licence; licentiousness.
licenciado(a) *adj* licensed; * *m(f)* graduate.
lícito(a) *adj* lawful, fair; permissible.
líder *m* or *f* leader.
liebre *f* hare.
lienzo *f* linen; canvas; face or front of a building.
liga *f* suspender; birdlime; league; coalition; alloy.
ligar *vt* to tie, to bind, to fasten; * ~se *vr* to commit oneself; * *vi* to mix, blend; (*sl*) to pick up.
ligero(a) *adj* light, swift; agile; superficial.
liguero *m* suspender belt.
lijar *vt* to smooth, to sandpaper.
lima *f* file; ~ de uñas nail file: — comer como una ~ to eat like a horse.
limitado(a) *adj* limited: — sociedad ~da limited company.
límite *m* limit, boundary.
limón *m* lemon.
limonada *f* lemonade.
limosna *f* alms *pl*, charity.
limpiar *vt* to clean; to cleanse; to purify; to polish; (*also fig*) to clean up.
linaza *f* linseed.
lince *m* lynx.
lindar *vi* to be adjacent.
lindo(a) *adj* pretty; lovely.
línea *f* line; cable; outline.
lino *m* flax.
linterna *f* lantern, lamp; torch.
lío *m* bundle, parcel; (*sl*) muddle, mess.
liquidar *vt* to liquidate; to settle (accounts).
líquido(a) *adj* liquid.
lirio *m* (botany) iris.
lirón *m* dormouse; (*fig*) sleepy-head.
liso(a) *adj* plain, even, smooth.
lisonja *f* adulation, flattery.
lista *f* list; register; catalogue; menu.
listo(a) *adj* ready; smart, clever.
litera *f* berth; bunk, bunk bed.
litigio *m* lawsuit.
litoral *adj* coastal; * *m* coast.
litro *m* litre (measure).
liviano(a) *adj* light; fickle; trivial.
llaga *f* wound.
llama *f* flame; llama (animal).
llamar *vt* to call; to name; to summon; to ring up, to telephone; * *vi* to knock at the door; * ~se *vr* to be named.
llano(a) *adj* plain; even, level, smooth; evident; * *m* plain.

llanta f (wheel) rim; tyre; inner (tube).

llanto m weeping; (fig) lamentation.

llanura f evenness, flatness; plain, prairie.

llave f key: ~ maestra master key.

llavero m keyring.

llegar vi to arrive; ~ a to reach; * ~se vr to approach.

llenar vt to fill; to cover; to fill in (a form); to satisfy, to fulfil; * ~se vr to gorge.

llevar vt to take; to wear; to carry; * ~se vr to carry off, to take away.

llorar vt, vi to weep, to cry.

llover vi to rain.

lo pron it; him; you; * art the.

lobo m wolf.

lóbulo m lobe.

local adj local; * m place, site.

loco(a) adj mad; * m(f) mad person.

locutor(a) m(f) (radio, TV) announcer, newsreader.

lodo m mud, mire.

lograr vt to achieve; to gain, to obtain.

lombarda f red cabbage.

lombriz f worm.

lomo m loin; back (of an animal); spine (of a book): — llevar or traer a ~ to carry on the back.

lona f canvas.

loncha f slice; rasher.

longaniza f pork sausage.

longitud f length; longitude.

loro m parrot.

los art mpl the; * pron them; you.

losa f flagstone.

lote m lot; portion.

loza f crockery.

lucero m morning star, bright star.

luchar vi to struggle; to wrestle.

luciérnaga f glow-worm.

lucir vt to light (up); to show off; * vi to shine; * ~se vr to make a fool of oneself.

luego adv next; afterwards: — desde ~ of course.

lugar m place, spot; village; reason: — en ~ de instead of, in lieu of.

lúgubre adj lugubrious; sad.

lujo m luxury; abundance.

lujoso(a) adj luxurious.

lujuria f lust.

lumbre f fire; light.

luminoso(a) adj luminous, shining.

luna f moon; glass plate for mirrors; lens.

lunar m mole, spot; * adj lunar.

lunes m invar Monday.

lupa f magnifying glass.

lupanar m brothel.

luto m mourning (dress); grief.

luz, luces f light.

M

maceta f flowerpot.

machacar vt to pound, crush; * vi to insist, to go on.

macho adj male; (fig) virile; * m male; (fig) he-man.

macizo(a) adj massive; solid; * m mass, chunk.

madera f timber, wood.

madrastra f stepmother.

madre f mother; womb.

madreselva f (botany) honeysuckle.

madriguera f burrow; den.

madrugada f early morning, small hours.

madrugar vi to get up early; to get ahead.

maduro(a) adj ripe, mature.

maestro(a) m(f) master; teacher; * adj masterly, skilled; principal.

magia f magic.

magisterio *m* teaching (profession); teachers *pl*.

magnetofón, magnetófono *m* tape recorder.

magnífico(a) *adj* magnificent, splendid.

mago(a) *m(f)* magician.

magullar *vt* to bruise; to damage; to bash (*sl*).

mahometano(a) *m(f)*, *adj* Muslim.

maíz *m* maize, Indian corn.

majadero(a) *adj* dull; silly, stupid; * *m* idiot.

majo(a) *adj* nice; attractive; smart.

majuelo *m* vine newly planted; hawthorn.

mal *m* evil; hurt; harm; damage; misfortune; illness; * *adj* (before masculine nouns) bad.

malcriado(a) *adj* rude, ill-behaved; naughty; spoiled.

maldad *f* wickedness.

maldecir *vt* to curse.

maldito(a) *adj* wicked; damned, cursed.

malecón *m* pier.

maleducado(a) *adj* bad-mannered, rude.

malestar *m* discomfort; (*fig*) uneasiness; unrest.

maleta *f* suitcase.

maletero *m* (car) boot.

maleza *f* weeds *pl*; thicket.

malgastar *vt* to waste, to ruin.

malhablado(a) *adj* foul-mouthed.

malhechor(a) *m(f)* malefactor; criminal.

malhumorado(a) *adj* cross, bad-tempered.

malla *f* mesh, network; ~s *fpl* leotard.

malo(a) *adj* bad; ill; wicked; * *m(f)* villain.

maltratar *vt* to ill-treat, abuse, mistreat.

malva *f* (botany) mallow.

malvado(a) *adj* wicked, villainous.

mama *f* teat; breast.

mamá *f* (*sl*) mum, mummy.

mamar *vt*, *vi* to suck.

mamífero *m* mammal.

manada *f* herd; pack; crowd.

manantial *m* source, spring.

manchado(a) *adj* dirty; spotted.

manchar *vt* to stain, to soil.

manco(a) *adj* one-armed; one-handed; maimed; faulty.

mancomunidad *f* union, fellowship; community; (law) joint responsibility.

mandar *vt* to command, to order; to bequeath; to send.

mandarina *f* tangerine.

mandíbula *f* jaw.

mandil *m* apron.

manera *f* manner, way; kind.

manga *f* sleeve; hose.

mango *m* handle; mango.

manguera *f* hose; pipe.

manifestación *f* manifestation; show; mass meeting.

manifestar *vt* to manifest, to declare.

maniobrar *vt* to manoeuvre; to handle.

manipular *vt* to manipulate.

maniquí *m* dummy: — *m* or *f* model.

manivela *f* crank.

mano *f* hand; hand (clock); foot, paw (animal); hand (at game): — a ~ by hand: — a ~s llenas liberally, generously.

manojo *m* handful, bunch.

manosear *vt* to handle; to mess up.

manso(a) *adj* tame; gentle, soft.

manta *f* blanket.

manteca *f* fat; ~ de cerdo lard.

mantel *m* tablecloth.

mantener *vt* to maintain, to support; to nourish; to keep; * ~se *vr* to hold one's ground; to support oneself.

mantequilla *f* butter.

manzana *f* apple.
manzanilla *f* camomile (tea); manzanilla sherry.
maña *f* handiness, dexterity, cleverness, cunning; habit, custom; trick.
mañana *f* morning; * *adv* tomorrow.
mapa *m* map.
maquillar *vt* to make up; * ~se *vr* to put on make-up.
máquina *f* machine; (railway) engine; camera; (*fig*) machinery; plan, project.
maquinilla *f*; ~ de afeitar razor.
maquinista *m or f* (railway) train driver; operator; (marine) engineer.
mar *m or f* sea.
maravilla *f* wonder.
marca *f* mark; stamp; marque.
marcar *vt* to mark; to dial; to score; to record; to set (hair); * *vi* to score; to dial.
marchar *vi* to go; to work; * ~se *vr* to go away.
marco *m* frame; framework; (sport) goalposts *pl*.
marea *f* tide.
marear *vt* (marine) to sail, navigate; to annoy, upset; * ~se *vr* to feel sick; to feel faint; to feel dizzy.
marfil *m* ivory.
margarina *f* margarine.
margarita *f* (botany) daisy.
margen *m* margin; border; * *f* bank (of river).
marido *m* husband.
marinero(a) *adj* sea (in compounds); seaworthy; * *m* sailor.
marioneta *f* puppet.
mariposa *f* butterfly.
mariquita *f* ladybird.
marisco *m* shellfish *pl*, seafood.
marisma *f* marsh, swamp.
mármol *m* marble.
marrano *m* pig, boar.
marrón *adj* brown.

martes *m invar* Tuesday.
martillo *m* hammer.
marzo *m* March.
mas *adv* but, yet.
más *adv* more; most; besides, moreover: — a ~ tardar at latest; ~ o menos more or less.
masa *f* dough; mortar; mass.
masaje *m* massage.
mascar *vt* to chew.
máscara *f* mask.
mascullar *vt* to mumble, to mutter.
masivo(a) *adj* mass.
mástil *m* (marine) mast.
mastín *m* mastiff.
mata *f* shrub; sprig, blade; grove, group of trees; mop of hair.
matadero *m* slaughterhouse.
matar *vt* to kill; to execute; to murder; * ~se *vr* to kill oneself, to commit suicide.
matasellos *m invar* postmark.
mate *m* checkmate; * *adj* matt.
material *adj* material, physical; * *m* equipment, materials *pl*.
maternidad *f* motherhood.
matinal *adj* morning (in compounds).
matiz *m* shade of colour; shading.
matorral *m* thicket.
matrícula *f* register, list; (car) registration number plate.
matrimonio *m* marriage, matrimony.
matriz *f* matrix; womb; mould, form.
maullar *vi* to mew.
mayonesa *f* mayonnaise.
mayo *m* May.
mayor *adj* main, chief; (music) major; biggest; eldest; greater, larger; elderly; * *m* chief, boss; adult: — al por ~ wholesale; ~es *mpl* forefathers.
mayoría *f* majority, greater part; ~ de edad coming of age.
mayúsculo(a) *adj* (*fig*)

tremendous; *f capital letter.
mazo m bunch; club, mallet; bat.
mazorca f ear of corn.
me pron me; to me.
mear vi (sl) to pee, piss; * ~se
vr de risa to laugh so much.
mecánico(a) adj mechanical,
repetitive.
mecanógrafo(a) m(f) typist.
mecer vt to rock; to dandle.
mechar vt to lard; to stuff.
mechón m lock of hair; large
bundle of threads or fibres.
medalla f medal.
media f stocking; sock;
average.
medianoche f midnight.
mediante prep by means of.
mediar vi to intervene; to
mediate.
medicamento m medicine.
médico(a) adj medical;
* m(f) doctor.
medida f measure.
medio(a) adj half: — a medias
partly; * m middle; average;
way, means; medium.
mediodía m noon, midday.
medir vt to measure;
* ~se vr to be moderate.
medrar vi to grow, to thrive,
to prosper; to improve.
médula f marrow; essence,
substance; pith.
medusa f jellyfish.
mejilla f cheek.
mejillón m mussel.
mejor adj, adv better; best.
mejorar vt to improve, to
ameliorate; to enhance;
* vi to improve; (medical) to
recover, to get better; * ~se
vr to improve, to get better.
melancólico(a) adj sad,
melancholy; dreamy.
melena f long hair (person);
mane (animal).
melindroso(a) adj prudish,
finicky.
mella f notch in edged tools; gap.

mellizo(a) adj, m(f) twin.
melocotón m peach.
melón m melon.
meloso(a) adj honeyed; mellow.
membrete m letterhead.
membrillo m quince (tree).
memoria f memory; report;
record; ~s fpl remembrances pl.
mendigar vt to beg.
menear vt to move from place
to place; (fig) to handle; * ~se
vr to move; to shake; to sway.
menguante f waning.
menor m or f young person,
juvenile; * adj less; smaller;
minor: — al por ~ retail.
menos adv less; least:
— al ~ or por lo ~ at least;
* prep except; minus.
menospreciar vt to undervalue;
to despise, to scorn.
mensaje m message.
mensual adj monthly.
menta f (botany) mint.
mente f mind; understanding.
mentecato(a) adj silly, stupid;
* m(f) idiot.
mentir vt to feign; to pretend;
* vi to lie.
mentira f lie, falsehood.
menudo(a) adj small; minute;
petty, insignificant:
— a ~ frequently, often.
meñique m little finger.
mercader m dealer, trader.
mercado m market(place).
mercancía f commodity;
~s fpl goods pl, merchandise.
mercurio m mercury.
merecer vt to deserve, to merit.
meridional adj southern.
merienda f (light) tea;
afternoon snack; picnic.
merluza f hake.
mermelada f jam.
mero m pollack (fish);
* ~(a) adj mere, pure.
mes m month.
mesa f table; desk; plateau;
~ redonda round table.

mestizo(a) *adj* of mixed race; crossbred; *$*m(f)$ half-caste.

meta *f* goal; finish.

metal *m* metal; (music) brass; timbre (of voice).

metálico(a) *adj* metallic.

meter *vt* to place, to put; to insert, to put in; to involve; to make, to cause; * ~se *vr* to meddle, interfere.

método *m* method.

metro *m* metre; underground.

mezclar *vt* to mix; * ~se *vr* to mix; to mingle.

mezquino(a) *adj* mean; small-minded, petty; wretched.

mezquita *f* mosque.

mi *adj* my.

mí *pron* me; myself.

miedo *m* fear, dread.

miel *f* honey.

miembro *m* member.

mientras *adv* meanwhile; * *conj* while; as long as.

miércoles *m invar* Wednesday.

mierda *f* (*sl*) shit.

miga *f* crumb; ~s *fpl* fried breadcrumbs *pl*.

mijo *m* (botany) millet.

mil *num* one thousand.

milagro *m* miracle, wonder.

milésimo(a) *adj, m* thousandth.

mili *f* (*sl*) military service.

milímetro *m* millimetre.

milla *f* mile.

millar *m* thousand: — a ~es in thousands.

millón *m* million.

mimado(a) *adj* spoiled.

mimar *vt* to spoil, to pamper.

mimbre *m* wicker.

mimo *m* caress; spoiling; mime.

mina *f* mine; underground passage.

minero(a) *m(f)* miner.

minifalda *f* miniskirt.

mínimo(a) *adj* minimum.

minoría *f* minority.

minucioso(a) *adj* meticulous; very detailed.

minúsculo(a) *adj* minute; * *f* small letter.

minusválido(a) *adj* (physically) handicapped; * *m(f)* (physically) handicapped person.

minuta *f* menu; fee.

minuto *m* minute.

mío(a) *poss adj* mine.

miope *adj* short-sighted.

mirar *vt* to look at; to observe; to consider; * *vi* to look; * ~se *vr* to look at oneself; to look at one another.

mirlo *m* blackbird.

misa *f* mass; ~ del gallo midnight mass.

miserable *adj* miserable; mean; squalid (place); (*sl*) despicable; * *m or f* rotter.

misericordia *f* mercy.

mismo(a) *adj* same; very.

mitad *f* half; middle.

mitin *m* (political) rally.

mixto(a) *adj* mixed.

mobiliario *m* furniture.

mochila *f* backpack.

mochuelo *m* red owl.

moco *m* snot; mucus.

moda *f* fashion, style.

modales *mpl* manners *pl*.

modelo *m or f* model, pattern.

módem *m* modem.

moderar *vt* to moderate, to restrain, to control.

módico(a) *adj* moderate.

modificar *vt* to modify.

modisto(a) *m(f)* dressmaker.

modo *m* mode, method, manner.

modorra *f* drowsiness.

mofarse *vr*; ~ de to mock, scoff at.

moflete *m* fat cheek.

mogollón *adj* (*sl*) loads, lots.

moho *m* rust; mould, mildew.

mojar *vt* to wet, moisten; * ~se *vr* to get wet.

mojón *m* landmark.

molde *m* mould; pattern; model.

moler *vt* to grind, to pound; to tire out; to annoy, to bore.

molestar *vt* to annoy, to bother; * *vi* to be a nuisance.

molino *m* mill.

momentáneo(a) *adj* momentary.

momento *m* moment.

momia *f* mummy.

mondadientes *m inv* toothpick.

mondar *vt* to clean; to cleanse; to peel; * ~se *vr* ~ de risa (*sl*) to split one's sides laughing.

mondo(a) *adj* clean; pure; ~ y lirondo bare, plain; pure and simple.

moneda *f* money; currency; coin.

monja *f* nun.

mono(a) *adj* lovely; pretty; nice; * *m(f)* monkey; ape; * *mpl* dungarees *pl*; overalls *pl*.

monopatín *m* skateboard.

monstruo *m* monster.

montacargas *f* service lift, freight elevator.

montaje *m* assembly; decor (of theatre); montage.

montaña *f* mountain.

montar *vt* to mount, to get on; to put together; to set up a business; to beat, whip (cookery); * *vi* to mount; to ride.

monte *m* mountain; woodland; ~ alto forest: ~ bajo scrub.

montón *m* heap, pile; mass; ~ones *pl* abundantly.

monumento *m* monument; memorial.

montura *f* mount; saddle.

monzón *m* monsoon.

moño *m* bun: — estar hasta el ~ to be fed up to the back teeth.

mora *f* (botany) blackberry; mulberry.

morado(a) *adj* violet, purple.

morcilla *f* black pudding.

mordaz *adj* biting, scathing; pungent.

morder *vt* to bite; to nibble; to corrode, to eat away.

mordisco *m* bite.

moreno(a) *adj* brown; swarthy; dark-skinned.

morir *vi* to die; to expire; to die down; * ~se *vr* to die; (*fig*) to be dying.

morisco(a) *adj* Moorish.

moroso(a) *adj* slow, sluggish; (commerce) slow to pay up.

morral *m* haversack.

morro *m* snout; nose (of plane, etc).

morsa *f* walrus.

mortal *adj* mortal; fatal, deadly.

mortero *m* mortar.

mosca *f* fly: — estar ~ to smell a rat.

mosquearse *vr* (*sl*) to get cross; (*sl*) to take offence.

mosquitero *m* mosquito net.

mosquito *m* gnat, mosquito.

mostaza *f* mustard.

mosto *m* must, grape juice.

mostrador *m* counter.

mostrar *vt* to show, to exhibit; to explain; * ~se *vr* to appear, to show oneself.

mote *m* nickname.

motivo *m* motive, cause, reason.

moto (*sl*), motocicleta *f* motorcycle.

motor *m* engine, motor.

motorismo *m* motorcycling.

mover *vt* to move; to shake; to drive; (*fig*) to cause; * ~se *vr* to move; (*fig*) to get a move on.

móvil *adj* mobile, movable; moving; * *m* motive.

mozo(a) *adj* young; * *m(f)* youth, young man or girl; waiter or waitress.

muchacho(a) *m(f)* boy or girl: — *f* maid, maidservant.

mucho(a) *adj* a lot of, much; * *adv* much, a lot; long.

mudar *vt* to change; to shed; * ~se *vr* to change one's clothes; to change house; * *vi* to change.

mudo(a) *adj* dumb; silent, mute.

mueble *m* piece of furniture:

~s *mpl* furniture.

mueca *f* grimace, funny face.

muela *f* tooth, molar.

muelle *m* spring; regulator; quay.

muérdago *m* (botany) mistletoe.

muerte *f* death.

mujer *f* woman.

mulato(a) *adj* mulatto.

muleta *f* crutch.

mullido(a) *adj* soft; springy.

mulo(a) *m(f)* mule.

multa *f* fine, penalty.

multitud *f* crowd.

mundial *adj* world-wide; world (*in compounds*).

mundo *m* world.

municipio *m* town council, corporation; town.

muñeca *f* wrist; child's doll.

muralla *f* (city) walls.

murciélago *m* bat.

murmullo *m* murmur, mutter.

murmurar *vi* to murmur; to gossip, to backbite.

muro *m* wall.

músculo *m* muscle.

museo *m* museum.

musgo *m* moss.

música *f* music.

muslo *m* thigh.

mustio(a) *adj* parched, withered; sad, sorrowful.

mutuo(a) *adj* mutual, reciprocal.

muy *adv* very; too; greatly; ~ bien all right.

N

nabo *m* turnip.

nácar *m* mother-of-pearl, nacre.

nacer *vi* to be born; to bud, to shoot (of plants); to rise; to grow.

nacimiento *m* birth; nativity.

nación *f* nation: — N~nes Unidas United Nations.

nada *f* nothing; * *adv* no way, not at all, by no means.

nadar *vi* to swim.

nadie *pron* nobody, no one.

nalgas *fpl* buttocks *pl*.

naranja *f* orange.

nariz *f* nose.

narrar *vt* to narrate, to tell.

nata *f* cream.

natillas *fpl* custard.

naturaleza *f* nature.

naufragar *vi* to be shipwrecked; to suffer ruin in one's affairs.

náutica *f* navigation.

navaja *f* penknife; razor.

nave *f* ship; nave; warehouse.

navegar *vt, vi* to navigate; to sail; to fly.

Navidad *f* Christmas.

nebuloso(a) *adj* misty; cloudy; hazy; drizzling; * *f* nebula.

neceser *m* toilet bag; holdall.

necesidad *f* need; ecessity.

necesitar *vt* to need; * *vi* to want, to need.

necio(a) *adj* ignorant; stupid, foolish; imprudent.

nefasto(a) *adj* unlucky.

negado(a) *adj* incapable, unfit.

negar *vt* to deny; to refuse; * ~se *vr* a hacer to refuse to do.

negativo(a) *adj* negative.

negocio *m* business, affair; transaction; firm; place of business.

negro(a) *adj* black; * *m* black: — *m(f)* Black.

nene(a) *m(f)* baby.

nervio *m* nerve; vigour.

neto(a) *adj* neat, pure; net.

neumático *adj* pneumatic; tyre; ~ de repuesto, de recambio spare tyre.

neutro(a) *adj* neutral; neuter.

nevar *vi* to snow.

nevera *f* icebox.

ni *conj* neither, nor.

nido *m* nest; hiding place.

niebla *f* fog; mist.

nieto(a) *m(f)* grandson, granddaughter.

nieve *f* snow.

ningún, **ninguno**, **na** *adj* no; * *pron* nobody; none; not one; neither.

niño(a) *adj* childish; * *pron* or *f* child; infant: —desde ~ from infancy, from a child: —*m* boy: — *f* girl; * *f* pupil (of eye).

nitidez *f* clarity; brightness; sharpness.

nivel *m* level; standard; height.

no *adv* no; not; * *excl* no!

no obstante *adv* nevertheless.

noche *f* night; evening; darkness: —N~ buena Christmas Eve: —N~ vieja New Year's Eve: — ¡buenas ~s! good night!

noción *f* notion, idea.

nocivo(a) *adj* harmful.

nogal *m* (botany) walnut tree.

nombrar *vt* to name; to nominate; to appoint.

nombre *m* name; reputation.

nómina *f* list; (commerce) payroll.

non *adj* odd, uneven; * *m* odd number.

nor(d)este *adj* northeast, northeastern; *m* northeast.

nórdico(a) *adj* northern; Nordic.

noria *f* water wheel; big wheel.

noroeste *adj* northwest, northwestern; *m* northwest.

norte *adj* north, northern; * *m* north; (*fig*) rule, guide.

nos *pron* us; to us; for us; from us; to ourselves.

nosotros, **nosotras** *pron* we; us.

nostalgia *f* homesickness.

nota *f* note; mark.

notar *vt* to note; to mark; to remark; * ~se *vr* to be obvious.

noticia *f* information; note; ~s *fpl* news.

noticiario *m* newsreel; news bulletin.

notificar *vt* to notify, to inform.

novato(a) *adj* inexperienced; * *m(f)* beginner.

novecientos(as) *adj* nine hundred.

novedad *f* novelty; modernness; newness; piece of news; change.

noveno(a) *adj* ninth.

noventa *adj*, *m* ninety.

noviembre *m* November.

novio(a) *m(f)* bridegroom; boyfriend; fiancé; bride; girlfriend; fiancée.

nube *f* cloud.

nublado(a) *adj* cloudy; * *m* storm cloud.

nuca *f* nape (of the neck).

nudillo *m* knuckle.

nudista *adj* nudist.

nudo *m* knot.

nuero(a) *m(f)* son-in-law; daughter-in-law.

nuestro(a) *adj* our; * *pron* ours.

nueve *m*, *adj* nine.

nuevo(a) *adj* new; modern; fresh; * *f* piece of news: — ¿qué hay de ~? is there any news?, what's new?

nuez *f* nut; walnut; Adam's apple; ~ moscada nutmeg.

número *m* number; cipher.

nunca *adv* never; ~ más never again.

nutria *f* otter.

nutrir *vt* to nourish; to feed.

Ñ

ñamé *m* yam

ñoñería *f* insipidity, spinelessness; stupid thing.

ñoño(a) *adj* characterless, insipid, insubstantial.

O

o *conj* or; either.

obedecer *vt* to obey.

obertura *f* overture.

obeso(a) *adj* obese, fat.
objetar *vi* to object.
objeto *m* object; aim.
obligar *vt* to force; * ~se *vr* to bind oneself.
obra *f* work; building, construction; play: —por ~ de thanks to.
obrero(a) *adj* working; labour (*in compounds*); * *m(f)* worker; labourer.
obsequiar *vt* to lavish attention on; ~ con to present with.
observar *vt* to observe; to notice.
obstáculo *m* obstacle, impediment, hindrance.
obstinarse *vr* to be obstinate; ~ en to persist in.
obstruir *vt* to obstruct; * ~se *vr* to be blocked up, to be obstructed.
obtener *vt* to obtain; to gain.
obviar *vt* to obviate; to remove.
oca *f* goose; juego de la ~ snakes and ladders.
ocasión *f* occasion, opportunity.
ocasionar *vt* to cause.
ocaso *m* sunset.
occidente *m* occident, west.
océano *m* ocean.
ochenta *m*, *adj* eighty.
ocho *m*, *adj* eight.
ocio *m* leisure; pastime.
octavilla *f* pamphlet.
octavo(a) *adj* eighth.
octubre *m* October.
ocultar *vt* to hide, to conceal.
oculto(a) *adj* hidden, secret.
ocupar *vt* to occupy; to hold (office); * ~se *vr* ~ de to concern oneself with.
ocurrencia *f* event; bright idea.
ocurrir *vi* to occur, to happen.
odiar *vt* to hate; * ~se *vr* to hate one another.
odontólogo(a) *m(f)* dentist.
oeste *adj* west, western; * *m* west.
ofender *vt* to offend; to injure; * ~se *vr* to be vexed; to take offence.

oferta *f* offer, proposal; ~s sales, bargains.
oficina *f* office.
oficio *m* employment; function; trade, business.
ofrecer *vt* to offer; to present; to exhibit; * ~se *vr* to offer oneself; to occur.
oído *m* hearing; ear.
oír *vt*, *vi* to hear; to listen (to).
ojal *m* buttonhole.
ojalá *conj* if only!, would that!
ojear *vt* to eye, to view; to glance.
ojera *f* bag under the eye.
ojo *m* eye; sight; eye of a needle; arch of a bridge.
ola *f* wave.
oleaje *m* swell.
oler *vt* to smell, to scent; * *vi* to smell; ~ a to smack of.
olfato *m* sense of smell.
olivo *m* (botany) olive tree.
oliva *f* olive: — aceite de ~ olive oil.
olla *f* pan; stew; ~ exprés, ~ a presion pressure cooker.
olmo *m* (botany) elm tree.
olor *m* smell, odour; scent.
olvidar *vt* to forget.
ombligo *m* navel.
once *m*, *adj* eleven.
onda *f* wave.
opaco(a) *adj* opaque; dark.
opción *f* option; alternative.
opinar *vt* to think; * *vi* to give one's opinion.
oponer *vt* to oppose; * ~se *vr* to be opposed; ~ a to oppose.
oportunidad *f* opportunity, chance.
oposición *f* opposition; ~ones *fpl* public examinations *pl*.
oprimir *vt* to oppress; to crush; to press; to squeeze.
optar *vt* to choose, to elect.
optativo(a) *adj* optional.
óptimo(a) *adj* best.
opuesto(a) *adj* opposite; contrary; adverse.

oración *f* prayer.
oral *adj*: — por vía ~ orally.
orar *vi* to pray.
orden *m* order; command.
ordenado(a) *adj* methodical; tidy.
ordenador *m* computer.
ordenar *vt* to arrange; to
  order; to ordain; * ~se *vr* to
  take holy orders.
ordinario(a) *adj* ordinary,
  usual; vulgar.
ordeñar *vt* to milk.
oreja *f* ear.
organizar *vt* to organise.
orgullo *m* pride, haughtiness.
oriental *adj* oriental, eastern.
orientar *vt* to orient; to point;
  * ~se *vr* to get one's bearings.
orificio *m* orifice; mouth.
origen *m* origin: — dar ~ to
  cause.
orilla *f* limit, border, margin;
  edge (of cloth); shore.
orín *m* rust.
orina *f* urine.
oro *m* gold; ~s *mpl* diamonds *pl*
  (at cards).
orquídea *f* (botany) orchid.
ortiga *f* (botany) nettle.
oruga *f* (zoo) caterpillar.
orzuelo *m* (medical) stye.
os *pron* you; to you.
osar *vi* to dare, venture.
oscuro(a) *adj* obscure; dark.
oso(a) *m(f)* bear; ~ blanco
  polar bear; Osa Mayor
  (Menor) Great (Little) Bear.
ostentar *vt* to show; * *vi* to
  boast, to brag.
ostra *f* oyster.
otear *vt* to observe; to look into.
otoño *m* fall, autumn.
otorgar *vt* to concede; to grant.
otro(a) *adj* another; other.
ovario *m* ovary.
oveja *f* sheep.
ovillo *m* ball of wool.
óvulo *m* ovum.
oxidar *vt* to rust; * ~se *vr* to go
  rusty.

oxígeno *m* oxygen.
oyente *m* or *f* listener, hearer.

P

pabellón *m* pavilion; block,
  section.
paciente *adj* patient.
pacificar *vt* to pacify, appease.
pacífico(a) *adj* peaceful:
  — Océano P~ Pacific Ocean
pacotilla *f*: — de ~ third-rate;
  cheap.
pactar *vt* to covenant; to
  contract; to stipulate.
padecer *vt* to suffer; to sustain
  (an injury); to put up with.
padrastro *m* stepfather.
padre *m* father: ~s *mpl* parents *pl*.
padrino *m* godfather: ~ de
  boda best man.
pagar *vt* to pay; to pay for;
  (*fig*) to repay; * *vi* to pay.
página *f* page.
pago *m* payment; reward.
país *m* country; region.
paisaje *m* landscape.
paisano(a) *adj* of the same
  country; * *m(f)* fellow-
  countryman or woman.
paja *f* straw; (*fig*) trash.
pajarita *f* bow tie.
pájaro *m* bird; sly, acute fellow.
pajita *f* (drinking) straw.
pala *f* spade, shovel.
palabra *f* word: — de ~ by word
  of mouth.
palabrota *f* swear-word.
palacio *m* palace; ~ de justicia
  court-house.
paladar *m* palate; taste, relish.
paladear *vt* to taste.
palanca *f* lever.
palangana *f* washbasin.
palco *m* box (in a theatre).
paleto(a) *m(f)* rustic.
pálido(a) *adj* pallid, pale.
palillo *m* small stick; toothpick;
  ~s *mpl* chopsticks *pl*.

palique *m*: — estar de ~ to have a chat.

paliza *f* beating, thrashing.

palma *f* palm tree; palm of the hand; palm leaf.

palmada *f* slap, clap; ~s *fpl* clapping of hands, applause.

palmera *f* palm tree.

palo *m* stick, a blow given by one; cudgel; post; bat; suit (at cards); ~s *mpl* masts.

paloma *f* pigeon, dove: ~ mensajera homing pigeon.

palomilla *f* moth; wing nut; angle iron.

palomitas *fpl* popcorn.

palpar *vt* to feel, ouch.

pámpano *m* vine branch.

pamela *f* sun hat.

pan *m* bread; loaf.

pana *f* corduroy.

panadería *f* baker's (shop).

pandereta *f* tambourine.

pandilla *f* group; gang; clique.

pantalla *f* screen; lampshade.

pantalón *m*, **pantalones** *mpl* trousers, pants *pl*.

pantano *m* marsh; reservoir; obstacle, difficulty.

pantorrilla *f* calf (of the leg).

panza *f* belly, paunch.

pañal *m* nappy.

pañuelo *m* handkerchief.

paño *m* cloth; duster, rag.

papá *m* (*sl*) dad, pop.

papada *f* double chin.

papel *m* paper; writing; part, role (in a play); ~ de estraza brown paper; ~ sellado stamped paper.

papeleo *m* red tape.

papelería *f* stationer's (shop).

paperas *fpl* mumps.

papilla *f* baby food: — estar hecho ~ to be dog tired.

paquete *m* packet; parcel; package tour.

par *adj* equal; alike; even; * *m* pair; couple; peer: — sin ~ matchless.

para *prep* for; to, in order to; towards.

parabrisas *m invar* windscreen.

parabólica *adj*: — antena ~ satellite dish.

paracaídas *m invar* parachute.

parada *f* halt; suspension; pause; stop; shutdown; ~ de autobús bus stop.

parado(a) *adj* motionless; at a standstill; stopped; standing (up); unemployed.

paraguas *m invar* umbrella.

parar *vi* to stop, to halt; * *vt* to stop, to detain: — sin ~ instantly, without delay; * ~se *vr* to stop, to halt; to stand up.

parecer *m* opinion, counsel; air, mien; * *vi* to appear; to seem; * ~se *vr* ~ a to resemble.

parecido(a) *adj* resembling, like.

pared *f* wall; ~ medianera party wall.

pareja *f* pair, couple, brace.

pariente(a) *m(f)* relative, relation.

parir *vt* to give birth to; * *vi* to give birth.

paro *m* strike; unemployment.

parpadear *vi* to blink.

párpado *m* eyelid.

parra *f* vine raised on stakes or nailed to a wall.

párrafo *m* paragraph.

parrilla *f* grill; grille.

parte *m* message; report; * *f* part; side; party: — de ocho días a esta ~ within these last eight days: — de ~ a ~ from side to side, through and through.

partera *f* midwife.

particular *adj* particular, special; * *m* private individual; particular matter or subject treated upon.

partida *f* departure; party; item in an account; parcel; game.

partido *m* (politics) party; game, match.

parto *m* birth.

partir *vt* to part; to divide, to separate; to cut; to break; * *vi* to depart; * ~se *vr* to break.

parvulario *m* nursery school.

pasa *f* raisin.

pasadizo *m* narrow passage.

pasado(a) *adj* past; bad; overdone; out of date; ~do mañana the day after tomorrow: —la semana ~da last week: — *m* past.

pasaje *m* passage; fare; passengers *pl*.

pasajero(a) *adj* transient; transitory; fugitive; * *m(f)* traveller; passenger.

pasamanos *m invar* (hand)rail.

pasar *vt* to pass; to surpass; to suffer; to strain; to dissemble; * *vi* to pass; to happen; * ~se *vr* to go over (to another party); to go bad or off.

pasarela *f* footbridge; gangway.

pasatiempo *m* pastime.

Pascua *f* Passover; Easter.

pasear *vt* to walk; * *vi* ~se *vr* to walk; to walk about.

pasmar *vt* to amaze; to numb; * ~se *vr* to be astonished.

paso *m* pace, step; passage; manner of walking; flight of steps; accident: — (railway) ~ a nivel level crossing: —al ~ on the way, in passing.

pasta *f* paste; dough; pastry; (*sl*) dough; ~s *fpl* pastries *pl*; pasta; ~ de dientes toothpaste.

pastel *m* cake; pie; crayon.

pastelería *f* cake shop.

pastilla *f* bar (of soap); tablet, pill.

pastor *m* shepherd; pastor.

pata *f* leg (of animal or furniture); foot: —meter la ~ to put one's foot in it.

patata *f* potato.

patear *vt* to kick; to stamp on.

patillas *fpl* sideburns *pl*.

patín *m* skate; runner.

patinar *vi* to skate; to skid; (*sl*) to blunder.

patio *m* courtyard; playground.

pato *m* duck.

patoso(a) *adj* (*sl*) clumsy.

patria *f* native land; mother country; ~ chica home town.

patrocinar *vt* to sponsor; to back, to support.

patrón(ona) *m(f)* boss, master, mistress; landlord, lady; patron saint; * *m* pattern.

patronal *adj* employers' organisation.

patrulla *f* patrol.

paulatino(a) *adj* gradual, slow.

pausa *f* pause; break.

pausar *vi* to pause.

pauta *f* guideline.

pavo *m* turkey: ~ real peacock.

pavor *m* dread, terror.

payaso(a) *m(f)* clown.

payo(a) *m(f)* non-gypsy (to a gypsy).

paz *f* peace; tranquillity, ease.

peaje *m* toll.

peana *f* pedestal; footstool.

peatón *m* pedestrian.

peca *f* freckle; spot.

pecado *m* sin.

pecera *f* goldfish bowl.

pecho *m* chest; breast(s) (*pl*); teat; bosom; (*fig*) courage, valour: —dar el ~ a to suckle: — tomar a ~ to take to heart.

pechuga *f* breast of a fowl; (*sl*) bosom.

pedal *m* pedal; ~ de embrague clutch; ~ de freno footbrake.

pedalear *vi* to pedal.

pedazo *m* piece, bit.

pedernal *m* flint.

pediatra *m* or *f* pediatrician.

pedicuro(a) *m(f)* chiropodist.

pedir *vt* to ask for; to petition; to order; to need; * *vi* to ask.

pedo *m* (*sl*) fart: — tirarse un ~ to fart (*sl*): — estar ~ to be pissed.

pegamento *m* glue.

pegar *vt* to cement; to join, to unite; to beat; ~ fuego a to set fire to; * *vi* to stick; to match; * ~se *vr* to intrude; to steal in.

pegatina *f* sticker.

peinar *vt* to comb; to style.

peine *m* comb.

pelar *vt* to cut (hair); to strip off (feathers); to peel; * ~se *vr* to peel off; to have one's hair cut.

pelas *fpl* (*sl*) money, pesetas.

peldaño *m* step (of a flight of stairs).

pelear *vt* to fight, to combat; * ~se *vr* to scuffle.

pelele *m* dummy; man of straw.

película *f* film.

peligro *m* danger, peril; risk.

pelirrojo(a) *m(f)* red-head; * *adj* red-haired.

pellejo *m* skin; hide, pelt; peel; wine skin; oilskin; drunkard.

pellizcar *vt* to pinch.

pelo *m* hair; pile; flaw (in precious stones).

pelota *f* ball.

peluca *f* wig.

peluquería *f* hairdresser's; barber's (shop).

pelusa *f* bloom (on fruit); fluff.

pena *f* punishment, pain: — duras ~s with great difficulty or trouble.

pendiente *f* slope, declivity; * *m* earring; * *adj* pending; unsettled.

pene *m* penis.

penetrante *adj* deep; sharp; piercing; searching; biting.

penique *m* penny.

penoso(a) *adj* painful.

pensar *vi* to think.

pensativo(a) *adj* pensive, thoughtful.

pensión *f* guest-house; pensione.

penúltimo(a) *adj* penultimate, last but one.

penumbra *f* half-light.

penuria *f* penury, poverty.

peña *f* frock, large stone.

peón *m* (day) labourer; foot soldier; pawn (at chess).

peor *adj*, *adv* worse: — de mal en ~ from bad to worse.

pepino *m* cucumber: — (no) me importa un ~ I don't care two hoots.

pepita *f* kernel; pip.

pepito *m* meat sandwich.

pequeño(a) *adj* little, small; young.

pera *f* pear.

percatarse *vr*: ~ de to notice.

percha *f* coat hook; coat hanger; perch.

percibir *vt* to receive; to perceive, to comprehend.

perder *vt* to lose; to waste; to miss; * ~se *vr* to go astray; to be lost; to be spoiled.

pérdida *f* loss, waste: — no tiene ~ you can't go wrong.

perdiz *f* partridge.

perdón *m* pardon; mercy: — ¡~! sorry!

perdonar *vt* to pardon, to forgive; to excuse.

perdurar *vi* to last; to still exist.

perecedero(a) *adj* perishable.

peregrino(a) *adj* (*fig*) strange; * *m* pilgrim.

perejil *m* parsley.

pereza *f* laziness, idleness.

perfecto(a) *adj* perfect.

perfil *m* profile.

perforar *vt* to perforate; * *vi* to drill.

perfume *m* perfume.

pergamino *m* parchment.

periódico(a) *adj* periodical; * *m* newspaper.

periodista *m* or *f* journalist.

periodo *m* period.

peripecia *f* vicissitude; sudden change.

periquito *m* budgie.

perito(a) *adj* skilful, experienced; * *m(f)* expert;

skilled worker; technician.
perjudicar *vt* to prejudice,
damage; to injure, hurt.
perjurar *vi* to perjure, to
swear falsely; to swear.
perla *f* pearl: — de ~s fine.
permanecer *vi* to stay; to
continue to be.
permiso *m* permission, leave.
permitir *vt* to permit, to allow.
permutar *vt* to exchange.
pernera *f* trouser leg.
perno *m* bolt.
pernoctar *vi* to spend the night.
pero *m* kind of apple;
* *conj* but, yet.
perogrullada *f* truism, platitude.
perol *m* large metal pan.
perro *m* dog.
perseguir *vt* to pursue; to
persecute; to chase after.
perseverar *vi* to persevere.
persiana *f* (Venetian) blind.
persistir *vi* to persist.
persona *f* person: — de ~ a ~ from
person to person.
personal *m* personal; personnel.
personaje *m* celebrity;
character.
persuadir *vt* to persuade;
* ~se *vr* to be persuaded.
pertenecer *vi*; ~ a to belong to;
to appertain, to concern.
pértiga *f* long pole or rod.
pertinaz *adj* pertinacious;
obstinate.
pertinente *adj* relevant;
appropriate.
perturbar *vt* to perturb, to
disturb.
pervertir *vt* to pervert; to
corrupt.
pesa *f* weight.
pesadez *f* heaviness, weight;
gravity; slowness; peevishness,
fretfulness; trouble; fatigue.
pesadilla *f* nightmare.
pesado(a) *adj* peevish;
troublesome; cumbersome;
tedious; heavy, weighty.

pesar *m* sorrow, grief;
repentance: — a ~ de in spite
of, notwithstanding; * *vi* to
weigh; to repent; * *vt* to weigh.
pescadería *f* fish shop.
pescado *m* fish (in general).
pescar *vt* to fish for, to catch
(fish); * *vi* to fish.
pescuezo *m* neck.
pésimo(a) *adj* very bad.
peso *m* weight, heaviness;
balance scales *pl*.
pesquisa *f* inquiry,
examination.
pestaña *f* eyelash.
pestañear *vi* to blink.
pestillo *m* bolt.
petardo *m* firecracker.
petróleo *m* oil, petroleum.
pez *m* fish; * *f* pitch.
pezón *m* nipple.
pezuña *f* hoof.
piadoso(a) *adj* pious; mild;
merciful; moderate.
piar *vi* to squeak; to chirp.
picado(a) *adj* pricked; minced,
chopped; bad (tooth); cross.
picadura *f* puncture, sting, bite.
picante *adj* hot, spicy; racy.
picaporte *m* door-handle; latch.
picar *vt* to prick; to sting; to
mince; to nibble; * *vi* to
prick; to sting; to itch;
* ~se *vr* to be piqued; to take
offence; to be moth-eaten; to
begin to rot.
pícaro(a) *adj* roguish;
mischievous, malicious; sly;
* *m(f)* rogue, knave.
pico *m* beak; bill, nib; peak;
pick-axe.
picor *m* itch.
pie *m* foot; leg; basis; trunk (of
trees); foundation; occasion:
— a ~ on foot.
piedad *f* piety; mercy, pity.
piedra *f* stone.
piel *f* skin; hide; peel.
pienso *m* fodder.
pierna *f* leg (human).

pieza f piece; room.
pila f battery; trough; font; sink; pile, heap: — **nombre de ~** first name.
píldora f pill.
pimentón m paprika.
pimienta f pepper.
pimiento m pepper, pimiento.
pincel m paintbrush.
pinchar vt to prick; to puncture.
pincho m thorn; snack.
ping-pong m table tennis.
pino m (botany) pine.
pintar vt to paint; to picture; to describe; to exaggerate; * vi to paint; (sl) to count, to be important; * **~se** vr to put on make-up.
pintura f painting.
pinza f claw; clothes peg; pincers pl; **~s** fpl tweezers pl.
piña f pineapple; fir cone; group.
piñón m pine nut; pinion.
piojo m louse; troublesome hanger-on.
pipa f pipe; sunflower seed.
piragua f canoe.
piropo m compliment; flattery.
piruleta f lollipop.
pisar vt to tread, to trample; to stamp on (the ground); to hammer down; * vi to tread, to walk.
piscina f swimming pool.
piso m flat, apartment; tread, trampling; floor, pavement; storey.
pisotear vt to trample, to tread under foot.
pista f trace, footprint; clue.
pita f (botany) agave.
pitar vt to blow; to whistle at; * vi to whistle; to toot one's horn.
pitillo m cigarette.
pito m whistle; horn.
pizarra f slate; blackboard.
pizca f mite; pinch.
placa f plate; badge.

placer m pleasure; delight; * vt to please.
plan m plan; design; plot; scheme.
plancha f plate; iron; gangway.
planchar vt to iron.
planear vt to plan; * vi to glide.
planicie f plain.
planificación f planning; **~ familiar** family planning.
plano(a) adj plain, level, flat; * m plan; ground plot; **~ inclinado** (railway) dead level.
plantación f plantation.
plantar vt to plant; to fix upright; to strike or hit (a blow); to found; to establish; * **~se** vr to stand upright.
plantilla f personnel; insole of a shoe.
plata f silver; plate (wrought silver); cash: — **en ~** briefly.
plátano m banana; plane tree.
plateado(a) adj silvered; plated.
platillo m saucer; **~s** mpl cymbals pl; **~ volador, ~ volante** flying saucer.
platino m platinum; **~s** mpl contact points pl.
plato m dish; plate.
playa f beach.
playera f T-shirt; * fpl canvas shoes pl.
plaza f square; place; office, employment; room; seat.
plazo m term; instalment; expiry date.
plegar vt to fold; to plait.
pleito m contract, bargain; dispute, debate; lawsuit.
plenilunio m full moon.
pleno(a) adj full; complete; * m plenum.
pliego m sheet of paper.
pliegue m fold; plait.
plisado(a) adj pleated; * m pleating.
plomero m plumber.
plomo m lead:

— **a** ~ perpendicularly.
pluma *f* feather, plume.
población *f* population; town.
pobre *adj* poor.
pobreza *f* poverty.
poco(a) *adj* little, scanty; few;
* *adv* little: ~o a ~o gently;
little by little; * *m* small
part; little.
podar *vt* to prune.
poder *m* power, authority;
command; force; * *vi* to be
able to.
podrido(a) *adj* rotten, bad;
(*fig*) rotten.
poesía *f* poetry.
polea *f* pulley; (marine)
tackle-block.
policía *m* or *f* policeman or
woman.
polideportivo *m* sports centre.
polifacético(a) *adj* many-
sided, versatile.
polilla *f* moth.
pollo *m* chicken.
polo *m* pole; ice lolly; polo;
polo neck.
polvo *m* powder, dust: — **estar**
hecho ~ to be exhausted.
pólvora *f* gunpowder.
pomada *f* cream, ointment.
pomelo *m* grapefruit.
pómez *f*: — **piedra** ~ pumice
stone.
pompa *f* pomp; bubble.
pómulo *m* cheekbone.
poner *vt* to put, place; to put
on; to impose; to lay (eggs);
* ~se *vr* to oppose; to set (of
stars); to become.
poniente *m* west; west wind.
ponzoña *f* poison.
popa *f* (marine) poop, stern.
por *prep* for; by; about;
through; on account of.
porción *f* part, portion; lot.
porfiar *vt* to dispute
obstinately; to persist in a
pursuit.
pormenor *f* detail.

poro *m* pore.
porque *conj* because; since; so
that.
porqué *m* reason, cause.
porquería *f* nastiness, rudeness.
porrón *m* spouted wine jar.
portada *f* portal, porch;
frontispiece.
portaequipajes *m invar* boot
(of car); baggage rack.
portal *m* vestibule, hall;
doorway, main door.
portarse *vr* to behave.
portatil *adj* portable.
portavoz *m* or *f* spokesman or
woman.
porte *m* transportation
charges *pl*; deportment,
demeanour, conduct.
portero *m* porter, gatekeeper.
porvenir *m* future.
posar *vi* to sit, to pose; * *vt* to
lay down (a burden); * ~se *vr*
to settle; to perch; to land.
posdata *f* postcript.
poseer *vt* to hold, to possess.
posesivo(a) *adj* possessive.
posibilitar *vt* to make
possible; to make feasible.
poso *m* sediment, dregs *pl*.
posponer *vt* to postpone.
postal *adj* postal; * *f* postcard.
poste *m* post, pillar.
postergar *vt* to leave behind;
to postpone.
posterior *adj* back, rear;
following, subsequent.
posterioridad *f*: — **con** ~
subsequently, later.
postigo *m* wicket; postern;
shutter.
postizo(a) *adj* artificial (not
natural); * *m* wig.
postrar *vt* to humble, to
humiliate; * ~se *vr* to
prostrate oneself.
postre *m* dessert: — **llegar a**
los ~s to come too late.
postura *f* position; attitude;
bet, wager; agreement.

potable *adj* drinkable.

potaje *m* thick vegetable soup.

potro(a) *m(f)* colt; foal.

pozo *m* well.

practicar *vt* to practise.

práctico(a) *adj* practical; skilful, experienced.

prado *m* lawn; meadow.

precaver *vt* to prevent; to guard against.

preceder *vt* to precede, to go before.

preciado(a) *adj* esteemed, valued.

precinto *m* seal.

precio *m* price; value.

precioso(a) *adj* precious; (*sl*) beautiful.

precipicio *m* cliff; precipice.

precipitación *m* haste; rainfall.

precisamente *adv* precisely.

precisar *vt* to compel, to oblige; to need.

preciso(a) *adj* necessary, accurate; abstracted.

precoz *adj* precocious.

precursor(a) *m(f)* harbinger, forerunner.

predecir *vt* to foretell.

predicar *vt* to preach.

predilecto(a) *adj* darling, favourite.

predisponer *vt* to predispose; to prejudice.

predominar *vi* to predominate, to prevail.

preferir *vt* to prefer.

pregón *m* proclamation; hue and cry.

preguntar *vt* to ask; to question; to demand; to inquire.

prejuicio *m* prejudgement; preconception; prejudice.

premiar *vt* to reward, to remunerate.

premura *f* pressure, haste, hurry.

prenda *f* pledge; garment; sweetheart; person or thing dearly loved; ~s *fpl* accomplishments, talents *pl*.

prender *vt* to seize, to catch, to imprison; * ~se *vr* to catch fire; * *vi* to take root.

prensar *vt* to press.

preñada *adj* pregnant.

preocupar(se) *vt* (*vr*) to worry.

preparar *vt* to prepare; * ~se *vr* to be prepared.

prepucio *m* foreskin.

presa *f* capture, seizure; dike, dam.

presagio *m* omen.

prescindir *vi*; ~ de to do without; to dispense with.

presenciar *vt* to attend; to be present at; to witness.

presentar *vt* to present; to introduce; to offer; to show; * ~se *vr* to present oneself; to appear; to run (as candidate); to apply.

presente *m* present; gift: — tener ~ to remember, to bear in mind.

presentir *vt* to have a premonition of.

preservativo *m* condom, sheath.

presidiario *m* convict.

presilla *f* clip; loop (in clothes).

presión *f* pressure, pressing.

presionar *vt* to press; (*fig*) to put pressure on.

preso(a) *m(f)* prisoner.

prestar *vt* to lend.

presto(a) *adj* quick; prompt; ready; * *adv* soon; quickly.

presumir *vt* to presume, conjecture; * *vi* to be conceited.

presunto(a) *adj* so-called.

presupuesto *m* budget.

pretender *vt* to claim; to try.

pretendiente *m* pretender; suitor.

pretexto *m* pretext; excuse.

prevalacer *vi* to prevail; to triumph; to take root.

prevenir *vt* to prepare; to foresee; to prevent; to warn; * ~se *vr* to be prepared; to be predisposed.

prever *vt* to foresee, forecast.

previo(a) *adj* previous.

previsión *f* foresight, prevision.

primario(a) *adj* primary.

primavera *f* spring (the season).

primero(a) *adj* first; former; * *adv* first; rather, sooner.

primicias *f* first fruits *pl*.

primo(a) *m* cousin; * *f* bonus.

primogénito(a) *adj*, *m(f)* first-born.

princesa *f* princess.

príncipe *m* prince.

principiante *m* beginner, learner.

principio *m* beginning, commencement; principle.

pringoso(a) *adj* greasy; sticky.

prisa *f* speed; promptness.

prismáticos *mpl* binoculars *pl*.

privación *f* deprivation, want.

privado(a) *adj* private; particular.

probador *m* fitting room.

probar *vt* to try; to prove; to taste; * *vi* to try.

probeta *f* test tube.

procedente *adj* reasonable; proper; ~ de coming from.

procesador *m*; ~ de textos word processor.

procesar *vt* to put on trial.

procurar *vt* to try; to obtain; to produce.

prodigar *vt* to waste, lavish.

producir *vt* to produce; to produce as evidence; * ~se *vr* to come about; to arise; to be made; to break out.

proeza *f* prowess, bravery.

profanar *vt* to profane, to desecrate.

profesor(a) *m(f)* teacher.

prófugo *m* fugitive.

profundidad *f* depth.

profundo(a) *adj* profound.

programa *m* programme.

progre *adj* (*sl*) liberal.

prohibir *vt* to prohibit, to forbid; to hinder.

prójimo *m* fellow creature; neighbour.

prole *f* offspring, progeny; race.

prólogo *m* prologue.

promedio *m* average; middle.

prometer *vt* to promise; to assure; * ~se *vr* to become engaged.

promiscuo(a) *adj* promiscuous; confusedly mingled.

promover *vt* to promote, to advance; to stir up.

promulgar *vt* to promulgate, to publish.

pronosticar *vt* to predict, to foretell; to conjecture.

pronto(a) *adj* prompt; ready; * *adv* promptly.

pronunciamiento *m* (law) publication; insurrection, sedition.

pronunciar *vt* to pronounce; to deliver; * ~se *vr* to rebel.

propaganda *f* propaganda; advertising.

propagar *vt* to propagate.

propasar *vt* to go beyond, to exceed.

propenso(a) *adj* prone, inclined.

propiamente *adv* properly; really.

propiciar *vt* to favour; to cause.

propiedad *f* possessions *pl*; right of property; propriety.

propietario(a) *m(f)* owner.

propina *f* tip.

propio(a) *adj* proper; own; typical; very.

proponer *vt* to propose.

proporción *f* proportion; ratio: ~es dimensions.

proporcionar *vt* to provide.

propósito *m* aim, purpose: — a ~ on purpose.

propuesta *f* proposal, offer; representation.

propulsar *vt* to propel; (*fig*) to promote.

prórroga *f* prolongation;

extension; extra time.

prorrumpir *vi* to break forth.

prosa *f* prose.

proscrito(a) *adj* banned.

proseguir *vt* to continue;
* *vi* to continue, go on.

prospección *f* exploration;
prospecting.

prosperar *vi* to prosper, to
thrive.

proteger *vt* to protect.

protestar *vt* to protest; to
make public declaration (of
faith); * *vi* to protest.

provecho *m* profit; advantage.

proveedor(a) *m(f)* supplier.

provenir *vi* to arise, to
originate; to issue.

provincia *f* province; region.

provisión *f* provision; supply.

provocar *vt* to provoke; to
lead to; to excite.

próximamente *adv* soon.

próximo(a) *adj* next;
neighbouring; close, nearby.

proyectar *vt* to throw; to cast;
to screen; to plan.

proyecto *m* plan, project.

prueba *f* proof; reason;
experiment; attempt; taste.

púa *f* sharp point, prickle;
shoot; pick.

pubertad *f* puberty.

publicar *vt* to publish; to
make public.

publicidad *f* publicity;
advertising.

público(a) *adj* public;
* *m* public; audience; crowd.

puchero *m* pot; stew.

púdico(a) *adj* chaste, pure.

pudiente *adj* rich, opulent.

pudor *m* bashfulness.

pudrir *vt* to rot, putrefy;
* ~se *vr* to decay, to rot.

pueblo *m* people *pl*; town,
village; population; populace.

puente *m* bridge.

puenting *m* bungee jumping.

puerco(a) *adj* nasty; filthy,

dirty; rude, coarse; * *m* pig,
hog; ~ espín porcupine.

pueril *adj* childish; puerile.

puerro *m* leek.

puerta *f* door; doorway;
gateway: ~ trasera back door.

puerto *m* port, harbour; pass.

pues *adv* then; therefore; well:
— ¡~! well, then.

puesto *m* place; particular
spot; post, employment;
barracks *pl*; stand.

púgil *m* boxer.

pujante *adj* powerful, strong;
robust; stout, strapping.

pulga *f* flea: — tener malas ~s
to be easily piqued; to be ill-
tempered.

pulgada *f* inch.

pulgar *m* thumb.

pulir *vt* to polish; to put the
last touches to.

pulmón *m* lung.

pulmonía *f* pneumonia.

pulpa *f* pulp; soft part (of fruit).

pulpo *m* octopus.

pulsar *vt* to touch; to play; to
press.

pulsera *f* bracelet.

pulso *m* pulse; wrist; firmness
or steadiness of the hand.

pulular *vi* to swarm.

pulverizador *m* spray gun.

punta *f* point; end; trace.

puntada *f* stitch.

puntal *m* prop, stay; buttress.

puntapié *m* kick.

puntería *f* aiming.

puntiagudo(a) *adj* sharp-pointed.

puntilla *f* narrow lace edging:
— de ~s on tiptoe.

punto *m* point; end; spot;
stitch; full stop.

puntual *adj* punctual; exact;
reliable.

punzada *f* prick; sting; pain;
compunction.

punzante *adj* sharp.

puñado *m* handful.

puñal *m* dagger.

puño *m* fist; handful; wristband; cuff, handle.

pupila *f* pupil (of eye).

puro(a) *adj* pure; mere; clear; genuine.

púrpura *f* purple.

purulento(a) *adj* purulent.

puta *f* whore.

PVP *abbrev* (precio de venta al público) RRP.

Q

que *pron* that; who; which; what; * *conj* that; than.

¿qué? *adj* what? which? * *pron* what?; which?.

quebrantar *vt* to break; to crack; to burst; to pound, to grind; to violate; to fatigue; to weaken.

quedar *vi* to stay; * ~se *vr* to remain.

quedo(a) *adj* quiet, still; * *adv* softly, gently.

quejarse *vr* to complain of.

quemadura *f* burn, scald; ~ de sol sunburn.

quemar *vt* to burn; to kindle; * ~se *vr* to be parched with heat; to burn oneself; * *vi* to be too hot.

querella *f* charge; dispute; complaint.

querer *vt* to want; to desire; to will; to love; * *m* will, desire.

querido(a) *adj* dear, beloved; * *m(f)* darling; lover: ~do mío, ~da mía my dear, my love, my darling.

queso *m* cheese.

quicio *m* hook, hinge (of a door).

quien *pron* who; whom.

¿quién? *pron* who? whom?

quienquiera *adj* whoever.

quieto(a) *adj* still, peaceable.

quilla *f* keel.

química *f* chemistry.

quina *f* Peruvian bark, quinine.

quince *adj, m* fifteen; fifteenth.

quinceañero(a) *adj* fifteen-year-old; teenager.

quincena *f* fortnight.

quiniela *f* football pools.

quinta *f* country house; levy, draft of soldiers.

quinto *adj* fifth: — *m* fifth; drafted soldier.

quiosco *m* bandstand; newsstand.

quirúrgico(a) *adj* surgical.

quiste *m* cyst.

quitamanchas *m invar* stain remover.

quitanieves *m invar* snowplough.

quitar *vt* to take away; to take off; to relieve; to annul; * ~se *vr* to take off (clothes, etc); to withdraw.

quitasol *m* parasol.

quizá, quizás *adv* perhaps.

R

rábano *m* radish.

rabia *f* rage, fury.

rabo *m* tail.

racha *f* gust of wind: —buena or mala spell of good or bad luck.

racimo *m* bunch of grapes.

ración *f* portion.

racional *adj* reasonable; rational.

radiografía *f* x-ray.

ráfaga *f* gust; flash; burst.

raído(a) *adj* scraped; worn-out; impudent.

raíz *f* root; base, basis; origin.

raja *f* splinter, chip (of wood); chink, fissure.

rajatabla *adv*: —a ~ strictly.

rallar *vt* to grate.

rama *f* branch.

ramo *m* bouquet.

rampa *f* ramp.

rana *f* frog.

rancho *m* grub; ranch; small farm.

rancio(a) *adj* rank; rancid.
ranura *f* groove; slot.
rapar *vt* to shave; to plunder.
rapaz(a) *adj* rapacious;
* *m(f)* young boy or girl.
rápido(a) *adj* quick, rapid, swift.
rapiña *f* robbery.
raptar *vt* to kidnap.
raquítico(a) *adj* stunted; (*fig*)
inadequate.
raro(a) *adj* rare, scarce;
extraordinary.
ras *m*: — **a ~ de** level with: — **a
~ de tierra** at ground level.
rascacielos *m invar*
skyscraper.
rascar *vt* to scratch, to scrape.
rasgar *vt* to tear, to rip.
rasgo *m* dash, stroke; grand or
magnanimous action;
~s *mpl* features *pl*.
rasguño *m* scratch.
raso *m* satin; glade;
* **~(a)** *adj* plain; flat:
— **al ~** in the open air.
raspa *f* beard (of an ear of
corn); backbone (of fish);
stalk (of grapes); rasp.
raspar *vt* to scrape, to rasp.
rastrear *vt* to trace; to inquire
into; * *vi* to skim along close
to the ground (of birds).
rastrillo *m* rake.
rastro *m* track; rake; trace.
rata *f* rat.
rato *m* moment: — **a ~s
perdidos** in leisure time.
ratón *m* mouse.
raya *f* stroke; line; part;
frontier; ray (fish); roach
(fish).
rayar *vt* to draw lines on; to
cross out; to underline; to
cross; to rifle.
rayo *m* ray, beam (of light).
raza *f* race, lineage; quality.
razonar *vi* to reason; to talk.
reacción *f* reaction: — **avión a
~** jet plane.
reaccionar *vi* to react.

real *adj* real, actual; royal;
* *m* (military) camp.
realidad *f* reality; sincerity.
realizador(a) *m(f)* producer (in
TV, etc).
realzar *vt* to raise, to elevate;
to emboss; to heighten.
reanimar *vt* to cheer, to
encourage; to reanimate.
reanudar *vt* to resume.
rebaja *f* abatement;
deduction; **~s** *fpl* sale.
rebanada *f* slice.
rebaño *m* flock, herd.
rebasar *vt* to exceed.
rebatir *vt* to resist; to parry,
to refute; to repress.
rebeca *f* cardigan.
rebelarse *vr* to revolt.
rebosar *vi* to overflow; to abound.
rebotar *vt* to bounce; to clinch;
to repel; * *vi* to rebound.
rebozar *vt* to wrap up; to fry in
batter or breadcrumbs.
rebuznar *vi* to bray.
recado *m* message; errand.
recaída *f* relapse.
recalcar *vt* to emphasise.
recalentar *vt* to heat again; to
overheat.
recambio *m* spare; refill.
recapacitar *vt* to reflect.
recargar *vt* to overload; to
recharge; to charge again.
recatado(a) *adj* prudent;
circumspect; modest.
recaudar *vt* to gather; to
obtain; to recoven.
recelo *m* dread; suspicion,
mistrust.
receta *f* recipe; prescription.
rechazar *vt* to refuse; to
repulse; to contradict.
recibir *vt* to receive, to accept;
to let in; to go to meet;
* **~se** *vr* **~ de** to qualify as.
recibo *m* receipt.
recién *adv* recently, lately.
reciente *adj* recent; new,
fresh; modern.

recio (a) *adj* strong, robust;
* *adv* strongly, stoutly:
— **hablar** ~ to speak loud.

recipiente *m* container.

reclamación *f* claim;
reclamation; protest.

recluir *vt* to shut up.

reclutar *vt* to recruit.

recobrar *vt* to recover; * ~**se** *vr*
to recover (from illness).

recodo *m* corner or angle
jutting out.

recoger *vt* to collect; to take
back; to get; to gather; to
shelter; to compile; * ~**se** *vr*
to take shelter or refuge; to
retire; to withdraw.

recompensa *f* compensation;
recompense, reward.

reconfortar *vt* to comfort.

reconocer *vt* to recognise; to
examine closely; to
acknowledge; to consider.

reconstituyente *m* tonic.

reconversión *f*; ~ **industrial**
industrial rationalisation.

recopilar *vt* to compile.

récord *adj* record: — **batir el** ~
to break the record.

recordar *vt* to remember; to
remind; * *vi* to remember.

recorrer *vt* to run over, to
peruse; to cover.

recorrido *m* run; journey.

recortar *vt* to cut out.

recostar *vt* to lean, recline;
* ~**se** *vr* to lie down.

recoveco *m* cubby hole; bend.

recreo *m* recreation; playtime
(school).

rectangular *adj* rectangular

rectángulo *m* rectangle.

rectitud *f* straightness;
justness, honesty; exactitude.

recto (a) *adj* straight; right; just,
honest; * *m* rectum; *f* straight
line.

rector (a) *m(f)* superior of a
community or establishment;
curate, rector; * *adj* governing.

recuadro *m* box; inset.

recuento *m* inventory.

recuerdo *m* souvenir; memory.

recuperar *vt* to recover; * ~**se**
vr to recover (from illness).

recurrir *vi*; ~ **a** to resort to.

red *f* net; network; snare.

redactar *vt* to draft; to edit,

redada *f*: ~ **policial** police raid.

redimir *vt* to redeem; to
ransom.

redoblar *vt* to redouble; to rivet.

redondo (a) *adj* round; complete.

reducir *adj* to reduce; to limit;
* ~**se** *vr* to diminish.

redundancia *f* superfluity,
redundancy, excess.

reembolso *m* reimbursement;
refund: — **contra** ~ COD.

referir *vt* to refer, to relate, to
report; * ~**se** *vr* to refer or
relate to.

refinado (a) *adj* refined; subtle,
artful.

reflejar *vt* to reflect.

reflejo *m* reflex; reflection.

reflujo *m* reflux, ebb:
— **flujo y** ~ the tides *pl*.

reformar *vt* to reform; to
correct; to restore;
* ~**se** *vr* to mend; to have
one's manners reformed or
corrected.

reforzar *vt* to strengthen, to
fortify; to encourage.

refrán *m* proverb.

refrescar *vt* to refresh;
* ~**se** *vr* to get cooler; to go
out for a breath of fresh air;
* *vi* to cool down.

refriega *f* affray, skirmish, fray.

refrigerador *m* refrigerator.

refuerzo *m* reinforcement.

refugiar *vt* to shelter;
* ~**se** *vr* to take refuge.

refunfuñar *vi* to snarl; to
growl; to grumble.

regadera *f* watering can.

regalar *vt* to give (as present);
to pamper; to caress.

REGALO

<cyan>regalo</cyan> m gift, present.
<cyan>regaliz</cyan> m licorice.
<cyan>regalo</cyan> m present, gift;
pleasure; comfort.
<cyan>regañadientes</cyan>: — * a ~ adv
reluctantly.
<cyan>regañar</cyan> vt to scold; * vi to
growl; to grumble; to quarrel.
<cyan>regar</cyan> vt to water, to irrigate.
<cyan>regata</cyan> f irrigation ditch;
regatta.
<cyan>regatear</cyan> vt (commercial) to
bargain over; to be mean with;
* vi to haggle; to dribble
(sport).
<cyan>regazo</cyan> m lap.
<cyan>regentar</cyan> vt to rule; to govern.
<cyan>régimen</cyan> m regime; diet; (gr)
rules pl of verbs.
<cyan>registrar</cyan> vt to survey; to
inspect, to examine; to
record, to enter in a register;
* ~se vr to register; to happen.
<cyan>regla</cyan> f rule, ruler; period.
<cyan>reglamentar</cyan> vt to regulate.
<cyan>regocijar</cyan> vt to gladden;
* ~se vr to rejoice.
<cyan>regordete</cyan> adj chubby, plump.
<cyan>regresar</cyan> vi to return.
<cyan>reguero</cyan> m small rivulet; trickle
of spilt liquid; drain, gutter.
<cyan>regulación</cyan> f regulation;
adjustment; ~ del tráfico
traffic control.
<cyan>regular</cyan> vt to regulate, to adjust;
* adj regular; ordinary.
<cyan>rehen</cyan> m or f hostage.
<cyan>rehuir</cyan> vt to avoid.
<cyan>rehusar</cyan> vt to refuse, to decline.
<cyan>reimpresión</cyan> f reprint.
<cyan>reina</cyan> f queen.
<cyan>reincidir</cyan> vi: ~ en to relapse
into, to fall back into.
<cyan>reino</cyan> m kingdom, reign.
<cyan>reintegrar</cyan> vt to reintegrate,
to restore; * ~se vr to be
reinstated or restored.
<cyan>reintegro</cyan> m refund.
<cyan>reir(se)</cyan> vi (vr) to laugh.
<cyan>reiterar</cyan> vt to reiterate.

<cyan>reivindicar</cyan> vt to claim.
<cyan>reja</cyan> f ploughshare; lattice,
grating.
<cyan>rejoneador</cyan> m mounted
bullfighter.
<cyan>relación</cyan> f relation;
relationship; report; account.
<cyan>relajar</cyan> vt to relax, to slacken;
* ~se vr to relax.
<cyan>relamerse</cyan> vr to lick one's lips;
to relish.
<cyan>relámpago</cyan> m flash of lightning.
<cyan>relatar</cyan> vt to relate, to tell.
<cyan>relato</cyan> m story; recital.
<cyan>relegar</cyan> vt to relegate; to
banish, to exile.
<cyan>relente</cyan> m evening dew.
<cyan>relevo</cyan> m relief: — carrera de
~s relay race.
<cyan>relieve</cyan> m relief; (fig)
prominence.
<cyan>religión</cyan> f religion.
<cyan>religioso(a)</cyan> religious;
* m(f) monk, nun.
<cyan>relinchar</cyan> vi to neigh.
<cyan>reliquia</cyan> f residue, remains pl;
(saintly) relic.
<cyan>rellano</cyan> m landing (of stairs).
<cyan>rellenar</cyan> vt to fill up; to stuff.
<cyan>reloj</cyan> m clock; watch.
<cyan>relucir</cyan> vi to shine, to glitter;
to excel, to be brilliant.
<cyan>relumbrar</cyan> vi to sparkle, to
shine.
<cyan>remachar</cyan> vt to rivet; (fig) to
drive home.
<cyan>remanente</cyan> m remainder;
(commerce) balance; surplus.
<cyan>remanso</cyan> m stagnant water;
quiet place.
<cyan>remar</cyan> vi to row.
<cyan>rematar</cyan> vt to terminate, to
finish; to sell off cheaply;
* vi to end.
<cyan>remediar</cyan> vt to remedy; to
assist, to help; to free from
danger; to avoid.
<cyan>remesa</cyan> f shipment; remittance.
<cyan>remilgado(a)</cyan> adj prim; affected.
<cyan>remitente</cyan> m sender.

remojar *vt* to steep; to dunk.
remolacha *f* beet.
remolear *vt* to tow.
remordimiento *m* remorse.
remoto(a) *adj* remote, distant.
remover *vt* to stir; to move around.
remozar *vt* to rejuvenate; to renovate.
renacer *vi* to be born again; to revive.
renacuajo *m* tadpole.
rencor *m* rancour, bitterness.
rendija *f* crack; aperture.
rendir *vt* to subject, to subdue; * ~se *vr* to yield; to surrender; to be tired out.
renegar *vt* to deny; to disown; to detest, to abhor; * *vi* to blaspheme; to curse.
renglón *m* line.
renombre *m* renown.
renovar *vt* to renew; to renovate; to reform.
renta *f* income; rent; profit.
reñir *vt, vi* to wrangle, quarrel; to scold, to chide.
reo *m* offender, criminal.
reparar *vt* to repair; to consider, to observe; to parry; * *vi* ~ en to notice; to pass (at cards).
reparo *m* scruple: — poner ~s to raise objections.
repartir *vt* to distribute; to deliver.
repasar *vt* to revise; to check; to mend.
repente: — de ~ *adv* suddenly.
repercutir *vi* to reverberate; to rebound.
repetir *vt, vi* to repeat.
repiquetear *vt* to ring merrily.
repisa *f* pedestal, stand; shelf, windowsill.
repleto(a) *adj* replete, very full.
replicar *vi* to reply.
repoblar *vt* to repopulate; to reafforest.
repollo *m* cabbage.

reponer *vt* to replace; to restore; * ~se *vr* to recover lost health or property.
reportaje *m* report, article.
reposar *vi* to rest, to repose.
repostería *f* confectioner's (shop).
reprender *vt* to reprimand.
represa *f* dam; lake.
representar *vt* to represent; to play on the stage; to look (age).
reprimir *vt* to repress; to check; to contain.
reprobable *adj* reprehensible.
reprochar *vt* to reproach.
repuesto *m* supply; spare part.
repugnancia *f* reluctance; repugnance; disgust.
requerir *vt* to intimate, to notify; to request; to require.
requesón *m* cottage cheese.
requiebro *m* endearing expression.
res *f* head of cattle.
resaca *f* surge, surf; (*fig*) backlash; (*sl*) hangover.
resaltar *vi* to rebound; to jut out; to be evident; to stand out.
resbaladizo(a) *adj* slippery.
resbalar(se) *vi* (*vr*) to slip, slide.
rescindir *vt* to rescind, to annul.
resecarse *vr* to dry up.
resentirse *vr*; ~ de to suffer; ~ con to resent.
reseña *f* review; account.
reservar *vt* to keep; to reserve; * ~se *vr* to preserve oneself, to keep to oneself
resfriado *m* cold.
resguardar *vt* to preserve, to defend; * ~se *vr* to be on one's guard.
residir *vi* to reside, to dwell.
residuo *m* residue, remainder.
resistir *vt* to resist, to oppose; to put up with; * *vi* to resist; to hold out.
resol *m* glare (of the sun).
resollar *vi* to wheeze; to take breath.

resolver *vt* to resolve, to decide; to analyse; * ~se *vr* to resolve, to determine.

resoplar *vi* to snore; to snort.

resorte *m* spring.

respaldo *m* backing; endorsement; back of a seat.

respecto *m*: — al ~ on this matter: — con ~ a, de with regard to, in relation to.

respetar *vt* to respect; to revere.

respingo *m* start; jump.

respiradero *m* vent, breathing hole; rest, repose.

respirar *vi* to breathe.

respiro *m* breathing (*fig*) respite, rest.

resplandecer *vi* to shine; to glisten.

resplandor *m* splendour, brilliance.

responder *vt* to answer; * *vi* to answer; to correspond; ~ de to be responsible for.

responso *m* prayer for the dead.

respuesta *f* answer, reply.

resquemor *m* resentment.

restablecer *vt* to re-establish; * ~se *vr* to recover.

restallar *vi* to crack; to click.

restar *vt* to subtract, take away; * *vi* to be left.

restaurar *vt* to restore.

restituir *vt* to restore; to return.

resto *m* remainder, rest.

restregar *vt* to scrub, rub.

restringir *vt* to restrict, limit; to restrain.

resuelto(a) *adj* resolute; prompt.

resultar *vi* to be; to turn out; to amount to.

resumir *vt* to summarise.

retahila *f* range, series.

retal *m* remnant.

retar *vt* to challenge.

retener *vt* to retain, keep back.

retentiva *f* memory.

retirar *vt* to withdraw, to retire; to remove; * ~se *vr* to retire, to retreat; to go to bed.

reto *m* challenge; menace.

retocar *vt* to retouch; to mend; to finish off (work).

retoñar *vi* to sprout.

retorcer *vt* to twist; to wring.

retozar *vi* to frisk, to skip.

retraído(a) *adj* shy.

retransmitir *vt* to broadcast; to relay; to retransmit.

retraso *m* delay; slowness; backwardness; lateness: — (railway) el tren ha tenido ~ the train is overdue or late.

retrato *m* portrait, effigy.

retrete *m* toilet, lavatory.

retribuir *vt* to repay.

retroceder *vi* to go backwards, to fly back; to back down.

retrovisor *m* rear-view mirror.

retumbar *vi* to resound, to jingle.

reuma *f* rheumatism.

reunir *vt* to reunite; to unite; * ~se *vr* to gather, to meet.

revancha *f* revenge.

revelar *vt* to reveal; to develop (photographs).

reventar *vi* to burst, to crack; to explode; to toil, to drudge.

reventón *m* blowout, flat tyre.

reverdecer *vi* to grow green again; to revive.

revés *m* back; wrong side; disappointment, setback.

revisar *vt* to revise, to review.

revisor *m* inspector; ticket collector.

revista *f* review; magazine.

revolcarse *vr* to wallow.

revolotear *vi* to flutter.

revoltoso(a) *adj* rebellious.

revolver *vt* to move about; to turn around; to mess up; to revolve; ~se *vr* to turn round; to change (of the weather).

revuelta *f* turn; disturbance, revolt.

rey *m* king; king (in cards or chess).

rezagar *vt* to leave behind; to

defer; * ~se vr to remain behind.
rezar vi to pray.
rezumar vt to ooze, to leak.
ría f estuary.
riada f flood.
ribera f shore, bank.
rico(a) adj rich; delicious; lovely; cute.
ridículo(a) adj ridiculous: — hacer el ~lo to make a fool of oneself.
riego m irrigation.
rienda f rein of a bridle: — dar ~ suelta to give free rein to.
riesgo m risk, danger.
rifa f raffle, lottery.
rígido(a) adj rigid, inflexible.
riguroso(a) adj rigorous.
rimar vi to rhyme.
rimel, rimmel m mascara.
rincón m (inside) corner.
rinoceronte m rhinoceros.
riña f quarrel, dispute.
riñón m kidney.
río m river, stream.
riqueza f riches pl, wealth.
risa f laugh, laughter.
risco m steep rock.
ritmo m rhythm.
rito m rite.
rizo m curl; ripple (on water).
robar vt to rob; to steal; to break into.
roble m oak tree.
robusto(a) adj robust, strong.
roca f rock.
rociar vt to sprinkle; to spray.
rocío m dew.
rodaja f slice.
rodaje m filming: — en ~ (car) running in.
rodear vi to make a detour; * vt to surround, to enclose.
rodilla f knee: — de ~s on one's knees.
rodillo m roller; rolling pin.
roer vt to gnaw; to corrode.
rogar vt, vi to ask for; to beg, to entreat; to pray.
rojizo(a) adj reddish.

rojo(a) adj red; ruddy.
rol m list, roll, catalogue; role.
rollo m roll; coil; (sl) bore: — ¡qué ~! what a carry-on!
romántico(a) adj romantic.
romería f pilgrimage.
romero m (botany) rosemary.
rompecabezas m invar riddle; jigsaw.
romper vt to break; to tear up; to wear out; to break up (land); * vi to break (of waves); to break through.
ron m rum.
roncar vi to snore; to roar.
ronco(a) adj hoarse; husky; raucous.
ronda f night patrol; round (of drinks, cards, etc).
ronronear vi to purr.
roña f scab, mange; grime; rust.
roñica adj (sl) skinflint.
ropa f clothes pl; clothing.
rosa f (botany) rose; * adj pink.
rosado(a) adj pink; rosy.
rosca f thread (of a screw); coil, spiral.
rosquilla f doughnut.
rostro m face.
roto(a) adj broken, destroyed; debauched.
rótula f kneecap; ball-and-socket joint.
rotulador m felt-tip pen.
rótulo m inscription; label, ticket; placard, poster.
rotundo(a) adj round; emphatic.
rozar vt to rub; to chafe; to nibble (the grass); to scrape; to touch lightly.
rubio(a) adj fair-haired, blond(e); * m(f) blond(e).
rubor m blush; bashfulness.
rudimento m principle; beginning; ~s mpl rudiments pl.
rudo(a) adj rough, coarse; plain, simple; stupid.
rueda f wheel; circle; slice.
ruedo m rotation; border, selvage; arena, bullring.

ruego m request, entreaty.
rugir vi to roar, to bellow.
rugoso(a) adj wrinkled.
ruido m noise; din, row; fuss.
ruin adj mean, despicable;
stingy.
ruina f ruin, collapse; downfall,
destruction; ~s fpl ruins pl.
ruiseñor m nightingale.
rulo m curler.
rumor m low sound; murmur,
buzz.
rumbo m (marine) course,
bearing; route; ostentation.
rumboso(a) adj generous, lavish.
rupestre adj rock: — **pinturas**
~s cave painting.
rústico(a) adj rustic;
* m(f) peasant.
ruta f route, itinerary.
rutina f routine; habit.

S

sábado m Saturday; (Jewish)
Sabbath.
sabana f savannah.
sábana f sheet; altar cloth.
sabañón m chilblain.
sábelotodo m or f invar know-all.
saber vt to know; to be able to;
to find out, learn; to
experience; * vi ~ a to taste
of; * m learning, knowledge.
sabiduría f learning,
knowledge; wisdom.
sabio(a) adj sage, wise;
* m(f) sage, wise person.
sablazo m sword wound; (sl)
sponging; scrounging.
sabor m taste, savour, flavour.
sabroso(a) adj tasty,
delicious; pleasant; salted.
sabueso m bloodhound.
sacacorchos m invar corkscrew.
sacapuntas m invar pencil
sharpener.
sacar vt to take out, to
extract; to get out; to bring

out (a book etc); to take off
(clothes); to receive, get;
(sport) to serve.
sacarina f saccharin(e).
sacerdote m priest.
saciar vt to satiate; to satisfy.
saco m bag, sack; jacket.
sacudir vt to shake, to jerk; to
beat, to hit.
saeta f arrow; sacred song in
flamenco style.
sagaz adj shrewd, clever,
sagacious.
sagrado(a) adj sacred, holy.
sal f salt.
sala f large room; (theatre)
auditorium; public hall; law-
court; (medical) ward.
salado(a) adj salted; witty.
salario m salary.
salchicha f sausage.
salchichón m (salami-type)
sausage.
saldo m settlement; balance;
remainder; ~s mpl sale.
salida f exit; departure;
production, output;
(commerce) sale; sales outlet.
saliente adj projecting; rising;
(fig) outstanding.
salir vi to go out; to set out; to
appear; to prove; * ~se vr to
escape, to leak.
salmo m psalm.
salmonete m red mullet.
salmuera f brine.
salón m living room, lounge;
public hall.
salpicadero m dashboard.
salpicar vt to sprinkle, to
splash, to spatter.
salpicón m splashing; fish and
seafood salad.
salsa f sauce.
saltamontes m invar
grasshopper.
saltar vt to jump, to leap; to
skip, to miss out; * vi to leap,
to jump; to bounce; (fig) to
explode, to blow up.

saltimbanqui *m or f* acrobat.
salubre *adj* healthy.
salud *f* health.
saludar *vt* to greet; (military) to salute.
salvado *m* bran.
salvaguardar *vt* to safeguard.
salvaje *adj* savage.
salvar *vt* to save; to rescue; to overcome; to cross, to jump across; to cover, to travel; to exclude; * **se** *vr* to escape from danger.
salvavidas *adj invar*:
— **bote ~, chaleco ~** or **cinturón ~** lifeboat, life jacket, life belt.
salvia *f* (botany) sage.
salvo *adj* safe; * *adv* save, except (for).
San(ta) *adj* Saint (as title).
sanar *vt, vi* to heal.
sandalia *f* sandal.
sandez *f* folly, stupidity.
sandía *f* watermelon.
sangre *f* blood: — **a ~ fría** in cold blood: — **a ~ y fuego** without mercy.
sangriento(a) *adj* bloody, bloodstained, gory; cruel.
sano(a) *adj* healthy, fit; intact, sound.
santo(a) *m(f)* holly; saint's day: — **hacer su ~ta voluntad** to do as one jolly well pleases: — **se le fue el ~to al cielo** he forgot what he was about to say.
saña *f* anger, passion.
sapo *m* toad.
saquear *vt* to ransack, to plunder.
sarampión *m* measles.
sarna *f* itch; mange; (medical) scabies.
sarpullido *m* (medical) rash.
sarro *m* (medical) tartar.
sarta *f* string of beads, etc; string, row.
sartén *f* frying pan.

sastre *m* tailor.
satisfacer *vt* to satisfy; to pay (a debt); * **~se** *vr* to satisfy oneself; to take revenge.
sauce *m* (botany) willow.
saúco *m* (botany) elder.
savia *f* sap.
sazonar *vt* to ripen; to season.
se *pron r* himself; herself; itself, yourself; themselves; yourselves; each other; one another; oneself.
septiembre *m* September.
sebo *m* fat, grease.
secano *m* dry, arable land which is not irrigated.
secar *vt* to dry; * **~se** *vr* to dry up; to dry oneself.
seco(a) *adj* dry; dried up; skinny; cold (of character); brusque, sharp; bare.
secuestrar *vt* to kidnap; to confiscate.
sed *f* thirst: — **tener ~** to be thirsty.
seda *f* silk.
sedal *m* fishing line.
sede *f* see; headquarters.
sediento(a) *adj* thirsty; eager.
seducir *vt* to seduce; to bribe; to charm, to attract.
segar *vt* to reap; to mow.
seguido(a) *adj* continuous; successive; long-lasting; * *adv* straight (on); after; often.
seguir *vt* to follow, to pursue; to continue; * *vi* to follow; to carry on; * **~se** *vr* to follow, to ensue.
según *prep* according to.
segundo(a) *adj* second; * *m* second (of time).
seguro(a) *adj* safe, secure; sure, certain; firm, constant; * *adv* for sure; * *m* safety device; insurance; safety, certainty.
seis *adj, m* six; sixth.
seiscientos(as) *adj* six hundred.

seísmo *m* earthquake.
sello *m* seal; stamp.
selva *f* forest.
semáforo *m* traffic lights *pl*; signal.
semana *f* week.
semanal *adj* weekly.
sembrar *vt* to sow; to sprinkle, to scatter.
semejante *adj* similar, like; * *m* fellow-man.
semestral *adj* half-yearly.
semestre *m* period of six months; semester.
semila *f* seed.
semiseco *m* medium-dry.
sémola *f* semolina.
sencillo(a) *adj* simple; natural; unaffected; single.
senda *f*, **sendero** *m* footpath.
seno *m* bosom; lap; womb; hole, cavity; sinus; ~s *mpl* breasts *pl*.
sensación *f* sensation; sense.
sensato(a) *adj* sensible.
sensible *adj* sensitive; perceptible; regrettable.
sentado(a) *adj* sitting, seated; sedate; settled.
sentar *vt* to seat; (*fig*) to establish; * *vi* to suit; * ~se *vr* to sit down.
sentido *m* sense; feeling; meaning; * ~(a) *adj* regrettable; sensitive.
sentir *vt* to feel; to hear; to perceive; to sense; to suffer from; to regret, to be sorry for; * ~se *vr* to feel; to feel pain; to crack (of walls, etc); * *m* opinion, judgement.
seña *f* sign, token; signal; password; ~s *fpl* address.
señal *f* sign, token; symptom; signal; landmark; (commerce) deposit.
señalar *vt* to stamp, to mark; to signpost; to point out; to fix, to settle; * ~se *vr* to distinguish oneself, to excel.
señor *m* man; gentleman; master; Mr; sir.
señora *f* lady; Mrs; madam; wife.
señorita *f* Miss; young lady.
señorito *m* young gentleman; rich kid.
separar *vt* to separate; * ~se *vr* to separate; to come away, to come apart; to withdraw.
septentrional *adj* north, northern.
séptimo(a) *adj* seventh.
sepultar *vt* to bury, to inter.
sequía *f* dryness; thirst; drought.
séquito *m* retinue, suite; group of supporters; aftermath.
ser *vi* to be; to exist; ~ de to come from; to be made of, to belong to; * *m* being.
serenata *f* (music) serenade.
sereno *m* night watchman; * ~(a) *adj* serene, calm, quiet.
serie *f* series; sequence.
serio(a) *adj* serious; grave; reliable.
serpentear *vi* to wriggle; to wind, snake.
serpiente *f* snake.
serranía *f* mountainous country.
serrar *vt* to saw.
serrín *m* sawdust.
servicial *adj* helpful, obliging.
servilleta *f* napkin, serviette.
servir *vt* to serve; to wait on; * *vi* to serve; to be of use; to be in service; * ~se *vr* to serve oneself, to help oneself; to deign, to please; to make use of.
sesenta *m*, *adj* sixty; sixtieth.
seso(s) *m* brain(s).
sestear *vi* to take a nap.
seta *f* mushroom.
setenta *adj*, *m* seventy.
seto *m* fence; enclosure; hedge.
severo(a) *adj* strict; grave.
sexto(a) *adj*, *m* sixth.
si *conj* whether; if.
sí *adv* yes; certainly; indeed; * *pron* oneself; himself; herself, itself; yourself; themselves; yourselves; each

other; one another.
siderúrgico(**a**) *adj* iron and steel (*in compounds*); * *f* **la siderúrgica** the iron and steel industry.
sidra *f* cider.
siempre *adv* always; all the time; ever; still; ~ **jamás** for ever and ever.
sierra *f* saw; range of mountains.
siesta *f* siesta; nap.
siete *adj, m* seven.
sigilo *m* secrecy.
sigla(**s**) *f* acronym, initials; abbreviation.
siglo *m* century.
significado *m* significance.
significativo(**a**) *adj* significant.
signo *m* sign, mark.
siguiente *adj* following, next.
silbar *vt, vi* to hiss; to whistle.
silencio *m* silence: — ¡~! quiet!
silla *f* chair; saddle; seat; ~ **de ruedas** wheelchair.
sillón *m* armchair, easy chair.
silo *m* silo; underground store for wheat.
silueta *f* silhouette; outline; figure.
silvestre *adj* wild, uncultivated; rustic.
símbolo *m* symbol.
simio *m* ape.
simpático(**a**) *adj* pleasant; kind.
simpatizar *vi*: ~ **con** to get on well with.
simular *vt* to simulate.
sin *prep* without.
sindicato *m* trade(s) union; syndicate.
sinfín *m*: — **un** ~ **de** a great many.
singular *adj* singular; exceptional; peculiar, odd.
siniestro(**a**) *adj* left; (*fig*) sinister; * *m* accident.
sino *conj* but; except; save; only; * *m* fate.
sinsabor *m* unpleasantness; disgust.
síntoma *m* symptom.

sintonía *f* tuning; signature tune.
sinuoso(**a**) *adj* sinuous; wavy.
sinvergüenza *m* or *f* rogue.
siquiera *conj* even if, even though; * *adv* at least.
sirena *f* mermaid; siren, hooter.
sitio *m* place; spot; site, location; room, space; job, post; (military) siege, blockade.
situar *vt* to place, to situate; to invest; * ~**se** *vr* to be established in place or business.
smoking *m* dinner jacket.
s/n *abrev* **sin número** no number.
sobaco *m* armpit, armhole.
sobar *vt* to handle, to soften; to knead; to massage, to rub hard; to rumple (clothes); to fondle.
soberbia *f* pride, haughtiness; magnificence.
sobornar *vt* to suborn, to bribe.
sobrante *adj* remaining; * *m* surplus, remainder.
sobrar *vt* to exceed, to surpass; * *vi* to be more than enough; to remain, to be left.
sobre *prep* on; on top of; above, over; more than; besides; * *m* envelope.
sobrecargar *vt* to overload; (commerce) to surcharge.
sobredosis *f* overdose.
sobre(**e**)**ntender** *vt* to deduce; * ~**se** *vr*: — **se sobre**(**e**)**ntiende que**... it is implied that.
sobrellevar *vt* to carry; to tolerate.
sobremesa *f* immediately after dinner.
sobrenombre *m* nickname.
sobrepasar *vt* to surpass.
sobresalto *m* sudden shock.
sobrevenir *vi* to happen, to come unexpectedly; to supervene.
sobrevivir *vi* to survive.
sobreviviente *adj* surviving;

* *m* or *f* survivor.

sobrevolar *vt* to fly over.

sobrino(a) *m(f)* nephew or niece.

sobrio(a) *adj* sober, frugal.

socarrón(a) *adj* sarcastic; ironic(al).

socavar *vt* to undermine.

socio(a) *m(f)* associate, member.

socorrista *m* or *f* first aider; lifeguard.

socorro *m* help, aid, assistance, relief: — ¡~! help!

soez *adj* dirty, obscene.

sofá *m* sofa.

soga *f* rope.

soja *f* soya.

sol *m* sun; sunshine, sunlight.

solamente *adv* only, solely.

solapa *f* lapel.

solar *m* building site; piece of land; ancestral home of a family; * *adj* solar.

soldado *m* or *f* soldier.

soldar *vt* to solder; to weld; to unite.

soledad *f* solitude; loneliness.

soleado(a) *adj* sunny.

soler *vi* to be accustomed to, to be in the habit of.

solicitar *vt* to ask for, to seek; to apply for (a job); to canvass for; to chase after, to pursue.

solidario(a) *adj* joint; mutually binding.

soliloquio *m* soliloquy.

solista *m* or *f* soloist.

solitario(a) *adj* solitary; * *m(f)* hermit.

sollozar *vi* to sob.

solo *m* (music) solo; * ~**(a)** *adj* alone, single: — **a solas** unaided.

sólo *adv* only.

solomillo *m* sirloin.

soltar *vt* to untie, to loosen; to set free, to let out; * ~**se** *vr* to get loose; to come undone.

soltero(a) *m(f)* bachelor or single woman; * *adj* single, unmarried.

soltura *f* looseness, slackness; agility, activity; fluency.

solucionar *vt* to solve; to resolve.

sombra *f* shade; shadow.

sombrero *m* hat.

sombrilla *f* parasol.

sombrío(a) *adj* shady; sad.

somero(a) *adj* superficial.

someter *vt* to conquer (a country); to subject to one's will; to submit; to subdue; * ~**se** *vr* to give in, to submit.

somnífero *m* sleeping pill.

sonar *vt* to ring; * *vi* to sound; to make a noise; to be pronounced; to be talked of; to sound familiar; * ~**se** *vr* to blow one's nose.

sondeo *m* sounding; boring; (*fig*) poll.

soneto *m* sonnet.

sonido *m* sound.

sonreir(se) *vi* (*vr*) to smile.

sonrisa *f* smile.

sonrojarse *vr* to blush.

sonsacar *vt* to wheedle; to cajole; to obtain by cunning.

soñar *vt, vi* to dream.

sopa *f* soup; sop.

sopetón *m*: — **de** ~ suddenly.

soplar *vt* to blow away, to blow off, to blow up, to inflate; * *vi* to blow, to puff.

soplón(ona) *m(f)* telltale.

soportal *m* portico.

soportar *vt* to suffer, to tolerate; to support.

sorber *vt* to sip; to inhale; to swallow; to absorb.

sorbete *m* sherbet; iced fruit drink.

sordo(a) *adj* deaf; silent, quiet; * *m(f)* deaf person.

sorprender *vt* to surprise.

sorteo *m* draw; raffle.

sortija *f* ring; ringlet, curl.

sortilegio *m* sorcery.

sosegar *vt* to appease, to calm;

* *vi* to rest.

soso(a) *adj* insipid, tasteless; dull.

sospechar *vt* to suspect.

sostén *m* support; bra; sustenance.

sostener *vt* to sustain, to maintain; * ~se *vr* to support or maintain oneself; to contrive, to remain.

sota *f* knave (at cards).

sótano *m* basement, cellar.

su *pron* his, her, its, one's; their; your.

suave *adj* smooth, soft; delicate; gentle; mild, meek.

subalterno(a) *adj* secondary; auxiliary.

subasta *f* auction.

subeampeón(ona) *m(f)* runner-up.

subestimar *vt* to underestimate.

subir *vt, vi* to raise, to lift up; to go up; to climb, to ascend; to increase, to swell; to get in, to get on, to board; to rise (in price).

súbito(a) *adj* sudden, hasty; unforeseen.

sublevar *vt* to excite; to incite; * ~se *vr* to revolt.

submarino(a) *adj* underwater; * *m* submarine.

subrayar *vt* to underline.

subsanar *vt* to excuse; to mend, to repair; to overcome.

subsidio *m* subsidy, aid; benefit, allowance.

subterráneo(a) *adj* subterranean; underground; * *m* underground passage; underground (railway).

suburbio *m* slum quarter; suburbs *pl*.

subvencionar *vt* to subsidise.

sucedáneo(a) *adj* substitute; * *m* substitute (food).

suceder *vt* to succeed, inherit; * *vi* to happen.

suceso *m* event; incident.

sucesor(a) *m(f)* successor; heir.

sucio(a) *adj* dirty, filthy; obscene; dishonest.

sucursal *f* branch (office).

sudar *vt, vi* to sweat.

sudeste *adj* south-east, south-eastern; * *m* south-east.

sudoeste *adj* south-west, south-western; * *m* south-west.

suegro(a) *m(f)* father-in-law or mother-in-law.

suela *f* sole of the shoe.

sueldo *m* wages *pl* salary.

suelo *m* ground; floor; soil, surface.

suelto(a) *adj* loose; free; detached; swift; * *m* loose change.

sueño *m* sleep; dream.

suerte *f* fate, good luck; kind, sort.

sufrir *vt* to suffer; to bear, to put up with; to support.

sugerir *vt* to suggest.

sujetador *m* fastener; bra.

sujetar *vt* to fasten, to hold down; to subdue; to subject; * ~se *vr* to subject oneself.

sujeto(a) *adj* fastened, secure; subject, liable; * *m* subject; individual.

sumamente *adv* extremely.

sumar *vt* to add, to add up; to collect, to gather; * *vi* to add up.

sumergir *vt* to submerge, to sink; to immerse.

sumidero *m* sewer, drain.

suministrar *vt* to supply, furnish.

sumiso(a) *adj* submissive.

sumo(a) *adj* great, extreme; highest, greatest: — **a lo ~** at most; * *f* addition.

super *f* four-star (petrol).

superar *vt* to surpass; to overcome; to exceed.

superficial *adj* shallow.

superficie *f* surface; area.

superior *adj* superior; upper; higher; better; * *m* or *f* superior.

supermercado *m* supermarket.

superviviente *m* or *f* survivor;
* *adj* surviving.
suplente *m* or *f* substitute.
suplicar *vt* to beg (for), to plead
(for); to beg; to plead with.
suplicio *m* torture.
suplir *vt* to supply; to make good,
to make up for; to replace.
suponer *vt* to suppose; * *vi* to
have authority.
suprimir *vt* to suppress; to
abolish; to remove; to delete.
supuesto *m* assumption;
* ~(a) *adj* supposed;
* **por ~ que** *conj* since,
granted that.
sur *adj* south, southern;
* *m* south; south wind.
surco *m* furrow; groove.
surgir *vi* to emerge; to crop up.
surtido *m* assortment, supply.
surtir *vt* to supply, to furnish,
to provide; * *vi* to spout, to
spurt.
suscitar *vt* to excite, to stir up.
susodicho(a) *adj* above-
mentioned.
suspender *vt* to suspend, to
hang up; to stop; to fail (e.g.
an exam).
suspicaz *adj* suspicious,
mistrustful.
suspirar *vi* to sigh.
sustancia *f* substance.
sustentar *vt* to sustain; to
support, to nourish.
susto *m* fright, scare.
sustraer *vt* to remove; (maths)
to subtract; * ~se *vr* to avoid;
to withdraw.
susurrar *vi* to whisper; to
murmur; to rustle; * ~se *vr* to
be whispered about.
sutil *adj* subtle; thin; delicate;
very soft; keen, observant.
suyo(a) *adj* his; hers; theirs;
one's; his; her; its own; one's
own; their own; * **los ~s** *mpl*
his own, near friends,
relations, family, supporters.

T

tabaco *m* tobacco; (*sl*)
cigarettes *pl*.
tábano *m* horsefly.
tabarra *f* nuisance: — **dar la ~**
to be a pain in the neck.
tabique *m* thin wall; partition
wall.
tabla *f* board; shelf; plank;
slab; index of a book; bed of
earth in a garden.
tablero *m* plank, board;
chessboard; dashboard;
bulletin board; gambling den.
taburete *m* stool.
tacaño(a) *adj* mean, stingy;
crafty.
tachar *vt* to find fault with; to
erase.
tachuela *f* tack, nail.
tácito(a) *adj* tacit, silent;
implied.
taco *m* stopper, plug; heel (of a
shoe); wad; book of coupons;
billiard cue.
tacón *m* heel.
tacto *m* touch, feeling; tact.
taimado(a) *adj* sly, cunning,
crafty.
tajo *m* cut, incision; cleft;
sheer drop; working area;
chopping block.
tal *adj* such: — **con ~ que**
provided that: — **no hay ~** no
such thing.
taladro *m* drill; borer, gimlet.
talante *m* mood; appearance;
aspect; will.
talar *vt* to fell (trees); to
desolate.
talla *f* raised work; sculpture;
stature, size; measure (of
anything); hand, draw, turn
(at cards).
tallar *vt* to cut, chop; to carve
in wood; to engrave; to
measure.
tallarín *m* noodle.

taller *m* workshop, laboratory.
tallo *m* shoot, sprout.
talón *m* heel; receipt; cheque.
tamaño *m* size, shape, bulk.
tambalearse *vr* to stagger, to waver.
también *adv* also, as well; likewise; besides.
tambor *m* drum; drummer; eardrum.
tamiz *m* fine sieve.
tampoco *adv* neither, nor.
tan *adv* so.
tanto *m* certain sum or quantity; point; goal; * ~(a) *adj* so much, as much; very great; * *adv* so much, as much; so long, as long.
tapa *f* lid; top; cover; snack.
tapar *vt* to stop up, to cover; to conceal, to hide.
tapia *f* wall.
tapicería *f* tapestry; upholstery; upholsterer's shop.
tapiz *m* tapestry; carpet.
tapón *m* cork, plug, bung.
taquigrafía *f* shorthand.
taquilla *f* booking office; locker.
tardar *vi* to delay; to take a long time; to be late.
tarde *f* afternoon; evening; * *adv* late.
tarea *f* task.
tarima *f* platform; step.
tarjeta *f* card; visiting card; ~ postal postcard.
tarro *m* pot.
tarta *f* cake.
tartamudear *vi* to stutter, stammer.
tarugo *m* wooden peg or pin.
tasar *vt* to appraise, to value.
tatarabuelo(a) *m(f)* great-great-grandfather, mother.
tataranieto(a) *m(f)* great-great-grandson, daughter.
tatuaje *m* tattoo; tattooing.
taurino(a) *adj* bullfighting (*in compounds*).

taza *f* cup; basin of a fountain.
te *pron* you.
té *m* (botany) tea.
teatro *m* theatre, playhouse.
tebeo *m* comic.
techo *m* roof; ceiling.
tecla *f* key (of an organ, piano, etc).
técnico(a) *adj* technical.
tedio *m* boredom; dislike, abhorrence.
tejado *m* roof covered with tiles.
tejer *vt* to weave.
tejo *m* quoit; (botany) yew tree.
tejón *m* badger.
tela *f* cloth; material.
telaraña *f* cobweb.
telefax *m invar* fax(machine).
telesilla *f* chairlift.
telesquí *m* ski-lift.
televisor *m* television set.
telón *m* curtain, drape.
tema *m* theme.
temblar *vi* to tremble.
temer *vt* to fear, to doubt; * *vi* to be afraid.
temerario(a) *adj* rash.
temible *adj* dreadful, terrible.
témpano *m* ice-floe.
templado(a) *adj* temperate, tempered.
templar *vt* to temper, to moderate, to cool; to tune; * ~se *vr* to be moderate.
temple *m* tempera; temperament; tuning: — al ~ painted in distemper.
temporada *f* time, season; epoch, period.
temprano(a) *adj* early, anticipated; * *adv* early; very early, prematurely.
tenaz *adj* tenacious; stubborn.
tenaza(s) *f* (*fpl*) tongs *pl*, pincers *pl*.
tender *vt* to stretch out; to expand; to extend; to hang out; to lay; * ~se *vr* to stretch oneself out.
tendero(a) *m(f)* shopkeeper.

tendón m tendon, sinew.
tenebroso(a) adj dark, obscure.
tenedor m fork.
tener vt to have; to take; to hold; to possess; * ~se vr to stand upright; to stop, to halt; to resist; to adhere.
tenia f tapeworm.
tensar vt to tauten; to draw.
tentar vt to touch; to try; to tempt; to attempt.
tentempié m (sl) snack.
tenue adj thin; tenuous, slender.
teñir vt to tinge, dye.
terapia f therapy.
tercero(a) adj third; * m (law) third party.
tercio(a) adj third; * m third part.
terceto m trio.
terciopelo m velvet.
terco(a) adj obstinate.
tergiversar vt to distort.
terminar vt to finish; to end; to terminate; * vi to end; to stop.
termo m flask.
ternero(a) m(f) calf, veal; heifer.
ternilla f gristle.
ternura f tenderness.
terrado m terrace.
terrateniente m or f landowner.
terraza f balcony; (flat) roof, terrace (in fields).
terremoto m earthquake.
terreno(a) adj earthly, terrestrial; * m land, ground, field.
terrón m lump; ~ de azucar lump sugar.
terror m terror, dread.
terso(a) adj smooth, glossy.
tertulia f club, assembly, circle.
tesorero m treasurer.
tesoro m treasure; exchequer.
testamento m will, testament.
testar vt, vi to make one's will.
testarudo(a) adj obstinate.
testificar vt to attest, to witness.
testigo m or f witness.
teta f breast.
tetera f teapot.
tetilla f nipple; teat (of a bottle).
tétrico(a) adj gloomy, sullen, surly.
tez f complexion, hue.
ti pron you; yourself
tibio(a) adj lukewarm.
tiburón m shark.
tiempo m time; term; weather; (gr) tense; occasion, opportunity; season.
tienda f tent; awning; tilt; shop.
tierno(a) adj tender.
tierra f earth; land, ground; native country.
tieso(a) adj still, hard, firm; robust; valiant; stubborn.
tiesto m earthen pot.
tigre m tiger.
tijeras fpl scissors pl.
tilde f tilde.
tilo m (botany) lime tree.
timar vt to con; to swindle.
timbre m stamp; bell; timbre; stamp duty.
timido(a) adj timid; cowardly.
timón m helm, rudder.
tímpano m ear-drum; small drum.
tina f tub; bath (tub).
tinieblas fpl darkness; shadows pl.
tino m skill; judgment, prudence.
tinta f ink; tint, dye; colour.
tinte m tint, dye; dry cleaner's.
tinto(a) adj dyed; * vino ~ m red wine.
tío(a) m(f) uncle, aunt; (sl) guy, bird.
tiovivo m merry-go-round.
tipo m type; norm; pattern; guy.
tiquismiquis m invar fussy person.
tira f abundance; strip.
tirachinas m invar catapult.

tirado(a) *adj* dirt-cheap; (*sl*) very easy; * *f* cast; distance; series; edition.

tirano(a) *m(f)* tyrant.

tirante *m* joist; stay; strap; brace; * *adj* taut, extended, drawn.

tirar *vt* to throw; to pull; to draw; to drop; to tend, to aim at; * *vi* to shoot; to pull; to go; to tend to.

tirita *f* (sticking) plaster.

tiritar *vi* to shiver.

títere *m* puppet; ridiculous little fellow.

titubear *vi* to stammer; to stagger; to hesitate.

titular *adj* titular; * *m* or *f* occupant; *m* headline; * *vt* to title; * ~**se** *vr* to obtain a title.

tiza *f* chalk.

tiznar *vt* to stain; to tarnish.

tizón *m* half-burnt wood.

toalla *f* towel.

tobillo *m* ankle.

tobogán *m* toboggan; rollercoaster; slide.

tocadiscos *m invar* record player.

tocado *m* head-dress, headgear.

tocar *vt* to touch; to strike; (music) to play; to ring (a bell); * *vi* to belong; to concern; to knock; to call; to be a duty or obligation.

tocino *m* bacon.

todavía *adv* even; yet, still.

todo(a) *adj* all, entire; every; * *pron* everything, all; * *m* whole.

todopoderoso(a) *adj* almighty.

toldo *m* awning; parasol.

tomar *vt* to take; to seize, to grasp; to understand; to interpret, to perceive; to drink; to acquire; * *vi* to drink; to take.

tomillo *m* (botany) thyme.

tomo *m* bulk; tome; volume.

tonada *f* tune, melody.

tonel *m* cask, barrel.

tonelada *f* ton; (marine) tonnage duty.

tónico(a) *adj* tonic, strengthening; * *m* tonic: — *f* tonic (water); (music) tonic; (*fig*) keynote.

tontería *f* foolery, nonsense.

tonto(a) *adj* stupid, foolish.

topar *vt* to run into; to find.

topo *m* mole; stumbler.

tórax *m* thorax.

torbellino *m* whirlwind.

torcer *vt* to twist, curve; to turn; to sprain; * ~**se** *vr* to bend; to go wrong; * *vi* to turn off.

torcido(a) *adj* oblique; crooked.

tordo *m* thrush; * ~**(a)** *adj* speckled black and white.

torear *vt* to avoid; to tease; * *vi* to fight bulls.

tormenta *f* storm, tempest.

tornar *vt* to return; to restore; * ~**se** *vr* to become; * *vi* to return: ~ **a hacer** to do again.

tornasolado *adj* iridescent; shimmering.

torneo *m* tournament.

tornillo *m* screw.

torno *m* winch; revolution.

toro *m* bull.

toronja *f* grapefruit.

torpe *adj* dull, heavy; stupid.

torre *f* tower; turret; steeple.

torrefacto(a) *adj* roasted.

torta *f* cake; (*sl*) slap.

tortilla *f* omelet; pancake.

tortuga *f* tortoise; turtle.

tos *f* cough.

tosco(a) *adj* coarse, ill-bred, clumsy.

toser *vi* to cough.

tostado(a) *adj* parched; sunburnt; light yellow; light brown; * *f* toast.

tostar *vt* to toast, roast.

total *m* whole, totality; * *adj* total, entire; * *adv* in short.

tóxico(a) *adj* toxic; *m poison.

trabajar *vt* to work, to labour; to persuade; to push; *vi* to strive.

trabalenguas *m invar* tonguetwister.

trabar *vt* to join, unite; to take hold of; to fetter, shackle.

tracción *f* traction; ~ **delantera** (**trasera**) frontwheel (rear-wheel) drive.

traducir *vt* to translate.

traer *vt* to bring, to carry; to attract; to persuade; to wear; to cause.

traficar *vi* to trade, do business, deal.

tragaluz *m* skylight.

tragaperras *f invar* slot machine.

tragar *vt* to swallow; to swallow up.

trago *m* drink; gulp; adversity, misfortune.

traicionar *vt* to betray.

traje *m* suit; dress; costume.

trajinar *vt* to carry; *vi* to bustle about; to travel around.

trama *f* plot; weft.

tramitar *vt* to transact; to negotiate; to handle.

tramo *m* section; piece of ground; flight of stairs.

tramoya *f* scene, theatrical decoration; trick.

trampa *f* trap, snare; trapdoor; fraud.

trampolín *m* trampoline; diving board.

tramposo(a) *adj* deceitful, swindling.

tranca *f* bar, crossbeam.

trance *m* danger; last stage of life; trance.

tranquilizar *vt* to calm; to reassure.

tranquilo(a) *adj* tranquil, calm, quiet.

transbordador *m* ferry.

transbordo *m* transfer:

— **hacer** ~ to change (trains).

transcurrir *vi* to pass; to turn out.

transeúnte *adj* transitory; *m passer-by.

transigir *vi* to compromise.

tránsito *m* passage; transition; road, way; change; removal; death of holy or virtuous persons.

transmitir *vt* to transmit; to broadcast.

transparente *adj* transparent; see-through.

transpirar *vt* to perspire; to transpire.

tranvía *m* tram.

trapo *m* rag, tatter.

tráquea *f* windpipe.

tras *prep* after, behind.

trascender *vi* to smell; to come out; ~ **a** to reach; to have an effect on.

trasegar *vt* to move about; to decant.

trasero(a) *adj* back; *m bottom.

trasfondo *m* background.

trasgredir *vt* to contravene.

trashumante *adj* migrating.

trasladar *vt* to transport; to transfer; to postpone; to transcribe; *~se *vr* to move.

trasnochar *vi* to watch, to sit up the whole night.

traspasar *vt* to remove, to transport; to transfix, to pierce; to return; to exceed (the proper bounds); to transfer.

traste *m* fret (of a guitar): — **dar al** ~ **con algo** to ruin something.

trastero *m* lumber room.

trastienda *f* back room behind a shop.

trasto *m* piece of junk; useless person.

trastornar *vt* to overthrow, to overturn; to confuse; *~se *vr* to go crazy.

116

trastrocar *vt* to invert (the order of).

tratar *vt* to traffic, to trade; to use; to treat; to handle; to address; * ~se *vr* to treat each other.

trato *m* treatment; manner, address; trade, traffic; conversation; (commercial) agreement.

través *m* (*fig*) reverse: — de ~, al ~ across, crossways; * a ~ de *prep* across; over; through.

travesía *f* crossing; cross-street; trajectory; (marine) side wind.

travieso(a) *adj* restless, uneasy, fidgety; lively; naughty.

trayecto *m* road; journey, stretch; course.

trazar *vt* to plan out; to project; to trace.

trípode *f* trivet, tripod.

trébol *m* trefoil, clover.

trece *adj*, *m* thirteen; thirteenth.

trecho *m* space, distance of time or place: — a ~s at intervals.

tregua *f* truce, cessation of hostilities.

treinta *adj*, *m* thirty.

tremendo(a) *adj* terrible, formidable; awful, grand.

tren *m* train, retinue; show, ostentation; (railway) train; ~ de gran velocidad fast or express train; ~ de mercancías freight train.

trenza *f* plait (in hair), plaited silk.

trepar *vi* to climb; to crawl.

tres *adj*, *m* three.

tresillo *m* three-piece suite; (music) triplet.

tricotar *vi* to knit.

trigésimo(a) *adj*, *m* thirtieth.

trigo *m* wheat.

trillado(a) *adj* beaten; trite, hackneyed.

trinar *vi* to trill, to quaver; to be angry.

trinchar *vt* to carve, to divide (meat).

trineo *m* sledge.

trino *m* trill.

tripa *f* gut, intestine: — *fpl* guts; tripe.

tripulación *f* crew.

tripular *vt* to man; to drive.

tris *m invar*: — estar en un ~ de to be on the point of.

triste *adj* sad, mournful, melancholy.

triturar *vt* to reduce to powder; to grind, to pound.

triza *f*: — hacer ~s to smash to bits; to tear to shreds.

trocar *vt* to exchange.

trompa *f* trumpet; proboscis; large top.

trompazo *m* heavy blow; accident.

trompeta *f* trumpet; * *m* trumpeter.

tronar *vi* to thunder; to rage.

tronco *m* trunk; log of wood; stock.

tropel *m* confused noise; hurry; bustle, confusion; heap; crowd: — en ~ in a tumultuous and confused way.

tropezar *vi* to stumble; * *vt* to meet accidentally.

trotamundos *m invar* globe-trotter.

trotar *vi* to trot.

trozo *m* piece.

trucha *f* trout.

truco *m* knack; trick.

trufa *f* truffle.

trueno *m* thunderclap.

trueque *m* exchange.

truncar *vt* to truncate, to maim.

tu *adj* your.

tú *pron* you.

tubería *f* pipe; pipeline.

tubo *m* tube.

tuerca *f* nut.

tumba *f* tomb.
tumbar *vt* to knock down;
* *vi* to tumble, fall down;
* ~se *vr* to lie down to sleep.
tumbona *f* easy chair; beach chair.
tunda *f* beating.
tupido(a) *adj* dense.
turbar *vt* to disturb, to trouble;
* ~se *vr* to be disturbed.
turbio(a) *adj* muddy; troubled.
turno *m* turn; shift; opportunity.
turrón *m* nougat (almond cake).
tutear *vt* to address as familiar 'tú'; * ~se *vr* to be on familiar terms.
tutor *m* guardian, tutor.
tuyo(a) *adj* yours; ~s *mpl* friends and relations of the person addressed.

U

u *conj* or (instead of o before an o or ho).
ubicar *vt* to place; * ~se *vr* to be located.
ufanarse *vr* to boast.
últimamente *adv* lately.
ultimar *vt* to finalise; to finish.
último(a) *adj* last; latest; bottom; top.
ultrajar *vt* to outrage; to despise; to abuse.
ultramar *adj*, *m* overseas.
umbral *m* threshold.
un, una *art* a, an; * *adj*, *m* one (for uno).
ungir *vt* to anoint.
ungüento *m* ointment.
únicamente *adv* only, simply.
único(a) *adj* only; singular, unique.
unidad *f* unity; unit, conformity; union.
unificar *vt* to unite.
uniforme *adj* uniform, equal, even; * *m* uniform.
unir *vt* to join, to unite; to

mingle; to bind, to tie;
* ~se *vr* to associate.
uno *m* one; * ~(a) *adj* one; sole, only; ~ a ~ one by one.
untar *vt* to anoint; to grease; (*sl*) to bribe.
uña *f* nail; hoof, claw, talon.
urbanidad *f* urbanity, politeness.
urbanismo *m* town planning.
urbanización *f* housing estate.
urdir *vt* to warp; to contrive.
urgencia *f* urgency; emergency; need, necessity.
urinario(a) *adj* urinary;
* *m* urinal.
urna *f* urn; ballot box.
urraca *f* magpie.
usado(a) *adj* used; experienced; worn.
usar *vt* to use, to make use of; to wear; * ~se *vr* to be used.
usted *pron* you (formal).
usuario *m* user.
útero *m* uterus, womb.
útil *adj* useful, profitable;
* *m* utility.
utilizar *vt* to use; to make useful.
uva *f* grape: ~ pasa raisin:
— estar de mala ~ to be in a bad mood.

V

vaca *f* cow; beef.
vacaciones *fpl* vacation; holidays *pl*.
vacante *adj* vacant; * *f* vacancy.
vaciar *vt* to empty, to clear; to mould; * *vi* to fall, to decrease (of waters);
* ~se *vr* to empty.
vacilar *vi* to hesitate; to falter; to fail.
vacío(a) *adj* void, empty; unoccupied; concave; vain; presumptuous; * *m* vacuum; emptiness.

vacuno(a) *adj* bovine, cow (*in compounds*); * ~**a** *f* vaccine.

vagar *vi* to rove or loiter about; to wander.

vago(a) *adj* vagrant; restless; vague.

vagón *m* (railway) wagon; carriage; ~ **de mercancías** goods wagon.

vaho *m* steam, vapour.

vaina *f* pod, husk.

vaivén *m* fluctuation, instability; giddiness.

vajilla *f* crockery.

vale *m* OK; promissory note, IOU.

valer *vi* to be valuable; to be deserving; to cost; to be valid; to be worth; to produce; to be current; * *vt* to protect, to favour; to be equivalent to; * ~**se** *vr* to employ, to make use of, to have recourse to.

valiente *adj* robust, vigorous; valiant, brave; boasting.

valija *f* suitcase: ~ **diplomática** diplomatic bag.

valioso(a) *adj* valuable.

valla *f* fence; hurdle; barricade.

valle *m* valley.

valor *m* value; price; validity; force; power; courage, valour.

valorar *vt* to value; to evaluate.

vals *m invar* waltz.

válvula *f* valve.

vanidoso(a) *adj* vain, showy; haughty; conceited.

vano(a) *adj* vain; useless, frivolous; arrogant; futile: — **en** ~ in vain.

vapor *m* vapour, steam; breath.

vaquero *m* cow-herd; * ~**(a)** *adj* belonging to a cowman; * ~**s** *mpl* jeans *pl*.

vara *f* rod; pole, stall; stick.

variar *vt* to vary; to modify; to change; * *vi* to vary.

varices *fpl* varicose veins *pl*.

varilla *f* small rod; curtain rod; spindle, pivot.

variable *adj* variable.

variación *adj* variation: — **sin** ~ unchanged.

vario(a) *adj* varied, different; vague; variegated; ~**s** *pl* some; several.

varón *m* man, male.

vasco(a) *adj*, *m(f)* Basque.

vasija *f* vessel.

vaso *m* glass; vessel; vase.

vástago *m* bud, shoot; offspring.

vasto(a) *adj* vast, huge.

vaticinar *vt* to divine, foretell.

vatio *m* watt.

vecindad *f* inhabitants of a place; neighbourhood.

vecino(a) *adj* neighbouring; near; * *n*, *m* neighbour, inhabitant.

vehículo *m* vehicle.

veinte *adj*, *m* twenty.

veintena *f* twentieth part; score.

vejar *vt* to vex; to humiliate.

vejez *f* old age.

vejiga *f* bladder.

vela *f* watch; watchfulness; night guard; candle; sail: — **hacerse a la** ~ to set sail.

velar *vi* to stay awake; to be attentive; * *vt* to guard, to watch.

velero(a) *adj* swift-sailing.

veleta *f* weathercock.

vello *m* down; gossamer; short downy hair.

velo *m* veil; pretext.

velocidad *f* speed; velocity.

vena *f* vein.

venado *m* deer; venison.

vencer *vt* to defeat; to conquer, to vanquish; * *vi* to win; to expire.

vendaje *m* bandage, dressing for wounds.

vendaval *m* gale.

vender *vt* to sell.

vendimia *f* grape harvest; vintage.

veneno *m* poison, venom.

venerar *vt* to venerate, to worship.

venganza *f* vengeance, revenge.

vengar *vt* to revenge, to avenge; * ~se *vr* to take revenge.

venida *f* arrival; return; overflow of a river.

venidero(a) *adj* future.

venir *vi* to come, to arrive; to follow, to succeed; to happen; to spring from.

venta *f* sale.

ventaja *f* advantage.

ventana *f* window; window shutter; nostril.

ventilar *vt* to ventilate; to fan; to discuss.

ventisca *f* snowstorm.

ventosidad *f* flatulence.

ver *vt* to see, to look at; to observe; to visit; * *vi* to understand; to see; * ~se *vr* to be seen; to be conspicuous; to find oneself; * ~se con uno *vr* to have a bone to pick with someone; * *m* sense of sight; appearance.

verano *m* summer; summer holiday.

veras *fpl* truth, sincerity: — de ~ in truth, really.

veraz *adj* truthful.

verbena *f* fair; dance.

verdad *f* truth, veracity; reality; reliability.

verdadero(a) *adj* true; real; sincere.

verde *m, adj* green; unripe; dirty: — chiste ~ blue joke.

verdura *f* verdure; vegetables *pl*, greens *pl*.

vereda *f* path; pavement.

vergüenza *f* shame; bashfulness; confusion.

verificar *vt* to check, verify; * ~se *vr* to happen.

verruga *f* wart.

vertedero *m* sewer, drain; tip.

verter *vt* to pour; to spill; to empty; * *vi* to flow.

vértice *m* vertex, zenith; crown (head).

vertiente *f* slope; waterfall, cascade.

vertiginoso(a) *adj* giddy.

vespertino(a) *adj* evening (*in compounds*).

vestíbulo *m* vestibule, lobby; foyer.

vestido *m* dress; clothes *pl*.

vestir *vt* to put on; to wear; to dress; to adorn; to cloak, to disguise; * *vi* to dress; * ~se *vr* to get dressed.

vestuario *m* clothes *pl*; uniform; vestry; changing room.

veta *f* vein (in mines, wood, etc); streak; grain.

veterano(a) *adj* experienced, practised; * *m* veteran, old soldier.

vez *f* time; turn; return: — cada ~ each time: — una ~ once: — a veces sometimes, by turns.

vía *f* way; road, route; mode, manner, method; (railway) line.

viajante *m* or *f* sales representative.

viajar *vi* to travel.

víbora *f* viper.

vibrar *vt, vi* to vibrate.

vicio *m* vice.

vid *f* (botany) vine.

vida *f* life.

video *m* video.

vidriera *f* stained-glass window; shop window.

vidrio *m* glass.

vieira *f* scallop.

viejo(a) *adj* old; ancient, antiquated.

viento *m* wind; air.

vientre *m* belly.

viernes *m invar* Friday: — V~ Santo Good Friday.

viga *f* beam; girder.

vigente *adj* in force.

vigésimo(a) *adj*, *m* twentieth.

vigía *f* (marine) lookout; * *m* watchman.

vigilar *vt* to watch over; * *vi* to keep watch.

vil *adj* mean, sordid, low; worthless; infamous; ungrateful.

vilipendiar *vt* to despise, to revile.

villancico *m* Christmas carol.

vilo: — **en ~** *adv* in the air; in suspense.

vinagre *m* vinegar.

vincular *vt* to link.

vino *m* wine; ~ **tinto** red wine.

viñedo *m* vineyard.

violar *vt* to rape; to violate; to profane.

violentar *vt* to force.

violento(a) *adj* violent; forced; absurd; embarrassing.

violeta *f* violet.

violón *m* double bass.

virar *vi* to swerve.

viril *adj* virile, manly.

virtud *f* virtue.

viruela *f* smallpox.

visa *f*, **visado** *m* visa.

viscoso(a) *adj* viscous, glutinous.

visillos *mpl* net curtains *pl*.

visión *f* sight, vision; fantasy.

visitar *vt* to visit.

vislumbrar *vt* to catch a glimpse of; to perceive indistinctly.

visón *m* mink.

víspera *f* eve; evening before; ~**s** *pl* vespers.

vista *f* sight, view; vision; eyesight; appearance; looks *pl*; prospect; intention; (law) trial; *m* customs officer.

vistazo *m* glance.

vistoso(a) *adj* colourful, attractive, lively.

vitalicio(a) *adj* for life.

vitorear *vt* to shout, to applaud.

vitrina *f* showcase.

viudo(a) *m(f)* widower, widow.

vivaz *adj* lively.

víveres *mpl* provisions.

vivero *m* nursery (for plants); fish farm.

vivienda *f* housing; flat, apartment.

viviente *adj* living.

vivir *vt* to live through; to go through; * *vi* to live; to last.

vivo(a) *adj* alive; lively: — **al ~** to the life; very realistically.

vocablo *m* word, term.

vocal *f* vowel; *m* or *f* member (of a committee); * *adj* vocal, oral.

vociferar *vt* to shout; to proclaim in a loud voice; * *vi* to yell.

volante *adj* flying; * *m* (car) steering wheel; note; pamphlet; shuttlecock.

volar *vi* to fly; to pass swiftly (of time); to rush, to hurry; * *vt* to blow up, to explode.

volcán *m* volcano.

volcar *vt* to upset, overturn; to make giddy; to empty out; to exasperate; * ~**se** *vr* to tip over.

volquete *m* tipper truck.

voltear *vt* to turn over; to overturn; * *vi* to roll over, to tumble.

voltereta *f* tumble; somersault.

voluble *adj* unpredictable; fickle.

volumen *m* volume; size.

vomitar *vt*, *vi* to vomit.

voluntad *f* will, willpower; wish, desire.

volver *vt* to run (over); to turn upside down; to turn inside out; * *vi* to return, to go back; * ~**se** *vr* to turn around.

vos *pron* you (formal).

vosotros, vosotras *pron pl* you.

votar *vi* to vow; to vote.

voz *f* voice; shout; rumour;

word, term.

vuelo *m* flight; wing; projection of a building; ruffle, frill: — **cazar al ~** to catch in flight; **~ charter** charter flight.

vuelta *f* turn; circuit; return; row of stitches; cuff; change; bend, curve; reverse, other side; return journey.

vuestro(a) *adj* your; ** pron* yours.

W

windsurf *m* windsurfing.

X

xenofobia *f* xenophobia.
xilófono *m* xylophone.

Y

y *conj* and.
ya *adv* already; now; immediately; at once; soon; ** conj* **~ que** since, seeing that: — ¡~! of course!, sure!
yacimiento *m* deposit.
yate *m* yacht, sailing boat.
yedra *f* (botany) ivy.
yegua *f* mare.
yema *f* bud; leaf; yolk; **~ del dedo** tip of the finger.
yerno *m* son-in-law.
yeso *m* gypsum; plaster; **~ mate** plaster of Paris.
yo *pron* I: **~ mismo** myself.
yodo *m* iodine.
yogur *m* yogurt.
yunque *m* anvil.
yute *m* jute.

Z

zafiro *m* sapphire.
zaguán *m* porch, hall.
zalamero(a) *adj* flattering; ** m(f)* wheedler.
zamarra *f* sheepskin (jacket).
zambullirse *vr* to plunge, dive.
zampar *vt* to gobble down; to put away hurriedly; ** ~se vr* to thrust oneself suddenly into any place; to crash, to hurtle.
zanahoria *f* carrot.
zancada *f* stride.
zancudo(a) *adj* long-legged; ** m* mosquito.
zángano *m* drone; idler, slacker.
zanja *f* ditch, trench.
zapata *f* boot; **~ de freno** (car) brake shoe.
zapatería *f* shoe-shop.
zapatilla *f* slipper; pump (shoe); (sport) trainer, training shoe.
zapato *m* shoe.
zarandear *vt* to shake vigorously.
zarcillo *m* earring; tendril.
zarpar *vi* to weigh anchor.
zarza *f* (botany) bramble.
zarzuela *f* Spanish light opera.
zócalo *m* plinth, base; baseboard.
zona *f* zone; area, belt.
zopenco(a) *adj* dull, very stupid.
zoquete *m* block; crust of bread; (*sl*) blockhead.
zorro(a) *m* or *f* fox; cunning person.
zozobrar *vi* (marine) to founder; to capsize; (*fig*) to fail; to be anxious.
zueco *m* wooden shoe; clog.
zumbar *vt* to hit; ** ~se vr* to hit each other; ** vi* to buzz.
zumo *m* juice.
zurcir *vt* to darn; (*fig*) to join, unite; to hatch (lies).
zurdo(a) *adj* left; left-handed.
zurrar *vt* (*sl*) to flog, to lay into; (*fig*) to criticise harshly.

ENGLISH SPANISH
INGLÉS ESPAÑOL

A

a *indefinite art* un, uno, una;
  * *prep* a, al, en.
abandon *vt* abandonar, dejar.
abash *vt* avergonzar, causar
  confusión.
abbey *n* abadía *f*.
abbot *n* abad *m*.
abbreviate *vt* abreviar, acortar.
abbreviation *n* abreviatura *f*.
abdicate *vt* abdicar; renunciar.
abdication *n* abdicación *f*,
  renuncia *f*.
abdomen *n* abdomen, *m* bajo
  vientre *m*.
abduct *vt* secuestrar.
aberration *n* error *m*;
  aberración *f*.
abet *vt*: — to aid and ~ ser
  cómplice de.
abide *vt* soportar, sufrir.
ability *n* habilidad *f*, capacidad *f*.
ablaze *adj* en llamas.
able *adj* capaz, hábil.
able-bodied *adj* robusto(a),
  vigoroso(a).
ably *adv* con habilidad.
abnormal *adj* anormal.
abnormality *n* anormalidad *f*.
aboard *adv* a bordo.
abode *n* domicilio *m*.
abolish *vt* abolir, anular.
abolition *n* abolición *f*,
  anulación *f*.
abominable *adj* abominable.
abomination *n* abominación *f*.
aboriginal *adj* aborigen.
abort *vi* abortar.
abortion *n* aborto *m*.
abound *vi* abundar.
about *prep* acerda de, acerca.
above *prep* encima.
above-board *adj* legitimo(a).
abrasion *n* abrasión *f*.
abrasive *adj* abrasivo(va).

abroad *adv* en el extranjero.
abrupt *adj* brusco(a).
abscess *n* absceso *m*.
abscond *vi* fugarse; huir.
absence *n* ausencia.
absent *adj* ausente.
absentee *n* ausente *m* or *f*.
absent-minded *adj* distraído(a).
absolute *adj* absoluto(a).
absorb *vt* absorber.
abstain *vi* abstenerse.
abstinence *n* abstinencia *f*.
abstinent *adj* abstinente.
abstract *adj* abstracto(a);
  * *n* resumen *m*.
abstraction *n* abstracción *f*.
absurd *adj* absurdo(a).
abundance *n* abundancia *f*.
abundant *adj* abundante.
abuse *vt* abusar; maltratar.
abusive *adj* abusivo(a);
  ofensivo(a).
abysmal *adj* abismal.
abyss *n* abismo *m*.
acacia *n* (botany) acacia *f*.
academic *adj* académico(a).
academy *n* academia *f*.
accede *vi* acceder.
accelerate *vt* acelerar.
accelerator *n* acelerador *m*.
accent *n* acento *m*; tono *m*.
accentuate *vt* acentuar.
accept *vt* aceptar; admitir.
acceptable *adj* aceptable.
acceptance *n* aceptación *f*.
access *n* acceso *m*; entrada *f*.
accessible *adj* accesible.
accession *n* aumento *f*;
  adquisición *f*.
accessory *n* accessorio *m*.
accident *n* accidente *m*;
  casualidad *f*.
acclaim *vt* aclamar, aplaudir.
accommodate *vt* alojar;
  complacer.
accommodation *n* alojamiento *m*.
accompany *vt* acompañar.

accomplice n cómplice m or f.

accomplish vt efectuar, completar.

accord n acuerdo m, convenio m.

accordance n: in ~ with de acuerdo con.

according prep según, conforme.

accordion n (music) acordeón m.

account n cuenta f.

accountability n responsabilidad f.

accountancy n contabilidad f.

accountant n contable m or f, contador m.

accrue vi resultar, provenir.

accumulate vt acumular; amontonar.

accuracy n exactitud f.

accurate adj exacto(a).

accursed adj maldito(a).

accuse vt acusar; culpar.

accustom vt acostumbrar.

ache n dolor m; * vi doler.

achieve vt realizar; obtener.

achievement n realización f.

acid adj ácido(a); agrio(a); * n ácido m.

acknowledge vt reconocer, agradecer.

acne n acné m.

acorn n bellota f.

acoustics n acústica f.

acquaint vt informar, avisar.

acquaintance n conocimiento m; conocido m.

acquire vt adquirir.

acquisition n adquisición f.

acquit vt absolver.

acquittal n absolución f.

acre n acre m.

acrid adj acre.

acrimony n acrimonio m.

across adv a través de.

action n acción f.

activate vt activar.

active adj activo(a).

activity n actividad f.

actor n actor m.

actress n actriz f.

actual adj real; efectivo(a).

actuary n actuario(a) de seguros m.

acumen n agudeza f.

acute adj agudo(a); ingenioso(a).

ad abbrev (advertisement n) aviso m.

adage n proverbio m, refrán f.

adamant adj inflexible.

adapt vt adaptar.

adaptor n adaptador m.

add vt añadir, agregar: — to ~ up sumar.

adder n culebra f, víbora f.

addict n drogadicto(a).

addiction n dependencia.

addition n adición f.

additional adj adicional.

additive n aditivo m.

address vt dirigir; * n dirección f.

adenoids npl vegetaciones; adenoideas fpl.

adept adj hábil.

adequacy n idoneidad f.

adequate adj adecuado(a); suficiente.

adhere vi adherir.

adhesion n adhesión.

adhesive adj pegajoso(a); adhesivo(a).

adhesiveness n adhesividad.

adieu adv adiós; * n despedida.

adjacent adj adyacente; contiguo(a).

adjective n adjetivo m.

adjoining adj contiguo(a).

adjournment n prórroga f.

adjudicate vi adjudicar.

adjust vt ajustar, acomodar.

adjustable adj ajustable.

adjustment n modificación f; arreglo m.

ad lib vt improvisar.

administer vt administrar.

administration n

administración *f*.
administrative *adj*
administrativo(a).
admirable *adj* admirable.
admiral *n* almirante *m*.
admire *vt* admirar.
admirer *n* admirador(a) *m(f)*;
pretendiente *m* or *f*.
admission *adj* entrada *f*.
admit *vt* admitir.
admittance *n* entrada *f*.
admittedly *adj* de acuerdo que.
admonish *vt* amonestar.
ad nauseam *adv* hasta el
cansancio.
adolescence *n* adolescencia *f*.
adopt *vt* adoptar.
adorable *adj* adorable.
adore *vt* adorar.
adorn *vt* adornar.
adrift *adv* a la deriva.
adult *adj* adulto(a).
adulterate *vt* adulterar,
corromper.
adulterer *n* adúltero(a) *m(f)*.
adultery *n* adulterio *m*.
advance *vt* avanzar; promover.
advantage *n* ventaja *f*.
advantageous *adj*
ventajoso(a).
adventure *n* aventura *f*.
adventurous *adj* intrépido(a).
adverb *n* adverbio *m*.
adversary *n* adversario(a)
m(f); enemigo(a) *m(f)*.
adversity *n* calamidad *f*,
infortunio *m*.
advertise *vt* anunciar.
advertisement *n* aviso *m*;
anuncio *m*.
advice *n* consejo *m*; aviso *m*.
advisability *n* prudencia *f*.
advise *vt* aconsejar; avisar.
advocacy *n* defensa *f*.
advocate *n* abogado(a) *m(f)*;
protector(a) *m(f)*.
aerial *n* antena *f*.

aerobics *npl* aerobic *m*.
aerosol *n* aerosol *m*.
afar *adv* lejos, distante.
affair *n* asunto *m*; negocio *m*.
affect *vt* conmover; afectar.
affection *n* cariño *m*.
affidavit *n* declaración jurada *f*.
affiliate *vt* afiliar.
affiliation *n* afiliación *f*.
affinity *n* afinidad *f*.
affirm *vt* afirmar, declarar.
affirmation *n* afirmación *f*.
affirmative *adj* afirmativo(a).
affix *vt* pegar.
afflict *vt* afligir.
affliction *n* aflicción *f*, dolor *m*.
affluence *n* opulencia *f*.
affluent *adj* opulento(a).
affray *n* asalto *m*; tumulto *m*.
aflame *adv* en llamas.
afloat *adv* flotante, a flote.
afore *prep* antes; * *adv* primero.
afraid *adj* temeroso(a).
afresh *adv* de nuevo, otra vez.
after *prep* después.
afterbirth *n* placenta *f*.
after-effects *npl*
consecuencias *fpl*.
afterlife *n* vida después de la
muerte *f*.
aftermath *n* consecuencias *fpl*.
afternoon *n* tarde *f*.
aftershave *n* aftershave *m*.
aftertaste *n* regusto *m*.
afterwards *adv* después.
again *adv* otra vez.
against *prep* en contra.
agate *n* ágata *f*.
age *n* edad *f*; vejez *f*.
agency *n* agencia *f*.
agenda *n* orden del día *m*.
agent *n* agente *m* or *f*.
aggrandisement *n*
engrandecimiento *m*.
aggravate *vt* agravar, exagerar.
aggregate *n* agregado *m*.
aggregation *n* agregación *f*.

aggression *n* agresión *f*.

aggressor *n* agresor(a) *m(f)*.

aggrieved *adj* ofendido(a).

aghast *adj* horrorizado(a).

agile *adj* ágil; diestro(a).

agitate *vt* agitar.

ago *adv* pasado.

agonising *adj* angustioso(a).

agony *n* agonía *f*; angustia *f*.

agree *vt* convenir; * *vi* estar de acuerdo.

agreeable *adj* agradable; amable; simpático(a).

agreement *n* acuerdo *m*.

agriculture *n* agricultura *f*.

ah! *excl* ¡ah! ¡ay!

ahead *adv* más allá, delante de otro.

aid *vt* ayudar, socorrer.

AIDS *n* SIDA *m*.

ail *vt* afligir, molestar.

ailment *n* dolencia *f*, indisposición *f*.

aim *vt* apuntar aspirar a; intentar.

air *n* aire *m*; * *vt* airear; ventilar.

air balloon *n* globo aerostático *m*.

airborne *adj* en el aire.

air-conditioning *n* climatización *f*, aire acondicionado *m*.

aircraft *n* avión *m*.

air force *n* fuerzas aéreas *fpl*.

airline *n* línea aérea *f*.

airmail *n*: — by ~ por avión.

airplane *n* avión *m*.

airport *n* aeropuerto *m*.

airstrip *n* pista de aterrizaje *f*.

airy *adj* bien ventilado(a).

aisle *n* nave *f*; pasillo *m*.

akin *adj* parecido(a).

alabaster *n* alabastro *m*.

alarm *n* alarma *f*; * *vt* alarmar; inquietar.

alas *adv* desgraciadamente.

albeit *conj* aunque.

album *n* album *m*.

alchemy *n* alquimia *f*.

alcohol *n* alcohol *m*.

alcoholic *adj* alcohólico(a).

alcove *n* nicho *m*.

alder *n* (botany) aliso *m*.

ale *n* cerveza *f*.

alert *adj* vigilante; alerta.

algae *n* alga *f*.

algebra *n* álgebra *f*.

alias *adj* alias.

alibi *n* (law) coartada *f*.

alien *adj* ajeno(a).

alienate *vt* enajenar.

alight *vi* apearse.

align *vt* alinear.

alike *adj* semejante, igual.

alive *adj* vivo(a), viviente; activo(a).

alkali *n* álcali *m*.

alkaline *adj* alcalino(a).

all *adj* todo(a).

allay *vt* aliviar.

allegation *n* alegación *f*.

allege *vt* alegar; declarar.

allegiance *n* lealtad *f*, fidelidad *f*.

allegorical *adj* alegórico(a).

allegory *n* alegoría *f*.

allergy *n* alergia *f*.

alley *n* callejuela *f*.

alliance *n* alianza *f*.

allied *adj* aliado(a).

alligator *n* caimán *m*.

allocate *vt* repartir.

allot *vt* asignar.

allow *vt* conceder; permitir; dar.

allowance *n* concesión *f*.

alloy *n* aleación *f*.

allspice *n* pimienta de Jamaica *f*.

allude *vt* aludir.

allure *n* fascinación *f*.

allusion *n* alusión *f*.

allusive *adj* alusivo(a).

alluvial *adj* aluvial.

ally *n* aliado(a) *m(f)*; * *vt* aliar.

almanac *n* almanaque *m*.

almighty *adj* omnipotente; todopoderoso(a).

almond *n* almendra *f.*
almost *adv* casi; cerca de.
aloft *prep* arriba.
alone *adj* solo(a).
along *adv* a lo largo.
aloof *adv* lejos.
alphabet *n* alfabeto *m.*
alphabetical *adj* alfabético(a).
alpine *adj* alpino(a).
already *adv* ya.
also *adv* también, además.
altar *n* altar *m.*
altarpiece *n* retablo *m.*
alter *vt* modificar.
alteration *n* alteración *f.*
alternate *adj* alterno(a);
 * *vt* alternar, variar.
alternator *n* alternador *m.*
alternative *n* alternativa *f.*
although *conj* aunque, no
 obstante.
altitude *n* altitud *f*, altura *f.*
altogether *adv* del todo, en
 conjunto.
aluminium *n* aluminio *m.*
always *adv* siempre,
 constantemente.
am (morning) *adv* de la mañana.
amalgam *n* amalgama *f.*
amalgamate *vt* (*vi*)
 amalgamar(se).
amaryllis *n* (botany) amarilis*m.*
amass *vt* acumular, amontonar.
amateur *n* aficionado(a) *m(f).*
amateurish *adj* torpe.
amaze *vt* asombrar.
amazon *n* amazona *f.*
ambassador *n* embajador(a) *m(f).*
amber *n* ámbar *m.*
ambidextrous *adj* ambidextro(a).
ambiguity *n* ambigüedad *f*,
 duda *f.*
ambiguous *adj* ambiguo;
 * ~ly *adv* ambiguamente.
ambition *n* ambición *f.*
amble *vi* andar sin prisa.
ambulance *n* ambulancia *f.*

ambush *n* emboscada *f.*
amenable *adj* sensible.
amend *vt* enmendar.
amendment *n* enmienda *f.*
amends *npl* compensación *f.*
amenities *npl* comodidades *fpl.*
America *n* América *f.*
amethyst *n* amatista *f.*
amiability *n* amabilidad *f.*
amiable *adj* amable.
amiably *adv* amablemente.
amicable *adj* amigable,
 amistoso(a).
amid(st) *prep* entre, en medio de.
amiss *adv*: — something is ~
 pasa algo malo.
ammonia *n* amoníaco *m.*
ammunition *n* municiones *fpl.*
amnesia *n* amnesia *f.*
amnesty *n* amnistía *f.*
amoral *adv* amoral.
amorous *adj* amoroso(a).
amount *n* importe *m*; cantidad *f.*
amp(ere) *n* amperio *m.*
amphibian *n* anfibio *m.*
amphibious *adj* anfibio(a).
amphitheatre *n* anfiteatro *m.*
ample *adj* amplio(a).
amplifier *n* amplificador *m.*
amplify *vt* ampliar, extender.
amplitude *n* amplitud *f*,
 extensión *f.*
amputate *vt* amputar.
amuse *vt* entretener, divertir.
amusement *n* diversión *f.*
amusing *adj* divertido(a).
an *indefinite art* un, uno, una.
anachronism *n* anacronismo *m.*
anaemia *n* anemia *f.*
anaesthetic *n* anestesia *f.*
analogy *n* analogía *f.*
analyse *vt* analizar.
anarchy *n* anarquía *f.*
anatomical *adj* anatómico(a).
anatomy *n* anatomía *f.*
ancestor *n*: ~s *pl* antepasados
 mpl.

ancestral *adj* ancestral.
ancestry *n* ascendencia *f.*
anchor *n* ancla *f;* * *vi* anclar.
anchovy *n* anchoa *f.*
ancient *adj* antiguo(a).
and *conj* y, e.
anecdote *n* anécdota *f.*
anemone *n* (botany) anénona *f.*
angel *n* ángel *m.*
anger *n* cólera *f;* * *vt* enojar,
 irritar.
angle *n* ángulo *m;* * *vt* pescar
 con caña.
anglicism *n* anglicismo *m.*
angry *adj* enojado(a).
anguish *n* ansia *f,* angustia *f.*
angular *adj* angular.
animal *n, adj* animal *m.*
animation *n* animación *f.*
aniseed *n* anís *m.*
ankle *n* tobillo *m.*
annals *n* anales *mpl.*
annex(e) *vt* anexar; * *n* anexo *m.*
annihilate *vt* aniquilar.
annihilation *n* aniquilación *f.*
anniversary *n* aniversario *m.*
annotate *vi* anotar.
announce *vt* anunciar, publicar.
announcement *n* anuncio *m.*
annoy *vt* molestar.
annual *adj* anual.
annunciation *n* anunciación *f.*
anoint *vt* untar, ungir.
anomaly *n* anomalía *f,*
 irregularidad *f.*
anon *adv* más tarde.
anonymity *n* anonimato *m.*
anonymous *adj* anónimo(a).
anorexia *n* anorexia *f.*
another *adj* otro(a).
answer *vt* responder;
 * *n* respuesta *f.*
answering machine *n*
 contestador automático *m.*
ant *n* hormiga *f.*
antagonist *n* antagonista,
 adversario(a).

Antarctic *adj* antártico(a).
antelope *n* antílope *m.*
antenna *npl* antena *f.*
anterior *adj* anterior,
 precedente.
anthem *n* himno *m.*
anthology *n* antología *f.*
anthropology *n* antropología *f.*
antibiotic *n* antibiótico *m.*
antibody *n* anticuerpo *m.*
Antichrist *n* Anticristo *m.*
anticipate *vi* anticipar,
 prevenir.
anticipation *n* anticipación *f.*
antidote *n* antídoto *m.*
antipodes *npl* antípodas *f* or *m pl.*
antiquarian *n* anticuario *m.*
antiquated *adj* anticuado(a).
antiquity *n* antigüedad *f.*
antiseptic *adj* antiséptico(a).
antler *n* cornamenta *f.*
anvil *n* yunque *m.*
anxiety *n* ansiedad *f,* ansia *f.*
anxious *adj* ansioso(a).
any *adj, pron* cualquier(a);
 alguno(a).
apart *adv* aparte,
 separadamente.
apartment *n* apartamento *m.*
apathy *n* apatía *f.*
ape *n* mono *m.*
apologise *vt* disculpar.
apology *n* disculpa *f,* excusa *f.*
apostrophe *n* apóstrofe *m.*
appal *vt* espantar, aterrar.
apparatus *n* aparato *m.*
apparent *adj* evidente, aparente.
apparition *n* aparición *f,* visión *f.*
appeal *vi* apelar.
appear *vi* aparecer.
appease *vt* aplacar.
append *vt* añadir.
appendicitis *n* apendicitis *f.*
appendix *n* apéndice *m.*
appetite *n* apetito *m.*
applaud *vi* aplaudir.
apple *n* manzana *f.*

appliance *n* aparato *m*.
applicable *adj* aplicable.
applicant *n* aspirante *m* or *f*,
  candidato(a) *m(f)*.
application *n* solicitud *f*.
applied *adj* aplicado(a).
apply *vt* solicitar.
appoint *vt* nombrar.
appointment *n* cita *f*;
  nombramiento *m*.
apportion *vt* repartir.
appraisal *n* estimación *f*,
  evaluación *f*.
appraise *vt* tasar; estimar,
  valorar.
appreciate *vt* apreciar;
  agradecer.
apprehend *vt* arrestar.
apprehension *n* aprensión *f*.
apprehensive *adj* aprensivo(a).
apprentice *n* aprendiz *m*.
approach *vt* (*vi*) aproximar(se).
appropriate *vt* apropiarse de;
  * *adj* apropiado(a).
approve (of) *vt* aprobar.
April *n* abril *m*.
apron *n* delantal *m*.
apse *n* ábside *m*.
apt *adj* apto(a); idóneo(a).
aptitude *n* aptitud *f*.
aquarium *n* acuario *m*.
Aquarius *n* Acuario *m*.
aqueduct *n* acueducto *m*.
arable *adj* cultibable.
arbitrate *vt* arbitrar.
arcade *n* arcada, *f*; galería
  comercial *f*.
arch *n* arco *m*.
archaeology *n* arqueología *f*.
archaic *adj* arcaico(a).
archbishop *n* arzobispo *m*.
archer *n* arquero(a) *m(f)*.
architect *n* arquitecto(a) *m(f)*.
architecture *n* arquitectura *f*.
archives *npl* archivos *mpl*.
Arctic *adj* ártico(a).
area *n* área *f*, espacio *m*.

arena *n* arena *f*.
arguably *adv* posiblemente.
argue *vi* discutir.
argument *n* argumento *m*,
  controversia *f*.
arid *adj* árido(a), estéril.
aridity *n* aridez *f*.
Aries *n* Aries *m*.
arise *vi* levantarse.
aristocracy *n* aristocracia *f*.
arithmetic *n* aritmética *f*.
ark *n* arca *f*.
arm *n* brazo *m*; arma *f*.
armament *n* armamento *m*.
armchair *n* sillón *m*.
armour *n* armadura *f*.
armpit *n* sobaco *m*.
army *n* ejército *m*.
aroma *n* aroma *m*.
around *prep* alrededor de.
arouse *vt* despertar; excitar.
arraign *vt* acusar.
arraignment *n* acusación *f*,
  proceso criminal *m*.
arrange *vt* organizar.
arrangement *n* colocación *f*,
  arreglo *m*.
arrant *adj* consumado(a).
array *n* serie *f*.
arrears *npl* retraso en un pago
  m; atraso *m*.
arrest *n* arresto *m*; * *vt* detener,
  arrestar.
arrival *n* llegada *f*.
arrive *vi* llegar.
arrogance *n* arrogancia *f*,
  presunción *f*.
arrogant *adj* arrogante,
  presuntuoso(a);
  * ~ly *adv* arrogantemente.
arrogate *vt* arrogarse.
arrogation *n* arrogación *f*.
arrow *n* flecha *f*.
arsenal *n* (military) arsenal *m*.
arsenic *n* arsénico *m*.
art *n* arte *m*.
arterial *adj* arterial.

artery *n* arteria *f*.
artful *adj* ingenioso(a).
art gallery *n* pinacoteca *f*.
arthritis *n* artritis *f*.
artichoke *n* alcachofa *f*.
article *n* artículo *m*.
articulate *vt* articular.
artifice *n* artificio *m*.
artillery *n* artillería *f*.
artisan *n* artesano(a) *m(f)*.
artist *n* artista *m* or *f*.
artistry *n* habilidad *f*.
artless *adj* sencillo, simple.
artlessness *n* sencillez *f*.
as *conj* como; mientras.
asbestos *n* asbesto *m*, amianto *m*.
ascend *vi* ascender, subir.
ascribe *vt* atribuir.
ash *n* (botany) fresno *m*; ceniza *f*.
ashamed *adj* avergonzado(a).
ashtray *n* cenicero .
Ash Wednesday *n* miércoles de
  ceniza *m*.
ask *vt* pedir, rogar, preguntar
  por.
askew *adv* sesgado(a);
  ladeado(a).
asleep *adj* dormido(a).
asparagus *n* espárrago *m*.
aspect *n* aspecto *m*.
aspen *n* álamo temblón *m*.
asphalt *n* asfalto *m*.
asphyxia *n* (medical) asfixia *f*.
asphyxiate *vt* asfixiar.
asphyxiation *n* asfixia *f*.
aspiration *n* aspiración *f*.
aspire *vi* aspirar, desear.
aspirin *n* aspirina *f*.
ass *n* asno *m*.
assassin *n* asesino *m*.
assassinate *vt* asesinar.
assault *n* asalto *m*.
assemble *vt* reunir, juntar.
assembly *n* asamblea *f*.
assert *vt* afirmar; *vr* imponerse.
assess *vt* valorar; calcular.
assessment *n* valoración *f*.

assets *npl* bienes *mpl*.
assign *vt* asignar.
assimilate *vt* asimilar.
assist *vt* asistir, ayudar.
assistance *n* asistencia *f*.
assistant *n* asistente,
  ayudante *m* or *f*.
associate *vt* asociar.
association *n* asociación *f*,
  sociedad *f*.
assortment *n* surtido *m*.
assume *vt* asumir; suponer.
assurance *n* promesa *f*.
assure *vt* asegurar.
asterisk *n* asterisco *m*.
asthma *n* asma *f*.
asthmatic *adj* asmatico(a).
astonish *vt* pasmar, asombrar.
astringent *adj* astringente.
astrologer *n* astrólogo(a) *m(f)*.
astrology *n* astrología *f*.
astronaut *n* astronauta *m* or *f*.
astronomer *n* astrónomo(a) *m(f)*.
astronomy *n* astronomía *f*.
astute *adj* astuto(a).
asylum *n* asilo, refugio *m*.
at *prep* a; en.
atheism *n* ateísmo *m*.
atheist *n* ateo(a).
athlete *n* atleta *m* or *f*.
atlas *n* atlas *m*.
atmosphere *n* atmósfera *f*.
atom *n* átomo *m*.
atomic *adj* atómico(a).
atrocious *adj* atroz.
atrocity *n* atrocidad *f*,
  enormidad *f*.
attach *vt* adjuntar.
attaché *n* agregado *m*.
attack *vt* atacar; acometer.
attempt *vt* intentar; probar,
  experimentar.
attend *vt* servir; asistir.
attendant *n* sirviente(a) *m(f)*.
attention *n* atención *f*, cuidado *m*.
attentive *adj* atento(a);
  cuidadoso(a).

attest vt atestiguar.

attic n desván m; altillo m.

attorney n abogado(a) m(f).

attract vt atraer.

attraction n atracción f.

auburn adj moreno(a); castaño(a).

auction n subasta f.

auctioneer n subastador(a) m(f).

audacious adj audaz.

audible adj audible.

audience n audiencia f.

audit n auditoría f.

augment vt aumentar, acrecentar.

August n agosto m.

august adj augusto(a).

aunt n tía f.

au pair n canguro m.

aura n aura f.

auspicious adj propicio(a).

austere adj austero(a); severo(a).

authentic adj auténtico(a).

authenticate vt autenticar.

authenticity n autenticidad f.

author n autor(a) m(f); escritor(a) m(f).

authority n autoridad f.

authorisation n autorización f.

authorise vt autorizar.

auto n auto m, coche m.

autograph n autógrafo m.

automatic adj automático(a).

autonomy n autonomía f.

autopsy n autopsia f.

autumn n otoño m.

auxiliary adj auxiliar, asistente.

available adj disponible.

avalanche n avalancha f, alud m.

avarice n avaricia f.

avenue n avenida f.

avert vt desviar, ăpartar.

aviary n pajarera f.

avoid vt evitar, escapar.

await vt aguardar.

awake vt despertar.

award vt otorgar; * n premio m.

aware adj consciente; enterado(a).

away adv ausente, fuera.

awe n miedo m, temor m.

awful adj tremendo(a); horroroso(a).

awhile adv un rato, algún tiempo.

awkward adj torpe, rudo(a).

awning n (marine) toldo m.

awry adv oblicuamente, torcidamente.

axe n hacha f.

axiom n axioma m.

axis n eje m.

axle n eje m.

B

baby n niño(a) pequeño(a); bebé m.

bachelor n soltero(a) m(f); bachiller m.

back n dorso m, espalda f.

backbone n hueso dorsal m, espinazo m.

backer n partidario(a) m(f).

backgammon n juego de chaquete o tablas m (juego de mesa).

background n fondo m; antecedentes f; experiencia f.

backlash n reacción f (en contra).

backpack n mochila f.

backside n trasero m.

backward adj hacia atrás; atrasado(a).

bacon n tocino m, panceta f.

bad adj mal, malo(a).

badge n insignia f; placa f.

badger n tejón m.

badminton n bádminton m.

baffle vt confundir.

bag n saco m; bolsa f, bolso m.

baggage *n* equipaje *m*.

bail *n* fianza *f*.

bailiff *n* alguacil *m*.

bake *vt* cocer en horno, hornear.

bakery *n* panadería *f*.

baking powder *n* levadura (en polvo) *f*.

balance *n* balanza *f*, equilibrio *m*.

balcony *n* balcón *m*.

bald *adj* calvo(a).

ball *n* bola *f*, pelota *f*; baile *m*.

ballad *n* balada *f*.

ballerina *n* bailarina *f*.

ballet *n* ballet *m*.

balloon *n* globo *m*.

ballpoint (pen) *n* bolígrafo *m*.

balm balsam *n* bálsamo *m*.

balustrade *n* balaustrada *f*.

bamboo *n* (botany) bambú *m*.

ban *n* prohibición *f*; * *vt* prohibir.

banal *adj* vulgar.

banana *n* plátano *m*.

band *n* faja *f*; cuadrilla *f*; banda *f*.

bandage *n* venda *f*; vendaje *m*.

bandit *n* bandido(a) *m(f)*.

bang *n* golpe *m*.

bangle *n* brazalete *m*.

banister(s) *npl* barandilla *f*, pasamanos *m*.

banjo *n* banjo *m*.

bank *n* orilla (de río) *f*; terraplén *m*; banco *m*.

bank account *n* cuenta de banco *f*.

bankrupt *adj* insolvente.

banner *n* bandera *f*.

banquet *n* banquete *m*.

baptise *vt* bautizar.

bar *n* bar *m*; barra *f*.

barbecue *n* barbacoa *f*.

barber *n* peluquero *m*.

bare *adj* desnudo(a); descubierto(a).

barely *adv* apenas.

bargain *n* ganga *f*.

barge *n* barcaza *f*.

bark *n* corteza *f*.

barley *n* cebada *f*.

barn *n* granero *m*.

barometer *n* barómetro *m*.

baron *n* barón *m*.

baroness *n* baronesa *f*.

barracks *npl* cuartel *m*.

barrel *n* barril *m*.

barren *adj* estéril, infructuoso(a).

barrier *n* barrera *f*, obstáculo *m*.

base *n* fondo *m*; base *f*.

baseball *n* béisbol *m*.

basement *n* sótano *m*.

basic *adj* básico(a).

basin *n* palangana *f*; lavabo *m*.

basis *n* base *f*; fundamento *m*.

basket *n* cesta *f*, canasta *f*.

basketball *n* baloncesto *m*.

bastard *n*, *adj* bastardo(a) *m(f)*; (*sl*) hijo(a) de puta *m(f)*.

bat *n* murciélago *m*.

batch *n* lote *m*; remesa *f*.

bath *n* baño *m*, bañera *f*.

bathe *vt* (*vi*) bañar(se); lavar.

bathing suit *n* traje de baño *m*, bañador *m*.

bathroom *n* (cuarto de) baño *m*.

baths *npl* piscina *f*.

battery *n* batería *f*, pila *f*.

battle *n* batalla *f*.

bawdy *adj* indecente.

bay *n* bahía *f*; laurel *m*.

bazaar *n* bazar *m*.

be *vi* ser; estar.

beach *n* playa *f*.

beacon *n* faro *f*.

beagle *n* sabueso *m*.

beak *n* pico *m*.

beam *n* rayo de luz *m*; travesaño *m*.

bean *n* haba *f*.

beansprouts *npl* brotes de soja *mpl*.

bear *vt* llevar alguna cosa como carga; sostener; soportar.

bear *n* oso *m*.

beard *n* barba *f*.
bearer *n* portador(a) *m(f)*, titular *m* or *f*.
beast *n* bestia *f*.
beat *vt* golpear; tocar (un tambor).
beatify *vt* beatificar, santificar.
beautiful *adj* hermoso(a), bello(a).
beauty *n* hermosura *f*, belleza *f*.
because *conj* porque, a causa de.
bed *n* cama *f*.
bedroom *n* dormitorio *m*.
bee *n* abeja *f*.
beech *n* (botany) haya *f*.
beef *n* carne de vaca *f*.
beefburger *n* hamburguesa *f*.
beefsteak *n* bistec *m*.
beeline *n* línea recta *f*.
beer *n* cerveza *f*.
beetle *n* escarabajo *m*.
befall *vi* suceder, acontecer.
before *adv*, *prep* antes de; delante.
beg *vt* mendigar.
beggar *n* mendigo(a) *m(f)*.
begin *vt*, *vi* comenzar, empezar.
beginning *n* principio *m*.
begrudge *vt* envidiar.
behave *vi* comportarse.
behind *prep* detrás; atrás.
beige *adj* color *m*, beige.
belch *vi* eructar.
belief *n* fe *f*, creencia *f*.
believe *vt* creer.
believer *n* creyente, fiel *m* or *f*.
bell *n* campana *f*.
bellows *npl* fuelle *m*.
belly *n* vientre *m*; panza *f*, barriga *f*.
belong *vi* pertenecer.
beloved *adj* querido(a); amado(a).
below *adv*, *prep* debajo, inferior; abajo.
belt *n* cinturón *m*, cinto *m*.
bench *n* banco *m*.
bend *vt* encorvar, inclinar, plegar.
beneath *adv*, *prep* debajo, abajo.
benefit *n* beneficio *m*; utilidad *f*, provecho *m*.
benevolence *n* benevolencia *f*.
benevolent *adj* benévolo(a).
benign *adj* benigno(a).
bent *n* inclinación *f*.
bereave *vt* privar.
bereavement *n* pérdida *f*.
beret *n* boina *f*.
berry *n* baya *f*.
beset *vt* acosar.
beside(s) *prep* al lado de; excepto.
best *adj* mejor.
bestial *adj* bestial, brutal.
bestow *vt* otorgar, conceder.
bestseller *n* bestseller *m*, éxito de ventas *m*.
bet *n* apuesta *f*.
betray *vt* traicionar.
betting *n* juego *m*; apuesta *f*.
between *prep* entre, en medio de.
beverage *n* bebida *f*.
beware *vi* guardarse.
bewitch *vt* encantar, hechizar.
beyond *prep* más allá de.
bias *n* predisposición *f*.
bib *n* babero *m*.
Bible *n* Biblia *f*.
bibliography *n* bibliografía *f*.
bicycle *n* bicicleta *f*.
bid *vt* mandar, ordenar; ofrecer.
biennial *adj* bienal.
bifocals *npl* anteojos bifocales *mpl*.
big *adj* grande.
bigamist *n* bígamo(a).
bigamy *n* bigamia *f*.
bigot *n* fanático(a).
bike *n* bici *f*.
bikini *n* bikini *m*.
bile *n* bilis *f*.
bilingual *adj* bilingüe.
bill *n* cuenta *f*, factura *f*; pico de ave *m*; billete *m*.
billet *n* alojamiento *m*.

billiards *npl* billar *m*.

billion *n* billón *f*.

bin *n* cubo de la basura *m*; papelera *f*.

binder *n* encuadernador(a) *m(f)*.

bingo *n* bingo *m*.

binoculars *npl* prismáticos *mpl*.

biographer *n* biógrafo(a) *m(f)*.

biography *n* biografía *f*.

biological *adj* biológico(a).

biology *n* biología *f*.

birch *n* (botany) abedul *m*.

bird *n* ave *f*; pájaro *m*.

birth *n* nacimiento *m*.

birthday *n* cumpleaños *mpl*.

biscuit *n* galleta *f*.

bishop *n* obispo *m*.

bit *n* bocado *m*; pedacito *m*.

bitch *n* perra *f*.

bite *vt* morder; picar.

bitter *adj* amargo(a).

bitumen *n* betún *m*.

bizarre *adj* raro(a).

blab *vi* chismorrear.

black *adj* negro(a); oscuro(a).

blackberry *n* zarzamora *f*.

blackbird *n* mirlo *m*.

blackboard *n* pizarra *f*.

blackmail *n* chantaje *m*; * *vt* chantajear.

black pudding *n* morcilla *f*.

blacksmith *n* herrero *m*.

bladder *n* vejiga *f*.

blade *n* hoja *f*; filo *m*.

blame *vt* culpar.

blameless *adj* inocente.

blank *adj* blanco(a).

blanket *n* manta *f*.

blaspheme *vt* blasfemar, jurar.

blasphemy *n* blasfemia *f*.

blatant *adj* descarado(a).

blaze *n* llama *f*.

bleed *vt*, *vi* sangrar.

blemish *vt* manchar.

bless *vt* bendecir.

blessing *n* bendición *f*.

blight *vt* arruinar.

blind *adj* ciego(a).

blink *vi* parpadear.

bliss *n* felicidad (eterna) *f*.

blister *n* ampolla *f*.

blitz *n* bombardeo aéreo *m*.

blizzard *n* huracán *m*, ventisca *f*.

bloated *adj* hinchado(a).

blob *n* gota *f*.

block *n* bloque *m*; obstáculo *m*.

blockade *n* bloqueo *m*; * *vt* bloquear.

blond *adj* rubio(a).

blood *n* sangre *f*.

blood group *n* grupo sanguíneo *m*.

blood poisoning *n* envenena- miento de la sangre *m*.

blood pressure *n* presión sanguínea *f*.

blood test *n* análisis de sangre *m*.

blood transfusion *n* transfusion de sangre *f*.

bloom *n* flor *f*, (*also fig*); * *vi* florecer.

blossom *n* flor *f*.

blot *vt* boorrar; manchar.

blotchy *adj* muy manchado(a).

blouse *n* blusa *f*.

blow *vi* soplar; sonar.

blubber *n* grasa de ballena *f*.

blue *adj* azul.

bluebell *n* (botany) campanilla *f*.

blueprint *n* (*fig*) anteproyecto *m*.

blunder *n* desatino *m*; metedura de pata *f*.

blunt *adj* desafilado(a); franco(a), directo(a).

blush *n* rubor *m*; sonrojo *m*.

boar *n* verraco *m*: — wild ~ jabalí *m*.

board *n* tablero *m*, mesa *f*.

boarder *n* huesped *m* or *f*.

boarding card *n* tarjeta de embarque *f*.

boast *vi* jactarse, ostentar.

boat *n* barco *m*.

bobsleigh *n* bob *m*, trineo de competición *m*.

bodice *n* corsé *m*, corpiño.
body *n* cuerpo *m*; individuo *m*; gremio *m*.
body-building *n* culturismo *m*.
bodyguard *n* guardaespaldas *mpl*.
boll *vi* hervir; bullir.
bold *adj* ardiente, valiente; audaz; negrita (type).
bolt *n* cerrojo *m*.
bomb *n* bomba *f*.
bond *n* ligadura *f*; fianza *f*.
bondage *n* esclavitud, servidumbre *f*.
bone *n* hueso *m*, espina *f*.
bonfire *n* hoguera *f*, fogata *f*.
bonny *adj* bonito(a).
bonus *n* cuota *f*, prima *f*.
book *n* libro *m*; * *vt* reservar.
bookcase *n* librería *f*, estante para libros *m*.
bookmark *n* registro *m*.
bookshop *n* librería *f*.
boom *n* trueno *m*.
boon *n* favor *m*, beneficio *m*.
booth *n* barraca *f*, cabina *f*.
booty *n* botín *m*; presa *f*; saqueo *m*.
border *n* orilla *f*, borde *m*.
borderline *n* frontera *f*.
bore *vt* taladrar; aburrir; fastidiar.
bored *adj* aburrido(a).
boredom *n* aburrimiento *m*.
borrow *vt* pedir prestado.
bosom *n* seno *m*, pecho *m*.
boss *n* jefe(a) *m(f)*; patrón(ona) *m(f)*.
botany *n* botánica *f*.
botch *vt* estropear, arruinar.
both *adj* ambos(as).
bother *vt* preocupar; fastidiar.
bottle *n* botella *f*.
bottom *n* fondo *m*.
bough *n* rama *f*.
boulder *n* canto rodado *m*.
bounce *vi* rebotar; ser rechazado.

bound *n* límite *m*; salto *m*.
boundary *n* límite *m*; frontera *f*.
bouquet *n* ramo de flores *m*.
bourgeois *adj* burgués(esa).
bout *n* ataque *m*.
bow *n* reverencia *f*; arco *m*; * *vi* inclinarse.
bowels *npl* intestinos *mpl*.
bowl *n* taza *f*, cuenco; * *vi* lanzar, arrojar la pelota.
bow tie *n* pajarita *f*.
box *n* caja *f*.
boxer *n* boxeador *m*.
boxing *n* boxeo *m*.
box office *n* taquilla *f*.
boy *n* muchacho *m*; niño *m*.
boycott *vt* boicotear; * *n* boicot *m*.
boyfriend *n* novio *m*.
bra *n* sujetador *m*.
bracelet *n* brazalete *m*, pulsera *f*.
bracket *n* puntal *m*; paréntesis *m*.
brag *n* jactancia *f*; * *vi* jactarse.
braid *n* trenza *f*; * *vt* trenzar.
brain *n* cerebro *m*.
brake *n* freno *m*; * *vt*, *vi* frenar.
bran *n* salvado *m*.
branch *n* rama *f*.
brand *n* marca *f*.
brandy *n* coñac *m*.
brass *n* latón *m*.
brassière *n* sujetador *m*.
brave *adj* bravo(a); valiente.
bravery *n* valor *m*.
brawl *n* pelea *f*.
brazier *n* brasero *m*.
breach *n* ruptura *f*.
bread *n* pan *m*.
breadcrumbs *n* migajas *fpl*; pan rallado *m*.
breadth *n* anchura *f*.
break *vt* romper; quebrantar.
breakage *n* rotura *f*.
breakfast *n* desayuno *m*; * *vi* desayunar.
breast *n* pecho *m*, seno *m*.
breastbone *n* esternón *m*.

breath *n* aliento *m*,
  respiración *f*, soplo de aire *m*.
breathe *vt*, *vi* respirar.
breathtaking *adj* pasmoso(a).
breed *n* casta *f*, raza *f*; * *vt* criar.
breeze *n* brisa *f*.
brevity *n* brevedad *f*.
brew *vt* hacer; elaborar, mezclar.
bribe *n* cohecho *m*, soborno *m*.
bribery *n* cohecho, soborno *m*.
bric-à-brac *n* baratijas *fpl*.
brick *n* ladrillo *m*.
bricklayer *n* albañil *m*.
bride *n* novia *f*.
bridegroom *n* novio *m*.
bridesmaid *n* madrina de boda *f*.
bridge *n* puente *m*.
brief *adj* breve, conciso(a)
  sucinto(a).
briefcase *n* cartera *f*.
brigade *n* (military) brigada *f*.
bright *adj* claro(a); reluciente,
  brillante.
brighten *vt* pulir, dar lustre.
brilliant *adj* brillante.
bring *vt* llevar, traer.
brisk *adj* vigoroso(a); alegre;
  jovial.
brisket *n* pecho (de un animal) *m*.
briskly *adv* vigorosamente.
bristle *n* cerda, seta *f*;
  * *vi* erizarse.
bristly *adj* cerdoso(a); lleno(a)
  de cerdas.
brittle *adj* quebradizo, frágil.
broach *vt* abordar.
broad *adj* ancho.
broad beans *npl* haba *f*.
broadcast *n* emisión *f*.
broadcasting *n* radiodifusión *f*.
broaden *vt* (*vi*) ensanchar(se).
broadly *adv* en general.
broad-minded *adj* tolerante.
brocade *n* brocado *m*.
broccoli *n* brécol *m*.
brochure *n* folleto *m*.
broil *vt* asar a la parrilla.

broken *adj* roto(a).
broker *n* corredor(a) *m*(*f*).
bronchial *adj* bronquial.
bronchitis *n* bronquitis *f*.
bronze *n* bronce *m*.
brooch *n* broche *m*.
brook *n* arroyo *m*.
broom *n* escoba *f*.
broth *n* caldo *m*.
brothel *n* burdel *m*.
brother *n* hermano *m*.
brother-in-law *n* cuñado *m*.
brow *n* cumbre *f*; cima *f*; frente *f*.
browbeat *vt* intimidar.
brown *adj* moreno(a); castaño(a).
browse *vt* ramonear.
bruise *vt* magullar.
brunette *n* morena *f*.
brush *n* cepillo *m*; escobilla *f*.
brusque *adj* brusco(a).
Brussels sprout *n* coles de
  Bruselas *fpl*.
brutal *adj* brutal.
brutality *n* brutalidad *f*.
brute *n* bruto(a) *m*(*f*).
bubble *n* burbuja *f*.
bubblegum *n* chicle *m*.
bucket *n* cubo, pozal *m*.
buckle *n* hebilla *f*.
bucolic *adj* bucólico(a).
bud *n* brote *m*, botón *m*;
  * *vi* brotar.
Buddhism *n* Budismo *m*.
buddy *n* compañero(a) *m*(*f*).
budge *vi* moverse.
budgerigar *n* periquito *m*.
budget *n* presupuesto *m*.
buff *n* entusiasta *m*.
buffalo *n* búfalo *m*.
buffet *n* buffet *m*.
buffoon *n* bufón *m*.
bug *n* chinche *m*.
bugle (horn) *n* trompa de caza *f*.
build *vt* edificar; construir.
building *n* edificio *m*;
  construcción *f*.
bulb *n* bulbo *m*; cebolla *f*.

bulge *vi* combarse; * *n* bombeo *m*.

bulk *n* bulto *m*; volumen *m*.

bulky *adj* vulminoso(a), abultado(a).

bull *n* toro *m*.

bulldog *n* dogo *m*.

bulldozer *n* escavadora *f*.

bullet *n* bala *f*.

bullfight *n* corrida de toros *f*.

bullfighter *n* torero *m*.

bullfighting *n* los toros *mpl*.

bullion *n* oro *m* or plata en barras *f*.

bullock *n* novillo capado *m*.

bullring *n* plaza de toros *f*, ruedo *m*.

bully *n* valentón *m*; * *vt* tiranizar.

bumblebee *n* abejorro *m*.

bump *n* hinchazón *f*, chichón *m*.

bun *n* bollo *m*; moño *m*.

bunch *n* ramo *m*.

bundle *n* fardo *m*, haz *m*.

bung *n* tapón *m*.

bungalow *n* bungalow *m*.

bunk *n* litera *f*.

bunker *n* refugio *m*; bunker *m*.

burden *n* carga *f*; * *vt* cargar.

bureau *n* cómoda *f*; escritorio *m*.

bureaucracy *n* burocracia *f*.

burglar *n* ladrón(ona).

burial *n* entierro *m*.

burial place *n* cementerio *m*.

burn *vt* quemar, abrasar, incendiar; * *vi* arder; * *n* quemadura *f*.

burner *n* quemador *m*; mechero *m*.

burning *adj* ardiente.

burrow *n* madriguera *f*.

bursar *n* tesorero(a) *m(f)*.

burse *n* bolsa *f*, lonja *f*.

burst *vi* reventar; abrirse.

bury *vt* enterrar, sepultar; esconder.

bus *n* autobús *m*.

bush *n* arbusto *m*, monte bajo *m*.

busily *adv* diligenternente, apresuradamente.

business *n* asunto *m*; negocios *mpl*.

businessman *n* hombre de negocios *m*.

bust *n* busto *m*.

bus-stop *n* parada de autobuses *f*.

bustle *vi* hacer ruido.

busy *adj* ocupado(a); entrometido(a).

busybody *n* entrometido *m*.

but *conj* pero; mas.

butcher *n* carnicero *m*.

butcher's (shop) *n* carnicería *f*.

butler *n* mayordomo *m*.

butter *n* mantequilla *f*.

buttercup *n* (botany) ranúnculo *m*.

butterfly *n* mariposa *f*.

buttocks *npl* nalgas *fpl*.

button *n* botón *m*.

buttonhole *n* ojal *m*.

buttress *n* estribo *m*; apoyo *m*.

buxom *adj* frescachón(ona).

buy *vt* comprar.

buzz *n* susurro, zumbido *m*; * *vi* zumbar.

buzzard *n* àguila ratonera *f*; ratonero común *m*.

buzzer *n* timbre *m*.

by *prep* por; a, en; de; cerca, al lado de.

bypass *n* carretera de circunvalación *f*.

by-product *n* derivado *m*.

bystander *n* mirador *m*.

byte *n* (computer) byte *m*.

byword *n* proverbio, refrán *m*.

C

cab *n* taxi *m*.

cabbage *n* berza *f*, col *f*.

cabin *n* cabaña *f*; camarote *m*.

cabinet *n* consejo de ministros

m; gabinete *m*; armario *m*.
cable *n* (marine) cable *m*.
cable-car *n* teleférico *m*.
cactus *n* cacto *m*.
cadet *n* cadete *m*.
cadge *vt* gorronear.
café *n* café *m*.
cage *n* jaula *f*; * *vt* enjaular.
cake *n* bollo *m*; pastel *m*.
calculate *vt* calcular.
calculator *n* calculadora *f*.
calendar *n* calendario *m*.
calf *n* ternero *m*.
call *vt* llamar, nombrar.
calligraphy *n* caligrafía *f*.
callous *adj* calloso(a);
  insensible; cruel.
calm *n* calma, tranquilidad;
  * *vt* calmar, tranquilizar.
calorie *n* caloría *f*.
Calvinist *n* calvinista *m or f*.
camel *n* camello *m*.
cameo *n* camafeo *m*.
camera *n* cámara *or* máquina
  fotográfica *f*.
camomile *n* manzanilla *f*.
camouflage *n* camuflaje *m*;
  * *vt* camuflar.
camp *n* campo *m*; * *vi* acampar.
campaign *n* campaña *f*.
camping *n* camping *m*.
campsite *n* camping *m*.
can *vi* poder; * *n* lata *f*.
canal *n* canal *m*.
cancel *vt* cancelar; anular.
cancer *n* cáncer *m*.
Cancer *n* Cáncer *m* (astrology).
candid *adj* cándido(a);
  sencillo(a).
candle *n* vela *f*, cirio *m*.
candlestick *n* candelero *m*.
candy *n* caramelo *m*.
cane *n* caña *f*, bastón *m*.
cannabis *n* canabis *f*.
cannibal *n* caníbal *m or f*.
cannibalism *n* canibalismo *m*.
cannon *n* cañón *m*.

canoe *n* canoa *f*.
canon *n* canon *m*; regla *f*.
can opener *n* abrelatas *m invar*.
canopy *n* dosel *m*; toldo *m*.
canteen *n* cantina *f*.
canter *n* medio galope *m*.
canvas *n* lona *f*, lienzo *m*;
  velamen *m*.
canyon *n* cañón *m*.
cap *n* gorra *f*.
capability *n* capacidad *f*.
capable *adj* capaz.
cape *n* cabo *m*, promontorio *m*.
capital *adj* capital; principal.
capitalism *n* capitalismo *m*.
Capitol *n* Capitolio *m*.
capitulate *vi* capitular.
Capricorn *n* Capricornio *m*
  (astrology).
capsule *n* cápsula *f*.
captain *n* capitán *m*.
captivate *vt* cautivar.
capture *n* captura *f*, presa *f*;
  * *vt* capturar.
car *n* coche *m*, carro *m*; vagón *m*.
carafe *n* garrafa *f*.
caramel *n* caramelo *m*.
carat *n* quilate *m*.
caravan *n* caravana *f*.
carbohydrates *npl* hidratos de
  carbono *mpl*, carbohidratos *mpl*.
carcass *n* cadáver *m*.
card *n* naipe *m*; carta *f*, tarjeta *f*.
cardboard *n* cartón *m*.
cardinal *adj* cardinal, principal.
care *n* cuidado *m*;
  preocupación *m*.
career *n* carrera *f*; profesión *f*.
caress *n* caricia *f*.
caretaker *n* portero(a) *m(f)*.
cargo *n* cargamento *m*; carga *f*.
caricature *n* caricatura *f*.
carnal *adj* carnal; sensual.
carnation *n* (botany) clavel *m*.
carnival *n* carnaval *m*.
carpenter *n* carpintero(a).
carpentry *n* carpintería *f*.

carpet *n* alfombra *f*.
carrier *n* portador(a) *m(f)*.
carrot *n* zanahoria *f*.
carry *vt* llevar, conducir.
cart *n* carro *m*; carreta *f*.
cartilage *n* cartílago *m*.
carton *n* caja *f*.
cartoon *n* dibujos animados *mpl*, tira cómica *f*.
carve *vt* cincelar; trinchar.
carving *n* escultura *f*.
case *n* caja *f*, maleta *f*; caso *m*.
cash *n* dinero efectivo *m*.
cashier *n* cajero *m*.
cashmere *n* cachemira *f*.
cask *n* barril *m*, tonel *m*.
casserole *n* cazuela *f*.
cassette *n* cassette *m*.
cassock *n* sotana *f*.
castanets *npl* castañuelas *fpl*.
castaway *n* náufrago *m* or *f*.
caste *n* casta *f*.
castigate *vt* castigar.
castle *n* castillo *m*.
castrate *vt* castrar.
castration *n* castración *m*.
casual *adj* casual.
cat *n* gato(a) *m(f)*.
catalogue *n* catálogo *m*.
catapult *n* catapulta *f*.
cataract *n* cascada *f*; catarata *f*.
catarrh *n* catarro *m*.
catastrophe *n* catástrofe *f*.
catch *vt* coger.
catchphrase *n* lema *m*.
catechism *n* catecismo *m*.
categorise *vt* clasificar.
category *n* categoría *f*.
caterpillar *n* oruga *f*.
cathedral *n* catedral *f*.
catholic *adj*, *n* católico(a) *m(f)*.
Catholicism *n* catolicismo *m*.
cattle *n* ganado *m*.
cauliflower *n* coliflor *f*.
cause *n* causa *f*, razón *f*; motivo *m*.
causeway *n* carretera elevada *m*, terraplén *m*.

caustic *adj*, *n* cáustico(a) *m(f)*.
cauterise *vt* cauterizar.
caution *n* prudencia *f*, precaución *f*.
cavalry *n* caballería *f*.
cave *n* caverna *f*, cueva *f*.
caviar *n* caviar *m*.
cease *vt* cesar.
cedar *n* (botany) cedro *m*.
cede *vt* ceder.
ceiling *n* techo *m*.
celebrate *vt* celebrar.
celery *n* apio *m*.
celibacy *n* celibato *m*.
cell *n* celdilla *f*; célula *f*, cueva *f*.
cellar *n* sótano *m*, bodega *f*.
cellophane *n* celofán *m*.
cement *n* cemento *m*.
cemetery *n* cementerio *m*.
cenotaph *n* cenotafio *m*.
censor *n* censor *m*; * *vt* censurar.
census *n* censo *m*.
cent *n* centavo *m*.
centigrade *n* centígrado *m*.
centilitre *n* centilitro *m*.
centimetre *n* centímetro *m*.
centipede *n* ciempiés *mpl invar*.
central *adj* central, céntrico(a).
centralise *vt* centralizar.
centre *n* centro *m*.
century *n* siglo *m*.
ceramic *adj* de cerámica.
ceremony *n* ceremonia *f*.
certain *adj* cierto(a), evidente.
certificate *n* certificado *m*, testimonio *m*.
certify *vt* certificar, afirmar.
cervical *adj* cervical.
chaffinch *n* pinzón *m*.
chain *n* cadena *f*.
chair *n* silla *f*.
chamber *n* cámara *f*.
chameleon *n* camaleón *m*.
champagne *n* champaña *m*.
championship *n* campeonato *m*.
chance *n* ventura, suerte *f*; oportunidad *f*.

chancellor *n* canciller *m*.
change *vt* cambiar.
channel *n* canal *m*.
chant *n* canto *m*; grito *m*.
chaos *n* caos *m*.
chapel *n* capilla *f*.
chaplain *n* capellán *m*.
chapter *n* capítulo *m*.
character *n* carácter *m*.
charcoal *n* carbón de leña *m*.
charge *vt* cargar; acusar,
 imputar.
charity *n* caridad *f*.
charlatan *n* charlatán(ana)*m(f)*.
charm *n* encanto *m*, atractivo *m*.
charter flight *n* vuelo charter *m*.
chauffeur *n* chófer *m*.
chauvinist *n* machista *m*,
 chovinista *m*.
cheap *adj* barato(a).
cheat *vt* engañar, defraudar.
checkmate *n* mate *m*.
checkout *n* caja *f*.
cheek *n* mejilla *f*.
cheese *n* queso *m*.
chef *n* jefe de cocina *m*.
chemical *adj* químico(a).
chemist *n* químico(a).
cheque *n* cheque *m*.
cheroot *n* puro *m*.
cherry *n* cereza *f*.
cherub *n* querubín *m*.
chess *n* ajedrez *m*.
chest *n* pecho *m*.
chestnut *n* castaña *f*.
chew *vt* mascar, masticar.
chewing gum *n* chicle *m*.
chicken *n* pollo *m*.
chickenpox *n* varicela *f*.
chickpea *n* garbanzo *m*.
chief *adj* principal.
chilblain *n* sabañón *m*.
child *n* niño(a) *m(f)*.
childhood *n* infancia *f*, niñez *f*.
children *npl* niños *mpl*.
chimney *n* chimenea *f*.
chimpanzee *n* chimpancé *m*.

chin *n* barbilla *f*.
chiropodist *n* pedicuro *m*.
chirp *vi* chirriar.
chlorine *n* cloro *m*.
chloroform *n* cloroformo *m*.
chocolate *n* chocolate *m*.
choice *n* elección *f*, preferencia *f*.
choir *n* coro *m*.
choke *vt* atragantarse.
cholera *n* cólera *m*.
choose *vt* escoger, elegír.
chop *vt* tajar, cortar;
 * *n* chuleta *f*.
chore *n* faena *f*.
Christ *n* Cristo *m*.
christen *vt* bautizar.
Christianity *n* cristianismo
 m; cristiandad *f*.
Christmas *n* Navidad *f*.
chrome *n* cromo *m*.
chronicle *n* crónica *f*.
chronological *adj*
 cronológico(a).
chubby *adj* rechoncho(a).
chunk *n* trozo *m*.
church *n* iglesia *f*.
churchyard *n* cementerio *m*.
cider *n* sidra *f*.
cigar *n* cigarro *m*.
cigarette *n* cigarrillo *m*.
cinder *n* carbonilla *f*.
cinema *n* cine *m*.
cinnamon *n* canela *f*.
circle *n* círculo *m*.
circumcise *vt* circuncidar.
circumcision *n* circuncisión *f*.
circumference *n* circunferencia *f*.
circumflex *n* acento
 circunflejo *m*.
circumstance *n* circunstancia *f*.
circus *n* circo *m*.
cistern *n* cisterna *f*.
cite *vt* citar.
citizen *n* ciudadano(a) *m(f)*.
city *n* ciudad *f*.
civic *adj* cívico(a).
civil *adj* civil, cortés.

civilisation *n* civilización *f*.

clairvoyant *n* clarividente *m* or *f*.

clam *n* almeja *f*.

clammy *adj* viscoso(a).

clamour *n* clamor *m*.

clan *n* familia *f*, tribu *f*, raza *f*, clan *m*.

clandestine *adj* clandestino(a).

clap *vt* aplaudir.

claret *n* clarete *m*.

clarify *vt* clarificar, aclarar.

clarinet *n* clarinete *m*.

clarity *n* claridad *f*.

class *n* clase *f*; orden *f*.

classic(al) *adj* clásico(a); * *n* autor clásico *m*.

classify *vt* clasificar.

classmate *n* compañero(a) de clase *m(f)*.

classroom *n* aula *f*.

clause *n* cláusula *f*.

claw *n* garra *f*.

clay *n* arcilla *f*.

clean *adj* limpio(a); * *vt* limpiar.

cleanse *vt* limpiar, purificar; purgar.

clear *adj* claro(a).

clemency *n* clemencia *f*.

clement *adj* clemente, benigno(a).

clergy *n* clero *m*.

clerical *adj* clerical, eclesiástico(a).

clerk *n* dependiente(a) *m*; oficinista *m* or *f*.

clever *adj* listo(a); hábil.

client *n* cliente *m* or *f*.

cliff *n* acantilado *m*.

climate *n* clima *m*.

climax *n* clímax *m*.

climb *vt* escalar, trepar.

cling *vi* colgarse, adherirse.

clinic *n* clínica *f*.

clip *n* horquilla *f*, sujetapapeles *m*, clip *m*; * *vt* cortar.

clique *n* camarilla *f*.

cloak *n* capa *f*.

cloakroom *n* guardarropa *m*.

clock *n* reloj *m*.

clog *n* zueco *m*.

cloister *n* claustro *m*, monasterio *m*.

close *vt* cerrar; concluir, terminar.

closet *n* armario *m*.

close-up *n* primer plano *m*.

clot *n* grumo *m*; embolia *f*.

cloth *n* paño *m*.

clothe *vt* vestir.

clothes *npl* ropa *f*.

clothes peg *n* pinza *f*.

cloud *n* nube *f*.

clout *n* tortazo *m*.

clove *n* (botany) clavo *m*.

clover *n* (botany) trébol *m*.

clown *n* payaso *m*.

coach *n* autocar *m*, autobús *m*.

coagulate *vt* coagular, cuajar.

coal *n* carbón *m*.

coalition *n* coalición *f*, confederación *f*.

coarse *adj* basto(a); grosero(a).

coast *n* costa *f*.

coastguard *n* guardacostas *m invar*.

coat *n* chaqueta *f*, abrigo *m*.

coat hanger *n* percha *f*.

cobbler *n* zapatero *m*.

cobweb *n* telaraña *f*.

cocaine *n* cocaína *f*.

cock *n* gallo *m*; macho *m*.

cockle *n* berberecho *m*.

cockpit *n* cabina *f*.

cockroach *n* cucaracha *f*.

cocktail *n* cóctel *m*.

cocoa *n* cacao *m*.

coconut *n* coco *m*.

cod *n* bacalao *m*.

code *n* código *m*.

cod-liver oil *n* aceite de hígado de bacalao *m*.

coffee *n* café *m*.

coffer *n* cofre *m*; caja *f*.

coffin *n* ataúd *m*.

cog n diente (de rueda) m.
cognac n coñac m.
cogwheel n rueda dentada f.
cohabit vi cohabitar.
coherence n coherencia f.
cohesion n cohesión m.
cohesive adj cohesivo(a).
coil n rollo m.
coin n moneda f.
coincide vi coincidir.
coke n coque m.
colander n colador m,
  escurridor m.
cold adj frío(a).
cold sore n herpes labial m,
  calentura f.
coleslaw n ensalada de col f.
colic n cólico m.
collaborate vt cooperar,
  colaborar.
collapse vi hundirse, colapsarse.
collapsible adj plegable.
collar n cuello m, collar m.
collarbone n clavícula f.
collate vt cotejar.
collateral adj colateral.
colleague n colega m.
collect vt recoger; coleccionar.
collection n colección f;
  recogida f.
college n colegio m.
collide vi chocar.
colloquial adj coloquial.
collusion n confabulación f.
colon n dos puntos mpl;
  (medical) colon m.
colonel n (military) coronel m.
colonial adj colonial.
colonise vt colonizar.
colony n colonia f.
colossal adj colosal.
colour n color m.
colt n potro m.
column n columna f.
columnist n columnista m or f.
coma n coma f.
comatose adj comatoso(a).

comb n peine m; * vt peinar.
combat n combate m.
combination n combinación f.
combine vt combinar.
combustion n combustión f.
come vi venir.
comedy n comedia f.
comet n cometa f.
comfort n confort m.
comfortable adj cómodo(a).
comma n coma f.
command vt mandar, ordenar.
commemorate vt
  conmemorar; celebrar.
commence vt, vi comenzar.
commencement n principio m.
commend vt recomendar.
commensurate adj
  proporcionado(a).
comment n comentario m.
commentator n comentador m.
commerce n comercio m.
commercial adj comercial.
commiserate vt compadecerse.
commission n comisión f.
commit vt cometer.
committee n comité m.
commodity n comodidad f.
common adj común.
commotion n tumulto m.
communicate vt comunicar.
communion n comunión f.
communism n comunismo m.
community n comunidad f.
commute vt conmutar.
compact adj compacto(a).
compact disc n disco compacto m.
companion n compañero(a) m(f).
company n compañía f,
  sociedad f.
compare vt comparar.
compartment n
  compartimiento m.
compass n brújula f.
compassion n compasión f.
compatriot n compatriota m or f.
compensate vt compensar.

compensation *n* compensación *f*.
compère *n* presentador(a) *m(f)*.
compete *vi* competir.
competent *adj* competente.
competition *n* competición *f*.
competitor *n* competidor(a) *m(f)*, rival *m* or *f*.
compilation *n* recopilación *f*.
complain *vi* quejarse, lamentarse.
complement *n* complemento *m*.
complex *adj* complejo(a).
complexion *n* tez *f*, aspecto *m*.
complicate *vt* complicar.
component *adj* componente.
compose *vt* componer.
composer *n* compositor(a).
composite *adj* compuesto(a).
composition *n* composición *f*.
comprehend *vt* comprender, entender.
compress *vt* comprimir.
comprise *vt* comprender.
compromise *n* compromiso *m*.
compulsive *adj* compulsivo(a).
computer *n* ordenador *m*.
comrade *n* compañero(a).
concave *adj* cóncavo(a).
conceal *vt* ocultar, esconder.
concede *vt* conceder.
conceit *n* concepto *m*, capricho *m*.
conceive *vt* concebir, comprender.
concentrate *vt* concentrar(se).
concept *n* concepto *m*.
conception *n* concepción *f*.
concern *vt* concernir, importar.
concert *n* concierto *m*.
concession *n* concesión *f*; privilegio *m*.
concise *adj* conciso(a).
conclude *vt* concluir.
conclusion *n* conclusión *f*.
concord *n* concordia *f*, armonía *f*.
concrete *n* concreto *m*.
concussion *n* concusión *f*.
condemn *vt* condenar.

condensation *n* condensación *f*.
condiment *n* condimento *m*; salsa *f*.
condition *vt* condicionar.
conditional *adj* condicional.
condom *n* condón *m*.
conduct *n* conducta *f*.
conductor *n* conductor(a) *m(f)*.
conduct *n* conducto *m*.
cone *n* cono *m*.
confection *n* confitura *f*.
confectioner's (shop) *n* pastelería *f*.
conference *n* conferencia *f*.
confess *vt* (*vi*) confesar(se).
confession *n* confesión *f*.
confessional *n* confesionario *m*.
comfetti *n* confeti *m*.
confidant *n* confidente *m* or *f*.
confide *vt*, *vi* confiar; fiarse.
confidence *n* confianza *f*, seguridad *f*.
confident *adj* seguro(a); confiado(a).
confine *vt* limitar; aprisionar.
confirm *vt* confirmar; ratificar.
confiscate *vt* confiscar.
conflagration *n* conflagración *f*.
conflict *n* conflicto *m*; combate *m*; pelea *f*.
conflicting *adj* contradictorio(a).
comfluence *n* confluencia *f*.
conform *vt* (*vi*) conformar(se).
conformity *n* conformidad *f*.
confound *vt* turbar, confundir.
confront *vt* afrontar; confrontar.
confrontation *n* enfrenta-miento *m*.
confuse *vt* confundir.
congeal *vt* (*vi*) helar, congelar(se).
congenial *adj* agradable.
congenital *adj* congénito(a).
congested *adj* atestado(a).
congestion *n* congestión *f*.
congratulate *vt* congratular,

felicitar.
congratulations *npl*
felicidades *fpl*.
congratulatory *adj*
congratulatorio(a).
congregate *vt* congregar.
congress *n* congreso *m*;
conferencia *f*.
congruity *n* congruencia *f*.
conifer *n* (botany) conífera *f*.
conjecture *n* conjetura *f*.
conjugal *adj* conyugal.
conjugate *vt* (grammar) conjugar.
conjunction *n* conjunción *f*.
conjuncture *n* coyuntura *f*.
conjure *vi* hacer juegos de manos.
con man *n* timador(a) *m(f)*.
connect *vt* juntar, unir.
connection *n* conexión *f*.
connivance *n* connivencia *f*.
connive *vi* tolerar.
connoisseur *n* conocedor(a);
experto(a).
conquer *vi* conquistar; vencer.
conqueror *n* vencedor(a) *m(f)*,
conquistador(a) *m(f)*.
conquest *n* conquista *f*.
conscience *n* conciencia *f*.
consciousness *n* conciencia *f*.
conscript *n* recluta *m*.
conscription *n* reclutamiento *m*.
consecrate *vt* consagrar.
consecration *n* consagración *f*.
consecutive *adj* consecutivo(a).
consensus *n* consenso *m*.
consent *n* consentimiento *m*;
aprobación *f*.
consequence *n* consecuencia *f*.
consequent *adj* consecutivo(a).
conservation *n* conservación *f*.
conservative *adj* conservativo(a).
conservatory *n* invernadero *m*.
conserve *vt* conservar.
consider *vt* considerar.
considerable *adj* considerable.
considerate *adj* considerado(a).
consideration *n* consideración *f*.

consign *vt* consignar.
consignment *n* envío *f*.
consist *vi* consistir.
consistency consistencia *f*.
consistent *adj* consistente.
consolation *n* consolación *f*,
consuelo *m*.
console *vt* consolar.
consolidate *vt* (*vi*) consolidar(se).
consolidation *n* consolidación *f*.
consonant *adj* consonante.
consort *n* consorte, socio(a).
conspicuous *adj* conspicuo(a).
conspiracy *n* conspiración *f*.
conspirator *n* conspirador(a)
m(f).
conspire *vi* conspirar.
constancy *n* constancia *f*.
constant *adj* constante.
eonstellation *n* constelación *f*.
constipated *adj* estreñido(a).
constituency *n* junta electoral *f*.
constituent *n* electo(a);
constituyente.
constitute *vt* constituir.
constitution *n* constitución *f*.
constitutional *adj*
constitucional.
constrict *vt* constreñir,
estrechar.
construct *vt* construir, edificar.
construction *n* construcción *f*.
consul *n* cónsul *m*.
consulate, consulship *n*
consulado *m*.
consult *vt* (*vi*) consultar(se).
consultation *n* consulta *f*.
consume *vt* consumir.
comsumer *n* consumidor(a) *m(f)*.
consumption *n* consumo *m*.
contact *n* contacto *m*.
contact lenses *npl* lentes de
contacto *mpl*, lentillas *fpl*.
contagious *adj* contagioso(a).
contain *vt* contener.
container *n* recipiente *m*.
contaminate *vt* contaminar.

contamination *n* contaminación *f*.

contemplate *vt* contemplar.

contemplation *n* contemplación *f*.

contempt *n* desprecio *m*, desdén *m*.

contend *vi* contender.

content *adj* contento(a); satisfecho(a).

contention *n* discusión *f*.

contest *n* comtienda *f*, *n* concurso *m*.

contestant *n* concursante *m* or *f*.

context *n* contexto *m*.

continent *adj* continente.

contingency *n* contingencia *f*.

contingent *n* contingente *m*.

continue *vi* continuar.

contort *vi* retorcer.

contortion *n* contorsión *f*.

contour *n* contorno *m*.

contraband *n* contrabando *m*.

contraception *n* contracepción *f*.

contraceptive *n* anticonceptivo *m*.

contract *vt* contraer; abreviar; contratar.

contraction *n* contracción *f*, abreviatura *f*.

contradict *vi* contradecir.

contradiction *n* contradicción *f*, oposición *f*.

contraption *n* artilugio *m*.

contrary *adj* contrario(a); opuesto(a).

contrast *n* ontraste *m*.

contrasting *adj* opuesto(a).

contributary *adj* contributario(a).

contribute *vt* contribuir, ayudar.

contrive *vt* inventar, idear.

control *n* control *m*; inspección *f*; * *vt* controlar; manejar; restringir; gobernar.

controversial *adj* controvertido(a).

controversy *n* controversia *f*.

conurbation *n* conturbación *f*.

convalesce *vi* convalecer.

convalescence *n* convalecencia *f*.

convene *vt* convocar; reunir.

convenient *adj* conveniente.

convent *n* convento *m*.

convention *n* convención *f*.

converge *vi* converger.

conversation *n* conversación *f*.

converse *vi* conversar.

conversely *adv* mutuamente, recíprocamente.

convert *vt* (*vi*) convertir(se).

convertible *adj* convertible.

convex *adj* convexo(a).

convey *vt* transportar; transmitir, transferir.

conveyance *n* transporte *m*.

conveyancer *n* notario *m*.

comviction *n* convicción *f*.

convince *vt* convencer.

convivial *adj* sociable; hospitalario(a).

convoke *vt* convocar.

convoy *n* convoy *m*.

convulse *vt* conmover, convulsionar.

convulsion *n* convulsión *f*.

convulsive *adj* convulsivo(a).

cook *n* cocinero(a); * *vi* cocinar.

cool *adj* fresco(a); indiferente.

co-operate *vi* cooperar.

co-operation *n* cooperación *f*.

co-ordinate *vt* coordinar.

co-ordination *n* coordinación *f*.

cop *n* (*sl*) poli *m*.

copier *n* copiadora *f*.

copious *adj* copioso(a); abundante.

copper *n* cobre *m*.

copulate *vi* copular.

copy *n* copia *f*.

coral *n* coral *m*.

cord *n* cuerda *f*, cable *m*.

cordial *adj* cordial.

corduroy *n* pana *f*.

core *n* centro *m*, núcleo *m*;
  meollo *m*.
cork *n* alcornoque *m*; corcho *m*.
corkscrew *n* sacacorchos *m*.
corn *n* maíz *m*; grano *m*; callo *m*.
corn cob *n* mazorca *f*.
cornea *n* córnea *f*.
corner *n* rincón *m*; esquina *f*.
cornet *n* corneta *f*.
cornflakes *npl* copos de maíz
  mpl, cornflakes *mpl*.
cornice *n* cornisa *f*.
coronary *n* infarto *m*.
coronation *n* coronación *f*.
coroner *n* juez de instrucción *m*.
corporation *n* corporación *f*.
corps *n* cuerpo (de ejército) *m*.
corpse *n* cadáver *m*.
correct *vt* corregir; enmendar.
correctness *n* exactitud *f*.
correspond *vi* corresponder.
correspondence *n* correspondencia *f*.
corridor *n* pasillo *m*.
corrode *vt* corroer.
corrosive *adj* corrosivo(a).
corrupt *vt* corromper;
  sobornar.
corruption *n* corrupción *f*,
  depravación *f*.
corset *n* corsé *m*.
cosily *adv* cómodamente.
cosmetic *adj* cosmético(a).
cosmic *adj* cósmico(a).
cosmonaut *n* cosmonauta *m* or *f*.
cosmopolitan *adj* cosmopolita.
cosset *vt* mimar.
cost *n* coste *m*, precio *m*;
  * *vi* costar.
costume *n* traje *m*.
cosy *adj* cómodo(a).
cottage *n* casita *f*, casa de
  campo *f*.
cotton *n* algodón *m*.
cotton wool *n* algodón hidrófilo *m*.
couch *n* sofá *m*.
couchette *n* litera *f*.

cough *n* tos *f*; * *vi* toser.
council *n* ayuntamiento *m*;
  consejo *m*.
counsel *n* consejo *m*, aviso *m*.
count *n* cuenta *f*; conde *m*;
  * *vt* contar, numerar; calcular.
counter *n* mostrador *m*; ficha *f*.
counterfeit *n* falsificación *f*;
  * *vt* falsificar.
counterpart *n* parte corres-
  pondiente *f*; homólogo(a) *m(f)*.
countersign *vt* refrendar.
countess *n* condesa *f*.
countless *adj* innumerable.
countrified *adj* rústico(a).
country *n* país *m*; campo *m*;
  región *f*; patria *f*.
county *n* condado *m*.
coup *n* golpe *m*.
couple *n* par *m*.
couplet *n* copla *f*; par *m*.
coupon *n* cupón *m*.
courage *n* coraje *m*, valor *f*.
courageous *adj* valiente;
  valeroso(a); * ~ly *adv*
  valerosamente.
courier *n* correo, mensajero(a)
  m(f), expreso *m*.
course *n* curso *m*; carrera *f*;
  camino *m*; ruta *f*.
court *n* corte *f*.
courteous *adj* cortés.
courtesy *n* cortesía *f*.
courthouse *n* palacio de
  justicia *m*.
courtyard *n* patio *m*.
cousin *n* primo(a).
cove *n* (marine) ensenada *f*,
  caleta *f*.
covenant *n* contrato *m*,
  convenio *m*.
cover *n* cubierta *f*; portada *f*,
  sobre *m*; * *vt* cubrir; abrigar.
covering letter *n* carta de
  explicación *f*.
covert *adj* encubierto(a);
  oculto(a); secreto(a).

cover-up *n* encubrimiento *m*.

covet *vt* codiciar.

cow *n* vaca *f*.

coward *n* cobarde *m or f*.

cowardice *n* cobardía *f*.

cowboy *n* vaquero *m*.

cower *vi* encogerse.

cow-herd *n* vaquero *m*.

crab *n* cangrejo *m*.

crab apple *n* manzana silvestre *f*.

crack *n* crujido *m*; grieta *f*;
* *vt* agrietar, romper.

cracker *n* galleta salada *f*.

crackle *vi* crepitar.

cradle *n* cuna *f*; * *vt* mecer,
acunar.

craft *n* arte *m*; embarcación *f*.

craftsman *n* artesano *m*.

craftsmanship *n* artesanía *f*.

crafty *adj* astuto(a);
artificioso(a).

cramp *n* calambre *m*.

cranberry *n* (botany) arándano *m*.

crane *n* grulla *f*; grua *f*.

crash accidente *m*; quiebra *f*;
* *vi* estallar.

crash helmet *n* casco *m*.

crass *adj* grosero(a),
maleducado(a).

crater *n* cráter *m*.

cravat(e) *n* pañuelo *m*.

crave *vt, vi* ansiar, anhelar.

craving *n* ansia *f*, antojo *m*.

crawl *vi* arrastrarse; gatear,
andar a gatas.

crayfish *n* cangrejo de río *m*.

crayon *n* lápiz *m*.

craze *n* manía *f*.

craziness *n* locura *f*.

crazy *adj* loco(a).

cream *n* crema *f*, nata *f*.

creamy *adj* cremoso(a).

crease *n* pliegue *m*.

create *vt* crear; causar.

creation *n* creación *f*.

creator *n* creador(a) *m(f)*.

creature *n* criatura *f*.

credence *n* creencia *f*, fe *f*.

credibility *n* credibilidad *f*.

credible *adj* creíble.

credit *n* crédito *m*.

creditable *adj* estimable.

credit card *n* tarjeta de crédito *f*.

creed *n* credo *m*.

creek *n* arroyo *m*.

creep *vi* arrastrar, deslizarse.

creeper *n* (botany) enredadera.

cremate *vt* incinerar.

cremation *n* incineración *f*,
cremación *f*.

crematorium *n* crematorio *m*.

crescent *n* calle en forma de
media luna *f*.

cress *n* berro *m*.

crest *n* cresta *f*.

crevasse *n* grieta (de glaciar) *f*.

crevice *n* raja, hendedura *f*.

crew *n* banda, tropa *f*.

crib *n* pesebre *m*; * *vt* plagiar,
copiar.

cricket *n* grillo *m*; criquet *m*.

crime *n* crimen *m*.

criminal *adj* criminal.

crimson *adj, n* carmesí *m*.

cripple *n, adj* cojo(a).

crisis *n* crisis *f*.

crisp *adj* crujiente.

crispness *n* encrespadura *f*.

criss-cross *adj* entrelazado(a).

criterion *n* criterio *m*.

critic *n* crítico(a) *m(f)*.

criticise *vt* criticar, censurar.

crochet *n* ganchillo *m*.

crockery *n* loza *f*.

crocodile *n* cocodrilo *m*.

crook *n* (sl) ladrón(ona) *m(f)*.

crooked *adj* torcido(a);
perverso(a).

cross *n* cruz *f*.

crossbar *n* travesaño *m*.

crossbreed *n* raza cruzada *f*.

cross-country *n* carrera a
campo traviesa *f*.

crossing *n* cruce *m*; paso a nivel *m*.

cross-reference *n* remisión *f.*

crossroad *n* encrucijada *f.*

crotch *n* entrepierna *f.*

crouch *vi* agacharse.

crow *n* cuervo *m.*

crowd *n* público *m;* muchedumbre *f.*

crown *n* corona *f.*

crown prince *n* príncipe real *m.*

crucial *adj* crucial.

crucible *n* crisol *m.*

crucifix *n* crucifijo *m.*

crucifixion *n* crucifixión *f.*

crude *adj* crudo(a), imperfecto(a).

cruel *adj* cruel.

cruelty *n* crueldad *f.*

cruet *n* vinagrera *f.*

cruiser *n* crucero *m.*

crumb *n* miga *f.*

crumble *vt* desmenuzar.

crumple *vt* arrugar.

crunchy *adj* crujiente.

crusade *n* cruzada *f.*

crush *n* aglomeración;
  * *vt* apretar, oprimir.

crust *n* costra *f*, corteza *f.*

crutch *n* muleta *f.*

crux *n* lo esencial.

cry *vt, vi* gritar; exclamar; llorar.

crypt *n* cripta (bóveda
  subterránea) *f.*

cryptic *adj* enigmático(a).

crystal *n* cristal *m.*

cub *n* cachorro *m.*

cube *n* cubo *m.*

cuckoo *n* cuco *m.*

cucumber *n* pepino *m.*

cuddle *vt* abrazar.

cudgel *n* garrote, palo *m.*

cue *n* taco (de billar) *m.*

cuff *n* bofetada *f;* puño *m.*

cull *n* matanza selectiva *f;*
  * *vt* entresacar.

culminate *vi* culminar.

culpable *adj* culpable.

cult *n* culto *f.*

cultivate *vi* cultivar.

cultivation *n* cultivo *m*, cultura *f.*

cultural *adj* cultural.

culture *n* cultura *f.*

cumulative *adj* cumulativo(a).

cunning *adj* astuto(a); intrigante.

cup *n* taza *f.*

cupboard *n* armario *m.*

curable *adj* curable.

curb *n* freno *m;* bordillo *m.*

curd *n* cuajada *f.*

cure *n* cura *f*, remedio *m.*

curiosity *n* curiosidad *f;*
  rareza *f.*

curious *adj* curioso(a);
  * ~ly *adv* curiosamente.

curl *n* rizo de pelo *m.*

curly *adj* rizado(a).

currant *n* pasa *f;* grosella *f.*

currency *n* moneda *f.*

current *adj* corriente.

current affairs *npl* noticias de
  actualidad *fpl.*

currently *adv* actualmente.

curriculum vitae *n*
  currículum (vitae) *m.*

curry *n* curry *m.*

curse *vt* maldecir.

cursor *n* cursor *m.*

curt *adj* seco(a).

curtail *vt* acortar.

curtain *n* cortina *f;* telón (en
  los teatros) *m.*

curvature *n* curvatura *f.*

curve *vt* encorvar; * *n* curva *f.*

cushion *n* cojín *m;* almohada *f.*

custard *n* natillas *fpl.*

custodian *n* guadián(ana) *m(f).*

custody *n* custodia *f.*

custom *n* costumbre *f*, uso *m.*

customary *adj* usual, acostumbrado(a), ordinario(a).

customer *n* cliente *m* or *f.*

customs *npl* aduana *f.*

customs duty *n* derechos de
  aduana *mpl.*

customs officer *n* aduanero(a)
  m(f).

cut vt cortar; separar.
cutback n reducción f;
 * vt podar, reducir.
cute adj lindo(a); (sl) mono(a).
cutlery n cubiertos mpl.
cutlet n chuleta f.
cut-rate adj a precio reducido.
cut-throat n asesino(a) m(f);
 * adj encarnizado(a).
cutting n reocorte m;
 * adj cortante; mordaz.
cyanide n cianuro m.
cycle n ciclo m; bicicleta f;
 * vi ir en bicicleta.
cycling n ciclismo m.
cyclist n ciclista m or f.
cyclone n ciclón m.
cygnet n pollo de cisne m.
cylinder n cilindro m; rollo m.
cylindric(al) adj cilíndrico(a).
cymbals n címbalo m.
cynic(al) adj cínico(a);
 * n cínico m (filósofo).
cynicism n cinismo m.
cypress n (botany) ciprés m.
cyst n quiste m.
czar n zar m.

D

dad(dy) n papá m.
daddy-long-legs n típula m.
daffodil n (botany) narciso m.
dagger n puñal m.
daily adj diario(a).
dainty adj delicado(a).
dairy n lechería f.
dairy produce n productos
 lácteos mpl.
daisy n (botany) margarita f.
damage n daño m; perjuicio m.
damask n damasco m.
damn vt condenar.
damnation n condenación f;
 maldición f.
damp adj húmedo(a); mojado(a).

dampen vt mojar.
dampness n humedad f.
dance n danza f, baile m.
dandelion n (botany) diente de
 león m.
dandruff n caspa f.
danger n peligro m.
dare vi atreverse, desafiar.
daredevil n atrevido(a) m(f).
dark adj oscuro(a).
darling n, adj querido(a) m(f).
darn vt zurcir.
dart n dardo m.
dartboard n diana f.
dash n chorrito m, gota f,
 pizca f, guión m; * vi irse
 apresuradamente.
dashboard n tablero de
 instrumentos m.
data n datos mpl.
database n base de datos f.
date n fecha f, cita f.
daughter n hija f; ~in-law
 nuera f.
dawn n alba f; * vi amanecer.
day n día m.
dazzle vt deslumbrar.
deacon n diácono m.
dead adj muerto(a).
deadline n fecha tope f.
deadlock n punto muerto m.
deaf adj sordo(a).
deal n convenio m; transacción f.
dean n deán m.
dear adj querido(a).
dearness n carestía f.
death n muerte f.
debacle n desastre m.
debar vt excluir.
debase vt degradar.
debate n debate m; polémica f.
debilitate vt debilitar.
debt n deuda f.
decade n década f.
decadence n decadencia f.
decaffeinated adj descafeinado(a).
decay vi decaer; pudrirse.

deceit *n* engaño *m*.

deceive *vt* engañar.

December *n* diciembre *m*.

decent *adj* decente.

decide *vt*, *vi* decidir; resolver.

deciduous *adj* (botany) de hoja caduca.

decimal *adj* decimal.

decipher *vt* descifrar.

decision *n* decisión *f*.

declare *vt* declarar.

decline *vt* (grammar) declinar; evitar.

decompose *vt* descomponer.

decorate *vt* decorar, adornar.

decoration *n* decoración *f*.

decorum *n* decoro *m*.

decrease *vt* disminuir.

decree *n* decreto *m*.

dedicate *vt* dedicar; consagrar.

dedication *n* dedicación *f*.

deduce *vt* deducir.

deep *adj* profundo(a).

deep-freeze *n* arcón congelador *m*.

deer *n* ciervo *m*.

defamation *n* difamación *f*.

defeat *n* derrota *f*; * *vt* derrotar.

defect *n* defecto *m*.

defend *vt* defender.

defence *n* defensa *f*.

defensive *adj* defensivo(a).

defer *vt* aplazar.

deficient *adj* insuficiente; defectuoso(a).

deficit *n* déficit *m*.

define *vt* definir.

definition *n* definición *f*.

deflate *vt* desinflar.

deflect *vt* desviar.

deform *vt* desfigurar.

defraud *vt* estafar.

defuse *vt* desactivar.

degenerate *vi* degenerar.

degrade *vt* degradar.

degree *n* grado *m*; título *m*.

dehydrated *adj* deshidratado(a).

deity *n* deidad *f*, divinidad *f*.

dejection *n* desaliento *m*.

delay *vt* demorar; * *n* retraso *m*.

delegate *vt* delegar; * *n* delegado(a) *m(f)*.

delete *vt* tachar; borrar.

delicacy *n* delicadeza *f*.

delicate *adj* delicado(a).

delicious *adj* delicioso(a).

delight *n* delicia *f*.

delinquent *n* delincuente *m* or *f*.

delirium *n* delirio *m*.

deliver *vt* entregar.

delivery *n* entrega *f*, reparto *m*; parto *m*.

delude *vt* engañar.

deluge *n* diluvio *m*.

demagogue *n* demagogo(a) *m(f)*.

demand *n* demanda *f*.

demean *vi* rebajarse.

demented *adj* demente.

demise *n* fallecimiento *m*.

democracy *n* democracia *f*.

democrat *n* demócrata *m* or *f*.

demolish *vt* demoler.

demon *n* demonio *m*, diablo *m*.

demonstrate *vt* demostrar; manifestarse.

demoralise *vt* desmoralizar.

demote *vt* degradar.

demure *adj* modesto(a).

den *n* guarida *f*.

denial *n* negación *f*, negativa *f*.

denims *npl* vaqueros *mpl*.

denomination *n* valor *m*.

denote *vt* denotar.

denounce *vt* denunciar.

dense *adj* denso(a).

density *n* densidad *f*.

dental *adj* dental.

dentist *n* dentista *m* or *f*.

dentures *npl* dentadura postiza *f*.

denunciation *n* denuncia *f*.

deny *vt* negar.

deodorant *n* desodorante *m*.

depart *vi* partir.

department *n* sección *f*,

departamento m.

department store n gran almacén m.

departure lounge n sala de embarque f.

depend vi depender.

depict vt pintar, retratar.

deplore vt deplorar, lamentar.

deport vt deportar.

deposit n depósito m; * vt depositar.

depositor n depositante m or f.

depot n depósito m.

deprave vt depravar.

depravity n depravación f.

deprecate vt lamentar.

depreciate vi depreciarse.

depreciation n depreciación.

depress vt deprimir(se).

depressed adj deprimido(a).

depression n depresión f.

deprivation n privación f.

deprive vt privar.

depth n profundidad f.

deputation n delegación f.

deputise vi suplir a.

deputy n diputado(a) m(f).

derelict adj abandonado(a).

deride vt ridiculizar, mofarse.

derision n mofa f.

derivative n derivado m.

derive vt (vi) derivar(se).

derogatory adj despectivo(a).

descend vi descender.

descendant n descendiente m or f.

descent n descenso m.

describe vt describir.

description n descripción f.

descriptive adj descriptivo(a).

desecrate vt profanar.

desert n desierto m.

deserve vt merecer.

design n diseño m; * vt diseñar.

designate vt nombrar, designar.

designedly adv de propósito.

designer n diseñador(a) m(f).

desirable adj deseable.

desire n deseo m.

desk n escritorio m.

desolate adj desierto(a).

despair n desesperación f.

desperado n bandido m.

desperate adj desesperado(a).

despise vt despreciar.

despite prep a pesar de.

despoil vt despojar.

despondency n abatimiento m.

despot n déspota m or f.

dessert n postre m.

destination n destino m.

destine vt destinar.

destiny n destino m; suerte f.

destitute adj indigente.

destroy vt destruir.

destruction n destrucción f.

detach vt separar.

detail n detalle m.

detain vt retener; detener.

detect vt detectar.

detection n descubrimiento m.

detective n detective m or f.

deter vt disuadir.

detergent n detergente m.

deteriorate vt deteriorar.

determination n resolución f.

determine vt determinar.

deterrent n fuerza de disuasión f.

detest vt detestar.

detonate vi detonar.

detonation n detonación f.

detour n desviación f.

detriment n perjuicio m.

devaluation n devaluación f.

devastate vt devastar.

develop vt desarrollar.

development n desarrollo m.

deviate vi desviarse.

deviation n desviación f.

device n mecanismo m.

devil n diablo m, demonio m.

devious adj taimado(a).

devise vt inventar.

devote vt dedicar.

devour vt devorar.

devout *adj* devoto(a).
dew *n* rocío *m*.
dexterity *n* destreza *f*.
diabetes *n* diabetes *f*.
diabetic *n* diabético(a) *m(f)*.
diadem *n* diadema *f*.
diagnosis *n* (medical) diagnosis *f*.
diagonal *adj*, *n* diagonal *f*.
diagram *n* diagrama *m*.
dial *n* dial *m*.
dialect *n* dialecto *m*.
dialogue *n* dialogo *m*.
diameter *n* diámetro *m*.
diamond *n* diamante *m*.
diaphragm *n* diafragma *m*.
diarrhoea *n* diarrea *f*.
diary *adj* diario(a).
dice *npl* dados *mpl*.
dictate *vt* dictar.
dictation *n* dictado *m*.
dictatorship *n* dictadura *f*.
diction *n* dicción *f*.
dictionary *n* diccionario *m*.
didactic *adj* didáctico(a).
die *vi* morir; * *n* dado *m*.
diesel *n* diesel *m*.
diet *n* dieta *f*, régimen *m*.
differ *vi* diferenciarse.
difference *n* diferencia *f*.
different *adj* diferente.
difficult *adj* difícil.
dig *vt* cavar.
digest *vt* digerir.
digestion *n* digestión *f*.
digger *n* excavadora *f*.
digit *n* dígito *m*.
digital *adj* digital.
dignity *n* dignidad *f*.
dike *n* dique *m*.
dilate *vt* (*vi*) dilatar(se).
dilemma *n* dilema *m*.
dilute *vt* diluir.
dim *adj* turbio(a).
dimension *n* dimensión *f*, extensión *f*.
diminish *vt*, *vi* disminuir.
dimple *n* hoyuelo *m*.

din *n* alboroto *m*.
dine *vi* cenar.
diner *n* restaurante (económico) *m*.
dinghy *n* lancha neumática *f*.
dingy *adj* sombrío(a).
dinner *n* cena *f*.
dinosaur *n* dinosaurio *m*.
diocese *n* diócesis *f*.
dip *vt* mojar.
diphtheria *n* difteria *f*.
diploma *n* diploma *m*.
diplomacy *n* diplomacia *f*.
diplomat *n* diplomático(a) *m(f)*.
dire *adj* calamitoso(a).
direct *adj* directo(a); * *vt* dirigir.
direction *n* dirección *f*.
directly *adj* directamente.
director *n* director(a) *m(f)*.
directory *n* guía *f*.
dirt *n* suciedad *f*.
disability *n* incapacidad *f*.
disabled *adj* minusválido(a).
disadvantage *n* desventaja *f*; * *vt* perjudicar.
disagree *vi* no estar de acuerdo, discrepar.
disappear *vi* desaparecer.
disappoint *vt* decepcionar.
disapprove *vt* desaprobar.
disaster *n* desastre *m*.
disbelieve *vi* desconfiar.
discard *vt* descartar.
discern *vt* discernir, percibir.
discharge *vt* descargar; pagar (una deuda).
disciple *n* discípulo(a) *m(f)*.
discipline *n* disciplina *f*; * *vt* disciplinar.
disclose *vi* revelar.
disco *n* discoteca *f*.
discomfort *n* incomodidad *f*.
discontent *n* descontento(a) *m(f)*.
discontinue *vi* interrumpir.
discord *n* discordia *f*.
discount *n* descuento *m*; rebaja *f*.
discover *vt* descubrir.

discreet *adj* discreto(a).
discriminate *vt* distinguir.
discuss *vt* discutir.
discussion *n* discusión *f.*
disease *n* enfermedad *f.*
disembark *vt, vi* desembarcar.
disentangle *vt* desenredar.
disfigure *vt* desfigurar.
disgrace *n* ignominia *f,*
  escándalo *m.*
disgruntled *adj* descontento(a).
disguise *vi* disfrazar.
disgust *n* aversión *f;*
  * *vt* repugnar.
dish *n* fuente *f,* plato *m.*
dishevelled *adj* desarreglado(a).
dishonest *adj* deshonesto(a).
dishonesty *n* falta de honradez *f.*
dishonour *n* deshonra *f,*
  ignominia *f.*
dishwasher *n* lavaplatos *m.*
disillusion *vt* desilusionar.
disillusioned *adj*
  desilusionado(a).
disincentive *n* freno *m.*
disinclination *n* aversión *f.*
disinclined *adj* reacio(a).
disinfect *vt* desinfectar.
disinfectant *n* desinfectante *m.*
disinherit *vt* desheredar.
disintegrate *vi* disgregarse,
  desintegrarse.
disinterested *adj* desintere-
  sado(a).
disjointed *adj* inconexo(a).
disk *n* disco *m,* disquete *m.*
diskette *n* disco *m,* disquete *m.*
dislike *n* aversión *f.*
dislocate *vt* dislocar.
dislocation *n* dislocación *f.*
dislodge *vt, vi* desalojar.
disloyal *adj* desleal.
disloyalty *n* deslealtad *f.*
dismal *adj* triste.
dismantle *vt* desmontar.
dismay *n* consternación *f;*
  * *vt* consternar.

dismember *vt* desmembrar.
dismiss *vt* despedir; destituir.
dismissal *n* despedida *f;*
  destitución.
disobedience *n* desobediencia.
disobedient *adj* desobediente.
disobey *vt* desobedecer.
disorderly *adj* desarreglado(a).
disorganised *adj*
  desorganizado(a).
disorientated *adj*
  desorientado(a).
disown *vt* renegar de.
disparage *vt* despreciar.
disparaging *adj* desprecia-
  tivo(a).
disparity *n* disparidad *f.*
dispassionate *adj*
  desapasionado(a).
dispatch *vt* enviar.
dispel *vt* disipar.
dispensary *n* dispensario *m.*
dispense *vt* dispensar; distribuir.
disperse *vt* disipersar.
dispirited *adj* desalentado(a).
displace *vt* desplazar;
  reemplazar.
display *n* exposición *f;*
  * *vt* exponer.
displeased *adj* disgustado(a).
displeasure *n* disgusto *m.*
disposable *adj* desechable.
disposal *n* venta *f;* traspaso *m.*
dispose *vt* disponer; arreglar.
disposition *n* disposición *f.*
dispossess *vt* desposeer.
disproportionate *adj*
  desproporcionado(a).
disprove *vt* refutar.
dispute *n* disputa *f,* controversia *f.*
disqualify *vt* incapacitar;
  desclasificar.
disregard *vt* desatender;
  * *n* desdén *m.*
disreputable *adj* de mala fama.
disrespectful *adj* irreverente.

disrobe vt desnudar.
disrupt vt interrumpir.
disruption n interrupción f.
dissatisfaction n descontento m, disgusto m.
dissatisfied adj insatisfecho(a).
dissect vt disecar.
dissection n disección.
dissent disentimiento m; * vi disentir.
dissertation n disertación f.
dissident n disidente m or f.
dissimilar adj distinto.
dissolution n disolución f.
dissolve vt disolver.
dissuade vt disuadir.
distance n distancia f: — at a ~ de lejos; * vt apartar.
distant adj distante.
distillery n destilería f.
distinct adj distinto(a).
distinction n distinción f.
distinctive adj distintivo(a).
distinguish vt distinguir.
distort vt retorcer.
distorted adj distorsionado(a).
distortion n deformación f, distorsión f.
distract vt distraer.
distracted adj distraído(a).
distraction n distracción f, confusión f.
distraught adj enloquecido(a).
distress n angustia f.
distribute vt distribuir, repartir.
distribution n distribución f.
district n distrito m.
disturb vt molestar.
disturbance n disturbio m.
disturbing adj inquietante.
disused adj abandonado(a).
ditch n zanja f.
ditto adv ídem, lo mismo.
diuretic adj (medical) diurético(a).
diver n buzo m.

diverge vi divergir.
diverse adj diverso(a), diferente.
diversion n desviación f.
diversity n diversidad f.
divert vt desviar.
divide vt (vi) dividir(se).
divine adj divino(a).
divinity n divinidad f.
divorce n divorcio m.
DJ n pinchadiscos m; disc jockey.
do vt hacer, obrar.
docile adj dócil, apacible.
dockyard n (marine) astillero m.
doctor n médico(a) m(f); doctor(a) m(f).
doctrine n doctrina f.
document n documento m.
documentary adj documental.
doe n gama f, cierva f, coneja f.
dog n perro m.
do-it-yourself n bricolaje m.
doll n muñeca f.
dollar n dólar m.
dolphin n delfín m.
dome n cúpula f.
domestic adj doméstico(a).
domesticity n vida casera f.
domicile n domicilio m.
dominant adj dominante.
dominate vi dominar.
domineer vi dominar.
dominion n dominio m.
dominoes npl dominó m.
donate vt donar.
donation n donación f.
donkey n asno m, borrico m.
donor n donante m or f.
door n puerta f.
doorbell n timbre m.
doorman n portero m.
doormat n felpudo m.
dormouse n lirón m.
dose n dosis f.
dossier n expediente m.
dot n punto m.
dote vi adorar.
double adj doble.

doubly *adj* doblemente.

doubt *n* duda *f*, sospecha *f*.

doubtfal *adj* dudoso(a).

doubtless *adv* sin duda.

dough *n* masa *f*.

douse *vt* apagar.

dove *n* paloma *f*.

dovecot *n* palomar *m*.

dowdy *adj* mal vestido(a), desaliñado(a).

down *n* plumón *m*; pelusa *f*; * *prep* abajo.

downfall *n* ruina *f*.

downhearted *adj* desanimado(a).

downpour *n* aguacero *m*.

downtown *adv* al centro (de la ciudad).

dowry *n* dote *f*.

doze *vi* dormitar.

dozen *n* docena *f*.

dozy *adj* soñoliento(a).

drab *adj* gris, monótono(a).

draft *n* borrador *m*.

dragon *n* dragón *m*.

dragonfly *n* libélula *f*.

drain *n* sumidero *m*; * *vt* desaguar, drenar.

drake *n* ánade macho *m*.

drama *n* drama *m*.

dramatic *adj* dramático(a).

dramatist *n* dramaturgo(a) *m(f)*.

dramatise *vt* dramatizar.

drape *vt* cubrir.

drastic *adj* drástico(a).

draw *vt* tirar; dibujar.

drawback *n* desventaja *f*.

drawer *n* cajón *m*.

drawing *n* dibujo *m*.

drawing room *n* salón *m*.

dread *n* terror *m*, espanto *m*; * *vt* temer.

dreadful *adj* espantoso(a).

dream *n* sueño *m*; * *vi* soñar.

drench *vt* empapar.

dress *vt* vestir; * *n* vestido *m*.

dresser *n* aparador *m*.

dressing gown *n* bata *f*.

dressing table *n* tocador *m*.

dressmaker *n* modisto(a) *m(f)*.

dried *adj* seco(a).

drill *n* taladro *m*, broca *f*.

drink *n* bebida *f*; * *vt*, *vi* beber.

drinkable *adj* potable.

drip *vi* gotear.

drive *vt* conducir.

driver *n* conductor(a) *m(f)*.

driveway *n* entrada *f*.

drizzle *vi* lloviznar.

droop *vi* decaer.

drop *n* gota *f*.

drought *n* seguía *f*.

drown *vt*, *vi* ahogar, ahogarse.

drowsiness *n* somnolencia *f*.

drowsy *adj* soñoliento(a).

drudgery *n* trabajo monótono *m*.

drug *n* droga *f*; * *vt* drogar.

drug addict *n* drogadicto(a) *m(f)*.

druggist *n* farmacéutico(a) *m(f)*.

drugstore *n* farmacia *f*.

drum *n* tambor *m*; * *vi* tocar el tambor.

drummer *n* batería *m*.

drumstick *n* palillo de tambor *m*.

drunk *adj* borracho(a).

drunkard *n* borracho(a) *m(f)*.

drunkenness *n* borrachera *f*.

dry *adj* seco(a); * *vt* secar.

dry rot *n* podredumbre *f*.

dual *adj* doble.

dubbed *adj* doblado(a).

dubious *adj* dudoso(a).

duck *n* pato *m*.

duckling *n* patito *m*.

due *adj* debido(a).

duel *n* duelo *m*.

duet *n* (music) dúo *m*.

dull *adj* lerdo(a); insípido(a).

duly *adv* debidamente; a su debido tiempo.

dumb *adj* mudo(a).

dumb bell *n* pesa *f*.

dumbfounded *adj* pasmado(a).

dummy *n* maniquí *m*; chupete *m*.

dumpling *n* bola de masa

hervida f.

dumpy adj gordito(a), regordete(a).

dunce n zopenco(a).

dune n duna f.

dung n estiércol m.

dungarees npl mono m.

dungeon n calabozo m.

dupe n víctima f; * vt engañar.

duplicity n doblez f, duplicidad f.

durability n durabilidad f.

durable adj duradero(a).

duration n duración f.

during prep mientras, durante el tiempo que.

dusk n crepúsculo m.

dust n polvo m.

duster n plumero m.

dutch courage n valor fingido m.

dutiful adj obediente; fiel, leal.

duty n deber m; obligación f.

dwarf n enano(a); * vt empequeñecer.

dwell vi habitar, morar.

dwelling n habitación f; domicilio m.

dwindle vi mermar, disminuirse.

dye vt teñir; * n tinte m.

dynamic adj dinámico(a).

dynamite n dinamita f.

dynamo n dinamo f.

dynasty n dinastía f.

dysentery n disentería f.

dyspepsia n (medical) dispepsia f.

E

each pron cada uno, cada una.

eager adj impaciente; entusiasmado(a).

eagle n águila f.

eaglet n aguilucho m.

ear n oreja f.

earache n dolor de oídos m.

eardrum n tímpano (del oído) m.

early adj temprano(a).

earn vt ganar; conseguir.

earnest adj serio(a).

earth n tierra f.

earthenware n loza de barro f.

earthquake n terremoto m.

erthworm n lombriz f.

earthy adj sencillo.

earwig n tijereta f.

ease n comodidad f, facilidad f.

easel n caballete m.

easily adv fácilmente.

east n este m; oriente m.

Easter n Pascua (de Resurrección) f.

Easter holidays npl Semana Santa f.

easterly adj del este, al este.

eastern adj del este, oriental.

easy adj fácil; cómodo(a).

easy chair n sillón m, butaca f.

eat vt comer.

ebb n reflujo m.

ebony n ébano m.

eccentric adj excéntrico(a).

echo n eco m.

eclectic adj ecléctico(a).

eclipse n eclipse m.

ecology n ecología f.

economics npl economía f.

economy n economía f.

ecstasy n éxtasis m.

eczema n eczema m.

eddy n remolino de agua m.

edge n filo m, borde m.

edict n edicto m, mandato m.

edit vt dirigir; redactar, editar.

edition n edición f.

editor n director(a) m(f); editor(a) m(f); redactor(a) m(f).

educate vt educar.

education n educación f.

eel n anguila f.

effect n efecto m.

effective adj eficaz.

effeminate adj afeminado(a).

effervescence n efervescencia f.

efficacy n eficacia f.

efficient *adj* eficaz.

effigy *n* efigie *f*, imagen *f*.

effort *n* esfuerzo *m*.

egg *n* huevo *m*.

eggplant *n* berenjena *f*.

ego(t)ist *n* egoísta *m* or *f*.

eight *num* ocho.

eighteen *num* dieciocho.

eighth *adj* octavo(a).

eighty *num* ochenta.

either *pron* cualquiera.

eject *vt* expeler, desechar.

elastic *adj* elástico(a).

elation *n* regocijo *m*, euforia *f*.

elbow *n* codo *m*.

elder *n* (botany) saúco *m*; * *adj* mayor.

elect *vt* elegir.

election *n* elección *f*.

electrician *n* electricista *m* or *f*.

electricity *n* electricidad *f*.

elegance *n* elegancia *f*.

elegant *adj* elegante, delicado(a).

elegy *n* elegía *f*.

element *n* elemento *m*.

elephant *n* elefante *m*.

elevate *vt* elevar, alzar.

elevator *n* ascensor *m*.

eleven *num* once.

eleventh *adj* undécimo(a).

elf *n* duende *m*.

elicit *vt* obtener algo de.

eligible *adj* elegible.

eliminate *vt* eliminar, descartar.

elk *n* alce *m*.

elm *n* (botany) olmo *m*.

elocution *n* elocución *f*.

elongate *vt* alargar.

elope *vi* escapar, fugarse.

elopement *n* fuga *f*.

eloquence *n* elocuencia *f*.

else *pron* otro(a).

elsewhere *adv* en otra parte.

elude *vt* eludir, evitar.

embargo *n* prohibición *f*.

embark *vt* embarcar.

embarrass *vt* avergonzar.

embarrassment *n* vergüenza *f*, azoramiento *m*.

embassy *n* embajada *f*.

embed *vt* empotrar; clavar.

embellish *vt* embellecer, adornar.

embers *npl* rescoldo *m*.

embezzle *vt* desfalcar, malversar.

embitter *vt* amargar.

emblem *n* emblema *m*.

embrace *vt* abrazar.

embroider *vt* bordar.

embroil *vt* embrollar; enredar(se).

embryo *n* embrión *m*.

emerald *n* esmeralda *f*.

emerge *vi* salir, proceder.

emergency *n* emergencia *f*.

emery board *n* lima de uñas *f*.

emigrant *n* emigrante *m*.

emigrate *vi* emigrar.

eminent *adj* eminente.

emission *n* emisión *f*.

emit *vt* emitir.

emotion *n* emoción *f*.

emperor *n* emperador *m*.

emphasis *n* énfasis *m*.

emphasise *vt* enfatizar, recalcar.

empire *n* imperio *m*.

employ *vt* emplear, ocupar.

employee *n* empleado(a) *m(f)*.

employer *n* patrón(ona) *m(f)*; empresario(a).

empress *n* emperatriz *f*.

empty *adj* vacío(a).

emulate *vt* emular.

emulsion *n* emulsión *f*.

enable *vt* capacitar.

enact *vt* promulgar.

enamel *n* esmalte *m*.

enchant *vt* encantar.

enchanting *adj* encantador(a).

encircle *vt* cercar, rodear.

enclose *vt* cercar, adjuntar.

encore *adv* otra vez, de nuevo.

encounter *n* encuentro *m*.

encourage *vt* animar.

encouragement *n* estímulo *m*,

fomento *m*.

encroach *vt* invadir, adueñarse de.

encumber *vt* estar cargado de.

encyclopedia *n* enciclopedia *f*.

end *n* fin *m*, extremo *m*.

endanger *vt* peligrar.

endear *vt* encarecer.

endeavour *vi* esforzarse; intentar.

endemic *adj* endémico(a).

ending *n* final *m*.

endive *n* (botany) escarola *f*, endibia *f*.

endless *adj* infinito(a).

endorse *vt* endosar; aprobar.

endow *vt* dotar.

endure *vt* aguantar, soportar.

enemy *n* enemigo(a).

energetic *adj* enérgico(a).

energy *n* energía, fuerza *f*.

enforce *vt* hacer cumplir.

engine *n* motor *m*; locomotora *f*.

engineer *n* ingeniero(a) *m(f)*.

engrave *vt* grabar.

enhance *vt* aumentar.

enigma *n* enigma *m*.

enjoy *vt* gozar.

enjoyment *n* disfrute *m*; placer *m*.

enlarge *vt* engrandecer.

enlist *vt* alistar.

enliven *vt* animar.

enmity *n* enemistad *f*, odio *m*.

enormous *adj* enorme.

enough *adv* bastante; basta.

enrage *vt* enfurecer.

enrapture *vt* arrebatar.

enrich *vt* enriquecer.

enrol *vt* inscribirse, matricularse.

enrolment *n* inscripción *f*.

ensign *n* (military) bandera *f*.

enslave *vt* esclavizar.

ensue *vi* seguirse.

ensure *vt* asegurar.

entangle *vt* enmarañar.

enter *vt* entrar; admitir.

enterprise *n* empresa *f*.

entertain *vt* divertir; hospedar.

entertainer *n* artista *m* or *f*.

entertainment *n* entretenimiento *m*, pasatiempo *m*.

enthralling *adj* cautivador(a).

enthusiasm *n* entusiasmo *m*.

entice *vt* tentar; seducir.

entire *adj* entero(a), completo(a).

entitle *vt* conferir algún derecho.

entity *n* entidad *f*.

entrance *n* entrada *f*.

entreat *vt* rogar, suplicar.

entrepreneur *n* empresario(a) *m(f)*.

entrust *vt* confiar.

entry *n* entrada *f*.

entwine *vt* entrelazar.

envelop *n* envolver.

envelope *vt* sobre *m*.

enviable *adj* envidiable.

environment *n* medio ambiente *m*.

environs *npl* vecindad *f*.

envisage *vt* prever; concebir.

envoy *n* enviado(a) *m(f)*.

envy *n* envidia *f*.

ephemeral *adj* efímero(a).

epic *adj* épico(a).

epidemic *adj* epidémico(a).

epilogue *n* epílogo *m*.

Epiphany *n* Epifanía *f*.

episcopacy *n* episcopado *m*.

episcopal *adj* episcopal.

episcopalian *n* anglicano(a) *m(f)*.

episode *n* episodio *m*.

epistle *n* epístola *f*.

epithet *n* epíteto *m*.

epoch *n* época *f*.

equal *adj* igual.

equalise *vt* igualar.

equality *n* igualdad *f*, uniformidad *f*.

equally *adv* igualmente.

equate *vt* equiparar (con).

equation *n* ecuación *f*.

equator *n* ecuador *m*.

equatorial *adj* ecuatorial.
equestrian *adj* ecuestre.
equilibrium *n* equilibrio *m*.
equinox *n* equinoccio *m*.
equip *vt* equipar.
equipment *n* equipaje *m*.
equitable *adj* equitativo(a).
equity *n* equidad *f*.
equivalent *adj, n* equivalente *m*.
era *n* era *f*.
eradicate *vt* eradicar.
eradication *n* extirpación *f*.
erase *vt* borrar.
eraser *n* goma de borrar *f*.
erect *vt* erigir; establecer.
ermine *n* armiño *m*.
erode *vt* erosionar.
erotic *adj* erótico(a).
err *vi* vagar, errar.
errand *n* recado *m*; mandato *m*.
erratic *adj* errático(a).
erroneous *adj* erróneo(a).
error *n* error *m*.
erudite *adj* erudito(a).
erupt *vi* entrar en erupción;
  hacer erupción.
eruption *n* erupción *f*.
escalate *vi* extenderse.
escalator *n* escalera mecánica *f*.
escapade *n* fuga *f*; escapatoria *f*.
escape *vt* evitar; escapar.
escapism *n* evasión *m*.
escort *n* escolta *f*; * *vt* escoltar.
esoteric *adj* esotérico(a).
especial *adj* especial.
essay *n* ensayo *m*.
essence *n* esencia *f*.
essential *adj* esencial,
  imprescindible.
establish *vt* establecer.
establishment *n* establecimiento *m*.
estate *n* estado *m*.
esteem *vt* estimar, apreciar.
estimate *vt* estimar, apreciar.
estuary *n* estuario *m*.
etch *vt* grabar al aguafuerte.

eternal *adj* eterno(a).
eternity *n* eternidad *f*.
ether *n* éter *m*.
ethical *adj* ético(a).
ethics *npl* ética *f*.
ethnic *adj* étnico(a).
ethos *n* sistema de valores *m*.
etiquette *n* etiqueta *f*.
etymology *n* etimología *f*.
Eucharist *n* Eucaristía *f*.
eulogy *n* elogio.
eunuch *n* eunuco *m*.
euphemism *n* eufemismo *m*.
evacuate *vt* evacuar.
evacuation *n* evacuación *f*.
evade *vt* evadir.
evaluate *vt* evaluar.
evangelical *adj* evangélico(a).
evaporate *vt* evaporar.
evasion *n* evasión *f*.
evasive *adj* evasivo(a).
eve *n* víspera *f*.
even *adj* llano(a), igual; par,
  semejante; * *adv* aun; aun
  cuando, supuesto que; no
  obstante.
evening *n* tarde *f*.
event *n* acontecimiento,
  evento *m*.
eventuality *n* eventualidad *f*.
ever *adv* siempre.
every *adj* cada uno(a).
evict *vt* desahuciar.
eviction *n* desahucio *m*.
evidence *n* evidencia *f*.
evil *adj* malo(a), depravado(a).
evocative *adj* sugestivo(a).
evoke *vt* evocar.
evolution *n* evolución *f*.
evolve *vt, vi* evolucionar.
ewe *n* oveja *f*.
exacerbate *vt* exacerbar.
exact *adj* exacto(a).
exacting *adj* exigente.
exaggerate *vt* exagerar.
exaggeration *n* exageración *f*.
exalt *vt* exaltar.

exaltation *n* exaltación *f*.
examination *n* examen *m*.
examine *vt* examinar.
examiner *n* examinador(a) *m(f)*.
example *n* ejemplo *m*.
excavate *vt* excavar.
excavation *n* excavación *f*.
exceed *vt* exceder.
exceedingly *adv* extrema-
mente, en sumo grado.
excel *vt* sobresalir.
excellence *n* excelencia *f*.
excellent *adj* excelente.
except *vt* exceptuar, excluir;
* ~ing *prep* excepto, a
excepción de.
exception *n* excepción *f*,
exclusión *f*.
exceptional *adj* excepcional.
excerpt *n* extracto *m*.
excess *n* exceso *m*.
excessive *adj* excesivo(a).
exchange *vt* cambiar; trocar.
exchange rate *n* tipo de
cambio *m*.
excitability *n* excitabilidad *f*.
excitable *adj* excitable.
excite *vt* excitar; estimular.
excited *adj* emocionado(a).
excitement *n* estímulo *m*,
excitación *f*.
exclaim *vi* exclamar.
exclamation *n* exclamación *f*.
exclamation mark *n* signo de
admiración *m*.
exclamatory *adj* exclamatorio(a).
exclude *vt* excluir; exceptuar.
exclusion *n* exclusión *f*.
exclusive *adj* exclusivo(a).
excommunicate *vt* excomulgar.
excommunicatiom *n*
excomunión *f*.
excrement *n* excremento *m*.
excruciating *adj* atroz.
excursion *n* excursión *f*.
excusable *adj* perdonable.
excuse *vt* disculpar.

execute *vt* ejecutar.
execution *n* ejecución *f*.
executioner *n* ejecutor(a) *m(f)*.
executive *adj* ejecutivo(a).
executor *n* testamentario(a)
m(f), albacea *m* or *f*.
exemplary *adj* ejemplar.
exemplify *vt* ejemplificar.
exempt *adj* exento(a).
exemption *n* exención *f*.
exercise *n* ejercicio *m*.
exercise book *n* cuaderno *m*.
exertion *n* esfuerzo *m*.
exhale *vt* exhalar.
exhaust *n* escape *m*.
exhausted *adj* agotado(a).
exhaustion *n* agotamiento *m*.
exhaustive *adj* exhaustivo(a).
exhibit *vt* exhibir; mostrar.
exhibition *n* exposición *f*.
exhilarating *adj* estimulante.
exhort *vt* exhortar.
exhume *vt* exhumar.
exile *n* destierro *m*, exilio *m*.
exist *vi* existir.
existence *n* existencia *f*.
exit *n* salida *f*; * *vi* hacer mutis.
exit ramp *n* vía de acceso *f*.
exodus *n* éxodo *m*.
exonerate *vt* exonerar.
exhorbitant *adj* exorbitante.
exorcise *vt* exorcizar, conjurar.
exorcism *n* exorcismo *m*.
exotic *adj* exótico(a).
expand *vt* extender, dilatar.
expatriate *n* expatriado(a);
* *vt* expatriar.
expect *vt* esperar.
expectant mother *n* mujer
encinta *f*.
expediency *n* conveniencia *f*.
expedition *n* expedición *f*.
expel *vt* expeler, desterrar.
expend *vt* gastar, consumir.
expendable *adj* prescindible.
expenditure *n* gasto *m*,
desembolso *m*.

expense *n* gasto *m*; coste *m*.
experience *n* experiencia *f*;
  práctica *f*.
experienced *adj*
  experimentado(a).
experiment *n* experimento *m*.
expert *adj* experto(a).
expertise *n* pericia *f*.
expiration *n* expiración *f*,
  vencimiento *m*.
expire *vi* expirar.
explain *vt* explicar.
explanation *n* explicación *f*.
expletive *n* imprecación *f*.
explicit *adj* explícito(a).
explode *vt*, *vi* estallar, explotar.
exploit *vt* explotar.
exploitation *n* explotación *f*.
exploration *n* exploración *f*.
exploratory *adj* exploratorio(a).
explore *vt* explorar.
explorer *n* explorador *m*.
explosion *n* explosión *f*.
explosive *ad* explosivo(a);
  * *n* explosivo *m*.
exponent *n* (maths) exponente *m*.
export *vt* exportar.
expose *vi* exponer; mostrar.
exposed *adj* expuesto(a).
exposition *n* exposición *f*.
expostulate *vi* debatir; contender.
exposure *n* exposición *f*.
expound *vt* exponer.
express *vt* exprimir; representar.
expression *n* expresión *f*
expressionless *adj* sin
  expresión (clara).
expressway *n* autopista *f*.
expulsion *n* expulsión *f*.
expurgate *vt* expurgar.
exquisite *adj* exquisito(a).
extend *vt* extender.
extension *n* extensión *f*.
extensive *adj* extenso(a).
extent *n* extensión *f*.
extenuate *vt* extenuar.
exterior *adj*, *n* exterior *m*.

extermimate *vt* exterminar.
extermination *n*
  exterminación *f*.
external *adj* externo(a).
extinct *adj* extinto(a).
extinction *n* extinción *f*.
extinguish *vt* extinguir, apagar.
extinguisher *n* extintor *m*.
extol *vt* alabar, ensalzar.
extort *vt* sacar a la fuerza.
extortion *n* extorsión *f*.
extortionate *adj* excesivo(a).
extra *adv* extra.
extract *n* extracto *m*;
  * *vt* extraer.
extracurricular *adj* extraescolar.
extradition *n* (law) extradición *f*.
extramarital *adj*
  extramatrimonial.
extraneous *adj* extraño(a).
extraordinary *adj*
  extraordinario(a).
extravagance *n* extravagancia *f*.
extravagant *adj* extravagante.
extreme *adj* extremo(a).
extremist *adj*, *n* extremista *m*
  or *f*.
extremity *n* extremidad *f*.
extrovert *adj*, *n* extrovertido(a).
exuberance *n* exuberancia *f*.
exuberant *adj* exuberante.
exult *vt* exultar.
exultation *n* exultación *f*,
  regocijo *m*.
eye *n* ojo *m*; * *vt* ojear,
  contemplar, observar.
eyeball *n* globo ocular *m*.
eyebrow *n* ceja *f*.
eyelash *n* pestaña *f*.
eyelid *n* párpado *m*.
eyesight *n* vista *f*.
eyewitness *n* testigo ocular *m*
  or *f*.
eyrie *n* aguilera *f*.

F

fabric n tejido m, tela f.
fabricate vt fabricar.
fabulous adj fabuloso(a).
façade n fachada f.
face n cara f, faz f; superficie f.
facet n faceta f.
facetious adj chistoso(a).
facile adj superficial.
facilitate vt facilitar.
facility n facilidad f.
facsimile n facsímil(e) m.
fact n hecho m.
factin n facción f.
factor n factor m.
factory n fabrica f.
faculty n facultad f.
fad n moda f, manía f.
fade vi decaer, desvanecerse.
fail vt suspender; fallar.
failure n fracaso m, suspenso m.
faint vi desmayarse, debilitarse.
faint-hearted adj apocado(a).
fair adj hermoso(a); rubio(a);
  claro(a); sereno(a); favorable;
  recto(a); justo(a); franco(a);
  * adv limpio; * n feria f.
fairly adv justamente.
fairy n hada f.
faith n fe f, dogma de fe m.
faithfulness n fidelidad f.
fake n falsificación f.
falcon n halcón m.
fall vi caer(se); * n catarata f.
fallacy n falacia f.
fallible adj falible.
false adj falso(a).
falsify vt falsificar.
fame n fama f.
famed adj famoso(a).
familiar adj familiar.
family n familia f.
famine n hambre m, carestía f.
famous adj famoso(a).
fan n abanico m; aficionado(a).

fanatic adj, n fanático(a) m(f).
fanciful adj imaginativo(a).
fancy n fantasía, imaginación f.
fanfare n (music) fanfarria f.
fang n colmillo m.
fantastic adj fantástico(a).
fantasy n fantasía f.
far adv lejos.
faraway adj remoto(a).
farce n farsa f.
fare n precio m; tarifa f.
farm n finca f, granja f.
farmer n granjero(a) m(f).
fascinate vt fascinar, encantar.
fascism n fascismo.
fashion n moda f; forma f.
fashionable adj a la moda.
fashion show n desfile de
  modelos m.
fast vi ayunar; * adv rápidamente.
fasten vt abrochar.
fastidious adj fastidioso(a).
fat adj gordo(a).
fatal adj fatal.
fate n sino m, destino m.
fateful adj fatídico(a).
father n padre m.
father-in-law n suegro m.
fatherland n patria f.
fathom n braza (medida) f.
fatigue n fatiga f.
fatty adj graso(a).
fault n falta f, culpa f.
fauna n fauna f.
faux pas n desacierto m.
favour n favor.
favourite n favorito(a) m(f).
fawn n cervato m.
fax n fax m.
fear vi temer; * n miedo m.
fearful adj temeroso(a).
feasible adj factible.
feast n banquete.
feat n hecho m.
feather n pluma f.
feature n característica f,
  rasgo m.

February *n* febrero *m*.
federal *adj* federal.
federalist *n* federalista *m* or *f*.
federation *n* federación *f*.
fed-up *adj* harto(a).
fee *n* honorarios *mpl*, cuota *f*.
feeble *adj* débil.
feed *vt* nutrir; alimentar.
feedback *n* reacción *f*.
feel *vt* sentir; tocar.
feign *vt* fingir.
feline *adj* felino(a).
fellowship *n* compañerismo *m*; beca *f*.
felon *n* criminal *m* or *f*.
felony *n* crimen *m*.
felt *n* fieltro *m*.
female *n* mujer *f*, hembra *f*; * *adj* femenino(a).
feminine *adj* femenino(a).
feminist *n* feminista *m* or *f*.
fence *n* cerca *f*; defensa *f*.
fennel *n* (botany) hinojo *m*.
fern *n* (botany) helecho *m*.
ferocious *adj* feroz.
ferret *n* hurón *m*.
ferry *n* barca de pasaje *f*.
fertile *adj* fértil, fecundo(a).
fester *vi* supurar.
festival *n* fiesta *f*, festival *m*.
fetch *vt* ir a buscar.
fête *n* fiesta *f*.
feud *n* riña *f*, pelea *f*.
feudal *adj* feudal.
fever *n* fiebre *f*.
feverish *adj* febril.
few *adj* poco(a).
fewer *adj* menos.
fewest *adj* los, las menos.
fiancé *n* novio *m*.
fiancée *n* novia *f*.
fib *n* mentirijilla *f*.
fibre *n* fibra *f*, hebra *f*.
fickle *adj* inconstante.
fiction *n* ficción *f*.
fiddle *n* violín *m*; trampa *f*.
fidelity *n* fidelidad *f*.

field *n* campo *m*.
fieldmouse *n* ratón de campo *m*.
fierce *adj* fiero(a), feroz.
fierceness *n* fiereza *f*, ferocidad *f*.
fiery *adj* ardiente; apasionado(a).
fifteen *num* quince.
fifteenth *num* decimoquinto(a).
fifth *num* quinto(a).
fiftieth *adj*, *n* quincuagésimo(a).
fifty *num* cincuenta.
fig *n* higo *m*.
fight *vt*, *vi* reñir; batallar; combatir.
fig-leaf *n* hoja de higuera *f*.
figurative *adj* figurativo(a).
figure *n* figura *f*.
filament *n* filamento *m*.
fill *vt* llenar; hartar.
fillet *n* filete *m*.
filling station *n* estación de servicio *f*.
fillip *n* (*fig*) estímulo *m*.
filly *n* potra *f*.
film *n* película *f*, film *m*.
filter *n* filtro *m*.
filth(iness) *n* suciedad *f*, porquería *f*.
fin *n* aleta *f*.
final *adj* final, último(a).
finalise *vt* concluir.
finance *n* fondos *mpl*, finanzas *fpl*.
financier *n* financiero(a) *m(f)*.
find *vt* hallar, descubrir.
finesse *n* sutileza *f*.
finger *n* dedo *m*.
fingernail *n* uña *f*.
finish *vt* acabar, terminar, concluir.
finite *adj* finito(a).
fir *n* (botany) abeto *m*.
fire *n* fuego *m*; incendio *m*.
firearm *n* arma de fuego *f*.
firefly *n* luciérnaga *f*.
firewood *n* leña *f*.
fireworks *npl* fuegos artificiales *mpl*.
firm *adj* firme, estable.

firmament *n* firmamento *m*.

firmness *n* firmeza *f*.

first *adj* primero(a).

fiscal *adj* fiscal.

fish *n* pez *m*.

fishbone *n* espina *f*.

fisherman *n* pescador(a) *m(f)*.

fishy *adj* (*fig*) sospechoso(a).

fist *n* puño *m*.

fitness *n* forma física *f*.

five *adj*, *n* cinco.

fix *vt* fijar.

fixation *n* obsesión *f*.

fizzy *adj* gaseoso(a).

flabbergasted *adj* pasmado(a).

flabby *adj* blando(a).

flaccid *adj* flojo(a); fofo(a).

flag *n* bandera *f*.

flagpole *n* asta de bandera *f*.

flagrant *adj* flagrante;
  notorio(a).

flagship *n* buque insignia *m*.

flair *n* aptitud especial *f*.

flake *n* copo *m*.

flamboyant *adj* vistoso(a).

flame *n* llama *f*.

flamingo *n* flamenco *m*.

flammable *adj* inflamable.

flank *n* flanco *m*, costado *m*.

flannel *n* franela *f*.

flare *vi* lucir, brillar.

flash *n* flash *m*.

flask *n* frasco *m*.

flat *adj* llano(a), plano(a);
  * *n* apartamento *m*, piso *m*.

flatness *n* llanura *f*.

flatten *vt* allanar.

flatter *vt* adular.

flattery *n* adulación *f*.

flatulence *n* (medical)
  flatulencia *f*.

flaunt *vt* ostentar.

flavour *n* sabor *m*.

flavourless *adj* soso(a);
  insípido(a).

flaw *n* falta *f*, defecto *m*.

flawless *adj* sin defecto.

flax *n* lino *m*.

flea *n* pulga *f*.

fleck *n* mota *f*.

flee *vt* huir de.

fleece *n* vellón *m*.

fleet *n* flota *f*.

flesh *n* carne *f*, pulpa *f*.

flex *n* cable *m*; * *vt* tensar.

flexibility *n* flexibilidad *f*.

flexible *adj* flexible.

flight *n* vuelo *m*.

flight attendant *n* auxiliar de
  vuelo *m* or *f*.

flimsy *adj* débil; fútil.

flinch *vi* encogerse.

fling *vt* lanzar.

flint *n* pedernal *m*.

flip *vt* arrojar.

flippant *adj* poco serio(a).

flipper *n* aleta *f*.

flirt *vi* coquetear; * *n* coqueta *f*.

flirtation *n* coquetería *f*.

flock *n* manada *f*, rebaño *m*.

flog *vt* azotar.

flogging *n* tunda *f*, zurra *f*.

flood *n* diluvio *m*; inundación *f*;
  * *vt* inundar.

flooding *n* inundación *f*.

floodlight *n* foco *m*.

floor *n* suelo *m*, piso *m*.

floorboard *n* tabla *f*.

flop *n* fracaso *m*; * *vi* fracasar.

floppy *adj* flojo(a).

flora *n* flora *f*.

floral *adj* floral.

florid *adj* florido(a).

florist *n* florista *m* or *f*.

florist's (shop) *n* floristería *f*.

flotilla *n* (marine) flotilla *f*.

flounder *n* platija (pez de mar) *f*.

flour *n* harina *f*.

flourish *vi* florecer.

flout *vt* burlarse de.

flow *vi* fluir.

flower *n* flor *f*.

flowerbed *n* macizo (en un
  jardín) *m*.

flowerpot *n* tiesto de flores *m*, maceta *f*.

flowery *adj* florido(a).

fluctuate *vi* fluctuar.

fluctuation *n* fluctuación *f*.

fluency *n* fluidez *f*.

fluent *adj* fluido(a).

fluff *n* pelusa *f*.

fluid *adj, n* fluido(a) *m(f)*.

fluidity *n* fluidez *f*.

fluke *n* (*sl*) chiripa *f*.

fluoride *n* fluoruro *m*.

flurry *n* ráfaga *f*, agitación *f*.

flute *n* flauta travesera *f*.

flutter *vi* revolotear; estar en agitación.

flux *n* flujo *m*.

fly *vt* pilotar; transportar; * *vi* volar.

flying saucer *n* platillo volante *m*.

foal *n* potro *m*.

foam *n* espuma *f*.

foamy *adj* espumoso(a).

focus *n* foco *m*.

fodder *n* forraje *m* pienso *m*.

foe *n* adversario(a), enemigo(a).

foetus *n* feto *m*.

fog *n* niebla *f*.

foggy *adj* nublado(a).

fold *n* redil *m*; pliegue *m*.

folder *n* carpeta *f*.

folding *adj* plegable.

foliage *n* follaje *m*.

folio *n* folio *m*.

folk *n* gente *f*.

folklore *n* folklore *m*.

folk song *n* canción folklórica *f*.

follow *vt* seguir; acompañar.

follower *n* seguidor(a).

following *adj* siguiente.

folly *n* extravagancia *f*.

foment *vt* fomentar.

fond *adj* cariñoso(a).

fondle *vt* acariciar.

fondness *n* gusto *m*; cariño *m*.

font *n* pila bautismal *f*.

food *n* comida *f*.

food mixer *n* batidora *f*.

food poisoning *n* intoxicación alimentaria *m*.

fool *n* loco(a), tonto(a) *m(f)*.

foolish *adj* bobo(a); tonto(a).

foolscap *n* papel tamaño folio *m*.

foot *n* pie *m*; pata *f*.

footage *n* imágenes *fpl*.

football *n* balón *m*; fútbol *m*.

footballer *n* futbolista *m or f*.

footnote *n* nota de pie de página *f*.

footpath *n* senda *f*.

footprint *n* huella *f*.

for *prep* por, a causa de; para.

forbid *vt* prohibir.

force *n* fuerza *f*, poder *m*, vigor *m*.

forced *adj* forzado(a).

forceful *adj* enérgico(a).

forceps *n* fórceps *m*.

ford *n* vado *m*; * *vt* vadear.

fore *n*: — to the ~ en evidencia.

forearm *n* antebrazo *m*.

foreboding *n* presentimiento *m*.

forecast *vt* pronosticar.

forecourt *n* patio *m*.

forefathers *npl* antepasados *mpl*.

forefinger *n* (dedo) índice *m*.

forefront *n*: — in the ~ of en la vanguardia de.

forego *vt* ceder.

foreground *n* delantera *f*.

forehead *n* frente *f*.

foreign *adj* extranjero(a); extraño(a).

foreigner *n* extranjero(a) *m(f)*, forastero(a) *m(f)*.

foreign exchange *n* divisas *fpl*.

foreleg *n* pata delantera *f*.

foreman *n* capataz *m*.

foremost *adj* principal.

forensic *adj* forense.

forerunner *n* precursor(a) *m(f)*.

foresee *vt* prever.

foresight *n* previsión *f*.

forest *n* bosque *m*; selva *f*.

forester *n* guardabosque *m or f*.

forestry *n* silvicultura *f*.

foretaste muestra *f*.
foretell *vt* predecir, profetizar.
forethought *n* providencia *f*.
forever *adv* para siempre.
foreword *n* prefacio *m*.
forfeit *n* prenda *f*; confiscación *f*.
forge *n* fragua *f*; fabrica de metales *f*.
forger *n* falsificador(a) *m*(*f*).
forgery *n* falsificación *f*.
forget *vt* olvidar.
forgetful *adj* olvidadizo(a).
forget-me-not *n* (botany) nomeolvides *m*.
forgive *vt* perdonar.
forgiveness *n* perdón *m*.
fork *n* tenedor *m*.
form *n* forma *f*, modelo *m*; modo *m*.
formal *adj* formal.
formality *n* formalidad *f*.
format *n* formato *m*.
formation *n* formación *f*.
formative *adj* formativo(a).
former *adj* precedente; anterior.
formidable *adj* formidable.
formula *n* fórmula *f*.
formulate *vt* formular.
forsake *vt* dejar, abandonar.
fort *n* fuerte *m*, castillo *m*.
forthright *adj* franco(a).
forthwith *adj* inmediatamente.
fortieth, *n* cuadragésimo(a) *m*(*f*).
fortification *n* fortificación *f*.
fortify *vt* fortificar.
fortitude *n* fortaleza *f*.
fortnight *n* quincena *f*.
fortress *n* (military) fortaleza *f*.
fortuitous *adj* fortuito(a).
fortunate *adj* afortunado(a).
fortune *n* fortuna *f*, suerte *f*.
fortune-teller *n* adivino(a) *m*(*f*).
forty *num* cuarenta.
forum *n* foro *m*.
forward *adj* avanzado(a); delantero(a).
forwardness *n* precocidad *f*, audacia *f*.

fossil *adj*, *n* fósil *m*.
foster *vt* criar.
foul *adj* sucio(a); puerco(a); impuro(a).
found *vt* fundar, establecer.
foundation *n* fundación *f*.
founder *n* fundador(a) *m* or *f*.
foundry *n* fundición *f*.
fount, fountain *n* fuente *f*.
fountain pen *n* pluma estilográfica *f*.
fountainhead *n* origen *m*, fuente *f*.
four *num* cuatro.
fourfold *adj* cuádruple.
fourteen *num* catorce.
fourteenth *num* decimocuarto(a).
fourth *num* cuarto(a); * ~ly *adv* en cuarto lugar.
fowl *n* ave (de corral) *f*.
fox *n* zorro(a) *m*(*f*).
foyer *n* vestíbulo *m*.
fracas *n* riña *f*.
fraction *n* fracción *f*.
fracture *n* fractura *f*.
fragile *adj* frágil; débil.
fragility *n* fragilidad *f*.
fragment *n* fragmento *m*.
fragrance *n* fragancia *f*.
fragrant *adj* fragante, oloroso(a).
frail *adj* frágil, débil.
frailty *n* fragilidad *f*, debilidad *f*.
frame *n* armazón *m*; marco *m*, cerco *m*.
franchise *n* sufragio *m*.
frank *adj* franco(a), liberal.
frankly *adv* francamente.
frantic *adj* frenético(a).
fraternity *n* fraternidad *f*.
fraternise *vi* hermanarse.
fraud *n* fraude *m*.
fraudulent *adj* fraudulento(a).
fraught *adj* cargado(a), lleno(a).
freak *n* fantasía *f*; fenómeno *m*.
freckle *n* peca *f*.
freckled *adj* pecoso(a).
free *adj* libre; liberal; suelto(a).

freedom *n* libertad *f*.
freehold *n* propiedad absoluta *f*.
free-for-all *n* riña general *f*.
freelance *adj, adv* por cuenta propia.
freemason *n* francmasón *m*.
freemasonry *n* francmasonería *f*.
freeway *n* autopista *f*.
freewheel *vi* ir en punto muerto.
freeze *vi* helar(se).
freezer *n* congelador *m*.
freight *n* carga *f*; flete *m*.
freighter *n* fletador *m*.
frenzy *n* frenesí *m*; locura *f*.
frequency *n* frecuencia *f*.
fresco *n* fresco *m*.
fresh *adj* fresco(a); nuevo(a).
freshly *adv* nuevamente.
freshman *n* novicio *m*.
freshwater *adj* de agua dulce.
fret *vi* agitarse.
friar *n* fraile *m*.
friction *n* fricción *f*.
Friday *n* viernes *m*:
— Good ~ Viernes Santo *m*.
friend *n* amigo(a) *m(f)*.
friendship *n* amistad *f*.
frieze *n* friso *m*.
frigate *n* (marine) fragata *f*.
fright *n* espanto *m*, terror *m*.
frighten *vt* espantar; aterrorizar.
frigid *adj* frío(a), frígido(a).
fringe *n* franja *f*.
frisk *vt* cachear.
frivolity *n* frivolidad *f*.
frock *n* vestido *m*.
frog *n* rana *f*.
frolic *vi* juguetear.
from *prep* de; después; desde.
front *n* parte delantera *f*, fachada *f*; paseo marítimo *m*; frente *m*.
frontal *adj* de frente.
frontier *n* frontera *f*.
frost *n* helada *f*, hielo *m*.
froth *n* espuma (de algún líquido) *f*.

frown *vt* mirar con ceño.
frozen *adj* helado(a).
fruit *n* fruta *f*, fruto *m*.
fruiterer *n* frutero *m*.
fruiterer's (shop) *n* frutería *f*.
fruit juice *n* zumo de fruta *m*.
fruitless *adj* estéril; inútil.
fruit salad *n* ensalada de frutas *f*, macedonia *f*.
fruit tree *n* árbol frutal *m*.
frustrate *vt* frustrar; anular.
fry *vt* freír.
frying pan *n* sartén *f*.
fuchsia *n* (botany) fucsia *f*.
fuel *n* combustible *m*.
fuel tank *n* depósito *m*.
fugitive *adj, n* fugitivo *m*.
fulfil *vt* cumplir; realizar.
fulfilment *n* cumplimiento *m*.
full *adj* lleno(a).
full moon *n* plenilunio *m*; luna llena *f*.
fulsome *adj* exagerado(a).
fumble *vi* manejar torpemente.
fume *vi* humear; encolerizarse.
fun *n* diversión *f*, alegría *f*.
function *n* función *f*.
functional *adj* funcional.
fund *n* fondo *m*.
fundamental *adj* fundamental.
funeral *n* funerales *mpl*.
fungus *n* hongo *m*; seta *f*.
funnel *n* embudo *m*.
funny *adj* divertido(a); curioso(a).
fur *n* piel *f*.
furious *adj* furioso(a).
furnace *n* horno *m*; hornaza *f*.
furnish *vt* amueblar.
furnishings *npl* muebles *mpl*.
furniture *n* muebles *mpl*.
furrow *n* surco *m*.
furry *adj* peludo(a); de peluche.
furthermore *adv* además.
fury *n* furor *m*; furia *f*, ira *f*.
fuse *vt, vi* fundir; derretirse.
fuse box *n* caja de fusibles *f*.
fusion *n* fusión *f*.

fuss *n* lío *m*; alboroto *m*.
fussy *adj* jactancioso(a).
futile *adj* fútil, frívolo(a).
futility *n* futilidad *f*.
future *adj* futuro(a).
fuzzy *adj* borroso(a); muy
rizado(a).

G

gable *n* aguilón *m*.
gag *n* mordaza *f*, chiste *m*.
gaiety *n* alegría *f*.
gain *n* ganancia *f*; * *vt* ganar.
gala *n* gala *f*.
galaxy *n* galaxia *f*.
gale *n* vendaval *m*.
gallant *adj* galante.
gallery *n* galería *f*.
gallom *n* galón *m* (medida).
gallop *n* galope *m*.
gallows *n* horca *f*.
galore *adv* en abundancia.
gambit *n* estrategia *f*, táctica *f*.
gamble *vi* jugar; apostar.
gambler *n* jugador(a) *m(f)*.
game *n* juego *m*; pasatiempo *m*.
gamekeeper *n* guardabosques
m or f.
gaming *n* juego *m*.
gammon *n* jamón, tocino
ahumado *m*.
gander *n* ganso *m*.
gang *n* pandilla *f*, banda *f*.
gamgrene *n* gangrena *f*.
gangster *n* gangster *m*.
gangway *n* pasarela *f*.
gap *n* hueco *m*; claro *m*;
intervalo *m*.
garage *n* garaje *m*.
garbage *n* basura *f*.
garden *n* jardín *m*.
gargoyle *n* gárgola *f*.
garish *adj* chillón(ona).
garland *n* guirnalda *f*.
garlic *n* ajo *m*.

garment *n* prenda *f*.
garnish *vt* aderezar, adornar.
garter *n* liga *f*.
gas *n* gas *m*; gasolina *f*.
gash *n* cuchillada *f*.
gasoline *n* gasolina *f*.
gasp *vi* jadear.
gastric *adj* gástrico(a).
gastronomic *adj*
gastronómico(a).
gate *n* puerta *f*.
gateway *n* puerta *f*.
gather *vt* recoger.
gathering *n* reunión *f*.
gaudy *adj* chillón(ona).
gauge *n* calibre *m*.
gauze *n* gasa *f*.
gay *adj* alegre; vivo(a); gay.
gazelle *n* gacela *f*.
gazette *n* gaceta *f*.
gazetteer *n* índice geográfico *m*.
gear *n* equipo *m*; engranaje *m*;
(of car) marcha *f*.
gearbox *n* caja de cambios *f*.
gel *n* gel *m*.
gelatine *n* gelatina *f*, jalea *f*.
gelignite *n* gelignita *f*.
gem *n* gema *f*, piedra preciosa *f*.
Gemini *n* Géminis *m*.
gender *n* género *m*.
gene *n* gen *m*.
genealogy *n* genealogía *f*.
general *adj* general, común.
generalise *vt* generalizar.
generation *n* generación *f*.
generic *adj* genérico(a).
generosity *n* generosidad *f*.
generous *adj* generoso(a).
genetics *npl* genética *f*.
genial *adj* genial.
genitals *npl* genitales *mpl*.
genius *n* genio *m*.
genteel *adj* refinado(a); elegante.
gentile *n* gentil.
gentle *adj* suave.
gentleman *n* caballero *m*.
gentry *n* alta burguesía *f*.

gents *n* aseos (de caballeros) *mpl.*

genuine *adj* genuino(a).

genus *n* género *m.*

geographer *n* geógrafo(a) *m(f).*

geography *n* geografía *f.*

geology *n* geología *f.*

geometry *n* geometría *f.*

geranium *n* (botany) geranio *m.*

germ *n* (biology) germen *m.*

germinate *vi* brotar, germinar.

gesticulate *vi* gesticular.

gesture *n* gesto *m.*

get *vt* ganar; conseguir, obtener.

geyser *n* géiser *m.*

ghastly *adj* espantoso(a).

gherkin *n* pepinillo *m.*

ghost *n* fantasma *m.*

ghostly *adj* fantasmal.

giant *n* gigante *m.*

giddy *adj* vertiginoso(a).

gift *n* regalo *m.*

giggle *vi* reírse tontamente.

gin *n* ginebra *f.*

ginger *n* jengibre *m.*

ginger-haired *adj* pelirrojo(a).

giraffe *n* jirafa *f.*

girl *n* muchacha *f,* chica *f.*

girlfriend *n* amiga *f,* novia *f.*

giro *n* giro postal *m.*

girth *n* circunferencia *f.*

give *vi, vi* dar.

glacier *n* glaciar *m.*

glad *adj* alegre, contento(a).

gladiator *n* gladiador(a) *m(f).*

glamour *n* encanto *m.*

gland *n* glándula *f.*

glare *n* deslumbramiento *m.*

glass *n* vidrio *m.*

glean *vt* recoger.

glee *n* alegría *f,* gozo *m.*

glib *adj* con poca sinceridad, elocuente pero falso.

glide *vi* resbalar, deslizarse.

glimmer *n* vislumbre *f.*

glimpse *n* luz tenue *f.*

glint *n* destello *m;* * *vi* centellear.

glisten, glitter *vi* relucir, brillar.

gloat *vi* ojear con admiración.

global *adj* mundial, global.

globe *n* globo *m;* esfera *f.*

gloom, gloominess *n* oscuridad *f;* melancolía.

glorify *vt* glorificar, celebrar.

glory *n* gloria *f,* fama *f,* celebridad *f.*

gloss *n* brillo *m,* lustre *m.*

glossary *n* glosario *m.*

glove *n* guante *m.*

glow *vi* brillar.

glower *vi* mirar con ceño.

glue *n* cola *f;* pegamento *m;* * *vt* pegar.

glum *adj* abatido(a), triste.

glut *n* superabundancia *f.*

gluttony *n* glotonería *f.*

glycerine *n* glicerina *f.*

gnarled *adj* nudoso(a).

gnash *vt, vi* rechinar; crujir los dientes.

gnat *n* mosquito *m.*

gnaw *vt* roer.

gnome *n* gnomo *m.*

go *vi* ir, irse.

goal *n* meta *f,* fin *m.*

goalkeeper *n* portero *m.*

gobble *vt* engullir, tragar.

go-between *n* mediador(a); intermediario(a).

goblet *n* copa *f.*

goblin *n* duende *m.*

God *n* Dios *m.*

godchild *n* ahijado(a) *m(f).*

goddaughter *n* ahijada *f.*

goddess *n* diosa *f.*

godfather *n* padrino *m.*

godmother *n* madrina *f.*

godsend *n* don del cielo *m.*

godson *n* ahijado *m.*

goggle-eyed *adj* bizco(a).

goggles *npl* anteojos *mpl,* gafas *fpl.*

gold *n* oro *m.*

goldfish *n* pez de colores *m.*

gold-plated *adj* chapado(a) en oro.

golf *n* golf *m*.

golf course *n* campo de golf *m*.

golfer *n* golfista *m* or *f*.

gondolier *n* gondolero(a) *m(f)*.

gone *adj* ido(a); perdido(a);
pasado(a); gastado(a);
muerto(a).

gong *n* gong *m*.

good *adj* bueno(a).

goodbye! *excl* ¡adiós!

Good Friday *n* Viernes Santo *m*.

good-looking *adj* guapo(a).

goodness *n* bondad *f*.

goodwill *n* benevolencia *f*,
bondad *f*.

goose *n* ganso *m*; oca *f*.

gooseberry *n* grosella espinosa *f*.

gorge *n* barranco *m*.

gorgeous *adj* maravilloso(a).

gorilla *n* gorila *m*.

gorse *n* (botany) aulaga *f*, tojo *m*.

gory *adj* sangriento(a).

goshawk *n* azor *m*.

gospel *n* evangelio *m*.

gossamer *n* gasa *f*.

gossip *n* charla *f*, cotilleo *m*.

gothic *adj* gótico(a).

gout *n* gota *f* (enfermedad).

govern *vt* gobernar, dirigir.

governess *n* gobernadora *f*.

government *n* gobierno *m*.

governor *n* gobernador *m*.

gown *n* toga *f*.

grab *vt* agarrar.

grace *n* gracia *f*.

graceful *adj* gracioso(a).

gracious *adj* amable.

gradation *n* gradación *f*.

grade *n* grado *m*.

gradient *n* (rail) pendiente.

gradual *adj* gradual.

graduate *vi* graduarse.

graduation *n* graduación *f*.

graffiti *n* pintadas *fpl*.

graft *n* injerto *m*.

grain *n* grano *m*.

gram *n* gramo *m* (peso).

grammar *n* gramática *f*.

granary *n* granero *m*.

grand *adj* grande, ilustre.

grandchild *n* nieto(a) *m(f)*.

grandad *n* abuelito *m*.

gramddaughter *n* nieta *f*.

grandeur *n* grandeza *f*.

grandfather *n* abuelo *m*.

gramdiose *adj* grandioso(a).

grandma *n* abuelita *f*.

grandmother *n* abuela *f*.

grandparents *npl* abuelos *mpl*.

grand piano *n* piano de cola *m*.

grandson *n* nieto *m*.

grandstand *n* tribuna *f*.

granite *n* granito *m*.

granny *n* abuelita *f*.

grant *vt* conceder.

granule *n* gránulo *m*.

grape *n* uva *f*: — bunch of ~s
racimo de uvas *m*.

grapefruit *n* pomelo *m*, toronja *f*.

graph *n* gráfica *f*.

graphics *n* artes gráficas *fpl*;
gráficos *mpl*.

grasp *vt* empuñar.

grass *n* hierba *f*.

grasshopper *n* saltamontes *mpl*.

grassland *n* pampa *f*, pradera *f*.

grass snake *n* culebra *f*.

gratify *vt* contentar; gratificar.

gratifying *adj* grato(a).

grating *n* rejilla *f*.

gratis *adv* gratis.

gratitude *n* gratitud *f*.

grave *n* sepultura *f*.

gravel *n* grava *f*.

gravestone *n* lápida *f*.

graveyard *n* cementerio *m*.

gravity *n* gravedad *f*.

gravy *n* jugo de carne *f*, salsa *f*.

graze *vt* pacer.

grease *n* grasa *f*; * *vt* untar.

greasy *adj* grasiento(a).

great *adj* gran, grande.

greatcoat *n* sobretodo *m*.

greatness *n* grandeza *f*.

greedily *adv* vorazmente, con avidez.

greediness, greed *n* gula *f*, codicia *f*.

Greek *n* griego (idioma) *m*.

green *adj* verde.

greengrocer *n* verdulero(a) *m(f)*.

greenhouse *n* invernadero *m*.

greet *vt* saludar, congratular.

greeting *n* saludo *m*.

greeting(s) card *n* tarjeta de felicitación *f*.

grenade *n* (military) granada *f*.

grenadier *n* granadero *m*.

grey *adj* gris.

greyhound *n* galgo *m*.

greyish *adj* pardusco(a).

grid *n* reja *f*, red *f*.

grief *n* dolor *m*.

grieve *vt* afligirse, acongojarse.

grievous *adj* doloroso(a), grave.

griffin *n* grifo *m*.

grill *n* parrilla *f*.

grim *adj* lúgubre.

grimace *n* mueca *f*.

grime *n* mugre *f*.

grin *n* sonrisa abierta *f*.

grind *vt* moler.

grinder *n* molinillo *m*.

grip *n* asimiento (de manos) *m*, apretón *m*.

grisly *adj* horroroso(a).

gristle *n* cartílago *m*.

grit *n* gravilla *f*; valor *m*.

groam *vi* gemir, suspirar.

grocer *n* tendero(a) *m(f)*.

groceries *npl* comestibles *mpl*.

groin *n* ingle *f*.

groom *n* mozo de cuadra *m*.

groove *n* ranura *f*.

gross *adj* grueso(a).

grotesque *adj* grotesco(a).

grotto *n* gruta *f*.

ground *n* tierra *f*, suelom.

ground floor *n* planta baja *f*.

group *n* grupo *m*.

grouse *n* urogallo *m*; * *vi* quejarse.

grove *n* arboleda *f*.

grovel *vi* arrastrarse.

grow *vt* cultivar; * *vi* crecer, aumentarse.

growl *vi* regañar, gruñir.

grown-up *n* adulto(a) *m(f)*.

grub *n* gusano *m*.

grubby *adj* sucio(a).

grudge *n* rencor *m*, odio *m*; envidia *f*; * *vt*, *vi* envidiar.

gruesome *adj* horrible.

gruff *adj* brusco(a).

grumble *vi* gruñir; murmurar.

grunt *n* gruñido *m*; * *vi* gruñir.

G-string *n* tanga *f*.

guarantee *n* garantía *f*.

guard *n* guardia *f*.

guardianship *n* tutela *f*.

guerrilla *n* guerrillero(a) *m(f)*.

guess *vt*, *vi* conjeturar; adivinar; suponer.

guest *n* huésped *m* or *f*.

guffaw *n* carcajada *f*.

guide *vt* guiar, dirigir; * *n* guía *m*.

guidebook *n* guía *f*.

guild *n* gremio *m*.

guile *n* astucia *f*.

guilt *n* culpabilidad *f*.

guilty *adj* culpable.

guinea pig *n* cobaya *f*.

guise *n* manera *f*.

guitar *n* guitarra *f*.

gulf *n* golfo *m*.

gull *n* gaviota *f*.

gullet *n* esófago *m*.

gullible *adj* crédulo(a).

gully *n* barranco *m*.

gulp *n* trago *m*.

gum *n* goma *f*.

gum tree *n* árbol gomero *m*.

gun *n* pistola *f*, escopeta *f*.

gunboat *n* cañonero *m*.

gunpowder *n* pólvora *f*.

gumshot *n* escopetazo *m*.

gurgle *vi* gorgotear.

guru *n* gurú *m*.

gush *vi* chorrear.

gusset *n* escudete *m*.
gut *n* intestino *m*.
gutter *n* canalón *m*; arroyo *m*.
guy *n* tío *m*; tipo *m*.
gym(nasium) *n* gimnasio *m*.
gymnast *n* gimnasta *m* or *f*.
gynaecologist *n* ginecólogo(a) *m(f)*.
gypsy *n* gitano(a) *m(f)*.
gyrate *vi* girar.

H

haberdasher *n* camisero(a).
habit *n* costumbre *f*.
habitable *adj* habitable.
habitat *n* hábitat *m*.
habitual *adj* habitual.
haddock *n* especie de merluza *f*.
haemorrhage *n* hemorragia *f*.
haemorrhoids *npl* hemorroides *mpl*, almorranas *fpl*.
hag *n* bruja *f*.
hail *n* granizo *m*.
hair *n* pelo *m*; cabello *m*.
hairbrush *n* cepillo *m*.
haircut *n* corte de pelo *m*.
hairdresser *n* peluquero(a) *m(f)*.
hairdryer *n* secador de pelo *m*.
hairspray *n* laca *f*.
hairstyle *n* peinado *m*.
half *n* mitad *f*.
half-caste *adj* mestizo(a).
hall *n* vestíbulo *m*.
hallow *vt* consagrar, santificar.
hallucination *n* alucinación *f*.
halo *n* aureola *f*.
halt alto *m*, parada *f*; * *vi* parar.
halve *vt* partir por mitad.
ham *n* jamón *m*.
hamburger *n* hamburguesa *f*.
hamlet *n* aldea *f*.
hammer *n* martillo *m*.
hammock *n* hamaca *f*.
hamper *vt* estorbar; * *n* cesto *f*.
hand *n* mano *f*.

handbag *n* cartera *f*.
handful *n* puñado *m*.
handicap *n* desventaja *f*.
handicraft *n* artesanía *f*.
handkerchief *n* pañuelo *m*.
handle *n* mango *m*, puño *m*; asa *f*; pomo *m*.
handshake *n* apretón de manos *m*.
handsome *adj* guapo(a).
handwriting *n* letra *f*.
handy *adj* práctico(a).
hang *vt* colgar.
hanger *n* percha *f*.
hangover *n* resaca *f*.
happen *vi* pasar; acontecer.
happiness *n* felicidad *f*.
happy *adj* feliz.
harass *vt* acosar, hostigar.
harbinger *n* precursor(a) *m(f)*.
harbour *n* puerto *m*.
hard *adj* duro(a), firme.
harden *vt*, (*vi*) endurecer(se).
hardiness *n* robustez *f*.
hardly *adv* apenas.
hardship *n* penas *fpl*.
hard-up *adj* sin plata, sin un duro.
hardy *adj* fuerte.
hare *n* liebre *f*.
harelip *n* labio leporino *m*.
haricot *n* alubia *f*.
harlequin *n* arlequín *m*.
harm *n* mal, daño *m*.
harmful *adj* perjudicial.
harmless *adj* inocuo(a).
harmonic *adj* armónico(a).
harmonious *adj* armonioso(a).
harmonise *vt* armonizar.
harmony *n* armonía *f*.
harp *n* arpa *f*.
harpoon *n* arpón *m*.
harsh *adj* duro(a); austero(a).
harvest *n* cosecha *f*.
harvester *n* cosechadora *f*.
hash *n* hachís *m*.
hassock *n* cojín de paja *m*.
haste *n* apuro *m*.
hasten *vt* acelerar.

hasty *adj* apresurado(a).

hat *n* sombrero *m*.

hatch *vt* incubar; tramar.

hatchet *n* hacha *f*.

hatchway *n* (marine) escotilla *f*.

hate *n* odio *m*.

hateful *adj* odioso(a).

hatred *n* odio, aborrecimiento *m*.

haughty *adj* altanero(a), orgulloso(a).

haul *vt* tirar; * *n* botín *m*.

hauler *n* transportista *m* or *f*.

haunch *n* anca *f*.

haunt *vt* frecuentar, rondar.

have *vt* haber; tener, poseer.

haven *n* asilo *m*, refugio *m*.

havoc *n* estrago *m*.

hawk *n* halcón *m*.

hawthorn *n* (botany) espino blanco *m*.

hay *n* (botany) heno *m*.

hazard *n* riesgo *m*.

haze *n* neblina *f*.

hazel *n* (botany) avellano *m*.

hazelnut *n* avellana *f*.

hazy *adj* brumoso(a).

he *pron* él.

head *n* cabeza *f*.

headache *n* dolor de cabeza *m*.

headlight *n* faro *m*.

headline *n* titular *m*.

headmaster *n* director(a) *m(f)*.

headphones *npl* auriculares *mpl*.

heal *vt, vi* curar, cicatrizar.

health *n* salud *f*.

healthy *adj* sano(a).

heap *n* montón *m*.

hear *vt* oír; escuchar.

hearing *n* oído *m*.

hearing aid *n* audífono *m*.

hearse *n* coche fúnebre *m*.

heart *n* corazón *m*.

heart attack *n* infarto *m*.

heartburn *n* acedía *f*.

hearth *n* hogar *m*.

heartily *adv* sinceramente.

heartless *adj* cruel.

hearty *adj* cordial.

heat *n* calor *m*.

heater *n* calentador *m*.

heathen *n* pagano(a) *m(f)*.

heating *n* calefacción *f*.

heatwave *n* ola de calor *f*.

heave *n* cielo *m*.

heavily *adv* pesadamente.

heavy *adj* pesado(a).

Hebrew *n* hebreo *m*.

heckle *vt* interrumpir.

hectic *adj* agitado(a).

hedge *n* seto *m*.

hedgehog *n* erizo *m*.

heed *vt* hacer caso de.

heedless *adj* descuidado(a).

heel *n* talón *m*.

hefty *adj* grande.

heifer *n* ternera *f*.

height *n* altura *f*, altitud *f*.

heinous *adj* atroz.

heir *n* heredero(a) *m(f)*.

heirloom *n* reliquia de familia *f*.

helicopter *n* helicóptero *m*.

hell *n* infierno *m*.

helm *n* (marine) timón *m*.

helmet *n* casco *m*.

help *vt, vi* ayudar, socorrer.

helper *n* ayudante *m*.

helpful *adj* útil.

helping *n* ración *f*.

helpless *adj* indefenso(a).

hem *n* dobladillo *m*.

he-man *n* macho *m*.

hemisphere *n* hemisferio *m*.

hemp *n* cáñamo *m*.

hen *n* gallina *f*.

henchman *n* secuaz *m*.

henceforth, henceforward *adv* de aquí en adelante.

hepatitis *n* hepatitis *f*.

her *pron* su; ella; de ella; a ella.

herald *n* precursor(a) *m(f)*.

heraldry *n* heráldica *f*.

herb *n* hierba *f*.

herbaceous *adj* herbáceo(a).

herbalist *n* herbolario *m*.

herbivorous *adj* herbívoro(a).
herd *n* rebaño *m*.
here *adv* aquí, acá.
hereabout(s) *adv* aquí alrededor.
hereafter *adv* en el futuro.
hereby *adv* por esto.
hereditary *adj* hereditario(a).
heresy *n* herejía *f*.
heretic *n* hereje *m* or *f*.
heritage *n* patrimonio *m*.
hermetic *adj* hermético(a).
hermit *n* ermitaño(a).
hermitage *n* ermita *f*.
hernia *n* hernia *f*.
hero *n* héroe *m*.
heroic *adj* heroico(a).
heroin *n* heroína *f* (droga).
heroine *n* heroína *f*.
heroism *n* heroísmo *m*.
heron *n* garza *f*.
herring *n* arenque *m*.
herself *pron* ella misma.
hesitant *adj* indeciso(a).
hesitate *vt* dudar; tardar.
heterosexual *adj*, *n*
  heterosexual *m*.
hew *vt* tajar; cortar.
heyday *n* apogeo *m*.
hi *excl* ¡hola!
hiatus *n* hiato *m*.
hibernate *vi* invernar.
hiccup *n* hipo *m*.
hickory *n* nogal americano *m*.
hide *vt* esconder.
hideaway *n* escondite *m*.
hideous *adj* horrible.
hierarchy *n* jerarquía *f*.
hieroglyphic *adj* jeroglífico *m*.
hi-fi *n* estéreo, hi-fi *m*.
high *adj* alto(a); elevado(a).
highlight *n* punto culminante *m*.
highway *n* carretera *f*.
hike *vi* ir de excursión.
hijack *vt* secuestrar.
hilarious *adj* alegre.
hill, hillock *n* colina *f*.
him *pron* le, lo, el.

himself *pron* él mismo; sí mismo.
hinder *vt* impedir.
hindrance *n* impedimento *m*,
  obstáculo *m*.
hinge *n* bisagra *f*.
hip *n* cadera *f*.
hippopotamus *n* hipopótamo *m*.
hire *vt* alquilar.
his *pron* su, suyo, de él.
Hispanic *adj* hispano(a);
  hispánico(a).
hiss *vt*, *vi* sisear, silbar.
historian *n* historiador(a) *m*(*f*).
history *n* historia *f*.
hit *n* golpe *m*, éxito *m*;
  * *vt* golpear.
hitch *vt* atar.
hitch-hike *vi* hacer autostop.
hive *n* colmena.
hoax *n* trampa *f*.
hobble *vi* cojear.
hobby *n* pasatiempo *m*.
hockey *n* hockey *m*.
hodge-podge *n* mezcolanza *f*.
hoe *n* azadón *m*.
hog *n* cerdo *m*, puerco *m*.
hoist *n* grúa *f*; * *vt* alzar.
hold *vt* tener; detener; contener.
hole *n* agujero *m*.
holiday *n* día de fiesta *m*; ~s *pl*
  vacaciones *fpl*.
hollow *adj* hueco(a).
holly *n* (botany) acebo *m*.
hollyhock *n* malva loca *f*.
holocaust *n* holocausto *m*.
holster *n* pistolera *f*.
holy *adj* santo(a).
holy week *n* semana santa *f*.
homage *n* homenaje *m*.
home *n* casa *f*, hogar *m*.
homeless *adv* sin casa.
home address *n* domicilio *m*.
homely *adj* casero(a).
homeopathist *n* homeopatista
  m or *f*.
homeopathy *n* homeopatía *f*.
homesick *adj* nostálgico(a).

homework *n* deberes *mpl*.
homicide *n* homicidio *m*; homicida *m*.
homosexual *adj, n* homosexual *m*.
honest *adj* honrado(a).
honesty *n* honradez.
honey *n* miel *f*.
honeycomb *n* panal *m*.
honeymoon *n* luna de miel *f*.
honeysuckle *n* (botany) madreselva *f*.
honorary *adj* honorario(a).
honour *n* honra *f*, honor *m*; * *vt* honrar.
hood *n* capucha *f*.
hoof *n* pezuña *f*.
hook *n* gancho *m*.
hooligan *n* gamberro(a) *m(f)*.
hoop *n* aro *m*.
hooter *n* bocina *f*, sirena *f*.
hop *vi* saltar, brincar.
hope *n* esperanza *f*.
horde *n* horda *f*.
horizon *n* horizonte *m*.
horizontal *adj* horizontal.
hormone *n* hormona *f*.
horn *n* cuerno *m*.
hornet *n* avispón *m*.
horny *adj* calloso(a); cachondo(a).
horoscope *n* horóscopo *m*.
horrendous *adj* horrendo(a).
horrible *adj* horrible.
horrid *adj* horrible.
horrific *adj* horroroso(a).
horrify *vt* horrorizar.
horror *n* horror, terror *m*.
hors d'oeuvre *n* entremeses *mpl*.
horse *n* caballo *m*.
horse chestnut *n* castaño de Indias *m*.
horsefly *n* moscarda *f*.
horseradish *n* rábano silvestre *m*.
horticulture *n* horticultura *f*, jardinería *f*.
horticulturist *n* jardinero(a) *m(f)*.
hosepipe *n* manguera *f*.
hosiery *n* calcetería *f*.

hospital *n* hospital *m*.
hospitality *n* hospitalidad *f*.
host *n* anfitrión *m*; hostia *f*.
hostage *n* rehén *m*.
hostess *n* anfitriona *f*.
hostile *adj* hostil.
hot *adj* caliente; cálido(a).
hotbed *n* semillero *m*.
hotel *n* hotel *m*.
hotelier *n* hotelero(a).
hour *n* hora *f*.
hour-glass *n* reloj de arena *m*.
house *n* casa *f*.
household *n* familia *f*.
housewife *n* ama de casa *f*.
hovel *n* choza *f*, cabaña *f*.
hover *vi* flotar.
how *adv* cómo.
howl *vi* aullar.
hub *n* centro *m*.
hue *n* color *m*, matiz *m*.
hug *vt* abrazar; * *n* abrazo *m*.
huge *adj* vasto(a); enorme.
hum *vi* tatarear, canturrear.
human *adj* humano(a).
humane *adv* humano(a), humanitario(a).
humanist *n* humanista *m* or *f*.
humanitarian *adj* humanitario(a).
humanity *n* humanidad *f*.
humble *adj* humilde.
humid *adj* húmedo(a).
humidity *n* humedad *f*.
humiliate *vt* humillar.
humming-bird *n* colibrí *m*.
humorist *n* humorista *m* or *f*.
humorous *adj* gracioso(a).
humour *n* sentido del humor *m*.
hundred *num* ciento.
hundredth *adj* centésimo.
hundredweight *n* quintal *m*.
hunger *n* hambre *f*.
hunt *vt* cazar; perseguir.
hunter *n* cazador(a) *m(f)*.
hurdle *n* valla *f*.
hurricane *n* huracán *m*.

hurt *n* hacer daño; ofender.
hurtful *adj* dañino(a).
husband *n* marido *m*.
hush! *excl* ¡chitón!, ¡silencio!
husk *n* cáscara *f*.
hut *n* cabaña *f*.
hutch *n* conejera *f*.
hyacinth *n* (botany) jacinto *m*.
hydraulic *adj* hidráulico(a).
hydrofoil *n* aerodeslizador *m*.
hydrogen *n* hidrógeno *m*.
hyena *n* hiena *f*.
hygiene *n* higiene *f*.
hymn *n* himno *m*.
hypermarket *n* hipermercado *m*.
hyphen *n* guión *m*.
hypocrisy *n* hipocresia *f*.
hypocrite *n* hipócrita *m* or *f*.
hysterical *adj* histérico(a).
hysterics *npl* histeria *f*.

I

I *pron* yo.
ice *n* hielo *m*; * *vt* helar.
ice cream *n* helado *m*.
ice rink *n* pista de hielo *f*.
icicle *n* carámbano *m*.
idea *n* idea *f*.
ideal *adj* ideal.
identical *adj* idéntico(a).
identification *n* identificación *f*.
identify *vt* identificar.
ideology *n* ideología *f*.
idiom *n* idioma *m*.
idiosyncrasy *n* idiosincrasia *f*.
idiot *n* idiota *m* or *f*, necio(a) *m(f)*.
idiotic *adj* tonto(a); bobo(a).
idle *adj* holgazán(ana).
idol *n* ídolo *m*.
idolatry *n* idolatría *f*.
idyllic *adj* idilico(a).
i.e. *adj* esto es.
if *conj* si, aunque.
ignite *vt* encender.
ignoble *adj* innoble, vil.

ignorance *n* ignorancia *f*.
ignorant *adj* ignorante.
ignore *vt* ignorar.
ill *adj* malo(a); enfermo(a).
ill-advised *adj* imprudente.
illegal *adj*; * (~ly *adv*)
ilegal(mente).
illegible *adj* ilegible.
illegitimate *adj* ilegitimo(a).
ill-feeling *n* rencor *m*.
illiterate *adj* analfabeto(a).
illness *n* enfermedad *f*.
illogical *adj* ilógico(a).
illuminate *vt* iluminar.
illusion *n* ilusión *f*.
illustrate *vt* ilustrar.
illustration *n* ilustración *f*.
image *n* imagen *f*.
imagination *n* imaginación *f*.
imagine *vt* imaginarse.
imbalance *n* desequilibrio *m*.
imbecile *adj* imbecil.
imitate *vt* imitar, copiar.
imitation *n* imitación *f*, copia *f*.
immaculate *adj* inmaculado(a).
immature *adj* inmaduro(a).
immediate *adj* inmediato(a).
immense *adj* inmenso(a).
immigrant *n* inmigrante *m* or *f*.
immigration *n* inmigración *f*.
imminent *adj* inminente.
immodest *adj* desvergonzado(a).
immoral *adj* inmoral.
immortal *adj* inmortal.
immune *adj* inmune.
imp *n* diablillo *m*, duende *m*.
impact *n* impacto *m*.
impair *vt* perjudicar.
impartial *adj*; * (~ly *adv*)
imparcial(mente).
impatiemce *n* impaciencia *f*.
impede *vt* estorbar.
impel *vt* obligar.
impending *adj* inminente.
imperative *adj* imperativo(a).
imperfect *adj* imperfecto(a).
imperial *adj* imperial.

impersonal *adj*; * (~ly *adv*)
impersonal(mente).
impetus *n* ímpetu *m*.
impiety *n* impiedad.
implant *vt* implantar; injertar.
implement *n* herramienta *f*,
instrumento *m*.
implore *vt* suplicar.
imply *vt* suponer.
impolite *adj* maleducado(a).
import *vt* importar.
importance *n* importancia *f*.
important *adj* importante.
impose *vt* imponer.
impostor *n* impostor(a).
impotence *n* impotencia *f*.
impotent *adj* impotente.
impound *vt* embargar.
impoverish *vt* empobrecer.
impractical *adj* poco práctico(a).
imprecise *adj* impreciso(a).
impress *vt* impresionar.
impression *n* impresión *f*;
edición *f*.
impressive *adj* impresionante.
imprint *n* sello *m*; * *vt* imprimir;
estampar.
improbable *adj* improbable.
improper *adj* impropio(a).
improve *vt*, *vi* mejorar.
improvise *vt* improvisar.
impulse *n* impulso *m*.
impure *adj* impuro(a).
impurity *n* impureza *f*.
in *prep* en.
inability *n* incapacidad *f*.
inaccessible *adj* inaccesible.
inaccurate *adj* inexacto(a).
inadequate *adj* inadecuado(a);
defectuoso(a).
inadmissible *adj* inadmisible.
inadvertently *adv* sin querer.
inappropriate *adj* inapropiado(a).
inaudible *adj* inaudible.
inaugurate *vt* inaugurar.
in-between *adj* intermedio(a).
inborn, inbred *adj* innato(a).

incapable *adj* incapaz.
incarcerate *vt* encarcelar.
incarnation *n* encarnación.
incendiary *n* incendiario(a)
m(f); bomba incendiaria *f*.
incense *n* incienso *m*.
incentive *n* incentivo *m*.
incessant *adj* incesante.
incest *n* incesto *m*.
inch *n* pulgada *f*.
incident *n* incidente *m*.
incinerator *n* incinerador *m*.
inclination *n* inclinación *f*.
incline *vt* (*vi*) inclinar(se).
include *vt* incluir.
inclusive *adj* inclusive.
incognito *adv* de incógnito.
incoherent *adj* incoherente.
income *n* renta *f*.
incompatible *adj* incompatible.
incompetence *n* incompetencia *f*.
imcomplete *adj* incompleto(a).
incomprehensible *adj*
incomprensible.
inconceivable *adj* inconcebible.
incontinence *n* incontinencia *f*.
inconvenience *n* incomodidad *f*.
incorrect *adj* incorrecto(a).
increase *vt* acrecentar, aumentar.
incredible *adj* increíble.
incubate *vi* incubar.
incubator *n* incubadora *f*.
incurable *adj* incurable.
indecency *n* indecencia *f*.
indecent *adj*; * (~ly *adv*)
indecente(mente).
indecisive *adj* indeciso(a).
indeed *adv* verdaderamente,
de veras.
independence *n* independencia *f*.
independent *adj* independiente.
indescribable *adj* indescriptible.
index *n* índice *m*.
indicate *vt* indicar.
indifference *n* indiferencia *f*.
indigenous *adj* indígena.
indigestion *n* indigestión *f*.

indignation *n* indignación *f*.
indigo *n* añil *m*.
indirect *adj* indirecto(a).
indiscreet *adj* indiscreto(a).
indispensable *adj* indispensable.
indistinguishable *adj*
  indistinguible.
individual *adj* individual.
indoors *adv* dentro.
indulge *vt*, *vi* conceder; ser
  indulgente.
industrialist *n* industrial *m*.
industry *n* industria *f*.
inedible *adj* no comestible.
ineffective, ineffectual *adj*
  ineficaz.
inefficiency *n* ineficacia *f*.
ineligible *adj* ineligible.
inept *adj* incompetente,
  inepto(a).
inequality *n* desigualdad *f*.
inevitable *adj* inevitable.
inexpensive *adj* económico(a).
inexperience *n* inexperiencia *f*.
inexpert *adj* inexperto(a).
inexplicable *adj* inexplicable.
infallible *adj* infalible.
infamy *n* infamia *f*.
infancy *n* infancia *f*.
infant *n* niño(a).
infantile *adj* infantil.
infantry *n* infantería *f*.
infatuation *n* enamoramiento *m*.
infect *vt* infectar.
infection *n* infección *f*.
inferior *adj* inferior.
infernal *adj* infernal.
inferno *n* infierno *m*.
infest *vt* infestar.
infidelity *n* infidelidad *f*.
infinite *adj* infinito(a).
infinitive *n* infinitivo *m*.
infinity *n* infinito *m*; infinidad *f*.
infirm *adj* enfermo(a).
infirmary *n* hospital *m*,
  enfermería *f*.
infirmity *n* achaque *m*,

enfermedad *f*.
inflammation *n* inflamación *f*.
inflatable *adj* inflable.
inflate *vt* inflar, hinchar.
inflation *n* inflación *f*.
inflict *vt* imponer.
influence *n* influencia *f*.
influenza *n* gripe *f*.
inform *vt* informar.
informal *adj* informal.
information *n* información *f*.
infrastructure *n*
  infraestructura *f*.
infuriate *vt* enfurecer.
infusion *n* infusión *f*.
ingenious *adj* ingenioso(a).
ingenuity *n* ingeniosidad *f*.
ingot *n* barra de metal *f*.
ingrained *adj* arraigado(a).
ingratitude *n* ingratitud *f*.
ingredient *n* ingrediente *m*.
inhabit *vt*, *vi* habitar.
inhabitant *n* habitante *m*.
inhale *vt* inhalar.
inherent *adj* inherente.
inherit *vt* heredar.
inheritance *n* herencia *f*.
inhibit *vt* inhibir.
inhospitable *adj* inhospita-
  lario(a).
inhuman *adj* inhumano(a).
inhumanity *n* inhumanidad *f*,
  crueldad *f*.
initial *adj* inicial.
initiate *vt* iniciar.
initiative *n* iniciativa *f*.
inject *vt* inyectar.
injection *n* inyección *f*.
injure *vt* herir.
injury *n* daño *m*.
injustice *n* injusticia *f*.
ink *n* tinta *f*.
inkling *n* sospecha *f*.
inlaid *n* entarimado *m*.
in-laws *npl* suegros *mpl*.
inlay *vt* taracear, embutir.
inlet *n* ensenada *f*; cala *f*.

inmate *n* preso(a) *m(f)*.

inn *n* posada *f*; mesón *m*.

innkeeper *n* posadero(a) *m(f)*; mesonero(a) *m(f)*.

innocence *n* inocencia *f*.

innocent *adj* inocente.

innovate *vt* innovar.

innovation *n* innovación *f*.

innuendo *n* indirecta *f*, insinuación *f*.

inoffensive *adj* inofensivo(a).

inorganic *adj* inorgánico(a).

inpatient *n* paciente interno *m*.

input *n* entrada *f*.

inquest *n* encuesta judicial *f*.

inquire *vt*, *vi* preguntar.

inquiry *n* pregunta *f*; pesquisa *f*.

inquisition *n* inquisición *f*.

inquisitive *adj* curioso(a); fisgón(ona).

insane *adj* loco(a); demente.

insanity *n* locura *f*.

inscription *n* inscripción *f*.

inscrutable *adj* inescrutable.

insect *n* insecto *m*.

insecticide *n* insecticida *m*.

insecure *adj* inseguro(a).

insensitive *adj* insensible.

inseparable *adj* inseparable.

insert *vt* introducir.

insertion *n* inserción *f*.

inside *n* interior *m*; * *adv* dentro.

inside out *adv* al revés.

insignia *npl* insignias *fpl*.

insignificant *adj* insignificante.

insincere *adj* poco sincero(a).

insipid *adj* insípido(a).

insist *vi* insistir.

insole *n* plantilla *f*.

insolence *n* insolencia *f*.

insoluble *adj* insoluble.

insomnia *n* insomnio *m*.

insomuch *conj* puesto que.

inspect *vt* examinar, inspeccionar.

inspection *n* inspección *f*.

inspire *vt* inspirar.

instablilty *n* inestabilidad *f*.

instance *n* ejemplo *m*.

instant *adj* instantáneo(a); inmediato(a).

instead (of) *pron* por, en lugar de, en vez de.

instil *vt* inculcar.

instinct *n* instinto *m*.

instinctive *adj* instintivo(a).

institute *vt* establecer; * *n* instituto *m*.

institution *n* institución *f*.

instruct *vt* instruir, enseñar.

instruction *n* instrucción *f*.

instrument *n* instrumento *m*.

instrumental *adj* instrumental.

insufferable *adj* insoportable.

insufficient *adj* insuficiente.

insulate *vt* aislar.

insulin *n* insulina *f*.

insult *vt* insultar; * *n* insulto *m*.

insurance *n* (commerce) seguro *m*.

insure *vt* asegurar.

intact *adj* intacto(a).

integral *adj* íntegro(a); integral.

integrate *vt* integrar.

integrity *n* integridad *f*.

intellect *n* intelecto *m*.

intelligence *n* inteligencia *f*.

intend *vi* tener intención.

intense *adj* intenso(a).

intensity *n* intensidad *f*.

intention *n* intención *f*.

inter *vt* enterrar.

interaction *n* interacción *f*.

intercourse *n* relaciones sexuales *fpl*.

interest *vt* interesar.

interesting *adj* interesante.

interest rate *n* tipo de interés *m*.

interfere *vi* entrometerse, interferir.

interference *n* interferencia *f*.

interior *adj* interior.

interlude *n* intermedio *m*.

intermediate *adj* intermedio(a).

interment *n* entierro *m*.

intermission *n* descanso *m*.
intermittent *adj* intermitente.
internal *adj* interno(a).
international *adj* internacional.
interpret *vt* interpretar.
interpretation *n* interpretación *f*.
interpreter *n* intérprete *m* or *f*.
interregnum *n* interregno *m*.
interrelated *adj*
  interrelacionado(a).
interrogate *vt* interrogar.
interrogation *n* interrogatorio *m*.
interrogative *adj*
  interrogativo(a).
interrupt *vt* interrumpir.
interruption *n* interrupción *f*.
intersect *vi* (*vt*) cruzar(se).
intersection *n* cruce *m*.
intersperse *vt* esparcir;
  salpicar de.
intertwine *vt* (*vi*) entrelazar(se).
interval *n* intervalo *m*,
  descanso *m*.
intervene *vi* intervenir.
intervention *n* intervención *f*.
interview *vt* entrevistar;
  * *n* entrevista *f*.
interviewer *n* entrevistador(a)
  m(*f*).
intestine *n* intestino *m*.
intimacy *n* intimidad *f*.
intimate *n* amigo(a) *m*(*f*);
  íntimo(a) *m*(*f*).
intimidate *vt* intimidar.
into *prep* en, dentro, adentro.
intolerable *adj* intolerable.
intolerance *n* intolerancia *f*.
intoxicate *vt* embriagar.
intravenous *adj* intravenoso(a).
intrepid *adj* intrépido(a).
intricate *adj* intrincado(a).
intrigue *n* intriga *f*; * *vi* intrigar.
intriguing *adj* fascinante.
intrinsic *adj* intrínseco(a).
introduce *vt* introducir;
  presentar.
introduction *n* introducción *f*.

introvert *n* introvertido(a) *m*(*f*).
intrude *vi* entrometerse.
intruder *n* intruso(a) *m*(*f*).
intuition *n* intuición *f*.
intuitive *adj* intuitivo(a).
inundate *vt* inundar.
inundation *n* inundación *f*.
invade *vt* invadir.
invalid *adj* inválido(a).
invalidate *vt* invalidar, anular.
invaluable *adj* inestimable.
invariable *adj* invariable.
invariably *adv* invariablemente.
invasion *n* invasión *f*.
invent *vt* inventar.
invention *n* invento *m*.
inventor *n* inventor(a) *m*(*f*).
inventory *n* inventario *m*.
inversion *n* inversión *f*.
invert *vt* invertir.
invest *vt* invertir; dedicar.
investigate *vt* investigar.
investment *n* inversión *f*.
invigilate *vt* vigilar.
invigorating *adj* vigorizante.
invincible *adj* invencible.
invisible *adj* invisible.
invitation *n* invitación *f*.
invite *vt* invitar.
invoice *n* (commerce) factura *f*.
involuntarily *adv* involunta-
  riamente.
involve *vt* implicar.
involvement *n* compromiso *m*.
iodine *n* (chemistry) yodo *m*.
IOU (*abbrev* I owe you) *n* pagaré *m*.
irate *adj* enojado(a).
iris *n* iris *m*; (botany) lirio *m*.
irksome *adj* fastidioso(a).
iron *n* hierro *m*; * *adj* férreo(a);
  * *vt* planchar.
ironic *adj* irónico(a);
  * ~ly *adv* irónicamente.
ironwork *n* herraje *m*, herrería *f*.
irony *n* ironía *f*.
irradiate *vt* irradiar.
irrational *adj* irracional.

irreconcilable *adj* irreconciliable.
irregular *adj*; * (~ly *adv*)
  irregular(mente).
irrelevant *adj* irrelevante.
irreparable *adj* irreparable.
irresistible *adj* irresistible.
irresponsible *adj* irresponsable.
irrigate *vt* regar.
irrigation *n* riego *m*.
irritable *adj* irritable.
irritant *n* (medical) irritante *m*.
irritate *vt* irritar.
Islam *n* islam *m*.
island *n* isla *f*.
isle *n* isla *f*.
isolate *vt* aislar.
issue *n* asunto *m*.
it *pron* él, ella, ello, lo, la, le.
italic *n* cursiva *f*.
itch *n* picazón *f*; * *vi* picar.
item *n* artículo *m*.
itemise *vt* detallar.
itinerary *n* itinerario *m*.
its *pron* su, suyo.
itself *pron* él mismo, ella
  misma, sí mismo.
ivory *n* marfil *m*.
ivy *n* (botany) hiedra *f*.

J

jab *vt* dar un codazo a.
jabber *vi* farfullar.
jack *n* gato *m*; sota *f*.
jackal *n* chacal *m*.
jackboots *npl* botas militares *fpl*.
jackdaw *n* grajo *m*.
jacket *n* chaqueta *f*.
jack-knife *vi* colear.
jackpot *n* premio gordo *m*.
jade *n* jade *m*.
jagged *adj* dentado(a).
jaguar *n* jaguar *m*.
jail *n* cárcel *f*.
jam *n* conserva *f*; mermelada
  de frutas *f*; embotellamiento *m*.

jangle *vi* sonar.
January *n* enero *m*.
jargon *n* jerga *f*.
jasmine *n* (botany) jazmín *m*.
jaundice *n* ictericia *f*.
jaunt *n* excursión *f*.
jaunty *adj* alegre.
javelin *n* jabalina *f*.
jaw *n* mandíbula *f*.
jay *n* arrendajo *m*.
jazz *n* jazz *m*.
jealous *adj* celoso(a).
jealousy *n* celos *mpl*; envidia *f*.
jeans *npl* vaqueros *mpl*.
jeep *n* jeep *m*.
jeer *vi* abuchear.
jelly *n* jalea *f*, gelatina *f*.
jellyfish *n* medusa *f*.
jeopardise *vt* arriesgar.
jersey *n* jersey *m*.
jest *n* broma *f*.
jester *n* bufón(ona) *m(f)*.
Jesuit *n* jesuita *m* or *f*.
Jesus *n* Jesús *m*.
jet *n* avión a reacción *m*.
jettison *vt* desechar.
jetty *n* muelle *m*.
Jew *n* judío(a) *m(f)*.
jewel *n* joya *f*.
jewellery *n* joyería *f*.
Jewish *adj* judío(a).
jib *vi* plantarse.
jibe *n* mofa *f*.
jig *n* giga *f*.
jigsaw *n* rompecabezas *m*.
jilt *vt* dejar plantado.
job *n* trabajo *m*.
jockey *n* jinete *m* or *f*.
jocular *adj* jocoso(a), alegre.
jog *vi* hacer footing.
jogging *n* footing *m*.
join *vt* juntar, unir.
joiner *n* carpintero(a) *m(f)*.
joinery *n* carpintería *f*.
joint *n* articulación *f*.
jointly *adv* conjuntamente.
joke *n* broma *f*; * *vi* bromear.

joker *n* comodín *m.*
jollity *n* alegría *f.*
jolly *adj* alegre.
jolt *vt* sacudir; * *n* sacudida *f.*
jostle *vt* dar empujones.
journal *n* revista *f.*
journalism *n* periodismo *m.*
journalist *n* periodista *m(f).*
journey *n* viaje *m;* * *vt* viajar.
jovial *adj* jovial.
joy *n* alegría *f,* jubilo *m.*
jubilant *adj* jubiloso(a).
jubilation *n* júbilo *m,* regocijo *m.*
jubilee *n* jubileo *m.*
Judaism *n* judaísmo *m.*
judge *n* juez *m(f);* * *vt* juzgar.
judgment *n* juicio *m.*
judicial *adj;* * (~ly *adv*) judicial(mente).
judiciary *n* magistratura *f,* poder judicial *m.*
judicious *adj* prudente.
judo *n* judo *m.*
jug *n* jarro *m.*
juggle *vi* hacer juegos malabares.
juggler *n* malabarista *m* or *f.*
juice *n* jugo *m.*
juicy *adj* jugoso(a).
jukebox *n* gramola *f.*
July *n* julio *m.*
jumble *vt* revolver.
jump *vi* saltar.
jumper *n* suéter *m.*
jumpy *adj* nervioso(a).
juncture *n* coyuntura *f.*
June *n* junio *m.*
jungle *n* selva *f.*
junior *adj* más joven.
juniper *n* (botany) enebro *m.*
junk *n* basura *f;* baratijas *fpl.*
junta *n* junta *f.*
jurisdiction *n* jurisdicción *f.*
jurisprudence *n* jurisprudencia *f.*
jurist *n* jurista *m(f).*
jury *n* jurado *m.*
just *adj* justo(a); * *adv* sólo, exactamente.

justice *n* justicia *f.*
justification *n* justificación *f.*
justify *vt* justificar.
justly *adv* justamente.
jut *vi:* — to ~ out sobresalir.
jute *n* yute *m.*
juvenile *adj* juvenil.
juxtaposition *n* yuxtaposición *f.*

K

kaleidoscope *n* calidoscopio *m.*
kangaroo *n* canguro *m.*
karate *n* karate *m.*
kebab *n* pincho *m.*
keel *n* (marine) quilla *f.*
keen *adj* agudo(a); vivo(a).
keep *vt* mantener; guardar; conservar.
keeper *n* guardián(ana) *m(f).*
keepsake *n* recuerdo *m.*
keg *n* barril *m.*
kennel *n* perrera *f.*
kernel *n* fruta *f;* meollo *m.*
kerosene *n* keroseno *m.*
ketchup *n* ketchup *m.*
kettle *n* hervidor *m.*
key *n* llave *f;* (music) clave *f;* tecla *f.*
keyboard *n* teclado *m.*
keyhole *n* ojo de la cerradura *m.*
key ring *n* llavero *m.*
khaki *n* caqui *m.*
kick *n* patada *f;* * *vt, vi* patear.
kid *n* chico(a) *m(f).*
kidnap *vt* secuestrar.
kidnapper *n* secuestrador(a) *m(f).*
kidney *n* riñón *m.*
killer *n* asesino(a) *m(f).*
killing *n* asesinato *m.*
kiln *n* horno *m.*
kilobyte *n* kilobyte *m.*
kilo(gramme) *n* kilo *m.*
kilometre *n* kilómetro *m.*
kilt *n* falda escocesa *f.*
kin *n* parientes *mpl.*

kind *adj* cariñoso(a); * *n* género *m*.
kind-hearted *adj* bondadoso(a).
kindle *vt*, *vi* encender.
kindly *adj* bondadoso(a).
kindness *n* bondad *f*.
kindred *adj* emparentado(a).
kinetic *adj* cinético(a).
king *n* rey *m*.
kingdom *n* reino *m*.
kingfisher *n* martín pescador *m*.
kiosk *n* quiosco *m*.
kiss *n* beso *m*; * *vt* besar.
kit *n* equipo *m*.
kitchen *n* cocina *f*.
kite *n* cometa *f*.
kitten *n* gatito(a) *m(f)*.
knack *n* don *m*.
knapsack *n* mochila *f*.
knead *vt* amasar.
knee *n* rodilla *f*.
kneel *vi* arrodillarse.
knell *n* toque de difuntos *m*.
knife *n* cuchillo *m*.
knight *n* caballero *m*.
knit *vt*, *vi* tejer.
knitting needle *n* aguja de tejer *f*.
knitwear *n* prendas de punto *fpl*.
knob *n* bulto *m*.
knock *vt*, *vi* golpear.
knocker *n* aldaba *f*.
knock-kneed *adj* patizambo(a).
knock-out *n* K.O. *m*.
knoll *n* cima de una colina *f*.
knot *n* nudo *m*; lazo *m*;
  * *vt* anudar.
knotty *adj* complicado(a).
know *vt*, *vi* conocer; saber.
know-all *n* sabelotodo *m* or *f*.
know-how *n* conocimientos *mpl*.
knowing *adj* entendido(a);
  * ~ly *adv* a sabiendas.
knowledge *n* conocimiento *m*.
knowledgeable *adj* bien
  informado(a).
knuckle *n* nudillo *m*.

L

label *n* etiqueta *f*.
laboratory *n* laboratorio *m*.
laborious *adj* penoso(a).
labour *n* trabajo *m*, labor *f*.
labourer *n* peón *m*.
labyrinth *n* laberinto *m*.
lace *n* cordón *m*.
lacerate *vt* lacerar.
lack *n* falta *f*, carencia *f*;
  * *vt*, *vi* faltar.
lacquer *n* laca *f*.
lad *n* muchacho *m*.
ladder *n* escalera *f*.
ladle *n* cucharón *m*.
lady *n* señora *f*.
lag *vi* quedarse atrás.
lager *n* cerveza (rubia) *f*.
lagoon *n* laguna *f*.
lake *n* lago *m*.
lamb *n* cordero *m*.
lame *adj* cojo(a).
lament *vt* (*vi*) lamentar(se).
lamp *n* lámpara *f*.
lampoon *n* sátira *f*; * *vt* satirizar.
lampshade *n* pantalla *f*.
lance *n* lanza *f*.
lancet *n* lanceta *f*.
land *n* país *m*; tierra *f*.
landing *n* aterrizaje *m*;
  desembarco *m*.
landmark *n* lugar conocido *m*.
landscape *n* paisaje *m*.
lane *n* callejuela *f*.
language *n* lengua *f*, lenguaje *m*.
lank *adj* lacio(a).
lanky *adj* larguirucho(a).
lantern *n* linterna *f*, farol *m*.
lap *n* regazo *m*.
lapel *n* solapa *f*.
lapse *n* lapso *m*.
larceny *n* latrocinio *m*.
larch *n* alerce *m*.
lard *n* manteca de cerdo *f*.
larder *n* despensa *f*.

large *adj* grande.
lark *n* alondra *f*.
larva *n* larva *f*.
laryngitis *n* laringitis *f*.
larynx *n* laringe *f*.
lascivious *adj* lascivo(a).
laser *n* láser *m*.
lash *n* latigazo *m*.
lasso *n* lazo *m*.
last *adj* último(a).
lasting *adj* duradero(a),
  permanente.
latch *n* picaporte *m*.
late *adj* tarde; difunto(a).
latent *adj* latente.
lathe *n* torno *m*.
lather *vt* enjabonar; * *n* espuma *f*.
latitude *n* latitud *f*.
latter *adj* último(a).
lattice *n* celosía *f*, enrejado *m*.
laugh *n* risa *f*, carcajada *f*;
  * *vi* reir.
laughter *n* risa *f*.
launch *vt* (*vi*) lanzar(se);
  * *n* (marine) lancha *f*.
launch(ing) *n* lanzamiento *m*.
launder *vt* lavar.
laundry *n* lavandería *f*.
laurel *n* laurel *m*.
lava *n* lava *f*.
lavatory *n* wáter *m*, lavabo *m*.
lavender *n* (botany) espliego
  m, lavanda *f*.
lavish *adj* pródigo(a); * ~ly *adv*
  pródigamente; * *vt* disipar.
law *n* ley *f*, derecho *m*.
law court *n* tribunal *m*.
lawn *n* césped *m*.
lawn mower *n* cortacésped *m*.
lawsuit *n* pleito *m*.
lawyer *n* abogado(a) *m*(*f*).
laxative *n* laxante *m*.
lay *vt* poner.
layabout *n* vago(a) *m*(*f*).
layer *n* capa *f*.
layout *n* composición *f*.
laze *vi* holgazanear.

laziness *n* pereza *f*.
lazy *adj* perezoso(a).
lead *n* plomo *m*.
leader *n* jefe(a) *m*(*f*).
leaf *n* hoja *f*.
leaflet *n* folleto *m*.
league *n* liga *f*, alianza *f*.
leak *n* escape *m*, fuga *f*.
lean *vt* (*vi*) apoyar(se).
leap *n* saltro *m*; * *vi* saltar.
leap year *n* año bisiesto *m*.
learn *vt*, *vi* aprender.
lease *n* arriendo *m*; * *vt* arrendar.
leash *n* correa *f*.
least *adj* mínimo(a).
leather *n* cuero *m*.
leave *n* licencia *f*; permiso *m*;
  * *vt* dejar.
lecherous *adj* lascivo(a).
lecture *n* conferencia *f*.
ledge *n* reborde *m*.
ledger *n* (commerce) libro
  mayor *m*.
leech *n* sanguijuela *f*.
leek *n* (botany) puerro *m*.
left *adj* izquierdo(a).
left-handed *adj* zurdo(a).
leftovers *npl* sobras *fpl*.
leg *n* pierna *f*.
legacy *n* herencia *f*.
legal *adj* legal.
legalise *vt* legalizar.
legend *n* leyenda *f*.
legendary *adj* legendario(a).
legible *adj* legible.
legion *n* legión *f*.
legislate *vt* legislar.
legislation *n* legislación *f*.
leisure *n* ocio *m*: — at ~
  desocupado(a); * ~ly *adj* sin
  prisa.
lemon *n* limón *m*.
lemonade *n* limonada *f*.
lend *vt* prestar.
length *n* largo *m*; duración *f*.
lenient *adj* indulgente.
lens *n* lente *f*.

Lent *n* Cuaresma *f*.
lentil *n* lenteja *f*.
leopard *n* leopardo *m*.
leotard *n* leotardo *m*.
leper *n* leproso(a) *m(f)*.
leprosy *n* lepra *f*.
lesbian *n* lesbiana *f*.
less *adj* menor.
lesson *n* lección *f*.
let *vt* dejar, permitir.
lethal *adj* mortal.
lethargy *n* letargo *m*.
letter *n* letra *f*; carta *f*.
lettuce *n* lechuga *f*.
leukaemia *n* leucemia *f*.
level *adj* llano(a), igual.
lever *n* palanca *f*.
leverage *n* influencia *f*.
levy *n* impuesto *m*; * *vt* recaudar.
lexicon *n* léxico *m*.
liability *n* responsabilidad *f*.
liable *adj* sujeto(a); responsable.
liaise *vi* colaborar.
liaison *n* enlace *m*.
liar *n* embustero(a) *m(f)*.
libel *n* difamación *f*; * *vt* difamar.
liberal *adj* liberal.
liberate *vt* libertar.
liberation *n* liberación *f*.
liberty *n* libertad *f*.
Libra *n* Libra *f*.
librarian *n* bibliotecario(a) *m(f)*.
library *n* biblioteca *f*.
licence *n* licencia *f*.
lick *vt* lamer.
lid *n* tapa *f*.
lie *n* mentira *f*.
life *n* vida *f*.
lifejacket *n* chaleco salvavidas *m*.
lifelike *adj* natural.
lift *vt* levantar.
ligament *n* ligamento *m*.
light *n* luz *f*.
light bulb *n* foco *m*; bombilla *f*.
lighter *n* encendedor *m*.
lighthouse *n* (marine) faro *m*.
lightning *n* relámpago *m*.

like *prep* como; * *adj* semejante;
  igual; * *vt* gustar.
likeness *n* semejanza *f*.
lilac *n* lila *f*.
lily *n* (botany) lirio *m*, azucena *f*.
limb *n* miembro *m*.
lime *n* cal *f*, lima *f*.
limestone *n* piedra caliza *f*.
limit *n* límite *m*.
line *n* línea *f*.
linen *n* lino *m*.
liner *n* transatlántico *m*.
linger *vi* persistir; retrasarse.
lingerie *n* ropa interior *f*.
linguist *n* lingüista *m* or *f*.
lining *n* forro *m*.
link *n* eslabón *m*; conexión *f*,
  vínculo *m*; * *vt* vincular.
linoleum *n* linóleo *m*.
lintel *n* dintel *m*.
lion *n* león *m*.
lip *n* labio *m*.
liqueur *n* licor *m*.
liquid *adj* líquido(a).
liquor *n* licor *m*.
liquorice *n* regaliz *m*.
lisp *n* ceceo *m*.
list *n* lista *f*.
listen *vi* escuchar.
literature *n* literatura *f*.
lithe *adj* ágil.
lithograph *n* litografía *f*.
litigation *n* litigio *m*.
litre *n* litro *m*.
litter *n* litera *f*.
little *adj* pequeño(a), poco(a).
live *vi* vivir; habitar.
liver *n* hígado *m*.
livestock *n* ganado *m*.
living *n* vida *f*; * *adj* vivo(a).
living room *n* sala de estar *f*.
lizard *n* lagarto *m*.
load *vt* cargar.
loaf *n* barra de pan *f*.
loam *n* marga *f*.
loan *n* préstamo *m*; * *vt* prestar.
loathe *vt* aborrecer.

loathing *n* aversión *f*.
lobby *n* vestíbulo *m*.
lobe *n* lóbulo *m*.
lobster *n* langosta *f*.
local *adj* local.
locality *n* localidad *f*.
locate *vt* localizar.
location *n* situación *f*.
loch *n* lago *m*.
lock *n* cerradura *f*.
locker *n* casillero *m*.
locket *n* medallón *m*.
locomotive *n* locomotora *f*.
locust *n* langosta *f*.
loft *n* desván *m*.
lofty *adj* alto(a).
log *n* leño *m*.
logic *n* lógica *f*.
logo *n* logotipo *m*.
loiter *vi* merodear.
lollipop *n* pirulí *m*.
loneliness *n* soledad *f*.
long *adj* largo(a).
longitude *n* longitud *f*.
look *vi* mirar *f*.
looking-glass *n* espejo *m*.
loop *n* lazo *m*.
loose *adj* suelto(a).
loot *vt* saquear; * *n* botín *m*.
lop *vt* podar.
lord *n* señor *m*.
lose *vt* perder.
loss *n* pérdida *f*.
lotion *n* loción *f*.
lottery *n* lotería *f*.
loud *adj* fuerte; * ~ly *adv* fuerte.
loudspeaker *n* altavoz *m*.
lounge *n* salón *m*.
louse *n* piojo (*pl* lice) *m*.
lout *n* gamberro (a) *m(f)*.
love *n* amor *m*, cariño *m*;
  * *vt* amar, querer.
lovely *adj* encantador(a).
lover *n* amante *m*.
low *adj* bajo(a).
loyal *adj* leal; fiel.
lozenge *n* pastilla *f*.

lubricant *n* lubricante *m*.
lubricate *vt* lubricar.
luck *n* suerte *f*, fortuna *f*.
lucrative *adj* lucrativo(a).
ludricrous *adj* absurdo(a).
lug *vt* arrastrar.
luggage *n* equipaje *m*.
lull *vt* acunar; * *n* tregua *f*.
lullaby *n* nana *f*.
lumbago *n* lumbago *m*.
luminous *adj* luminoso(a).
lump *n* terrón *m*.
lunacy *n* locura *f*.
lunar *adj* lunar.
lunatic *adj* loco(a).
lunch, luncheon *n* almuerzo *m*,
  comida *f*.
lungs *npl* pulmones *mpl*.
luscious *adj* delicioso(a).
lush *adj* exuberante.
lust *n* lujuria, sensualidad *f*.
lustre *n* lustre *m*.
luxurious *adj* lujoso(a).
luxury *n* lujo *m*.
lymph *n* linfa *f*.
lynx *n* lince *m*.
lyrical *adj* lírico(a).
lyrics *npl* letra (de una canción) *f*.

M

macaroni *n* macarrones *mpl*.
macaroon *n* macarrón *m*.
mace *n* maza *f*.
machine *n* máquina *f*.
machinery *n* maquinaria,
  mecanismo *m*.
mackerel *n* caballa *f*.
mad *adj* loco(a), furioso(a).
madam *n* señora *f*.
madhouse *n* casa de locos *f*.
madness *n* locura *f*.
magazine *n* revista *f*.
maggot *n* gusano *m*.
magic *n* magia *f*.
magician *n* mago(a) *m(f)*.

magistrate *n* magistrado(a)*m(f)*.
magnet *n* imán *m*.
magnetic *adj* magnético(a).
magnificent *adj* magnífico(a).
magnify *vt* aumentar.
magnifying glass *n* lupa *f*.
magnitude *n* magnitud *f*.
magpie *n* urraca *f*.
mahogany *n* caoba *f*.
mail *n* correo *m*.
maim *vt* mutilar.
main *adj* principal.
maintain *vt* mantener.
maintenance *n* mantenimiento *m*.
maize *n* maíz *m*.
majesty *n* majestad *f*.
major *adj* principal, mayor.
make *vt* hacer, crear.
make-up *n* maquillaje *m*.
malaria *n* malaria *f*.
male *adj* masculino(a);
  * *n* macho *m*.
malice *n* malicia *f*.
malicious *adj* malicioso(a).
mall *n* centro comercial *m*.
malleable *adj* maleable.
mallet *n* mazo *m*.
mallows *n* (botany) malva *f*.
malnutrition *n* desnutrición *f*.
malpractice *n* negligencia *f*.
malt *n* malta *f*.
maltreat *vt* maltratar.
mammal *n* mamífero *m*.
mammoth *n* mamut *m*;
  * *adj* gigantesco(a).
man *n* hombre *m*.
manage *vt*, *vi* manejar, dirigir.
management *n* dirección *f*.
manager *n* director(a) *m(f)*.
mandate *n* mandato *m*.
mane *n* crin *f*.
manoeuvre *n* maniobra *f*.
mangle *n* escurridor *m*.
mangy *adj* sarnoso.
manhood *n* edad viril *f*.
mania *n* manía *f*.
maniac *n* maníaco(a) *m(f)*.

manipulate *vt* manipular.
mankind *n* género humano *m*,
  humanidad *f*.
man-made *adj* artificial.
manner *n* manera *f*; modo *m*.
mansion *n* mansión *f*.
mantelpiece *n* repisa de
  chimenea *f*.
manual *adj*, *n* manual *m*.
manufacture *n* fabricación *f*;
  * *vt* fabricar.
manufacturer *n* fabricante *m*.
manuscript *n* manuscrito *m*.
many *adj* muchos(as).
map *n* mapa *m*.
maple *n* arce *m*.
mar *vt* estropear.
marathon *n* maratón *m*.
marble *n* marmol *m*.
March *n* marzo *m*.
mare *n* yegua *f*.
margarine *n* margarina *f*.
margin *n* margen *m*; borde *m*.
marigold *n* (botany) caléndula *f*.
marijuana *n* marihuana *f*.
marine *adj* marino(a).
marital *adj* marital.
mark *n* marca *f*.
market *n* mercado *m*.
marmalade *n* mermelada de
  naranja *f*.
maroon *adj* granate;
  * *vt* naufragar.
marquee *n* carpa *f*.
marriage *n* matrimonio *m*.
marrow *n* medula *f*.
marry *vt (vi)* casar(se).
marsh *n* pantano *m*; marisma *f*.
marshy *adj* pantanoso.
martyr *n* mártir *m* or *f*.
marvel *n* maravilla *f*.
marvellous *adj* maravilloso(a).
marzipan *n* mazapán *m*.
mascara *n* rimel *m*.
masculine *adj* masculino(a).
mask *n* máscara *f*.
masochist *n* masoquista *m* or *f*.

mason n albañil m.
mass n masa f, misa f.
massacre n matanza f.
massage n masaje m.
massive adj enorme; masivo(a).
mast n mástil m.
masterpiece n obra maestra f.
masticate vt masticar.
mat n estera f.
match n fósforo m, cerilla f.
mate n compañero(a) m(f);
 * vt acoplar.
mathematics npl matemáticas
 fpl.
matinée n funcion de la tarde f.
mating n aparejamiento m.
matriculate vt matricular.
matriculation n matriculación f.
matt adj mate.
matter n materia f, substancia f.
mattress n colchón m.
mature adj maduro(a).
mauve adj de color malva.
maximum n máximo(a) m(f).
May n mayo m.
mayonnaise n mayonesa f.
mayor n alcalde m.
maze n laberinto m.
me pron me; mí.
meal n comida f, harina f.
mean adj tacaño(a).
meander vi serpentear.
meaning n sentido m,
 significado m.
meantime, meanwhile adv
 mientras tanto.
measles npl sarampión m.
measurement n medida f.
meat n carne f.
mechanic n mecánico(a) m(f).
mechanism n mecanismo m.
medal n medalla f.
media npl medios de
 comunicación mpl.
medical adj médico(a).
medicate vt medicar.
medicine n medicina f.

medieval adj medieval.
mediocre adj mediocre.
meditate vi meditar.
meditation n meditación f.
Mediterranean adj mediterráneo.
medium n medio m.
meet vt encontrar.
meeting n reunión f.
megaphone n megáfono m.
melancholy n melancolía f.
mellow adj maduro(a).
mellowness n madurez f.
melody n melodía f.
melon n melón m.
melt vt derretir.
member n miembro m.
membrane n membrana f.
memento n recuerdo m.
memoir n memoria f.
memorandum n memorandum m.
memorial n monumento
 conmemorativo m.
memory n memoria f, recuerdo m.
menace n amenaza f.
menagerie n casa de fieras f.
mend vt reparar.
menial adj bajo(a); servil.
meningitis n meningitis f.
menopause n menopausia f.
menstruation n menstruación f.
mental adj mental.
mention n mención f.
mentor n mentor m.
menu n menú m; carta f.
merchamdise n mercancía f.
merchant n comerciante m.
mercuiry n mercurio m.
mercy n compasión f.
mere adj simple, mero.
meridian n meridiano m.
merit n mérito m.
mermaid n sirena f.
merry adj alegre.
merry-go-round n tiovivo m.
mesh n malla f.
mesmerise vt hipnotizar.
mess n lío m, revoltijo m.

message *n* mensaje *m*.
metabolism *n* metabolismo *m*.
metal *n* metal *m*.
metallic *adj* metálico(a).
metamorphosis *n* metamorfosis *f*.
metaphor *n* metáfora *f*.
meteor *n* meteoro *m*.
meteorological *adj*
  meteorológico.
meteorology *n* meteorología *f*.
meter *n* medidor *m*.
method *n* método *m*.
methodical *adj* metódico(a).
Methodist *n* metodista *m or f*.
metre *n* metro *m*.
metric *adj* métrico.
metropolis *n* metrópoli *f*.
metropolitan *adj* metropolitano.
mettle *n* valor *m*.
mew *vi* maullar.
mezzanine *n* entresuelo *m*.
microbe *n* microbio *m*.
microphone *n* micrófono *m*.
microchip *n* microchip *m*.
microscope *n* microscopio *m*.
microwave *n* microondas *m*.
mid *adj* medio, mediado.
midday *n* mediodía *m*.
middle *adj* medio *m*.
midge *n* mosquito *m*.
midget *n* enano *m*.
midnight *n* medianoche *f*.
midst *n* entre, en medio de.
midsummer *n* pleno verano *m*.
midwife *n* comadrona *f*.
might *n* poder *m*; fuerza *f*.
mighty *adj* fuerte.
migraine *n* jaqueca *f*.
migrate *vi* emigrar.
migration *n* emigración *f*.
mike *n* micrófono *m*.
mild *adj* apacible; suave.
mildew *n* moho *m*.
mileage *n* kilometraje *m*.
milieu *n* ambiente *m*.
militant *adj* militante.
military *adj* militar.

milk *n* leche *f*.
milkshake *n* batido *m*.
milky *adj* lechoso;
  * M~ Way *n* Vía Lactea *f*.
mill *n* molino *m*.
millennium *n* milenio *m*.
miller *n* molinero *m*.
milligramme *n* miligramo *m*.
millilitre *n* mililitro *m*.
millimetre *n* milímetro *m*.
milliner *n* sombrerero(a) *m(f)*.
million *n* millón *m*.
millionaire *n* millonario(a) *m(f)*.
millionth *adj, n* millonésimo *m*.
mime *n* mimo *m*.
mimic *vt* imitar.
mince *vt* picar.
mind *n* mente *f*.
mine *pron* mío, mía, mi;
  * *n* mina *f*; * *vi* minar.
miner *n* minero(a) *m(f)*.
mineral *adj, n* mineral *m*.
mineral water *n* agua mineral *f*.
mingle *vt* mezclar.
miniature *n* miniatura *f*.
minimal *adj* mínimo(a).
minimum *n* mínimo(a) *m(f)*.
mining *n* explotación minera *f*.
minister *n* ministro(a) *m(f)*.
mink *n* visón *m*.
minnow *n* pececillo *m*.
minor *adj* menor.
mint *n* (botany) menta *f*.
minus *adv* menos.
minute *adj* diminuto(a).
minute *n* minuto *m*.
miracle *n* milagro *m*.
mirage *n* espejismo *m*.
mire *n* fango *m*.
mirror *n* espejo *m*.
mirth *n* alegría *f*.
misbehave *vi* portarse mal.
miscarry *vi* abortar.
miscellaneous *adj* varios, varias.
miser *n* avaro(a) *m(f)*.
miserable *adj* miserable.
miserly *adj* mezquino, tacaño.

misery n miseria f.
mislay vt extraviar.
mislead vt engañar.
misogynist n misógino m.
Miss n señorita f.
miss vt perder; echar de menos.
missile n misil m.
mission n misión f.
missionary n misionero(a) m(f).
mist n niebla f.
mistake n error m;
  * vt entender mal.
Mister n Señor m.
mistletoe n (botany) muérdago m.
mistress n amante f.
mistrust vt desconfiar.
mitigate vt mitigar.
mitigation n mitigación f.
mitre n mitra f.
mittens npl manoplas fpl.
mix vt mezclar.
mixer n licuadora f.
mixture n mezcla f.
moan n gemido m.
moat n foso m.
mob n multitud f.
mobile adj móvil.
mode n modo m.
model n modelo m.
moderate adj moderado(a).
moderation n moderación f.
modern adj moderno(a).
modernise vt modernizar.
modest adj modesto(a).
modesty n modestia f.
modify vt modificar.
module n módulo m.
mogul n magnate m or f.
mohair n mohair m.
moist adj húmedo(a).
moisture n humedad f.
mole n topo m.
molecule n molécula f.
molest vt importunar.
moment n momento m.
momentum n ímpetu m.
monarch n monarca m.

monarchy n monarquía f.
monastery n monasterio m.
Monday n lunes m.
monetary adj monetario.
money n moneda f; dinero m.
mongol n mongólico(a) m(f).
mongrel n perro cruzado m.
monk n monje m.
monkey n mono(a) m(f).
monopoly n monopolio m.
monotonous adj monotono(a).
monsoon n (marine) monzón m.
monster n monstruo m.
month n mes m.
monthly adj, adv
  mensual(mente).
monument n monumento m.
mood n humor m.
moody adj malhumorado.
moon n luna f.
moor(land) n páramo m.
moose n alce m.
mop n fregona f.
mope vi estar triste.
moped n ciclomotor m.
morality n ética f, moralidad f.
morbid adj morboso(a).
more adj, adv más.
moreover adv además.
morgue n depósito de
  cadáveres m; morgue f.
morning n mañana f: — good ~
  buenos días mpl.
moron n imbécil m or f.
morphine n morfina f.
Morse n morse m.
morsel n bocado m.
mortal adj mortal.
mortality n mortalidad f.
mortar n mortero m.
mortgage n hipoteca f.
mortify vt mortificar.
mortuary n depósito de
  cadáveres m.
mosaic n mosaico m.
mosque n mezquita f.
mosquito n mosquito m.

moss *n* (botany) musgo *m*.
most *adj* la mayoría de, la
  mayor parte de.
motel *n* motel *m*.
moth *n* polilla *f*.
mother *n* madre *f*.
mother-in-law *n* suegra *f*.
mother-of-pearl *n* nacar *m*.
motif *n* tema *m*.
motion *n* movimiento *m*.
motive *n* motivo *m*.
motor *n* motor *m*.
motorbike *n* moto *f*.
motorcycle *n* motocicleta *f*.
motor vehicle *n* automóvil *m*.
motto *n* lema *m*.
mould *n* molde *m*.
mount *n* monte *m*.
mountain *n* montaña *f*.
mountaineering *n*
  montañismo *m*.
mourn *vt* lamentar.
mourner *n* doliente *m*.
mourning *n* luto *m*.
mouse *n* (*pl* mice) ratón *m*.
mousse *n* mousse, espuma *f*.
moustache *n* bigote *m*.
mouth *n* boca *f*.
mouthful *n* bocado *m*.
mouthwash *n* enjuague *m*.
mouthwatering *adj* apetitoso(a).
move *vt* mover.
movement *n* movimiento *m*.
movie *n* película *f*.
moving *adj* conmovedor(a).
mow *vt* segar.
mower *n* cotacesped *m*.
Mrs *n* señora *f*.
much *adj*, *adv* mucho.
muck *n* suciedad *f*.
mucus *adj* mocosidad *f*, moco *m*.
mud *n* barro *m*.
muddle *vt* confundir *m*;
  * *n* confusión *f*.
muffle *vt* amortiguar.
mug *n* jarra *f*.
mulberry *n* (botany) mora *f*.

mule *n* mulo(a) *m(f)*.
multiple *adj* múltiple;
  * *n* múltiplo *m*.
multiplication *n* multiplicación *f*.
multiply *vt* multiplicar.
multitude *n* multitud *f*.
mum, mummy *n* mamá *f*.
mumble *vt*, *vi* refunfuñar.
mummy *n* momia *f*.
mumps *npl* paperas *fpl*.
munch *vt* mascar.
mundame *adj* trivial.
municipal *adj* municipal.
municipality *n* municipalidad *f*.
mural *n* mural *m*.
murder *n* asesinato *m*;
  homicidio *m*.
murky *adj* sombrío(a).
murmur *n* murmullo *m*.
muscle *n* músculo *m*.
muse *vi* meditar.
museum *n* museo *m*.
mushroom *n* (botany) seta *f*,
  champiñón *m*.
music *n* música *f*.
musician *n* músico *m*.
musk *n* almizcle *m*.
muslin *n* muselina *f*.
mussel *n* mejillón *m*.
must *verb aux* estar obligado;
  deber.
mustard *n* mostaza *f*.
mute *adj* mudo(a), silencioso(a).
mutilate *vt* mutilar.
mutter *vt*, *vi* murmurar.
mutton *n* carnero *m*.
mutual *adj* mutuo, mutual.
muzzle *n* bozal *m*.
my *pron* mi, mis; mío, mía;
  míos, mías.
myriad *n* miríada *f*.
myrrh *n* mirra *f*.
myrtle *n* (botany) mirto,
  arrayán *m*.
myself *pron* yo mismo.
mysterious *adj* misterioso(a).
mystery *n* misterio *m*.

mystic(al) *adj* místico(a).
mystify *vt* dejar perplejo, desconcertar.
mystique *n* misterio *m*.
myth *n* mito *m*.
mythology *n* mitología *f*.

N

nag *n* jaca *f*; * *vt* regañar.
nagging *adj* persistente.
nail *n* uña *f*, clavo *m*.
naïve *adj* ingenuo(a).
naked *adj* desnudo(a).
name *n* nombre *m*;
  * *vt* nombrar, poner nombre.
nameless *adj* anónimo(a).
namely *adv* a saber.
namesake *n* tocayo(a) *m(f)*.
nanny *n* niñera *f*.
nap *n* siesta *f*.
nape *n* nuca *f*.
napkin *n* servilleta *f*.
narcissus *n* (botany) narciso *m*.
narcotic *adj*, *n* narcótico *m*.
narrate *vt* narrar.
narrative *adj* narrativo(a).
narrow *adj* angosto(a), estrecho(a).
nasal *adj* nasal.
nasty *adj* sucio(a), antipático(a).
natal *adj* nativo(a); natal.
nation *n* nación *f*.
nationalism *n* nacionalismo *m*.
nationalist *adj*, *n* nacionalista *m(f)*.
nationality *n* nacionalidad *f*.
nationalise *vt* nacionalizar.
native *adj* nativo(a) *m(f)*.
native language *n* lengua materna *f*.
Nativity *n* Navidad *f*.
natural *adj* natural.
naturalist *n* naturalista *m(f)*.
naturalise *vt* naturalizar.
nature *n* naturaleza *f*.

naught *n* cero *m*.
naughty *adj* malo(a).
nausea *n* náusea *f*.
nauseous *adj* nauseabundo(a).
nautic(al), naval *adj* náutico(a), naval.
nave *n* nave (de la iglesia) *f*.
navel *n* ombligo *m*.
navigate *vi* navegar.
navigation *n* navegación *f*.
navy *n* marina *f*.
Nazi *n* nazi *m* or *f*.
near *prep* cerca de.
nearby *adj* cercano(a).
nearly *adv* casi.
near-sighted *adj* miope.
nebulous *adj* nebuloso.
necessarily *adv* necesariamente.
necessary *adj* necesario(a).
necessity *n* necesidad *f*.
neck *n* cuello *m*.
necklace *n* collar *m*.
nectar *n* nectar *m*.
need *n* necesidad *f*.
needle *n* aguja *f*.
needless *adj* superfluo(a), innecesario(a).
needlework *n* costura *f*.
needy *adj* necesitado(a).
negation *n* negación *f*.
negative *adj* negativo(a).
neglect *vt* desatender.
negligée *n* salto de cama *m*.
negligence *n* negligencia *f*.
negligible *adj* insignificante.
negotiate *vt*, *vi* negociar (con).
negotiation *n* negociación *f*, negocio *m*.
neighbour *n* vecino(a) *m(f)*.
neighbourhood *n* vecindad *f*; vecindario *m*.
neither *conj* ni; * *pron* ninguno.
neon *n* neón *m*.
neon light *n* luz de neón *f*.
nephew *n* sobrino *m*.
nepotism *n* nepotismo *m*.
nerve *n* nervio *m*; valor *m*.

nerve-racking *adj* angustioso(a).
nervous *adj* nervioso(a).
nervous breakdown *n* crisis nerviosa *f*.
nest *n* nido *m*.
nest-egg *n* (*fig*) ahorros *mpl*.
nestle *vt* acurrucarse.
net *n* red *f*.
netball *n* básquet *m*.
nettle *n* (botany) ortiga *f*.
network *n* red *f*.
neurosis *n* neurosis *f invar*.
neurotic *adj*, *n* neurótico(a) *m(f)*.
neuter *adj* neutro(a).
neutral *adj* neutral.
neutrality *n* neutralidad *f*.
neutron *n* neutrón *m*.
never *adv* nunca, jamás.
nevertheless *adv* no obstante.
new *adj* nuevo(a).
news *npl* novedad, noticias *fpl*.
newscaster *n* presentador(a) *m(f)*.
newspaper *n* periódico *m*.
next *adj* próximo(a).
nib *n* plumilla *f*.
nibble *vt* mordisquear.
nice *adj* simpatico(a), amable.
niche *n* nicho *m*.
nickel *n* níquel *m*.
nickname *n* mote *m*, apodo *m*.
nicotine *n* nicotina *f*.
niece *n* sobrina *f*.
niggling *adj* insignificante.
night *n* noche *f*.
nightclub *n* club *m*, discoteca *f*.
nightfall *n* anochecer *m*.
nightingale *n* ruiseñor *m*.
nightmare *n* pesadilla *f*.
nihilist *n* nihilista *m* or *f*.
nimble *adj* ligero(a), ágil.
nine *adj*, *n* nueve *m*.
nineteen *adj*, *n* diecinueve *m*.
nineteenth *adj*, *n* decimono-veno(a) *m(f)*.
ninety *adj*, *n* noventa *m*.
ninth *adj*, *n* nono(a), noveno(a) *m*.
nip *vt* pellizcar; morder.

nipple *n* pezón *m*; tetilla *f*.
nit *n* liendre *f*.
nitrogen *n* nitrógeno *m*.
no *adv* no.
nobility *n* nobleza *f*.
noble *adj* noble.
nobleman *n* noble *m*.
nobody *n* nadie, ninguna persona *f*.
nocturnal *adj* nocturno(a).
noise *n* ruido *m*.
noisy *adj* ruidoso(a).
nominate *vt* proponer.
nomination *n* nominación *f*.
nominee *n* candidato(a) *m(f)*.
non-alcoholic *adj* sin alcohol.
nonchalant *adj* indiferente.
nondescript *adj* anodino(a), soso(a).
none *adj* nadie, ninguno.
nonentity *n* nulidad *f*.
nonetheless *adv* sin embargo.
nonsense *n* disparate *m*.
noodles *npl* fideos *mpl*.
noon *n* mediodía *m*.
noose *n* lazo corredizo *m*.
nor *conj* ni.
normal *adj* normal.
north *n* norte *m*.
North America *n* América del Norte *f*.
northeast *n* nor(d)este *m*.
northerly, northern *adj* norteño(a).
North Pole *n* Polo Norte *m*.
northwest *n* nor(d)oeste *m*.
nose *n* nariz *f*.
nosebleed *n* hemorragia nasal *f*.
nostalgia *n* nostalgia *f*.
nostril *n* ventana de la nariz *f*.
not *adv* no.
notable *adj* notable.
notably *adv* especialmente.
notary *n* notario(a) *m(f)*.
notch *n* muesca *f*.
note *n* nota *f*, marca *f*.
notebook *n* libreta *f*.

noted *adj* afamado(a), célebre.
nothing *n* nada *f*.
notice *n* noticia *f*, aviso *m*.
notification *n* notificación *f*.
notify *vt* notificar.
notion *n* noción *f*.
notoriety *n* notoriedad *f*.
notwithstanding *conj* no
obstante, aunque.
nougat *n* turrón *m*.
nought *n* cero *m*.
noun *n* sustantivo *m*.
nourish *vt* nutrir, alimentar.
novel *n* novela *f*.
novelist *n* novelista *m* or *f*.
novelty *n* novedad *f*.
November *n* noviembre *m*.
novice *n* novato(a) *m(f)*.
now *adv* ahora.
nowadays *adv* hoy (en) día.
nowhere *adv* en ninguna parte.
noxious *adj* nocivo(a).
nozzle *n* boquilla *f*.
nuance *n* matiz *m*.
nuclear *adj* nuclear.
nucleus *n* núcleo *m*.
nude *adj* desnudo(a).
nudge *vt* dar un codazo a.
nudist *n* nudista *m* or *f*.
nudity *n* desnudez *f*.
null *adj* nulo.
nullify *vt* anular.
numb *adj* entumecido(a),
insensible.
number *n* número *m*.
numerous *adj* numeroso.
nun *n* monja *f*.
nunnery *n* convento de monjas *m*.
nuptial *adj* nupcial.
nurse *n* enfermera *f*.
nursery *n* guardería infantil *f*.
nursery rhyme *n* canción
infantil *f*.
nursery school *n* parvulario *m*.
nursing home *n* clínica de
reposo *f*.
nurture *vt* alimentar, nutrir.

nut *n* nuez *f*.
nutcrackers *npl* cascanueces *m*.
nutmeg *n* nuez moscada *f*.
nutritious *adj* nutritivo(a).
nutshell *n* cáscara de nuez *f*.
nylon *n* nylon *m*.

O

oak *n* (botany) roble *m*, encina.
oar *n* remo *m*.
oasis *n* oasis *f*.
oat *n* avena *f*.
oath *n* juramento *m*.
obedience *n* obediencia *f*.
obese *adj* obeso(a), gordo(a).
obey *vt* obedecer.
obituary *n* necrología *f*.
object *n* objeto *m*; * *vt* objetar.
objective *n* objetivo *m*;
* *adj* objetivo(a).
oblige *vt* obligar.
obliterate *vt* borrar.
oblivion *n* olvido *m*.
oblong *adj* oblongo(a).
obnoxious *adj* odioso(a).
oboe *n* oboe *m*.
obscene *adj* obsceno(a).
obscenity *n* obscenidad *f*.
obscure *adj* oscuro(a).
observatory *n* observatorio *m*.
observe *vt* observar, mirar.
obsess *vt* obsesionar.
obsolete *adj* obsoleto(a).
obstacle *n* obstáculo *m*.
obstinate *adj* obstinado(a).
obstruct *vt* obstruir; impedir.
obtan *vt* obtener, adquirir.
obvious *adj* obvio, evidente.
occasion *n* ocasión *f*.
occupant, occupier *n* inqui-
lino(a) *m(f)*, ocupante *m* or *f*.
occupation *n* ocupación *f*,
empleo *m*.
occupy *vt* ocupar.
occur *vi* pasar, ocurrir.

ocean *n* océano *m*: * ~-going
  adj de alta mar.
ochre *n* ocre *m*.
octave *n* octava *f*.
October *n* octubre *m*.
octopus *n* pulpo *m*.
odd *adj* impar.
oddity *n* singularidad *f*.
odious *adj* odioso(a).
odour *n* olor *m*.
of *prep* de.
off *adv* desconectado; apagado.
offence *n* ofensa *f*.
offend *vt* ofender.
offensive *adj* ofensivo(a).
offer *vt* ofrecer.
offering *n* ofrenda *f*.
office *n* oficina *f*, despacho *m*.
officer *n* oficial, empleado *m*.
official *adj* oficial.
offspring *n* prole *f*.
often *adv* a menudo, con
  frecuencia.
ogle *vt* comerse con los ojos.
oil *n* aceite *m*.
oil painting *n* pintura al óleo *f*.
oil rig *n* torre de perforación *f*.
oil tanker *n* petrolero *m*.
ointment *n* ungüento *m*.
OK, okay *excl* vale.
old *adj* viejo(a); antiguo(a).
old age *n* vejez *f*.
olive *n* (botany) olivo (tree) *m*;
  aceituna (fruit) *f*.
omelette *n* tortilla de huevos *f*.
omen *n* presagio *m*.
ominous *adj* de mal agüero.
omission *n* omisión *f*.
omit *vt* omitir.
omnipotence *n* omnipotencia *f*.
on *prep* sobre, encima, en; de; a.
one *adj* un, uno.
oneself *pron* sí mismo; sí misma,
  uno mismo, una misma.
ongoing *adj* continuo(a).
onion *n* cebolla *f*.
onlooker *n* espectador(a) *m*(*f*).

only *adj* único(a), solo(a);
  * *adv* solamente, sólo.
onus *n* responsabilidad *f*.
onwards *adv* (hacia) adelante.
opaque *adj* opaco(a).
open *adj* abierto(a); * *vi* abrir;
  * ~ up *vt*(*vr*) abrir(se).
open-minded *adj* de amplias
  miras, sin prejuicios.
opera *n* ópera *f*.
operate *vi* obrar.
operation *n* operación *f*.
operational *adj* operacional.
operative *adj* operativo(a).
operator *n* operario(a) *m*(*f*);
  operador(a) *m*(*f*).
ophthalmic *adj* oftálmico(a).
opinion *n* opinión *f*.
opinion poll *n* encuesta *f*,
  sondeo *m*.
opponent *n* adversario(a) *m*(*f*).
opportune *adj* oportuno.
opportunity *n* oportunidad *f*.
oppose *vt* oponerse.
opposite *adj* opuesto(a);
  contrario(a).
opposition *n* oposición *f*.
oppress *vt* oprimir.
oppression *n* opresión *f*.
optic(al) *adj* óptico(a).
optician *n* optico *m*.
optimist *n* optimista *m* or *f*.
optimum *adj* óptimo(a).
option *n* opción *f*.
opulent *adj* opulento(a).
or *conj* o; u.
oracle *n* oráculo *m*.
oral *adj* oral.
orange *n* naranja *f*.
orbit *n* órbita *f*.
orchard *n* huerto *m*.
orchestra *n* orquesta *f*.
orchid *n* (botany) orquídea *f*.
order *n* orden *f*; encargo *m*;
  * *vt* ordenar, encargar, pedir.
ordinary *adj* ordinario(a).
ore *n* mineral *m*.

organ *n* órgano *m*.
organic *adj* orgánico(a).
organism *n* organismo *m*.
organist *n* organista *m* or *f*.
organisation *n* organización *f*.
organise *vt* organizar.
orgasm *n* orgasmo *m*.
orgy *n* orgía *f*.
oriental *adj* oriental.
orifice *n* orificio *m*.
origin *n* origen *m*.
original *adj* original.
originate *vi* originar.
ornament *n* ornamento *m*.
ornate *adj* adornado.
orphan *adj*, *n* huérfano(a) *m(f)*.
orphanage *n* orfanato *m*.
orthodox *adj* ortodoxo(a).
orthopaedic *adj* ortopédico(a).
oscillate *vi* oscilar.
osprey *n* aguila marina *f*.
ostensibly *adv* aparentemente.
ostentatious *adj* ostentoso(a).
osteopath *n* osteópata *m*.
ostrich *n* avestruz *m*.
other *pron* otro(a).
otter *n* nutria *f*.
ouch *excl* ¡ay!
ought *verb aux* deber, ser
  menester.
ounce *n* onza *f*.
our, ours *pron* nuestro,
  nuestra, nuestros, nuestras.
ourselves *pron pl* nosotros
  mismos, nosotras mismas.
out *adv* fuera.
outbreak *n* erupción *f*.
outcast *n* paria *m* or *f*.
outcome *n* resultado *m*.
outcry *n* protesta *f*.
outdo *vt* superar.
outer *adj* exterior.
outermost *adj* extremo(a).
outfit *n* vestidos *mpl*; ropa *f*.
outline *n* contorno *m*.
outlook *n* perspectiva *f*.
out-of-date *adj* caducado;

pasado de moda.
outpatient *n* paciente externo *m*.
output *n* rendimiento *m*.
outrage *n* ultraje *m*.
outrageous *adj* estravagante,
  escandaloso(a).
outside *n* superficie *f*, exterior *m*.
outsider *n* forastero(a) *m(f)*.
outskirts *npl* alrededores *mpl*.
outstanding *adj* excepcional.
outwit *vt* ser más listo(a) que.
oval *n* óvalo *m*; * *adj* oval.
ovary *n* ovario *m*.
oven *n* horno *m*.
ovenproof *adj* resistente al horno.
over *prep* sobre, encima.
overbearing *adj* autoritario(a).
overcharge *vt* cobrar un precio
  excesivo.
overcoat *n* abrigo *m*.
overdose *n* sobredosis *f*.
overdue *adj* retrasado(a).
overeat *vi* atracarse.
overflow *vt*, *vi* inundar.
overhaul *vt* revisar.
overkill *n* capacidad excesiva
  de detrucción *f*.
overlap *vi* superponerse.
overleaf *adv* al dorso.
overload *vt* sobrecargar.
overpower *vt* predominar,
  oprimir.
overseas *adv* en ultramar;
  * *adj* extranjero(a).
oversee *vt* inspeccionar.
overshadow *vt* eclipsar.
overstate *vi* exagerar.
overstep *vt* exceder, pasar de.
overtake *vt* sobrepasar;
  adelantar.
overtime *n* horas extra *fpl*.
overtone *n* tono *m*.
owe *vt* deber.
owl *n* buho *m*.
own *adj* propio(a).
owner *n* dueño(a) *m(f)*,
  propietario(a) *m(f)*.

ownership *n* posesión *f*.
ox *n* buey *m*.
oxidise *vt* oxidar.
oxygen *n* oxígeno *m*.
oyster *n* ostra *f*.
ozone *n* ozono *m*.

P

pa *n* papá *m*.
pace *n* paso *m*.
pacemaker *n* marcapasos *m*.
pacific(al) *adj* pacífico(a);
  * *n* P~ Ocean Océano Pacífico.
pacify *vt* apaciguar.
package *n* paquete *m*.
packet *n* paquete *m*.
packing *n* embalaje *m*.
pact *n* pato *m*.
pad *n* bloc *m*.
paddle *vi* remar.
paddock *n* corral *m*.
paddy *n* arrozal *m*.
pagan *adj, n* pagano(a) *m(f)*.
page *n* página *f*.
pain *n* pena *f*, castigo *m*; dolor *m*.
painkiller *n* analgésico *m*.
paint *vt* pintar.
paintbrush *n* pincel *m*.
painter *n* pintor(a) *m(f)*.
painting *n* pintura *f*.
pair *n* par *m*.
pajamas *npl* pijama *m*.
palatial *adj* suntuoso(a).
pale *adj* pálido; claro.
pallet *n* pallet *m*.
palliative *adj, n* paliativo(a) *m(f)*.
pallid *adj* pálido(a).
pallor *n* palidez *f*.
palm *n* (botany) palma *f*.
Palm Sunday *n* Domingo de
  Ramos *m*.
palpable *adj* palpable.
paltry *adj* miserable;
  mezquino(a).
pamphlet *n* folleto *m*.

pan *n* sartén *f*.
pancake *n* panqueque *m*.
pandemonium *n* jaleo *m*.
pane *n* cristal *m*.
panel *n* panel *m*.
pang *n* remordimientos *m*.
panic *n* pánico *m*.
pansy *n* (botany) pensamiento *m*.
pant *vi* jadear.
panther *n* pantera *f*.
pantry *n* despensa *f*.
papacy *n* papado *m*.
papal *adj* papal.
paper *n* papel *m*.
paperback *n* libro de bolsillo *m*.
paperclip *n* clip *m*.
paperweight *n* pisapapeles *m*.
paprika *n* pimentón *m*.
parachute *n* paracaídas *m*.
paradise *n* paraíso *m*.
paradox *n* paradoja *f*.
paragon *n* modelo *m*.
paragraph *n* párrafo *m*.
parallel *adj* paralelo(a).
paralysis *n* parálisis *f*.
paralytic(al) *adj* paralítico(a).
paralyse *vt* paralizar.
paramedic *n* auxiliar
  sanitario *m* or *f*.
paramount *adj* supremo(a).
paranoid *adj* paranoico(a).
parasite *n* parásito *m*.
parasol *n* parasol *m*.
parcel *n* paquete *m*.
parch *vt* resecar.
pardon *n* perdón *m*.
parent *n* padre *m*; madre *f*.
parentage *n* parentela *f*.
parental *adj* paternal.
parenthesis *n* paréntesis *m*.
parish *n* parroquia *f*.
parity *n* paridad *f*.
park *n* parque *m*.
parliament *n* parlamento *m*.
parlour *n* salón *m*.
parody *n* parodia *f*.
parrot *n* papagayo *m*, loro *m*.

parsley *n* (botany) perejil *m*.
parsnip *n* (botany) chirivía *f*.
part *n* parte *f*.
participate *vi* participar (en).
particle *n* partícula *f*.
particular *adj* particular.
parting *n* separación *f*,
 despedida *f*.
partition *n* partición *f*.
partner *n* socio(a) *m(f)*,
 compañero(a) *m(f)*.
partridge *n* perdiz *f*.
party *n* partido *m*; fiesta *f*.
pass *vt* pasar.
passage *n* pasaje *m*.
passbook *n* libreta de depósitos *f*.
passenger *n* pasajero(a) *m(f)*.
passion *n* pasión *f*.
passionate *adj* apasionado(a).
passive *adj* pasivo(a).
Passover *n* Pascua *f*.
passport *n* pasaporte *m*.
password *n* contraseña *f*.
past *adj* pasado.
pasta *n* pasta *f*.
paste *n* pasta *f*; * *vt* pegar.
pastime *n* pasatiempo *m*.
pastor *n* pastor(a) *m(f)*.
pastry *n* pastel *m*.
pasture *n* pasto *m*.
patch *n* remiendo *m*; parche *m*.
patent *adj* patente.
path *n* senda *f*.
pathetic *adj* patético(a).
patience *n* paciencia *f*.
patient *adj* paciente.
patio *n* patio *m*.
patriot *n* patriota *m* or *f*.
patriotism *n* patriotismo *m*.
patrol *n* patrulla *f*.
patron *n* patrón *m*.
patronise *vt* patrocinar.
pattern *n* patrón *m*; dibujo *m*.
pauper *n* pobre *m*.
pause *n* pausa *f*.
pave *vt* pavimentar.
pavement *n* calzada *f*.

pavilion *n* pabellón *m*.
paw *n* pata *f*, garra *f*.
pay *vt* pagar.
pea *n* guisante *m*.
peace *n* paz *f*.
peach *n* melocotón *m*.
peacock *n* pavo real *m*.
peak *n* cima *f*, cumbre *f*; pico *m*.
peanut *n* cacahuete *m*.
pear *n* pera *f*.
pearl *n* perla *f*.
peasant *n* campesino(a) *m(f)*.
pebble *n* guijarro *m*.
peculiar *adj* peculiar.
pedal *n* pedal *m*.
pedestal *n* pedestal *m*.
pedestrian *n* peatón(ona) *m(f)*.
pedigree *n* genealogía *f*, pedigrí *m*.
peel *n* cáscara *f*; * *vt* pelar.
peg *n* clavija *f*.
pelican *n* pelícano *m*.
pen *n* bolígrafo *m*; pluma *f*.
penal *adj* penal.
pencil *n* lápiz *m*.
pendulum *n* péndulo *m*.
penetrate *vt* penetrar.
penguin *n* pingüino *m*.
penicillin *n* penicilina *f*.
peninsula *n* península *f*.
penis *n* pene *m*.
penitence *n* penitencia *f*.
penknife *n* navaja *f*.
penny *n* penique *m*.
pension *n* pensión *f*.
pensive *adj* preocupado(a).
Pentecost *n* Pentecostés *m*.
penthouse *n* ático *m*.
people *n* pueblo *m*; nación *f*;
 gente *f*.
pepper *n* pimienta *f*.
peppermint *n* menta *f*.
perceive *vt* percibir.
percemtage *n* porcentaje *m*.
perception *n* percepción *f*.
percolator *n* cafetera de filtro *f*.
percussion *n* percusión *f*, golpe *m*.
perennial *adj* perenne.

perfect *adj* perfecto(a).
perform *vt* ejecutar.
performance *n* ejecución *f*.
perfume *n* perfume *m*;
 fragancia *f*; * *vt* perfumar.
perhaps *adv* quizá, quizás.
peril *n* peligro *m*.
period *n* periodo *m*.
periodical *adj* periódico(a);
 * *n* periódico *m*, revista *f*.
perk *n* extra *m*.
perm *n* permanente *f*.
permanent *adj*; * (~ly *adv*)
 permanente(mente).
permissible *adj* lícito(a).
permission *n* permiso *m*.
permit *vt* permitir.
perplex *vt* dejar perplejo.
persecute *vt* perseguir.
persevere *vi* perseverar.
persist *vi* persistir.
person *n* persona *f*.
personality *n* personalidad *f*.
personnel *n* personal *m*.
perspective *n* perspectiva *f*.
perspiration *n* transpiración *f*.
perspire *vi* transpirar.
persuade *vt* persuadir.
perturb *vt* perturbar.
peruse *vt* leer, examinar.
perverse *adj* perverso(a).
pessimist *n* pesimista *m* or *f*.
pester *vt* molestar.
pet *n* animal doméstico *m*.
petal *n* (botany) pétalo *m*.
petition *n* petición *f*.
petroleum *n* petróleo *m*.
petticoat *n* enaguas *fpl*.
petty *adj* mezquino(a).
pewter *n* peltre *m*.
phantom *n* fantasma *m*.
pharmacist *n* farmaceutico(a)
 m(*f*).
pharmacy *n* farmacia *f*.
phase *n* fase *f*.
pheasant *n* faisán *m*.
phenomenon *n* fenómeno *m*.

phial *n* ampolla *f*.
philosopher *n* filosofo(a) *m*(*f*).
philosophy *n* filosofía *f*.
phlegm *n* flema *f*.
phobia *n* fobia *f*.
phone *n* teléfono *m*.
photocopier *n* fotocopiadora *f*.
photocopy *n* fotocopia *f*.
photograph *n* fotografía *f*;
 * *vt* fotografiar.
photographic *adj* fotográfico(a).
photography *n* fotografía *f*.
phrase *n* frase *f*.
physical *adj* físico(a).
physician *n* médico(a) *m*(*f*).
physicist *n* físico(a) *m*(*f*).
physiotherapy *n* fisioterapia *f*.
physique *n* físico *m*.
pianist *n* pianista *m* or *f*.
piano *n* piano *m*.
piccolo *n* flautín *m*.
pick *vt* escoger, elegir.
pickle *n* escabeche *m*.
picnic *n* comida, merienda *f*.
picture *n* pintura *f*.
picturesque *adj* pintoresco(a).
pie *n* pastel *m*; tarta *f*.
piece *n* pedazo *m*; pieza *f*.
pierce *vt* penetrar, agujerear.
pig *n* cerdo *m*.
pigeon *n* paloma *f*.
pigtail *n* trenza *f*.
pike *n* lucio *m*; pica *f*.
pile *n* montón *m*; * *vt* amontonar.
pilgrim *n* peregrino(a) *m*(*f*).
pill *n* píldora *f*.
pillar *n* pilar *m*.
pillow *n* almohada *f*.
pilot *n* piloto *m*.
pimple *n* grano *m*.
pin *n* alfiler *m*.
pinball *n* fliper *m*.
pincers *n* pinzas *fpl*.
pinch *vt* pellizcar.
pine *n* (botany) pino *m*.
pineapple *n* piña *f*.
pink *n* rosa *f*.

pinnacle *n* cumbre *f*.
pint *n* pinta *f*.
pioneer *n* pionero(a) *m(f)*.
pious *adj* piadoso(a).
pip *n* pepita *f*.
pipe *n* tubería *f*, cañería *f*.
pirate *n* pirata *m*.
pirouette *n* pirueta *f*.
Pisces *n* Piscis *m*.
piss *vi* mear.
pistol *n* pistola *f*.
piston *n* émbolo *m*; pistón.
pit *n* hoyo *m*; mina *f*.
pitcher *n* cántaro *m*; jarro *m*.
pitchfork *n* horca *f*.
pity *n* piedad *f*, compasión *f*.
pivot *n* eje *m*.
pizza *n* pizza *f*.
placard *n* pancarta *f*.
placate *vt* apaciguar.
place *n* lugar *m*, sitio *m*;
   * *vt* poner, colocar.
placid *adj* plácido(a).
plagiarism *n* plagio *m*.
plague *n* peste *f*, plaga *f*.
plaice *n* platija *f*.
plaid *n* tela de cuadros *f*.
plain *adj* liso(a), llano(a);
   claro(a), sencillo(a).
plaintiff *n* (law) demandante
   m or *f*.
plait *n* pliegue *m*; trenza *f*.
plan *n* plano *m*, plan *m*;
   * *vt* planear.
plane *n* avión *m*; plano *m*.
planet *n* planeta *m*.
plank *n* tabla *f*.
plant *n* planta *f*.
plantation *n* plantación *f*.
plaque *n* placa *f*.
plaster *n* yeso *m*.
plastic *n* plástico; * *adj* de
   plástico.
plate *n* plato *m*.
plateau *n* meseta *f*.
platform *n* plataforma *f*.
platinum *n* platino *m*.

platoon *n* (military) pelotón *m*.
play *n* juego *m*; * *vi* jugar.
playboy *n* playboy *m*.
player *n* jugador(a) *m(f)*.
plea *n* súplica *f*, petición *f*.
pleasant *adj* agradable.
please *vt* agradar.
pleasure *n* gusto *m*, placer *m*.
pleat *n* pliegue *m*.
plentiful *adj* copioso(a),
   abundante.
plethora *n* plétora *f*.
pleurisy *n* pleuresía *f*.
pliers *npl* alicates *mpl*.
plinth *n* plinto *m*.
plough *n* arado *m*; * *vt* arar.
ploy *n* truco *m*.
plug *n* tapón *m*, enchufe *m*.
plum *n* ciruela *f*.
plumage *n* plumaje *m*.
plumb *n* plomada *f*.
plumber *n* fontanero(a) *m(f)*.
plume *n* pluma *f*.
plump *adj* rechoncho(a),
   rollizo(a).
plunder *vt* saquear.
plunge *vi* (*vt*) sumergir(se),
   hundir(se).
pluperfect *n* pluscuamperfecto *m*.
plural *adj*, *n* plural *m*.
plus *n* signo de más *m*.
plush *adj* de felpa.
plutonium *n* plutonio *m*.
plywood *n* madera
   contrachapada *f*.
pneumatic *adj* neumático.
pneumonia *n* pulmonía *f*,
   neumonía *f*.
poach *vt* escalfar.
pocket *n* bolsillo *m*.
pod *n* vaina *f*.
poem *n* poema *m*.
poet *n* poeta *m*.
poetry *n* poesía *f*.
poignant *adj* conmovedor(a).
point *n* punta *f*; punto *m*.
point-blank *adv* a quemarropa.

poise *n* porte *m*; aplomo *m*.
poison *n* veneno *m*.
poker *n* atizador *m*; póker *m*.
polar *adj* polar.
pole *n* polo *m*.
police *n* policía *m or f*.
policy *n* política *f*; póliza *f*.
polio *n* polio *f*.
polish *vt* pulir, alisar.
polite *adj* cortés.
politician *n* político(a) *m(f)*.
politics *npl* política *f*.
polka *n* polca *f*.
pollen *n* (botany) polen *m*.
pollute *vt* contaminar.
pollution *n* polución,
  contaminación *f*.
polo *n* polo *m*.
polyester *n* poliester *m*.
polytechnic *n* politécnico *m*.
pomegranate *n* granada *f*.
pomp *n* pompa *f*, esplendor *m*.
pompom *n* borla *f*.
pompous *adj* pomposo(a).
pond *n* estanque *m*.
ponder *vt* meditar.
ponderous *adj* pesado(a).
pontoon *n* pontón *m*.
pony *n* poney *m*.
pool *n* charca *f*, piscina *f*.
poor *adj* pobre.
pop *n* ruido seco *m*.
popcorn *n* palomitas (de maíz) *fpl*.
Pope *n* Papa *m*.
poplar *n* (botany) álamo *m*.
poppy *n* (botany) amapola *f*.
popular *adj*; * (~ly *adv*)
  popular(mente).
populate *vi* poblar.
population *n* población *f*.
porcelain *n* porcelana *f*.
porch *n* pórtico *m*.
porcupine *n* puerco espín *m*.
pore *n* poro *m*.
pork *n* carne de cerdo *f*.
pornography *n* pornografía *f*.
porous *adj* poroso(a).

porpoise *n* marsopa *f*.
port *n* puerto *m* oporto (wine) *m*.
portable *adj* portatil.
portal *n* portal *m*.
porter *n* portero(a) *m(f)*.
portfolio *n* cartera *f*.
porthole *n* portilla *f*.
portico *n* pórtico *m*.
portion *n* porción *f*.
portly *adj* corpulento(a).
portrait *n* retrato *m*.
portray *vt* retratar.
pose *n* postura *f*; pose *f*.
posh *adj* elegante.
position *n* posición *f*.
positive *adj* positivo(a).
posse *n* pelotón *m*.
possess *vt* poseer.
possession *n* posesión *f*.
possibility *n* posibilidad *f*.
possible *adj* posible.
post *n* correo *m*; puesto *m*.
postage stamp *n* sello *m*.
postcard *n* tarjeta postal *f*.
poster *n* cartel *m*.
posterior *n* trasero *m*.
posterity *n* posteridad *f*.
postgraduate *n*
  posgraduado(a) *m(f)*.
posthumous *adj* póstumo(a).
postman *n* cartero(a) *m(f)*.
post office *n* correos *m*.
postpone *vt* aplazar, postergar.
posture *n* postura *f*.
posy *n* ramillete de flores *m*.
pot *n* olla *f*, maceta *f*.
potato *n* patata *f*.
potent *adj* potente.
potential *adj* potencial.
pothole *n* bache *m*.
potion *n* poción *f*, pócima *f*.
potter *n* alfarero(a) *m(f)*.
pottery *n* cerámica *f*.
pouch *n* bolsa *f*.
poultice *n* cataplasma *f*.
poultry *n* aves de corral *fpl*.
pound *n* libra *f*, libra esterlina *f*.

pour *vt* echar; servir.
pout *vi* hacer pucheros.
poverty *n* pobreza *f*.
powder *n* polvo *m*.
power *n* poder *m*.
practicable *adj* factible.
practical *adj* práctico(a);
 * ~ly *adv* prácticamente.
practicality *n* factibilidad *f*.
practice *n* práctica *f*.
pragmatic *adj* pragmático(a).
prairie *n* pampa *f*.
praise *n* alabanza *f*.
prattle *vi* charlar; * *n* charla *f*.
prawn *n* gamba *f*.
pray *vi* rezar.
prayer *n* oración *f*, rezo *m*.
preach *vi* predicar.
preacher *n* predicador(a) *m(f)*,
 pastor(a) *m(f)*.
precaution *n* precaución *f*.
precede *vt* preceder.
precious *adj* precioso(a).
precise *adj* preciso(a).
precision *n* precisión *f*.
preconception *n* idea
 preconcebida *f*.
predator *n* depredador *m*.
predict *vt* predecir.
prediction *n* predicción *f*.
predominant *adj* predominante.
predominate *vt* predominar.
preface *n* prefacio *m*.
prefer *vt* preferir.
preference *n* preferencia *f*.
prefix *n* prefijo *m*.
pregnancy *n* embarazo *m*.
pregnant *adj* embarazada.
prehistoric *adj* prehistórico(a).
prejudice *n* perjuicio *m*.
preliminary *adj* preliminar.
prelude *n* preludio *m*.
premature *adj* prematuro(a).
premier *n* primer(a)
 ministro(a) *m(f)*.
premises *npl* establecimiento *m*.
premium *n* premio *m*.

premonition *n* presentimiento *m*.
prepare *vt (vi)* preparar(se).
preposition *n* preposición *f*.
preposterous *adj* absurdo(a),
 ridículo(a).
prerequisite *n* requisito previo *m*.
prerogative *n* prerrogativa *f*.
prescribe *vi* prescribir; recetar.
prescription *n* prescripción *f*.
present *n* presente, actual;
 regalo *m*.
presentation *n* presentación *f*.
preservation *n* conservación *f*.
preservative *n* conservante *m*.
preserve *vt* preservar, proteger.
preside *vi* presidir.
presidency *n* presidencia *f*.
president *n* presidente *m* or *f*.
press *vt* empujar; * *n* prensa *f*.
pressure *n* presión *f*.
prestige *n* prestigio *m*.
presume *vt* presumir; suponer.
pretence *n* pretexto *m*;
 pretensión *f*.
pretend *vi* pretender.
preterite *n* pretérito *m*.
pretext *n* pretexto *m*.
pretty *adj* lindo(a), bonito(a).
prevent *vt* prevenir.
preview *n* preestreno *m*.
previous *adj* previo.
prey *n* presa *f*.
price *n* precio *m*; premio *m*.
prick *vt* pinchar, picar.
pride *n* orgullo *m*.
priest *n* sacerdote *m*.
priggish *adj* afectado(a).
prim *adj* remilgado(a).
primary *adj* primario(a).
primate *n* primate *m*.
primeval *adj* primitivo(a).
primitive *adj* primitivo(a).
primrose *n* (botany) prímula *f*.
prince *n* príncipe *m*.
princess *n* princesa *f*.
principle *n* principio *m*.
printer *n* impresora *f*.

prior *adj* anterior, previo.
priority *n* prioridad *f*.
priory *n* priorato *m*.
prism *n* prisma *m*.
prison *n* prisión *f*, carcel *f*.
prisoner *n* prisionero(a) *m(f)*.
pristine *adj* pristino(a).
privacy *n* soledad *f*; intimidad *f*.
private *adj* secreto(a),
   privado(a); particular.
private eye *n* detective privado *m*.
privet *n* alheña *f*.
privilege *n* privilegio *m*.
prize *n* premio *m*.
probability *n* probabilidad *f*.
probable *adj* probable.
probation *n* prueba *f*.
problem *n* problema *m*.
procedure *n* procedimiento *m*.
proceed *vi* proceder.
process *n* proceso *m*.
procession *n* procesión *f*.
proclaim *vt* proclamar.
proclamation *n* proclamación *f*.
procure *vt* procurar.
prod *vt* empujar.
prodigal *adj* pródigo(a).
prodigious *adj* prodigioso(a).
prodigy *n* prodigio *m*.
produce *vt* producir.
product *n* producto *m*; obra *f*,
   efecto *m*.
production *n* producción *f*.
profame *adj* profano(a).
profess *vt* profesar.
profession *n* profesión *f*.
professor *n* profesor(a) *m(f)*,
   catedrático(a) *m(f)*.
proficient *adj* proficiente.
profile *n* perfil *m*.
profit *n* ganancia *f*.
profound *adj* profundo(a).
profuse *adj* profuso(a).
program *n* programa *m*.
progress *n* progreso *m*.
prohibit *vt* prohibir.
project *vt* proyectar.

prominent *adj* prominente.
promiscuous *adj* promiscuo(a).
promise *n* promesa *f*.
promontory *n* promontorio *m*.
promote *vt* promover.
promotion *n* promoción *f*.
prone *adj* postrado(a).
prong *n* diente *m*.
pronoun *n* pronombre *m*.
pronounce *vt* pronunciar.
proof *n* prueba *f*.
propaganda *n* propaganda *f*.
propel *vt* impulsar.
propeller *n* hélice *f*.
propensity *n* propensión *f*.
proper *adj* propio(a).
property *n* propiedad *f*.
prophecy *n* profecía *f*.
prophesy *vt* profetizar.
prophet *n* profeta *m* or *f*.
prophetic *adj* profético(a).
proportion *n* proporción *f*.
proportional *adj* proporcional.
proposal *n* propuesta *f*.
propose *vt* proponer.
proposition *n* proposición *f*.
proprietor *n* propietario(a) *m(f)*.
propriety *n* propiedad *f*.
pro rata *adv* aprorrata.
prosaic *adj* prosaico(a).
prose *n* prosa *f*.
prosecute *vt* procesar.
prosecution *n* proceso *m*,
   causa *f*; acusación *f*.
prosecutor *n* acusador(a) *m(f)*.
prospect *n* perspectiva *f*,
   posibilidad *f*.
prospectus *n* prospecto *m*.
prosper *vi* prosperar.
prosperity *n* prosperidad *f*.
prostitute *n* prostituta *f*.
prostitution *n* prostitución *f*.
prostrate *adj* postrado(a).
protagonist *n* protagonista *m* or *f*.
protect *vt* proteger.
protection *n* protección *f*.
protective *adj* protector(a).

protector *n* protector(a) *m(f)*.
protege *n* protegido(a) *m(f)*.
protein *n* proteína *f*.
protest *vi* protestar.
Protestant *n* protestante *m* or *f*.
protester *n* manifestante *m* or *f*.
protocol *n* protocolo *m*.
prototype *n* prototipo *m*.
protracted *adj* prolongado(a).
protrude *vi* sobresalir.
proud *adj* soberbio(a),
  orgulloso(a).
prove *vt* probar.
proverb *n* proverbio *m*.
provide *vt* proveer.
provided *conj*: ~ that con tal que.
providence *n* providencia *f*.
province *n* provincia *f*.
provincial *adj*, *n* provincial *m*.
provision *n* provisión *f*.
proviso *n* estipulación *f*,
  condición *f*.
provocation *n* provocación *f*.
provocative *adj* provocativo(a).
provoke *vt* provocar.
prowess *n* destreza *f*.
prowl *vi* rondar, merodear.
proximity *n* proximidad *f*.
proxy *n* poder *m*; apoderado(a) *m(f)*.
prudence *n* prudencia *f*.
prudent *adj* prudente.
prudish *adj* gazmoño.
pry *vi* entrometerse (en).
psalm *n* salmo *m*.
pseudonym *n* (p)seudónimo *m*.
psyche *n* psique *f*.
psychiatrist *n* psiquiatra *m* or *f*.
psychiatry *n* psiquiatría *f*.
psychic *adj* psíquico(a).
psychoanalysis *n* psicoanálisis *m*.
psychoanalyst *n* psicoanalista
  m or *f*.
psychological *adj* psicológico(a).
psychologist *n* psicólogo(a) *m(f)*.
psychology *n* psicología *f*.
puberty *n* pubertad *f*.
public *adj* público.

publicity *n* publicidad *f*.
publicise *vt* hacer propaganda
  para.
publish *vt* publicar.
publisher *n* editor(a) *m(f)*;
  editorial *f*.
pucker *vt* arrugar, hacer pliegues.
pudding *n* pudín *m*; postre *m*.
puddle *n* charco *m*.
puff *n* soplo *m*.
pull *vt* tirar.
pulley *n* polea *f*.
pullover *n* jersey *m*.
pulp *n* pulpa *f*.
pulpit *n* púlpito *m*.
pulsate *vi* pulsar.
pulse *n* pulso *m*; legumbres *fpl*.
pumice *n* piedra pómez *f*.
pummel *vt* aporrear.
pump *n* bomba *f*.
pumpkin *n* calabaza *f*.
pun *n* juego de palabras *m*.
punch *n* puñetazo *m*;
  * *vt* golpear, dar un puñetazo.
punctual *adj* puntual.
punctuate *vi* puntuar.
punctuation *n* puntuación *f*.
pungent *adj* acre.
punish *vt* castigar.
punishment *n* castigo *m*.
punk *n* punki *m* or *f*.
punt *n* batea *f*.
pup *n* cachorro *m*.
pupil *n* alumno(a) *m(f)*.
puppet *n* títere *m* or *f*.
puppy *n* perrito *m*.
purchase *vt* comprar.
pure *adj* puro(a).
purée *n* puré *m*.
purification *n* purificación *f*.
purify *vt* purificar.
puritan *n* puritano(a) *m(f)*.
purity *n* pureza *f*.
purple *adj* morado(a).
purpose *n* intención *f*.
purr *n* ronroneo *m*; * *vi* ronronear.
purse *n* bolsa *f*, cartera *f*.

pursue *vi* perseguir.

pursuit *n* caza *f*.

purveyor *n* proveedor(a) *m(f)*.

push *vt* empujar.

pusher *n* traficante de drogas *m* or *f*.

push-up *vt* hacer subir.

put *vt* poner, colocar.

putrid *adj* podrido(a).

putty *n* masilla *f*.

puzzle *n* acertijo *m*.

puzzling *adj* extraño(a), misterioso(a).

pylon *n* torre de conducción eléctrica *f*.

pyramid *n* pirámide *f*.

python *n* pitón *m*.

Q

quack *n* graznido *m*; * *vi* graznar.

quadrangle *n* patio *m*.

quadrant *n* cuadrante *m*.

quadrilateral *adj* cuadrilátero.

quadruped *n* cuadrúpedo(a) *m(f)*.

quadruple *adj* cuadruple.

quadruplet *n* cuatrillizo(a) *m(f)*.

quagmire *n* lodazal *m*, cenegal *m*.

quail *n* codorniz *f*.

quaint *adj* extraño(a); pintoresco(a).

quake *n* temblor *m*; * *vi* temblar.

qualification *n* calificación *f*.

qualify *vt* calificar.

quality *n* calidad *f*.

qualm *n* escrúpulo *m*.

quandary *n* incertidumbre *f*.

quantitative *adj* cuantitativo(a).

quantity *n* cantidad *f*.

quarantine *n* cuarentena *f*.

quarrel *n* riña *f*, contienda *f*.

quarrelsome *adj* pendenciero(a).

quarry *n* cantera *f*.

quarter *n* cuarto *m*, cuarta parte *f*.

quarterly *adj* trimestral.

quartermaster *n* (military)

comisario *m*.

quartet *n* (music) cuarteto *m*.

quartz *n* (geology) cuarzo *m*.

quash *vt* invalidar, anular.

quay *n* muelle *m*.

queasy *adj* nauseabundo(a).

queen *n* reina *f*.

queer *adj* extraño(a).

quell *vt* calmar.

quench *vt* apagar.

query *n* cuestión.

quest *n* busqueda *f*.

question *n* pregunta *f*; cuestión *f*.

questionable *adj* discutible, dudoso(a).

question mark *n* punto de interrogación *m*.

questionnaire *n* cuestionario *m*.

quibble *vi* andar con sutilezas.

quick *adj* rápido(a).

quicken *vt* apresurar.

quicksand *n* arena movediza *f*.

quicksilver *n* azogue *m*; mercurio *m*.

quick-witted *adj* listo(a), despabilado(a).

quiet *adj* callado(a), tranquilo(a).

quinine *n* quinina *f*.

quintet *n* (music) quinteto *m*.

quintuple *adj* quintuplo.

quintuplet *n* quintillizo(a) *m(f)*.

quip *n* ocurrencia *f*; * *vt* echar pullas.

quirk *n* peculiaridad *f*.

quit *vt* dejar, abandonar, desocupar.

quite *adv* bastante.

quits *adv* ¡en paz!.

quiver *vi* estremecerse.

quixotic *adj* quijotesco.

quiz *n* concurso *m*.

quizzical *adj* burlón(ona).

quota *n* cuota *f*.

quotation *n* presupuesto *m*; cita *f*.

quotation marks *npl* comillas *fpl*.

quote *vt* citar.

quotient *n* cociente *m*.

R

rabbi *n* rabino *m*.
rabbit *n* conejo *m*.
rabble *n* gentuza *f*; chusma *f*.
rabid *adj* rabioso(a).
rabies *n* rabia *f*.
race *n* raza *f*; carrera *f*;
  * *vt* competir, correr.
rack *n* rejilla *f*.
racket *n* ruido *m*; raqueta *f*.
racy *adj* picante.
radiance *n* brillantez *f*;
  resplandor *m*.
radiant *adj* radiante.
radiate *vt*, *vi* radiar, irradiar,
  extenderse.
radiation *n* radiación *f*.
radiator *n* radiador *m*.
radical *adj*; * (~ly *adv*)
  radical(mente).
radio *n* radio *f*.
radioactive *adj* radioactivo(a).
radish *n* (botany) rábano *m*.
radius *n* radio *f*.
raffle *n* rifa *f*, sorteo *m*; * *vt* rifar.
raft *n* balsa *f*.
rafter *n* viga *f*.
rag *n* trapo *m*.
rage *n* rabia *f*; * *vi* rabiar, estar
  furioso.
raid *n* incursion *f*.
rail *n* barandilla *f*: — by ~ en tren.
railway *n* ferrocarril *m*, tren *m*.
rain *n* lluvia *f*.
rainbow *n* arco iris *m*.
raise *vt* levantar, alzar.
raisin *n* pasa *f*.
rake *n* rastrillo *m*.
ram *n* carnero *m*.
ramble *n* caminata *f*; * *vi* divagar.
ramification *n* ramificación *f*.
ramp *n* rampa *f*.
rampant *adj* estar muy
  extendido(a).
ramshackle *adj* destartalado(a).

ranch *n* hacienda *f*.
rancid *adj* rancio(a).
rancor *n* rencor *m*.
random *adj* fortuito(a),
  aleatorio(a).
range *n* cordillera *f*; serie *f*,
  surtido *m*; * *vt* colocar, ordenar.
ransack *vt* saquear.
ransom *n* rescate *m*.
rape *n* violacion *f*; * *vt* violar.
rapid *adj* rápido(a).
rapist *n* violador *m*.
rapture *n* rapto *m*.
rare *adj* raro(a).
rascal *n* pícaro(a) *m*(*f*).
rash *adj* precipitado(a);
  * *n* erupción (cutánea) *f*.
raspberry *n* frambuesa *f*.
rat *n* rata *f*.
rate *n* tasa *f*; precio *m*; valor *m*.
rather *adv* más bien; antes.
ratification *n* ratificación *f*.
ratify *vt* ratificar.
ratio *n* razón *f*, proporción *f*.
ration *n* racion *f*; * *vt* racionar.
rational *adj* racional.
ravage *vt* hacer estragos.
rave *vi* delirar; entusiasmarse,
  encolerizarse.
raven *n* cuervo *m*.
ravine *n* barranco *m*.
ravish *vt* encantar.
ravishing *adj* encantador(a).
raw *adj* crudo.
ray *n* rayo *m*; raya *f* (pez).
raze *vt* arrasar.
razor *n* navaja *f*; maquinilla
  de afeitar *f*.
reach *vt* alcanzar.
react *vi* reaccionar.
reaction *n* reacción *f*.
read *vt* leer.
readable *adj* legible.
reader *n* lector(a) *m*(*f*).
readjust *vt* reajustar.
ready *adj* listo(a), pronto.
real *adj* real.

reality *n* realidad *f*.
realisation *n* realización *f*.
realise *adv* darse cuenta de;
  realizar.
realm *n* reino *m*.
ream *n* resma *f*.
reap *vt* segar.
reappear *vi* reaparecer.
rear *n* parte trasera *f*.
rearmament *n* rearme *m*.
reason *n* razón *f*, causa *f*;
  * *vt*, *vi* razonar.
reassure *vt* tranquilizar.
rebel *n* rebelde *m(f)*.
rebellion *n* rebelión *f*.
rebound *n* rebote *m*; * *vi* rebotar.
rebuke *n* reprimenda *f*;
  * *vt* reprender.
rebut *vi* rebatir.
recede *vi* retroceder.
receipt *n* recibo *m*.
receive *vi* recibir.
recent *adj* reciente.
reception *n* recepción *f*.
recess *n* descanso *m*.
recession *n* retirada *f*
  (commerce) recesión *f*.
recipe *n* receta *f*.
recipient *n* recipiente *m*.
recital *n* recital *m*.
recite *vt* recitar.
reckless *adj* temerario(a).
reckon *vt* contar.
recline *vt* (*vi*) reclinar(se).
recluse *n* recluso(a) *m(f)*.
recognise *vt* reconocer.
recommend *vt* recomendar.
recommendation *n*
  recomendación *f*.
recompense *n* recompensa *f*.
reconcile *vt* reconciliar.
reconsider *vt* reconsiderar.
record *n* disco *m*; registro *m*;
  * *vt* registrar; grabar.
recourse *n* recurso *m*.
recover *vt* recobrar; recuperar.
recovery *n* convalecencia *f*;

  rescate *m*.
recreation *n* recreación *f*,
  recreo *m*.
recruit *vt* reclutar.
rectangle *n* rectángulo *m*.
rectify *vt* rectificar.
rectilinear *adj* rectilineo(a).
rector *n* rector(a) *m(f)*.
recur *vi* repetirse.
red *adj* rojo(a); tinto(a); * *n* rojo *m*.
redeem *vt* redimir.
redemption *n* redención *f*.
red-hot *adj* candente, ardiente.
redress *n* reparación *f*;
  * *vt* reparar.
reduce *vt* reducir.
reduction *n* reducción *f*.
reed *n* lengüeta *f*.
reek *n* mal olor *m*; * *vi* apestar.
refectory *n* comedor *m*.
refer *vt*, *vi* referir.
referee *n* árbitro *m*.
reference *n* referencia *f*.
refine *vt* refinar.
refit *vt* reparar.
reflect *vt*, *vi* reflejar.
reflection *n* reflexión *f*.
reflex *adj* reflejo.
reform *vt* (*vi*) reformar(se).
refresh *vt* refrescar.
refreshment *n* refresco *m*.
refrigerator *n* nevera *f*.
refuge *n* refugio *m*, asilo *m*.
refugee *n* refugiado(a) *m(f)*.
refund *vt* devolver.
refurbish *vt* restaurar.
refusal *n* negativa *f*.
refuse *vt* rehusar.
refute *vt* refutar, rebatir.
regal *adj* real.
regard *vt* considerar;
  * *n* respecto *m*.
regardless *adv* a pesar de todo.
regatta *n* regata *f*.
regime *n* régimen *m*.
region *n* región *f*.
register *n* registro *m*.

registrar *n* registrador(a) *m(f)*.
registration *n* declaración *f*;
  matrícula *f*.
registry *n* registro *m*.
regular *adj* regular.
regulation *n* regulación *f*.
reign *n* reinado *m*; * *vi* reinar.
reinforce *vt* reforzar.
reinstate *vt* reintegrar.
reject *vt* rechazar.
rejection *n* rechazo *m*.
rejoice *vi* (*vt*) regocijar(se),
  alegrar(se).
relapse *n* reincidencia *f*;
  * *vi* reincidir.
relate *vt, vi* relatar.
relation *n* relación *f*.
relationship *n* parentesco *m*;
  relación *f*.
relative *adj* relativo(a).
relax *vt, vi* relajar.
release *vt* soltar, libertar.
relic *n* reliquia *f*.
relief *n* alivio *m*.
relieve *vt* aliviar.
religion *n* religión *f*.
rely *vi* confiar en; contar con.
remain *vi* quedar.
remains *npl* restos *mpl*.
remark *n* comentario *m*;
  * *vt* comentar.
remedy *n* remedio *m*.
remember *vt* acordarse de;
  recordar.
remind *vt* recordar.
remt *vt, vi* remitir.
remorse *n* remordimiento *m*.
remote *adj* remoto(a).
remove *vt* quitar.
renew *vt* renovar.
renovate *vt* renovar, reanudar.
rent *n* renta *f*.
rental *n* alquiler *m*.
repair *vt* reparar.
repeat *vt* repetir.
repel *vt* repeler.
repetition *n* repetición *f*.

replace *vt* reemplazar.
reply *n* respuesta *f*.
repose *vt, vi* reposar.
represent *vt* representar.
reproduce *vt* reproducir.
reproduction *n* reproducción *f*.
reptile *n* reptil *m*.
republic *n* república *f*.
repugnance *n* repugnancia *f*.
repulse *vt* rechazar.
request *n* petición *f*.
require *vt* requerir.
rescue *vt* librar.
research *n* investigación *f*;
  * *vt* investigar.
resemble *vt* asemejarse,
  parecerse.
resent *vt* resentirse.
reserve *vt* reservar.
residence *n* residencia *f*.
resign *vt, vi* renunciar, dimitir.
resin *n* resina *f*.
resist *vt* resistir, oponerse.
resolve *vt, vr* resolver.
resort *vi* recurrir.
resource *n* recurso *m*; centro
  turístico *m*.
respect *n* respecto *m*.
respite *n* respiro *m*, prórroga *f*.
respond *vt* responder.
rest *n* reposo *m*.
restless *adj* inquieto(a).
restore *vt* restaurar.
restrict *vt* restringir.
result *vi* resultar.
resume *n* resumen *m*; * *vt* resumir.
resurrection *n* resurrección *f*.
resuscitate *vt* resucitar.
retail *n* venta al por menor *f*.
retain *vt* retener.
reticence *n* reticencia *f*.
retina *n* retina *f*.
retire *vt* (*vi*) retirar(se).
retreat *n* retirada *f*.
return *n* vuelta *f*, regreso *m*; * *vt*
  regresar; reaparecer; volver.
reveal *vt* revelar.

revenge *vt* vengar; * *n* venganza *f.*
revenue *n* renta *f.*
revere *vt* reverenciar.
reverse *n* contrario(a) *m(f)*;
  atrás; * *vt* dar marcha atrás.
review *vt* reseña.
revise *vt* corregir; repasar.
revival *n* reanimación *f.*
revolt *n* rebelión *f*; * *vi* rebelarse.
revolution *n* revolución *f.*
revolve *vt* girar, dar vueltas.
revue *n* revista *f.*
reward *n* recompensa *f.*
rheumatism *n* reumatismo *m.*
rhinoceros *n* rinoceronte *m.*
rhombus *n* rombo *m.*
rhubarb (botany) *n* ruibarbo *m.*
rhyme *n* rima *f.*
rhythm *n* ritmo *m.*
rib *n* costilla *f.*
ribbon *n* cinta *f.*
rice *n* arroz *m.*
rich *adj* rico(a).
riches *npl* riqueza *f.*
rickets *n* raquitismo *m.*
rid *vt* librar.
riddle *n* enigma *m.*
ride *vi* cabalgar.
ridge *n* cresta *f.*
ridiculous *adj* ridículo(a).
rifle *n* rifle *m.*
right *adj* derecho(a), recto(a);
  justo(a).
rigid *adj* rígido(a).
rigor *n* rigor *m.*
rind *n* corteza *f.*
rinse *vt* lavar, limpiar.
rise *n* cuesta *f*, pendiente *f*,
  altura *f*, subida *f*, alza *f*;
  * *vi* elevarse, subir, crecer.
risk *n* riesgo *m*, peligro *m.*
rite *n* rito *m.*
ritual *adj*, *n* ritual *m.*
rival *adj* rival.
river *n* río *m.*
road *n* camino *m.*
road sign *n* señal de tráfico *f.*

roar *vi* rugir.
roast *vt* asar.
rob *vt* robar.
robber *n* ladrón(ona) *m(f).*
robbery *n* robo *m.*
robust *adj* robusto(a).
rock *n* roca *f.*
rocket *n* cohete *m.*
rodent *n* roedor *m.*
rogue *n* bribón(ona) *m(f).*
roll *n* panecillo *m*; * *vt* enrollar.
Roman Catholic *adj*, *n*
  católico(a) *m(f)* romano(a).
romance *n* romance *m.*
roof *n* tejado *m.*
room *n* habitación *f*, sala *f.*
roomy *adj* espacioso(a).
root *n* raíz *f.*
rope *n* cuerda *f.*
rosary *n* rosario *m.*
rose *n* (botany) rosa *f.*
rosebed *n* rosaleda *f.*
rosebud *n* capullo de rosa *m.*
rosemary *n* (botany) romero *m.*
rosette *n* roseta *f.*
rot *vi* pudrirse.
rotten *adj* podrido(a).
rouble *n* rublo *m.*
rouge *n* colorete *m.*
rough *adj* áspero(a).
roulette *n* ruleta *f.*
round *adj* redondo(a).
rouse *vt* despertar.
route *n* ruta *f.*
routine *adj* rutinario(a);
  * *n* rutina *f.*
row *n* (line) hilera *f*, fila *f*;
  * *vt* (marine) remar, bogar.
royal *adj* real.
royalty *n* realeza *f*; derechos
  de autor *m.*
rub *vt* restregar, frotar.
rubber *n* caucho *m*, goma *f.*
rubber-band *n* goma *f*, gomita *f.*
rubbish *n* basura *f.*
rubric *n* rúbrica *f.*
ruby *n* rubí *m.*

rucksack *n* mochila *f*.
rudder *n* timón *m*.
rude *adj* rudo(a), brutal.
rudiment *n* rudimento *m*.
rue *vi* arrepentirse de.
rug *n* alfombra *f*.
rugby *n* rugby *m*.
ruin *n* ruina *f*.
ruinous *adj* ruinoso(a).
rule *n* mando *m*; regla *f*.
ruler *n* gobernador(a) *m(f)*; regla *f*.
rum *n* ron *m*.
rumour *n* rumor *m*.
run *vt* dirigir; organizar;
  * *vi* correr.
runaway *n* fugitivo(a) *m(f)*.
rung *n* escalón *m*.
runway *n* pista de aterrizaje *f*.
rupture *n* rotura *f*.
rural *adj* rural.
ruse *n* ardid *f*.
rush *n* (botany) junco *m*; prisa *f*,
  ímpetu *m*; * *vi* correr,
  precipitarse.
rusk *n* galleta *f*.
russet *adj* bermejo.
rust *n* herrumbre *f*.
rustic *adj* rústico(a).
rustle *vi* crujir; susurrar.
rut *n* celo *m*.
ruthless *adj* despiadado(a).
rye *n* (botany) centeno *m*.

S

Sabbath *n* domingo *m*;
  (Jewish) sábado *m*.
sabotage *n* sabotaje *m*.
saccharin *n* sacarina *f*.
sachet *n* sobrecito *m*.
sack *n* saco *m*; * *vt* despedir.
sacrament *n* sacramento *m*.
sacred *adj* sagrado(a).
sacredness *n* santidad *f*.
sacrifice *n* sacrificio *m*.
sacrilege *n* sacrilegio *m*.

sad *adj* triste.
saddle *n* silla (de montar) *f*;
  * *vt* ensillar.
sadness *n* tristeza *f*.
safari *n* safari *m*.
safe *adj* seguro(a); *n* caja fuerte *f*.
safety *n* seguridad *f*.
saffron *n* azafrán *m*.
sage *n* (botany) salvia *f*.
Sagittarius *n* Sagitario *m*.
sago *n* (botany) sagú *m*.
sail *n* vela *f*.
sailor *n* marinero(a) *m(f)*.
saint *n* santo(a) *m(f)*.
sake: — for the ~ of por motivo de.
salad *n* ensalada *f*.
salamander *n* salamandra *f*.
salary *n* sueldo *m*.
sale *n* venta *f*; saldo *m*.
salient *adj* sobresaliente.
saline *adj* salino(a).
saliva *n* saliva *f*.
salmon *n* salmón *m*.
salmon trout *n* trucha
  asalmonada *f*.
saloon *n* bar *m*.
salt *n* sal *f*.
salubrious *adj* salubre.
salutation *n* saludo *m*.
salute *vt* saludar.
same *adj* mismo(a), idéntico(a).
sample *n* muestra *f*; ejemplo *m*.
sanctify *vt* santificar.
sanctuary *n* santuario *m*.
sand *n* arena *f*.
sandal *n* sandalia *f*.
sandstone *n* piedra arenisca *f*.
sandwich *n* bocadillo *m*.
sane *adj* cuerdo(a), sensato(a).
sanitarium *n* sanatorio *m*.
sanity *n* cordura *f*.
sap *n* savia *f*.
sapling *n* arbolito *m*.
sapphire *n* zafiro *m*.
sarcasm *n* sarcasmo *m*.
sarcophagus *n* sarcófago.
sardine *n* sardina *f*.

Satan *n* Satanás *m*.
satchel *n* mochila *f*.
satellite *n* satélite *m*.
satin *n* raso *m*.
satire *n* sátira *f*.
satisfaction *n* satisfacción *f*.
satisfy *vt* satisfacer.
Saturday *n* sábado *m*.
satyr *n* sátiro(a) *m(f)*.
sauce *n* salsa *f*.
saucepan *n* cazo *m*.
saucer *n* platillo *m*.
sausage *n* salchicha *f*.
savage *adj* salvaje.
savagery *n* crueldad *f*.
savannah *n* sabana *f*.
save *vt* salvar, ahorrar, guardar.
saveloy *n* salchicha seca muy
  sazonada *f*.
Saviour *n* Salvador *m*.
savoury *adj* sabroso(a).
saw *n* sierra *f*.
saxophone *n* saxofón *m*.
say *vt* decir.
saying *n* dicho *m*.
scab *n* roña *f*; costra *f*.
scald *vt* escaldar.
scale *n* balanza *f*.
scalp *n* cabellera *f*.
scam *n* estafa *f*, timo *m*.
scampi *npl* gambas *fpl*.
scan *vt* escudriñar, registrar.
scandal *n* escándalo *m*.
scandalise *vt* escandalizar.
scar *n* cicatriz *f*.
scarce *adj* raro(a).
scare *vt* espantar.
scarf *n* bufanda *f*.
scarlet *n* escarlata *f*.
scarp *n* escarpa *f*.
scene *n* escena *f*.
scenery *n* vista *f*.
sceptic *n* escéptico(a) *m(f)*.
scepticism *n* escepticismo *m*.
schedule *n* horario *m*.
scheme *n* proyecto *m*, plan *m*.
schism *n* cisma *m*.

scholar *n* estudiante *m*.
school *n* escuela *f*.
schoolteacher *n* maestro(a)
  m(f); profesor(a) *m(f)*.
science *n* ciencia *f*.
scientist *n* científico(a) *m(f)*.
scissors *npl* tijeras *fpl*.
scooter *n* moto *f*.
scorch *vt* quemar.
scorn *n* desprecio *m*;
  * *vt, vi* despreciar.
Scorpio *n* Escorpión *m*
  (astrology).
scorpion *n* escorpión *m*,
  alacrán *m*.
Scotch *n* whisky escoces *m*.
scoundrel *n* canalla *m* or *f*.
scramble *n* subida *f*, pelea *f*;
  * *vi* pelear por.
scrap *n* pedacito *m*, pizca *f*;
  riña *f*, bronca *f*.
scrape *n* lío *m*, apuro *m*; * *vt*,
  raspar.
scraper *n* raspador *m*.
scratch *n* rasguño *m*, arañazo
  m; * *vt* arañar.
scrawl *vi* hacer garabatos.
scream, screech *n* chillido *m*;
  * *vi* chillar.
screen *n* pantalla *f*.
screenplay *n* guión *m*.
screw *n* tornillo *m*.
screwdriver *n* destornillador *m*.
scribble *vt* garabatear.
scribe *n* escritor *m*.
script *n* guion *m*; letra *f*.
Scripture *n* Sagradas
  Escrituras *fpl*.
scruffy *adj* desaliñado(a).
scruple *n* escrúpulo *m*.
scullery *n* fregadero *m*.
sculptor *n* escultor(a) *m(f)*.
sculpture *n* escultura *f*.
scum *n* espuma *f*, escoria *f*.
scurvy *n* escorbuto *m*.
scythe *n* guadaña *f*.
sea *n* mar *m* or *f*; * *adj* de mar.

sea breeze *n* brisa marina *f*.
seafood *n* mariscos *mpl*.
sea front *n* paseo marítimo *m*.
seagull *n* gaviota *f*.
sea horse *n* hipocampo *m*,
  caballito de mar *m*.
seal *n* sello *m*; foca *f*.
seam *n* costura *f*.
seaman *n* marinero *m*.
sea plane *n* hidroavión *m*.
sear *vt* cauterizar.
search *vt* examinar, buscar.
seashore *n* ribera *f*, litoral *m*.
seasick *adj* mareado(a).
season *n* estación *f*.
seasoning *n* condimento *m*.
seat *n* asiento *m*; silla *f*.
seat belt *n* cinturón de
  seguridad *m*.
seaweed *n* alga marina *f*.
seclude *vt* retirar.
seclusion *n* retiro *m*.
second *adj* segundo(a).
secondary *adj* secundario(a).
second-hand *n* segunda mano *f*.
secret *adj*, *n* secreto *m*.
secretary *n* secretario(a) *m(f)*.
sect *n* secta *f*.
section *n* sección *f*.
sector *n* sector *m*.
secular *adj* secular.
secure *adj* seguro(a).
security *n* seguridad *f*.
sedate *adj* tranquilo(a).
sedative *n* sedante *m*.
sedge *n* (botany) junco *m*.
sediment *n* sedimento *m*.
sedition *n* sedición *f*.
seduce *vt* seducir.
seducer *n* seductor(a) *m(f)*.
seduction *n* seducción *f*.
seductive *adj* seductor(a).
see *vt*, *vi* ver.
seed *n* semilla *f*.
seedy *adj* desaseado(a).
seek *vt*, *vi* buscar.
seem *vi* parecer.

seemliness *n* decencia *f*.
seesaw *n* balancín *m*.
seethe *vi* hervir.
segment *n* segmento *m*.
seize *vt* asir.
seizure *n* ataque *m*.
seldom *adv* raramente.
select *adj* selecto(a)
  escogido(a); * *vt* elegir.
selection *n* selección *f*.
self *n* uno(a) mismo(a) *m(f)*.
selfish *adj* egoísta.
self-portrait *n* autorretrato *m*.
self-same *adj* mismo(a).
sell *vt*, *vi* vender.
semen *n* semen *m*.
semester *n* semestre *m*.
semicircle *n* semicírculo *m*.
semicircular *adj* semicircular.
semicolon *n* punto y coma *m*.
seminary *n* seminario *m*.
senate *n* senado *m*.
senator *n* senador(a) *m(f)*.
send *vt* enviar.
sender *n* remitente *m* or *f*.
senile *adj* senil.
senior *n* mayor *m*.
senna *n* (botany) sena *f*.
sensation *n* sensación *f*.
sense *n* sentido *m*.
sensibility *n* sensibilidad *f*.
sensible *adj* sensato(a),
  juicioso(a).
sensitive *adj* sensitivo(a).
sensual, sensuous *adj* sensual.
sensuality *n* sensualidad *f*.
sentence *n* oración *f*, sentencia *f*.
sentiment *n* sentimiento *m*.
sentinel, sentry *n* centinela *m*.
separate *vt* (*vi*) separar(se).
separation *n* separación *f*.
September *n* se(p)tiembre *m*.
sepulchre *n* sepulcro *m*.
sequel *n* consecuencia *f*,
  resultado *m*.
sequence *n* sucesión *f*, serie *f*.
seraph *n* serafín *m*.

serenade *n* serenata *f.*

serene *adj* sereno(a).

serenity *n* serenidad *f.*

serf *n* siervo(a) *m(f).*

sergeant *n* sargento *m.*

serial *adj* telenovela *f*, novela por entregas *f.*

series *n* serie *f.*

serious *adj* serio(a), grave.

sermon *n* sermón *f.*

serpent *n* serpiente *f.*

serpentine *adj* serpentino(a).

serrated *adj* serrado.

serum *n* suero *m.*

servant *n* criado(a) *m(f).*

serve *vt, vi* servir.

service *n* servicio *m.*

servile *adj* servil.

session *n* junta *f*, sesión *f.*

set *vt* poner, colocar, fijar.

setter *n* setter *m.*

seven *adj, n* siete.

seventeen *adj, n* diez y siete, diecisiete.

seventeenth *adj, n* decimoséptimo(a).

seventh *adj, n* séptimo(a).

seventieth *adj, n* septuagésimo(a).

seventy *adj, n* setenta.

sever *vt, vi* cortar, romper.

several *adj, pron* varios(as).

severance *n* ruptura *f.*

severe *adj* severo(a).

severity *n* severidad *f.*

sew *vt, vi* coser.

sewer *n* alcantarilla *f.*

sex *n* sexo *m.*

sexist *adj, n* sexista *m* or *f.*

sexual *adj* sexual.

sexy *adj* sexy.

shade, shadow *n* sombra *f.*

shaft *n* astil *m*, eje *m.*

shake *vt* sacudir; agitar.

shallow *adj* poco profundo(a), superficial.

sham *n* fraude *m*, engaño *m*; * *vt* fingir.

shame *n* vergüenza *f.*

shamefaced *adj* vergonzoso(a).

shampoo *n* champú *m.*

shamrock *n* (botany) trébol *m.*

shank *n* pierna *f.*

shanty *n* chabola *f.*

shanty town *n* barrio de chabolas *m.*

shape *vt, vi* formar; *n* forma *m.*

shapeless *adj* informe.

shapely *adj* bien formado(a).

share *n* parte, porción *f*; * *vi* compartir.

shark *n* tiburón *m.*

sharp *adj* agudo(a).

shatter *vt* destrozar.

shave *vt* afeitar.

shaver *n* maquinilla de afeitar *f.*

shawl *n* chal *m.*

she *pron* ella.

sheaf *n* gavilla *f.*

shear *vt* esquilar.

sheath *n* vaina *f.*

shed *n* cobertizo *m*; * *vt* mudar, derramar.

sheen *n* brillo *m.*

sheep *n* oveja *f.*

sheer *adj* puro(a), claro(a).

sheet *n* sábana *f.*

sheet lightning *n* relámpago *m.*

shelf *n* estante *m.*

shell *n* cáscara *f*; concha *f.*

shelter *n* abrigo *m*, refugio *m*; amparo *m.*

shepherd *n* pastor *m.*

sherbet *n* sorbete *m.*

sheriff *n* sherif *m.*

sherry *n* jerez *m.*

shield *n* escudo *m.*

shift *n* cambio *m*, turno *m*; * *vi* cambiarse.

shinbone *n* espinilla *f.*

shine *vi* lucir, brillar.

shiny *adj* brillante.

ship *n* nave *f*, barco *m.*

shipwreck *n* naufragio *m.*

shirt *n* camisa *f.*

shit! *excl (sl)* ¡mierda!

shiver *vi* tiritar de frío.

shoal *n* banco *m*.

shock *n* choque *m*, descarga emocional *f*.

shock absorber *n* amortiguador *m*.

shoddy *adj* de pacotilla.

shoe *n* zapato *m*.

shoelace *n* cordón de zapato *m*.

shoemaker *n* zapatero *m*.

shoot *n* retoño *m*, vástago *m*; * *vt* tirar, disparar.

shop *n* tienda *f*.

shopper *n* comprador(a) *m(f)*.

shopping *n* compras *fpl*.

shopping centre *n* centro comercial *m*.

shore *n* costa, ribera *f*.

short *adj* corto(a), breve.

short-sighted *adj* corto de vista.

shot *n* tiro *m*.

shotgun *n* escopeta *f*.

shoulder *n* hombro *m*.

shout *vi* gritar, aclamar.

shove *vt, vi* empujar.

shovel *n* escavadora *f*.

show *vt* mostrar.

shower *n* chaparrón *m*, llovizna *f*, ducha *f*.

showy *adj* ostentoso(a).

shred *n* triza *f*, jirón *m*; * *vt* hacer trizas.

shrewd *adj* astuto(a).

shriek *n* chillido *m*; * *vt, vi* chillar.

shrimp *n* camarón *m*.

shrine *n* santuario *m*, sepulcro *m*.

shrink *vi* encogerse.

shroud *n* cubierta *f*.

Shrove Tuesday *n* martes de carnaval *m*.

shrub *n* arbusto *m*.

shrug *vt* encogerse de hombros.

shun *vt* rehuir, evitar.

shut *vt* cerrar.

shutter *n* contraventana *f*.

shuttle *n* lanzadera *f*.

shuttlecock *n* volante *m*.

shy *adj* tímido(a).

shyness *n* timidez *f*.

sick *adj* malo(a), enfermo(a).

sickle *n* hoz *f*.

sickness *n* enfermedad *f*.

side *n* lado *m*.

sideboard *n* aparador *m*.

siege *n* (military) sitio *m*.

sieve *n* tamiz *m*.

sift *vt* cribar.

sigh *vi* suspirar.

sight *n* vista *f*.

sightseeing *n* excursionismo, turismo *m*.

sign *n* señal *f*.

signal *n* señal *f*.

signature *n* firma *f*.

significance *n* importancia *f*.

signify *vt* significar.

signpost *n* indicador *m*.

silence *n* silencio *m*.

silk *n* seda *f*.

silky *adj* hecho de seda; sedoso(a).

sill *n* alféizar *m*.

silly *adj* tonto(a).

silver *n* plata *f*.

similar *adj* similar; semejante.

similarity *n* semejanza *f*.

simile *n* símil *m*.

simmer *vi* hervir a fuego lento.

simple *adj* simple.

simplicity *n* sencillez *f*.

simulate *vt* simular.

simulation *n* simulación *f*.

sin *n* pecado *m*.

since *adv* desde.

sincerity *n* sinceridad *f*.

sinew *n* tendón *m*.

sing *vi, vt* cantar.

singe *vt* chamuscar.

singer *n* cantor(a) *m(f)*, cantante *m* or *f*.

single *adj* solo(a); soltero(a).

singly *adv* uno po uno.

singular *adj* singular.

sinister *adj* siniestro(a).

sink *n* fregadero *m*; * *vi (vt)*

hundir(se).

sinner *n* pecador(a) *m(f)*.

sinus *n* seno *m*.

sip *vt* sorber; * *n* sorbo *m*.

siphon *n* sifón *m*.

sir *n* señor *m*.

siren *n* sirena *f*.

sister *n* hermana *f*.

sister-in-law *n* cuñada *f*.

sisterly *adj* en hermandad.

sit *vi* sentarse.

site *n* sitio *m*; * *vt* situar.

sit-in *n* ocupación *f*.

sitting room *n* sala de estar *f*.

situation *n* situación *f*.

six *adj, n* seis.

sixteen *adj, n* diez y seis, dieciseis.

sixteenth *adj, n* decimosexto(a).

sixth *adj, n* sexto(a).

sixtieth *adj, n* sexagésimo(a).

sixty *adj, n* sesenta.

size *n* tamaño *m*.

skate *n* patín *m*; * *vi* patinar.

skeleton *n* esqueleto *m*.

sketch *n* esbozo *m*.

ski *n* esquí *m*; * *vi* esquiar.

skid *n* patinazo *m*.

skill *n* destreza *f*.

skim *vt* desnatar.

skin *n* piel *f* cutis *m*.

skip *vi* saltar, brincar.

skirt *n* falda.

skittle *n* bolo *m*.

skulk *vi* (*vt*) esconder(se).

skull *n* calavera *f*, cráneo *m*.

sky *n* cielo *m*.

skyscraper *n* rascacielos *m invar*.

slab *n* losa *f*.

slack *adj* flojo(a), de poca actividad.

slag *n* escoria *f*.

slander *n* calumnia *f*, difamación *f*; * *vt* calumniar *f*.

slang *n* argot *m*.

slap *n* bofetada *f*.

slate *n* pizarra *f*.

slave *n* esclavo(a) *m(f)*.

slaver *n* baba *f*; * *vi* babosear.

slay *vt* matar.

sledge, sleigh *n* trineo *m*.

sleek *adj* lustroso(a).

sleep *vi* dormir.

sleeping bag *n* saco de dormir *m*.

sleeping pill *n* somnífero *m*.

sleepwalking *n* sonambulismo *m*.

sleet *n* aguanieve *f*.

sleeve *n* manga *f*.

slender *adj* delgado(a).

slice *n* rebanada *f*.

slide *vi* resbalar, deslizarse.

slight *adj* ligero(a).

slim *adj* delgado(a).

slime *n* lodo *m*.

slimy *adj* viscoso(a), limoso(a).

sling *n* honda *f*, cabestrillo *m*.

slip *n* resbalón *m*; * *vi* resbalar; escapar.

slipper *n* zapatilla *f*.

slogan *n* eslogan *m*, lema *m*.

slope *n* cuesta *f*.

slow *adj* lento(a), torpe.

slum *n* barrios bajos *mpl*.

slump *n* depresión (económica) *f*.

slur *n* calumnia *f*; * *vt* difamar; calumniar.

slut *n* marrana *f*.

sly *adj* astuto(a).

smack *n* manotada *f*, golpe *m*.

small *adj* pequeño(a).

smallpox *n* viruela *f*.

small-talk *n* cháchara *f*.

smart *adj* elegante; listo(a).

smash *vt* estrellarse, hacer pedazos.

smell *vt, vi* oler.

smile *vi* sonreir; * *n* sonrisa *f*.

smoke *n* humo *m*; * *vi* fumar.

smoker *n* fumador(a) *m(f)*.

smooth *adj* liso(a).

smug *adj* engreído(a).

smut *n* carbonilla *f*, hollín *m*, tizne *m*.

snack *n* bocado *m*, tentenpié *m*.

snag *n* problema *m*.

snail *n* caracol *m*.
snake *n* culebra *f*.
snap *vt*, *vi* partir, quebrar.
snapdragon *n* (botany)
  antirrino *m*.
snatch *vt* arrebatar.
sneeze *n* estornudo *m*;
  * *vi* estornudar.
sniff *vt* oler; * *vi* resnifar,
  sorber por la nariz.
snob *n* (e)snob *m* or *f*.
snore *vi* roncar.
snow *n* nieve *f*; * *vi* nevar.
snowdrop *n* (botany)
  campanilla blanca *f*.
snowman *n* figura de nieve *f*.
snub *vt* desairar.
snuff *n* rapé *m*.
so *adv* así; de este modo; tan.
soap *n* jabón *m*.
soap opera *n* telenovela *f*.
soar *vi* remontarse.
sob *n* sollozo *m*; * *vi* sollozar.
soccer *n* fútbol *m*.
sociable *adj* sociable.
social *adj* social.
socialism *n* socialismo *m*.
society *n* sociedad *f*.
sociologist *n* sociólogo(a) *m(f)*.
sociology *n* sociología *f*.
sock *n* calcetín *m*.
socket *n* enchufe *m*.
sod *n* cesped *m*.
soda *n* sosa *f*; soda *f*.
sofa *n* sofá *m*.
soft *adj* blando(a).
soil *vt* ensuciar; * *n* tierra *f*,
  suelo *m*.
solar *adj* solar.
soldier *n* soldado *m*.
sole *n* suela *f*; lenguado *m*;
  * *adj* único(a).
solemn *adj*; * (~ly *adv*)
  solemne(mente).
solicitor *n* abogado(a), agente *m(f)*.
solid *adj* sólido(a).
solitaire *n* solitario *m*;

diamante *m*.
solitude *n* soledad *f*.
solo *n* (music) solo *m*.
solstice *n* solsticio *m*.
soluble *adj* soluble.
solution *n* solución *f*.
solve *vt* resolver.
some *adj* algo de, un poco,
  algún, alguno, alguna, unos,
  pocos, ciertos.
somebody *pron* alguien *m*.
something *pron* alguna cosa, algo.
sometimes *adv* a veces.
somnambulism *n*
  sonambulismo *m*.
somnambulist *n* sonámbulo(a)
  m(f).
son *n* hijo *m*.
sonata *n* (music) sonata *f*.
song *n* canción *f*.
son-in-law *n* yerno *m*.
sonnet *n* soneto *m*.
soon *adv* pronto.
soot *n* hollín *m*.
soothe *vt* tranquilizar;
  calmar.
sop *n* sopa *f*.
sophisticate *vt* sofisticar.
sophisticated *adj* sofisticado(a).
sorcerer *n* hechicero *m*.
sorcery *n* hechizo *m*.
sordid *adj* sórdido(a).
sore *n* llaga, úlcera *f*.
sorrow *n* pesar *m*; tristeza *f*.
sorry *adj* triste.
soul *n* alma *f*.
sound *adj* sano(a); * *n* sonido *m*;
  * *vi* sonar.
soup *n* sopa *f*.
sour *adj* agrio(a).
souvemir *n* recuerdo *m*.
south *n* sur *m*.
sovereign *adj*, *n* soberano(a) *m(f)*.
sovereignty *n* soberanía *f*.
sow *n* puerca *f*; * *vt* sembrar.
space *n* espacio *m*.
spacious *adj* espacioso(a).

spade n pala f; (cards) picas fpl.
spaghetti n espaguetis mpl.
span n palmo m.
spangle n lentejuela f.
spaniel n perro de aguas m.
Spanish adj español(a).
spar n palo m.
spark n chispa f.
sparkle n centelleo m;
 * vi relucir, centellear.
sparrow n gorrión m.
sparse adj esparcido(a), escaso(a).
spasm n espasmo m.
spatula n espátula f.
spawn n huevas f;
 * vt, vi desovar, engendrar.
speak vt, vi hablar.
spear n lanza f.
special adj especial.
species npl especie f.
specific adj específico(a).
specimen n muestra f,
 espécimen m, ejemplar m.
spectacle n espectáculo m.
spectator n espectador(a) m(f).
spectre n espectro m.
speculate vi especular.
speculation n especulación f.
speed n prisa f, velocidad f.
spell n hechizo m; * vt deletrear.
spelling n ortografía f.
spend vt gastar.
sperm n esperma f.
spew (sl) vi vomitar.
sphere n esfera f.
spherical adj esférico(a).
spice n especia f.
spicy adj aromático(a), picante.
spider n araña f.
spike n espiga f; punta f.
spill vt derramar, verter.
spin n vuelta f, revolución f;
 * vt hilar; girar.
spinach n espinaca f.
spinal adj espinal.
spine n espinazo m, columna
 vertebral f.

spinster n soltera f.
spiral adj espiral.
spire n aguja f.
spirit n licores mpl; espíritu m,
 alma f.
spiritual adj; * (~ly) adv
 espiritual(mente).
spiritualist n espiritualista m or f.
spit n asador m; saliva f.
spite n rencor m; * vt fastidiar.
splash vt salpicar.
spleen n bazo m.
splendid adj espléndido(a).
splendor n esplendor m.
splint n tablilla f.
splinter n astilla f;
 * vi astillarse, hacer astillas.
split n hendedura f.
spoil vt dañar, estropear; echar
 a perder; mimar, consentir.
spoke n radio de la rueda m.
spokesman n portavoz m.
sponge n esponja f.
sponsor n patrocinador(a) m(f).
spontaneity n espontaneidad f.
spool n carrete m.
spoon n cuchara f.
spoonful n cucharada f.
sport n deporte m.
spot n mancha f.
spouse n cónyugue m or f.
sprain n torcedura f, esguince m.
sprat n arenque m.
sprawl vi tumbarse.
spray n rociada f, atomizador m.
spread vt extender.
spree n fiesta f, juerga f.
sprig n primavera f; fuente f,
 manantial m; * vi brotar.
sprinkle vt rociar.
spur n espuela f.
spurn vt despreciar.
spy n espía m or f.
squad n escuadra f.
squadron n (military) pelotón m.
squalid adj miserable.
squall n ráfaga f.

squalor n miseria f.

squander vt derrochar, despilfarrar.

square adj cuadrado(a); * n plaza f.

squash n calabaza f; * vt aplastar.

squaw n india f.

squeak vi chirriar, rechinar.

squeamish adj remilgado(a).

squeeze vt apretar.

squid n calamar m.

squint adj bizco(a).

squirrel n ardilla f.

stable n establo m.

stack n pila f, montón.

staff n personal m.

stag n ciervo m.

stage n etapa f, escena f.

stagnate vi estancarse.

stain n mancha f; * vt manchar.

stair n escaleras fpl, escalón m, peldaño m.

staircase n escalera f.

stale adj pasado(a), duro(a).

stalk tallo m, caña f.

stall n puesto (en un mercado) m; casilla f.

stallion n semental m.

stamina n resistencia f.

stammer vi tartamudear.

stamp vi estampar, poner sellos en; * n sello m.

stampede n estampida f.

stand vi estar de pie; * n posición f.

standard n estandarte m.

staple n grapa f.

star n estrella f.

starch n almidón m.

stark adj severo(a), escueto(a).

starling n estornino m.

start n principio m; * vi empezar.

startle vt sobresaltar.

starvation n hambre f.

state n estado m; condición f.

statement n afirmación f.

static adj estático(a).

station n estación f.

stationary adj estacionario(a), fijo(a).

stationery n papelería f.

statistics npl estadística f.

statuary n estatuario m.

statue n estatua f.

stature n estatura f.

statute n estatuto m.

stay n estancia f; * vi (vt) quedar(se), hospedar(se).

steak n filete m; bistec m.

steal vt, vi robar.

stealth n hurto m.

steam n vapor m.

steel n acero m.

steep adj escarpado(a), abrupto(a).

steeple n torre f; campanario m.

steer n novillo m; * vt manejar, conducir.

steering wheel n volante m.

stem n tallo m; * vt detener.

stench n hedor m.

stencil n cliché m.

stenographer n taquígrafo(a) m(f).

stenography n taquigrafía f.

step n paso, escalón m.

stepbrother n hermanastro m.

stepdaughter n hijastra f.

stepfather n padrastro m.

stepmother n madrastra f.

stepsister n hermanastra f.

stepson n hijastro m.

stereo n estéreo m.

stereotype n estereotipo m or f.

sterile adj estéril.

sterling n libras esterlinas fpl.

stethoscope n (medical) estetoscopio m.

stew vt estofar f.

steward n mayordomo m.

stick n palo m; * vi (vt) pegar(se).

stiff adj tieso(a).

stifle vt sofocar.

stigma n estigma m.

stigmatise vt difamar.

stiletto n estilete m.

still *adj* inmóvil(a); * *adv* todavía.
still-born *adj* nacido(a),
  muerto(a).
stilts *npl* zancos *mpl*.
stimulant *n* estimulante *m*.
stimulate *vt* estimular.
stimulus *n* estímulo *m*.
sting *n* picadura *f*; * *vt* picar o
  morder (un insecto).
stingy *adj* mezquino(a).
stink *vi* heder.
stint *n* tarea *f*.
stipulate *vt* estipular.
stipulation *n* estipulación *f*.
stir *vt* agitar.
stirrup *n* estribo *m*.
stitch *vt* coser.
stoat *n* armiño *m*.
stock *n* ganado *m*; caldo *m*.
stockbroker *n* agente de bolsa
  m or *f*.
stock exchange *n* bolsa *f*.
stocking *n* media *f*.
stock market *n* bolsa *f*.
stoical *adj* estoico(a).
stole *n* estola *f*.
stomach *n* estómago *m*.
stone *n* piedra *f*.
stop n parada *f*; * *vt* detener,
  parar.
stopwatch *n* cronómetro *m*.
store *n* provisión *f*, almacén *m*.
stork *n* cigüeña *f*.
storm *n* tempestad.
story *n* historia *f*.
stout *adj* sólido(a); * *n* cerveza
  negra *f*.
stove *n* estufa *f*.
straight *adj* derecho(a).
strain *vt* cansar, estirar;
  * *n* tensión *m*; raza *f*, linaje *f*.
strainer *adj* torcido(a);
  * *n* colador *m*.
strange *adj* raro(a), extranjero(a).
stranger *n* desconocido(a) *m(f)*;
  extranjero(a) *m(f)*.
strangle *vt* estrangular.

strap *n* correa *f*.
strapping *adj* robusto(a),
  fornido(a).
stratagem *n* estratagema *f*,
  astucia *f*.
strategic *adj* estratégico(a).
strategy *n* estrategia *f*.
stratum *n* estrato *m*.
straw *n* paja *m*; pajita *f*.
strawberry *n* fresa *f*.
stray *vi* extraviarse.
streak *n* raya.
stream *n* arroyo *m*, río *m*.
street *n* calle *f*.
strength *n* fuerza *f*.
strenuous *adj* arduo(a).
stress *n* presión *f*, estrés *m*.
stretch *vt*, *vi* extender.
stretcher *n* camilla *f*.
strew *vt* esparcir.
strict *adj* estricto(a).
stride *n* tranco *m*.
string *n* cuerda *f*, hilera *f*.
stringent *adj* astringente.
strip *n* tira *f*, franja *f*;
  * *vt* desnudar.
stripe *n* raya *f*.
strive *vi* esforzarse.
stroll *n* paseo.
strong *adj* fuerte.
strongbox *n* caja fuerte *f*.
structure *n* estructura *f*.
struggle *vi* esforzarse.
strum *vt* (music) rasguear.
strut *vi* pavonearse.
stubborn *adj* obstinado(a).
stucco *n* estuco *m*.
stud *n* corchete *m*.
student *n* estudiante *m* or *f*.
studio *n* estudio *m*.
studious *adj* estudioso(a).
study *n* estudio *m*.
stuff *n* materia *f*; cosas *fpl*.
stuffing *n* relleno *m*.
stumble *vi* tropezar.
stump *n* tocón *m*.
stun *vt* aturdir.

stunt *n* vuelo acrobático *m*; truco publicitario *m*.

stuntman *n* especialista *m*.

stupid *adj* estúpido(a).

sturdy *adj* fuerte.

sturgeon *n* esturión *m*.

stutter *vi* tartamudear.

sty *n* pocilga *f*.

stye *n* orzuelo *m*.

style *n* estilo *m*.

stylish *adj* elegante.

sub-divide *vt* subdividir.

subdue *vt* sojuzgar.

subject *adj* sujeto.

subjunctive *n* subjuntivo *m*.

sublime *adj* sublime.

submarine *adj* submarino(a).

submerge *vt* sumergir.

submit *vt* (*vi*) someter(se), presentar.

subordinate *adj* subordinado(a); * *vt* subordinar.

subscribe *vt*, *vi* suscribir.

subsequent *adj*; * (~ly *adv*) subsiguiente(mente).

subservient *adj* subordinado.

subside *vi* sumergirse.

subsidence *n* hundimiento *m*.

subsidiary *adj* subsidiario(a).

subsidise *vt* subvencionar.

subsidy *n* subvención *f*.

substance *n* substancia *f*.

substitute *vt* sustituir.

substratum *n* lecho *m*.

subterranean *adj* subterráneo(a).

subtitle *n* subtítulo *m*.

subtle *adj* sutil.

suburb *n* suburbio *m*.

subversion *n* subversión *f*.

subway *n* metro *m*, subterráneo *m*.

succeed *vt*, *vi* seguir; conseguir, lograr, tener éxito.

success *n* éxito *m*.

succumb *vi* sucumbir.

such *adj* tal.

suck *vt*, *vi* chupar.

sudden *adj* repentino(a), imprevisto(a).

sue *vt* demandar.

suède *n* ante *m*.

suffer *vt*, *vi* sufrir, padecer.

sufficient *adj* suficiente.

suffocate *vt* asfixiarse.

suffrage *n* sufragio *m*.

sugar *n* azucar *m*.

sugar cane *n* caña de azucar *f*.

suggest *vt* sugerir.

suggestion *n* sugestión *f*.

suicide *n* suicidio *m*.

suit *n* conjunto *m*; traje *m*.

suitcase *n* maleta *f*.

suitor *n* pretendiente *m* or *f*.

sultan *n* sultán *m*.

sultana *n* sultana *f*.

sum *n* suma *f*.

summary *adj*, *n* sumario *m*.

summer *n* verano *m*.

summit *n* cima *f*, cumbre *f*.

summon *vt* citar.

summons *n* citación *f*.

sumptuous *adj* suntuoso(a).

sun *n* sol *m*.

sunbathe *vi* tomar el sol.

Sunday *n* domingo *m*.

sundial *n* reloj de sol *m*.

sundry *adj* varios.

sunflower *n* girasol *m*.

sunglasses *npl* gafas de sol *fpl*.

sunlight *n* luz del sol *f*.

sunrise *n* amanecer *m*.

sunset *n* puesta del sol *f*.

sunshade *n* sombrilla *f*.

sunstroke *n* insolacion *f*.

suntan *n* bronceado *m*.

suntan oil *n* aceite bronceador *m*.

superb *adj* magnífico(a).

superficial *adj* superficial.

superfluous *adj* superfluo(a).

superior *adj*, *n* superior *m*.

supermarket *n* supermercado *m*.

supernatural *n* sobrenatural.

superpower *n* superpotencia *f*.

superstition *n* superstición *f*.

supertanker *n* superpetrolero *m*.
supervise *vt* inspeccionar.
supper *n* cena *f*.
supple *adj* flexible.
supplement *n* suplemento *m*.
supplementary *adj* adicional.
suppleness *n* flexibilidad *f*.
supplicant *n* suplicante *m* or *f*.
supplicate *vt* suplicar.
supplication *n* súplica *f*.
supplier *n* distribuidor(a) *m(f)*.
supply *vt* suministrar; suplir, completar; surtir;
* *n* provisión *f*; suministro *m*.
support *vt* sostener, asistir;
* *n* apoyo *m*.
supportable *adj* soportable.
supporter *n* partidario(a); aficionado(a) *m(f)*.
suppose *vt*, *vi* suponer.
supposition *n* suposición *f*.
suppress *vt* suprimir.
suppression *n* supresión *f*.
supremacy *n* supremacía *f*.
supreme *adj* supremo(a).
surcharge *vt* sobrecargar;
* *n* sobretasa *f*.
sure *adj* seguro(a), cierto(a); firme; estable: — to be ~ sin duda; ya se ve; * ~ly *adv* ciertamente, seguramente, sin duda.
sureness *n* certeza *f*; seguridad *f*.
surety *n* fianza *f*; fiador(a) *m(f)*.
surf *n* (marine) resaca *f*.
surface *n* superficie *f*; * *vt* revestir; * *vi* salir a la superficie.
surfboard *n* plancha (de surf) *f*.
surfeit *n* exceso *m*.
surge *n* ola *f*, oleaje *m*;
* *vi* avanzar en tropel.
surgeon *n* cirujano(a) *m(f)*.
surgery *n* cirujía *m*.
surgical *adj* quirúrgico(a).
surliness *n* mal humor *m*.
surly *adj* malhumorado(a).
surmise *vt* sospechar;
* *n* sospecha *f*.

surmount *vt* superar.
surmountable *adj* superable.
surname *n* apellido *m*, sobrenombre *m*.
surpass *vt* superar, exceder.
surpassing *adj* sobresaliente.
surplice *n* sobrepelliz *f*.
surplus *n* excedente *m*; sobrante *m*; * *adj* sobrante.
surprise *vt* sorprender;
* *n* sorpresa *f*.
surprising *adj* sorprendente.
surrender *vt*, *vi* rendir; ceder; rendirse; * *n* rendición *f*.
surreptitious *adj* subrepticio.
surrogate *n* sustituto *m*.
surrogate mother *n* madre portadora *f*.
surround *vt* circundar, cercar, rodear.
survey *vt* inspeccionar, examinar; * *n* inspección *f*, encuesta *f*.
survive *vi* sobrevivir;
* *vt* sobrevivir a.
survivor *n* sobreviviente *m* or *f*.
susceptibility *n* susceptibilidad *f*.
susceptible *adj* susceptible.
suspect *vt*, *vi* sospechar;
* *n* sospechoso(a) *m(f)*.
suspend *vt* suspender.
suspense *n* suspense *m*; incertidumbre *f*.
suspension *n* suspensión *f*.
suspension bridge *n* puente colgante *m*.
suspicion *n* sospecha *f*.
suspicious *adj* suspicaz;
* ~ly *adv* sospechosamente.
suspiciousness *n* suspicacia *f*.
sustain *vt* sostener, sustentar, mantener; apoyar.
sustenance *n* sustento *m*.
suture *n* sutura *f*, costura *f*.
swab *n* algodon *m*; frotis *m invar*.
swaddle *vt* fajar, envolver en pañales.
swagger *vi* pavonearse.

swallow *n* golondrina *f*;
* *vt* tragar, engullir.
swamp *n* pantano *m*.
swampy *adj* pantanoso.
swan *n* cisne *m*.
swap *vt* canjear; * *n* intercambio *m*.
swarm *n* enjambre *m*; gentío *m*;
hormiguero *m*; * *vi* pulular;
hormiguear.
swarthy *adj* moreno(a).
swarthiness *n* tez morena *f*.
swashbuckling *adj* aventurero(a).
swath *n* tranco *m*.
swathe *vt* vendar.
sway *vt* mover; * *vi* mecerse,
balancearse; * *n* balanceo *m*;
dominio *m*.
swear *vt*, *vi* jurar; hacer jurar;
juramentar.
sweat *n* sudor *m*; * *vi* sudar;
trabajar con fatiga.
sweater, sweatshirt *n* suéter *m*.
sweep *vt*, *vi* barrer; deshollinar.
sweeping *adj* dramático.
sweepstake *n* lotería *f*.
sweet *adj* dulce, grato(a),
gustoso(a); suave;
hermoso(a); amable; * ~ly
adv dulcemente, suavemente;
* *n* dulce *m*, caramelo *m*.
sweetbread *n* mollejas de
ternera *fpl*.
sweeten *vt* endulzar; suavizar;
aplacar; perfumar.
sweetener *n* edulcorante *m*.
sweetheart *n* novio(a) *m(f)*,
querida *f*.
sweetmeats *npl* dulces secos *mpl*.
sweetness *n* dulzura *f*, suavidad *f*.
swell *vi* hincharse; inflarse;
* *vt* hinchar, inflar, agravar;
* *n* marejada *f*; * *adj* (*sl*)
estupendo, fenomenal.
swelling *n* hinchazón *f*, tumor *m*.
swelter *vi* ahogarse de calor.
swerve *vi* vagar; desviarse.
swift *adj* veloz, ligero(a),

rápido(a); * *n* vencejo, *m*.
swiftly *adv* velozmente.
swiftness *n* velocidad *f*, rapidez *f*.
swill *vt* lavar, limpiar con
agua; * *n* bazofia *f*.
swim *vi* nadar; abundar en;
* *vt* pasar a nado.
swimming *n* natación *f*.
swimming pool *n* piscina *f*.
swimsuit *n* traje de baño *m*.
swindle *vt* estafar.
swindler *n* estafador(a) *m(f)*.
swine *n* puerco, cochino *m*.
swing *vi* balancear, columpiar-
se; *vt* columpiar; balancear;
girar; * *n* viraje *m*, balanceo *m*.
swinging *adj* (*sl*) alegre.
swing door *n* puerta giratoria *f*.
swirl *n* hacer remolinos (en el
agua).
switch *n* interruptor *m*; (railway)
aguja *f*; * *vt* cambiar de:
— to ~ off apagar; parar:
— to ~ on encender, prender.
switchboard *n* centralita (de
teléfonos) *f*.
swivel *vt* girar.
swoon *vi* desmayarse;
* *n* desmayo *m*, delirio *m*.
swoop *vi* caer en picado;
* *n* calada *f*, redada *f*:
— in one fell ~ de un golpe.
sword *n* espada *f*.
swordfish *n* pez espada *f*.
swordsman *n* guerrero *m*.
sycamore *n* (botany) sicomoro *m*.
sycophant *n* adulador(a) *m(f)*.
syllabic *adj* silábico.
syllable *n* sílaba *f*.
syllabus *n* programa de
estudios *m*.
syllogism *n* silogismo *m*.
sylph *n* silfo *m*; sílfide *f*.
symbol *n* símbolo *m*.
symbolic(al) *adj* simbólico(a).
symbolise *vt* simbolizar.
symmetrical *adj* simétrico(a);

* ~ly *adv* con simetria.
symmetry *n* simetría *f.*
sympathetic *adj* compasivo(a);
   * ~ally *adv* amablemente, con
   compasión.
sympathise *vi* compadecerse.
sympathy *n* compasión *f.*
symphony *n* sinfonía *f.*
symposium *n* simposio *m.*
symptom *n* síntoma *m.*
synagogue *n* sinagoga *f.*
synchronism *n* sincronismo *m.*
syndicate *n* sindicato *m.*
syndrome *n* síndrome *m.*
synod *n* sínodo *m.*
synonym *n* sinónimo *m.*
synonymous *adj* sinónimo(a);
   * ~ly *adv* con sinonímia.
synopsis *n* sinopsis *f,* sumario *m.*
synoptical *adj* sinóptico(a).
syntax *n* sintaxis *f.*
synthesis *n* síntesis *f.*
syringe *n* jeringa *f.*
system *n* sistema *m.*
systematic *adj* sistemático(a);
   * ~ally *adv* sistemáticamente.
systems analyst *n* analista de
   sistemas *m* or *f.*

T

table *n* mesa *f.*
tablecloth *n* mantel *m.*
tablespoon *n* cuchara grande *f.*
tablet *n* pastilla *f.*
table tennis *n* ping-pong *m.*
taboo *adj* tabú.
tacit *adj* tácito(a).
taciturn *adj* taciturno(a).
tack *n* tachuela *f.*
tact *n* tacto *m.*
tactician *n* táctico(a) *m(f).*
tactics *npl* táctica *f.*
tadpole *n* renacuajo *m.*
taffeta *n* tafetán *m.*
tag *n* etiqueta *f.*

tail *n* cola *f.*
tailor *n* sastre *m* or *f.*
tailor-made *adj* hecho a medida.
taint *vt* tachar; contaminar.
take *vt* tomar, coger.
take off *n* despegue *m;*
   * *vi* despegar.
takings *npl* ingresos *mpl.*
talc *n* talco *m.*
talent *n* talento *m.*
talisman *n* talismán *m.*
talk *vi* hablar.
talkative *adj* locuaz.
tall *adj* alto(a).
talon *n* garra de ave de rapiña *f.*
tambourine *n* pandereta *f.*
tame *adj* manso(a),
   domesticado(a).
tamper *vi* intentar forzar;
   falsificar.
tampon *n* tampón *m.*
tan *vt* broncear.
tang *n* sabor fuerte *m.*
tangerine *n* mandarina *f.*
tangle *vi* (*vt*) enredar(se).
tank *n* cisterna *f,* aljibe *m;*
   depósito *m.*
tanned *adj* bronceado(a).
tantrum *n* rabieta *f.*
tap *n* grifo *m.*
tape *n* cinta *f.*
tape measure *n* metro *m.*
tapestry *n* tapiz *f.*
tar *n* brea *f;* alquitrán *m.*
target *n* blanco *m* (para tirar).
tariff *n* tarifa *f.*
tarmac *n* pista de aterrizaje *f.*
tarnish *vt* deslustrar.
tarpaulin *n* alquitranado *m.*
tarragon *n* (botany) estragón *m.*
tartan *n* tela escocesa *f.*
tartar *n* tártaro *m.*
task *n* tarea *f.*
tassel *n* borla *f.*
taste *n* gusto *m;* sabor *m.*
tasty *adj* sabroso(a).
tattoo *n* tatuaje *m.*

taunt *vt* lanzar pullas.
Taurus *n* Tauro *m*.
tax *n* impuesto *m*.
taxi *n* taxi *m*.
tea *n* té *m*.
teach *vt* enseñar.
teacher *n* profesor(a) *m(f)*.
teak *n* teca *f*.
team *n* equipo *m*.
teamster *n* camionero *m*.
teapot *n* tetera *f*.
tear *vt* despedazar, rasgar;
  * *n* lágrima *f*.
tease *vi* tomar el pelo.
teaspoon *n* cucharita *f*.
teat *n* ubre *f*, teta *f*.
technical *adj* técnico(a).
technician *n* técnico *m*.
technique *n* técnica *f*.
technology *n* tecnología *f*.
teddy(bear) *n* osito de peluche *m*.
tedious *adj* tedioso(a).
tedium *n* tedio *m*.
tee-shirt *n* camiseta *f*.
telegram *n* telegrama *m*.
telegraph *n* telégrafo *m*.
telegraphic *adj* telegráfico(a).
telepathy *n* telepatía *f*.
telephone *n* teléfono *m*.
telescope *n* telescopio *m*.
telescopic *adj* telescópico(a).
television *n* televisión *f*.
tell *vi* decir.
temper *vi* templar; * *n* mal genio *m*.
temperament *n* temperamento *m*.
temperate *adj* templado(a).
temperature *n* temperatura *f*.
template *n* plantilla *f*.
temple *n* templo *m*.
temporary *adj* temporal.
tempt *vt* tentar.
temptation *n* tentación *f*.
ten *adj*, *n* diez.
tenacity *n* tenacidad *f*.
tenancy *n* alquiler *m*.
tenant *n* inquilino(a) *m(f)*.
tend *vt* cuidar, atender.

tendency *n* tendencia *f*.
tender *adj* tierno(a); * *vt* ofrecer.
tendon *n* tendón *m*.
tennis *n* tenis *m*.
tense *adj* tieso(a), tenso(a).
tension *n* tensión *f*.
tent *n* tienda de campaña *f*.
tentacle *n* tentáculo *m*.
tenth *adj*, *n* décimo.
tenure *n* posesión *f*.
tepid *adj* tibio(a).
term *n* término *m*.
terminal *adj* terminal.
termination *n* terminación *f*.
terminus *n* terminal *f*.
terrace *n* terraza *f*.
terrain *n* terreno *m*.
terrestrial *adj* terrestre.
terrible *adj* terrible.
terrier *n* terrier *m*.
terrific *adj* fantástico(a).
terrify *vt* aterrar.
territorial *adj* territorial.
territory *n* territorio, distrito *m*.
terror *n* terror *m*.
terrorism *n* terrorismo *m*.
test *n* examen *m*.
testament *n* testamento *m*.
testicles *npl* testículos *mpl*.
testify *vt* testificar.
testimony *n* testimonio *m*.
tetanus *n* tétanos *mpl*.
tether *vi* atar.
text *n* texto *m*.
textiles *npl* tejidos *mpl*.
texture *n* textura *f*.
than *adv* que, de.
thank *vt* agradecer.
thanks *npl* gracias *fpl*.
that *pron* aquel, aquello,
  aquella; que; ese, esos, esas.
thaw *n* deshielo *m*; * *vi* derretirse.
the *art* el, la, lo; los, las.
theatre *n* teatro *m*.
theft *n* robo *m*.
their *pron* su, suyo, suya; de
  ellos, de ellas; * ~s el suyo, la

suya, los suyos, las suyas; de ellos, de ellas.

them *pron* los, las, les; ellos, ellas.

theme *n* tema *m*.

themselves *pron pl* ellos mismos, ellas mismas; sí mismos.

then *adv* entonces, después.

theology *n* teología *f*.

theory *n* teoría *f*.

therapist *n* terapeuta *m or f*.

therapy *n* terapia *f*.

there *adv* allí, alla; ~ **is (are)** hay.

thermal *adj* termal.

thermometer *n* termómetro *m*.

thesaurus *n* tesoro *m*; diccionario de sinónimos *m*.

these *pron pl* estos, estas.

thesis *n* tesis *f*.

they *pron pl* ellos, ellas.

thick *adj* espeso(a), grueso(a).

thicken *vi* espesar.

thief *n* ladrón(ona) *m(f)*.

thigh *n* muslo *m*.

thimble *n* dedal *m*.

thin *adj* delgado(a).

thing *n* cosa *f*.

think *vi* pensar.

third *adj* tercero(a).

thirst *n* sed *f*.

thirteen *adj, n* trece.

thirteenth *adj, n* decimotercero(a).

thirtieth *adj, n* trigésimo(a).

thirty *adj, n* treinta.

this *adj* este, esta, esto; * *pron* éste, ésta, esto.

thorn *n* espina *f*.

those *pron pl* ésos, ésas; aquéllos, aquéllas; * *adj* esos, esas; aquellos, aquellas.

thought *n* pensamiento *m*.

thousand *adj, n* mil.

thousandth *adj, n* milésimo(a).

thrash *vi* dar una paliza a.

thread *n* hilo *m*.

threat *n* amenaza *f*.

threaten *vt* amenazar.

three *adj, n* tres.

threshold *n* umbral *m*.

thrifty *adj* económico(a).

thrill *n* emoción *f*; * *vt* emocionar.

thrive *vi* prosperar.

throat *n* garganta *f*.

throb *vi* latir, vibrar.

throne *n* trono *m*.

through *prep* por; durante; mediante.

throw *vt* echar.

thrush *n* tordo *m* (ave).

thrust *vt* empujar.

thug *n* gamberro(a) *m(f)*.

thumb *n* pulgar *m*.

thump *n* golpe *m*.

thunder *n* trueno *m*.

Thursday *n* jueves *m*.

thus *adv* así, de este modo.

thyme *n* (botany) tomillo *m*.

thyroid *n* tiroides *m*.

tiara *n* diadema *f*.

tic *n* tic *m*.

ticket *n* billete *m*.

tickle *vt* hacer cosquillas.

tidal *adj* (marine) de marea.

tide *n* marea *f*.

tidy *adj* ordenado(a).

tie *vt* anudar, atar; * *n* corbata *f*.

tiger *n* tigre *m*.

tight *adj* tirante, apretado(a).

tile *n* azulejo *m*.

till *n* caja registradora *f*; * *vt* cultivar.

timber *n* madera de construcción *f*.

time *n* tiempo *m*; época *f*.

timer *n* interruptor *m*, temporizador *m*.

timid *adj* tímido(a).

timidity *n* timidez *f*.

tin *n* estaño *m*.

tinfoil *n* papel de estaño *m*.

tinsel *n* oropel *m*.

tint *n* tinte *m*.

tiny *adj* pequeño(a), chico(a).

tip *n* punta *f*, extremidad *f*; propina *f*.

tire *vt* cansar, fatigar.
tissue *n* tejido *m*.
title *n* título *m*.
titular *adj* titular.
to *prep* a; para; por; de; hasta;
en; con; que.
toad *n* sapo *m*.
toadstool *n* (botany) seta
venenosa *f*.
toast *n* tostada *f*; * *vt* tostar;
brindar.
toaster *n* tostadora *f*.
tobacco *n* tabaco *m*.
tobacco shop *n* estanco *m*.
today *adv* hoy.
toe *n* dedo del pie *m*.
together *adv* juntos, al mismo
tiempo.
toilet *n* servicios *mpl*.
toilet paper *n* papel higiénico *m*.
token *n* señal *f*.
tolerate *vt* tolerar.
tomato *n* tomate *m*.
tomb *n* tumba *f*.
tomboy *n* marimacho *m*.
tombstone *n* piedra sepulcral *f*.
tomcat *n* gato *m*.
tomorrow *adv*, *n* mañana *f*.
ton *n* tonelada *f*.
tongs *npl* tenacillas *fpl*.
tongue *n* lengua *f*.
tonic *n* (medical) tónico.
tonight *adv*, *n* esta noche *f*.
tonsil *n* amígdala *f*.
too *adv* demasiado; también.
tool *n* herramienta *f*.
tooth *n* diente *m*.
toothache *n* dolor de muelas *m*.
top *n* cima *f*.
topaz *n* topacio *m*.
topic *n* tema *m*.
topless *adj* topless.
topographic(al) *adj* topográfico(a).
topography *n* topografía *f*.
torch *n* antorcha *f*.
torment *vt* atormentar.
tornado *n* tornado *m*.

torrent *n* torrente *m*.
torrid *adj* apasionado(a),
tórrido(a).
tortoise *n* tortuga *f*.
tortoiseshell *adj* de carey.
tortuous *adj* tortuoso(a).
torture *n* tortura *f*.
toss *vt* tirar, lanzar.
total *adj* total.
totalitarian *adj* totalitario(a).
totality *n* totalidad *f*.
totter *vi* tambalearse.
touch *vi* tocar.
touchdown *n* aterrizaje *m*.
touching *adj* patetico(a),
conmovedor.
tough *adj* duro(a).
toupée *n* tupé *m*, peluquín *m*.
tour *n* viaje *m*.
touring *n* viajes turísticos *mpl*.
tourism *n* turismo *m*.
tourist *n* turista *m* or *f*.
tourist office *n* oficina de
turismo *f*.
tournament *n* torneo *m*.
tow *n* remolque *m*; * *vt* remolcar.
towards *prep*, *adv* hacia.
towel *n* toalla *f*.
tower *n* torre *m*.
town *n* ciudad *f*.
town hall *n* ayuntamiento *m*.
toy *n* juguete *m*.
toyshop *n* juguetería *f*.
trace *n* huella *f*; * *vt* trazar.
trade *n* comercio *m*;
ocupación *f*.
trade(s) union *n* sindicato *m*.
tradition *n* tradición *f*.
traditional *adj* tradicional.
traffic *n* tráfico *m*.
traffic lights *npl* semáforo *m*.
tragedy *n* tragedia *f*.
tragic *adj* trágico(a).
trail *n* rastro *m*, pista *f*;
* *vt*, *vi* rastrear.
train *vt* entrenar; * *n* tren *m*.
trainee *n* aprendiz *m*.

trainer *n* entrenador(a) *m(f)*.
trait *n* rasgo *m*.
traitor *n* traidor(a) *m(f)*.
tram *n* tranvía *f*.
tramp *n* vagabundo(a) *m(f)*.
trample *vt* pisotear.
trampoline *n* trampolín *m*.
trance *n* trance *m*.
tranquil *adj* tranquilo(a).
tranquilliser *n* tranquilizante *m*.
transact *vt* tramitar.
transactiom *n* transacción *f*.
transatlantic *adj*
  transatlántico(a).
transcription *n* transcripción *f*.
transfer *vt* transferir.
transform *vt* transformar.
transformatio *n*
  transformación *f*.
transfusion *n* transfusión *f*.
transit *n* tránsito *m*.
transition *n* tránsito *m*;
  transición *f*.
translate *vt* traducir.
translation *n* traducción *f*.
translator *n* traductor(a) *m(f)*.
tramsmit *vt* transmitir.
transparent *adj* transparente.
transpire *vi* resultar, ocurrir,
  suceder.
transplant *vt* trasplantar.
transport *vt* transportar.
trap *n* trampa *f*.
trapeze *n* trapecio *m*.
trappings *npl* adornos *mpl*.
trash *n* basura *f*.
travel *vi* viajar.
trawler *n* pesquero de arrastre *m*.
tray *n* bandeja *f*.
treachery *n* traición *f*.
tread *n* paso *m*, pisada *f*; * *vi* pisar.
treason *n* traición *m*.
treasure *n* tesoro *m*.
treasurer *n* tesorero(a) *m(f)*.
treat *vt* tratar.
treatise *n* tratado *m*.
treatment *n* tratamiento *m*.

treaty *n* tratado *m*.
treble *adj* triple.
treble clef *n* clave de sol *f*.
tree *n* árbol *m*.
trellis *n* enrejado *m*.
tremble *vi* temblar
tremendous *adj* tremendo(a).
tremor *n* temblor *m*.
trench *n* zanja *f*, trinchera *f*.
trend *n* tendencia *f*.
trendy *adj* de moda.
trespass *vt* trespasar.
tress *n* guadeja *f*.
trestle *n* caballete *m*.
trial *n* proceso *m*, juicio *m*.
triangle *n* triángulo *m*.
triangular *adj* triangular.
tribal *adj* tribal.
tribe *n* tribu *f*.
tribunal *n* tribunal *m*.
tributary *adj*, *n* tributario *m*.
tribute *n* tributo *m*.
trice *n* momento *m*, tris *m*.
trick *n* engaño *m*.
trickle *vi* gotear.
tricky *adj* difícil.
tricycle *n* triciclo *m*.
trifle *n* bagatela *f*; postre de
  bizcocho, gelatina, frutas y
  natillas.
trigger *n* gatillo *m*.
trigonometry *n* trigonometría *f*.
trim *adj* aseado(a).
Trinity *n* Trinidad *f*.
trinket *n* baratija *f*.
trio *n* (music) trío *m*.
trip *vt* andar a paso ligero;
  * *n* viaje *m*, excursión *m*.
tripe *n* callos *mpl*.
triple *adj* triple.
triplets *npl* trillizos *mpl*.
triplicate *n* triplicado *m*.
tripod *n* trípode *m*.
triumph *n* triunfo *m*.
triumphal *adj* triunfal.
triumphant *adj* triunfante.
trivia *npl* trivialidades *fpl*.

trivial *adj* trivial.
trolley *n* carrito *m*.
trombone *n* trombón *m*.
trophy *n* trofeo *m*.
tropical *adj* tropical.
trot *n* trote *m*.
trouble *n* problema *f*, dificultad *f*; * *vt* molestar, preocupar, inquietar.
trough *n* abrevadero *m*.
trousers *npl* pantalones *mpl*.
trout *n* trucha *f*.
trowel *n* paleta *f*.
truce *n* tregua *f*.
truck *n* camión *m*.
true *adj* verdadero(a).
truffle *n* trufa *f*.
truly *adv* en verdad.
trumpet *n* trompeta *f*.
trunk *n* baúl *m*, cofre *m*; trompa *f*.
trust *n* confianza *f*.
truth *n* verdad *f*.
try *vt* examinar, intentar.
tub *n* balde *m*, cubo *m*.
tuba *n* tuba *f*.
tube *n* tubo *m*.
tuberculosis *n* tuberculosis *f*.
Tuesday *n* martes *m*.
tuition *n* enseñanza *f*.
tulip (botany) tulipán *m*.
tumble *n* caída *f*; * *vi* caer.
tumbler *n* vaso *m*.
tummy *n* barriga *f*.
tumour *n* tumor *m*.
tumultuous *adj* tumultuoso(a).
tuna *n* atún *m*.
tune *n* tono *m*.
tunic *n* túnica *f*.
tunnel *n* tunel *m*.
turban *n* turbante *m*.
turbine *n* turbina *f*.
turbulence *n* turbulencia *f*.
tureen *n* sopera *f*.
turf *n* césped *m*.
turgid *adj* pesado(a).
turkey *n* pavo *m*.
turmoil *n* desorden *m*, alboroto *m*.

turn *n* turno *m*, curva *f*; * *vi* volver.
turncoat *n* renegado(a) *m(f)*.
turnip *n* nabo *m*.
turnover *n* facturación *f*.
turnstile *n* torniquete *m*.
turpentine *n* trementina *f*.
turquoise *n* turquesa *f*.
turret *n* torreón *m*.
turtle *n* galápago *m*.
turtledove *n* tórtola *f*.
tusk *n* colmillo *m*.
tussle *n* pelea *f*.
tutor *n* tutor(a) *m(f)*.
tuxedo *n* smoking *m*.
twang *n* tañido *m*, timbre nasal *m*.
tweezers *npl* tenacillas *fpl*.
twelfth *adj*, *n* duodécimo(a).
twelve *adj*, *n* doce.
twentieth *adj*, *n* vigesimo(a).
twenty *adj*, *n* veinte.
twice *adv* dos veces.
twig *n* ramita *f*; * *vi* caer en la cuenta.
twilight *n* crepúsculo *m*.
twin *n* gemelo(a) *m(f)*.
twist *vt* torcer.
twit *n* (*sl*) tonto(a) *m(f)*.
twitch *vi* moverse nerviosamente.
two *adj*, *n* dos.
two-faced *adj* falso(a).
tycoon *n* magnate *m*.
type *n* tipo *m*; letra *f*, modelo *m*; * *vt* escribir a máquina.
typewriter *n* máquina de escribir *f*.
typical *adj* típico(a).
tyrannical *adj* tiránico(a).
tyranny *n* tiranía *f*.
tyrant *n* tirano(a) *m(f)*.

U

ubiquitous *adj* ubicuo(a).
udder *n* ubre *f*.
ugh *excl* ¡uf!

ugliness *n* fealdad *f*.

ugly *adj* feo(a); peligroso(a).

ulcer *n* úlcera *f*.

ulterior *adj* ulterior.

ultimate *adj* último(a).

ultimatum *n* ultimatum *m*.

umbrella *n* paraguas *m invar*.

umpire *n* árbitro *m*.

unable *adj* incapaz.

unaccompanied *adj* sin
acompañamiento.

unaccustomed *adj*
desacostumbrado(a).

unamimity *n* unanimidad *f*.

unanimous *adj* unánime.

unanswerable *adj*
incontrovertible.

unapproachable *adj* inaccesible.

unbearable *adj* insoportable.

unbecoming *adj* indecente,
indecoroso(a).

unbutton *vt* desabotonar.

uncanny *adj* extraordinario.

unchanged *adj* sin alterar.

uncharitable *adj* nada
caritativo(a).

uncle *n* tío.

uncomfortable *adj* incómodo(a).

uncommon *adj* raro(a).

uncompromising *adj*
intransigente.

unconscious *adj* inconsciente.

unconventional *adj* poco
convencional.

uncork *vt* destapar.

uncouth *adj* grosero(a).

uncover *vt* descubrir.

undaunted *adj* in dejarse
desanimar por.

under *prep* debajo de.

under-age *adj* menor de edad.

underdeveloped *adj*
subdesarrollado(a).

underdog *n* desvalido(a) *m(f)*.

underestimate *vt* subestimar.

undergo *vt* sufrir.

undergraduate *n* estudiante *m* or *f*.

underground *n* movimiento
clandestino *m*; subterráneo *m*.

underline *vt* subrayar.

underpaid *adj* mal pagado(a).

understand *vt* entender,
comprender.

understatement *n*
subestimación *f*.

underwear *n* ropa interior *f*.

underworld *n* hampa *f*.

undetermined *adj*
indeterminado(a), indeciso(a).

undigested *adj* indigesto(a).

undisciplined *adj*
indisciplinado(a).

undismayed *adj* intrépido(a).

undisputed *adj* incontestable.

undisturbed *adj* ininterrumpido.

undivided *adj* indiviso(a),
entero(a).

undo *vt* deshacer.

undoubted *adj* indudable.

undress *vi* desnudarse.

undue *adj* indebido(a).

undulating *adj* ondulante.

unduly *adv* excesivamente.

undying *adj* eterno.

unearth *vt* desenterrar.

uneasy *adj* inquieto(a).

uneducated *adj* ignorante.

unemployed *adj* parado(a).

unemployment *n* paro *m*.

unenlightened *adj* no iluminado.

unenviable *adj* poco envidiable.

unequal *adj* desigual.

unequalled *adj* incoraparable.

uneven *adj* desigual.

unexpected *adj* inesperado(a).

unexplored *adj* inexplorado(a).

unfair *adj* injusto(a).

unfaithful *adj* infiel.

unfamiliar *adj* desconocido(a).

unfashionable *adj* pasado de
moda.

unfasten *vt* desatar.

unfavourable *adj* desfavorable.

unfeeling *adj* insensible.

unfit *adj* en baja forma.
unfold *vt* desplegar.
unforeseen *adj* imprevisto(a).
unforgettable *adj* inolvidable.
unforgivable *adj* imperdonable.
unforgiving *adj* implacable.
unfortunate *adj* desafortunado(a).
unfounded *adj* sin fundamento.
unfriendly *adj* antipático.
unfruitful *adj* estéril;
  infructuoso(a).
unfurnished *adj* sin muebles.
ungrateful *adj* ingrato(a).
unhappily *adv* desgraciadamente.
unhappy *adj* triste, desgraciado(a).
unhealthy *adj* malsano(a),
  insalubre.
unhook *vt* desenganchar;
  descolgar; desabrochar.
unhoped(-for) *adj* inesperado(a).
unhurt *adj* ileso(a).
unicorn *n* unicornio *m*.
uniform *adj* uniforme;
  * *n* uniforme *m*.
uniformity *adj* uniformidad.
unify *vt* unificar.
unimaginable *adj* inimaginable.
unimportant *adj* sin
  importancia.
uninformed *adj* ignorante.
uninhabitable *adj* inhabitable.
uninhabited *adj*
  despoblado(a), desierto(a).
uninjured *adj* ileso(a).
unintelligible *adj* ininteligible.
unintentional *adj* involuntario(a).
uninterested *adj* desinteresado(a).
uninteresting *adj* poco
  interesante.
uninvited *adj* sin invitación.
union *n* unión *f*, sindicato *m*.
unionist *n* unitario *m*.
unique *adj* único, singular.
unit *n* unidad *f*.
unite *vt* (*vi*) unir(se), juntarse.
United States (of America) *npl*
  Estados Unidos (de América) *mpl*.

unity *n* unidad *f*.
universal *adj* universal.
universe *n* universo *m*.
university *n* universidad *f*.
unjust *adj* injusto(a).
unkind *adj* poco amable.
unknown *adj* desconocido(a).
unlawful *adj* ilícito(a), ilegal.
unless *conj* a menos que, si no.
unload *vt* descargar.
unlucky *adj* desafortunado(a).
unmarried *adj* soltero(a).
unmerited *adj* desmerecido(a).
unmistakable *adj* inconfundible.
unmoved *adj* firme.
unnatural *adj* antinatural.
unnecessary *adj* inútil,
  innecesario(a).
unnoticed *adj* desapercibido(a).
unobserved *adj* inadertido(a).
unobtainable *adj* inasequible.
unobtrusive *adj* discreto(a).
unoccupied *adj* desocupado(a).
unofficial *adj* no oficial.
unpack *vt* desempacar;
  desenvolver.
unpaid *adj* sin pagar, impagado(a).
unpleasant *adj* desagradable.
unpopular *adj* poco popular.
unpractised *adj* inexperto(a).
unprecedented *adj* sin
  precedentes.
unpredictable *adj* imprevisible.
unprepared *adj* improvisado.
unprofitable *adj* poco
  lucrativo(a), poco provechoso.
unpunished *adj* impune.
unqualified *adj* sin títulos;
  incondicional.
unquestionable *adj* indudable.
unravel *vt* desenredar.
unrealistic *adj* poco realista.
unreasonable *adv*
  irracionalmente.
unrelated *adj* sin relacion;
  inconexo(a).
unrelenting *adj* implacable.

unreliable *adj* poco fiable.
unrestrained *adj*
  desenfrenado(a); ilimitado(a).
unripe *adj* inmaduro(a).
unrivaled *adj* sin rival.
unroll *vt* desenrollar.
unsafe *adj* inseguro(a).
unsatisfactory *adj*
  insatisfactorio(a).
unscrew *vt* destornillar.
unscrupulous *adj* sin escrúpulos.
unseemly *adj* indecente.
unseen *adj* oculto(a).
unselfish *adj* desinteresado(a).
unsettle *vt* perturbar.
unshaken *adj* increbantable,
  estable.
unskilled *adj* no cualificado(a).
unsociable *adj* insociable.
unspeakable *adj* indecible,
  incalificable.
unstable *adj* instable, inconstante.
unsteady *adj* inestable.
unsuccessful *adj* sin éxito,
  desafortunado.
unsuitable *adj* inapropiado(a);
  inoportuno(a), inconveniente.
unsure *adj* inseguro(a).
unsympathetic *adj* poco
  comprensivo(a).
untapped *adj* sin explotar.
untenable *adj* insostenible.
unthinkable *adj* inconcebible.
unthinking *adj* irreflexivo(a).
untidiness *n* desaliño *m*,
  desorden *m*.
untidy *adj* desordenado(a);
  desaliñado(a).
untie *vt* desatar, deshacer, soltar.
until *prep* hasta; * *conj* hasta que.
untimely *adj* inoportuno(a).
untiring *adj* incansable.
untold *adj* nunca dicho;
  indecible; incalculable.
untouched *adj* intacto(a).
untoward *adj* impropio(a);
  adverso(a).

untried *adj* no probado(a).
untroubled *adj* no
  perturbado(a), tranquilo(a).
untrue *adj* falso(a).
untrustworthy *adj* poco fiable.
untruth *n* falsedad *f*, mentira *f*.
unused *adj* sin usar, nuevo(a).
unusual *adj* inusitado(a), raro(a);
  * ~ly *adv* inusitadamente,
  raramente.
unveil *vt* quitar el velo, descubrir.
unwavering *adj* inquebrantable.
unwelcome *adj* molesto(a),
  inoportuno(a).
unwell *adj* indispuesto(a).
unwieldy *adj* difícil de manejar.
unwilling *adj* poco dispuesto(a)
  a hacer algo; * ~ly *adv* de
  mala gana.
unwillingness *n* mala gana *f*,
  repugnancia *f*.
unwind *vt* desenvolver;
  * *vi* relajarse.
unwise *adj* imprudente.
unwitting *adj* inconsciente.
unworkable *adj* impracticable.
unworthy *adj* indigno(a).
unwrap *vt* desenvolver.
unwritten *adj* no escrito(a).
up *adv* arriba, en lo alto;
  levantado(a); * *prep* hacia; hasta.
upbringing *n* educación *f*.
update *vt* poner al día.
upheaval *n* agitación *f*.
uphill *adj* difícil, penoso;
  * *adv* cuesta arriba.
uphold *vt* sostener, apoyar.
upholstery *n* tapicería *f*.
upkeep *n* manteninimiento *m*.
uplift *vt* levantar.
upon *prep* sobre, encima.
upper *adj* superior; más elevado.
upper-class *adj* de la clase alta.
upper-hand *n* (*fig*) superioridad *f*.
uppermost *adj* más alto,
  supremo(a): — to be ~
  predominar.

upright *adj* derecho(a),
  vertical; honrado(a).
uprising *n* sublevación *f*.
uproar *n* tumulto *m*, alboroto *m*.
uproot *vt* desarraigar.
upset *vt* trastornar; derramar,
  volcar; * *n* revés *m*; trastorno *m*;
  * *adj* molesto(a); preocupado(a).
upshot *n* resultado *m*.
upside-down *adv* de arriba abajo.
upstairs *adv* arriba.
upstart *n* advenedizo(a) *m(f)*.
uptight *adj* nervioso(a).
up-to-date *adj* al día.
upturn *n* mejora *f*.
upward *adj* ascendente;
  * ~s *adv* hacia arriba.
urban *adj* urbano(a).
urbane *adj* cortés.
urchin *n* golfillo(a) *m(f)*.
urge *vt* animar; * *n* impulso *m*;
  deseo *m*.
urgency *n* urgencia *f*.
urgent *adj* urgente.
urinal *n* orinal *m*.
urinate *vi* orinar.
urine *n* orina *f*.
urn *n* urna *f*.
us *pron* nos; nosotros.
usage *n* tratamiento *m*; uso *m*.
use *n* uso *m*; utilidad, práctica
  f; * *vi* usar, emplear.
used *adj* usado(a).
useful *adj*; * (~ly *adv*) útil(mente).
usefulness *n* utilidad *f*.
useless *adj*; * (~ly *adv*)
  inútil(mente).
uselessness *n* inutilidad *f*.
user-friendly *adj* fácil de utilizar.
usher *n* ujier *m*; acomodador *m*.
usherette *n* acomodadora *f*.
usual *adj* usual, común, normal;
  * ~ly *adv* normalmente.
usurer *n* usurero *m*.
usurp *vt* usurpar.
usury *n* usura *f*.
utensil *n* utensilio *m*.

uterus *n* útero *m*.
utility *n* utilidad *f*.
utilise *vt* utilizar.
utmost *adj* mayor, sumo(a);
  último(a).
utter *adj* total; todo(a);
  entero(a); * *vt* proferir;
  expresar; publicar.
utterance *n* expresión *f*,
  declaración *f*.
utterly *adv* completamente,
  totalmente.

V

vacancy *n* cuarto libre *m*;
  vacante *f*.
vacant *adj* vacío(a);
  desocupado(a).
vacate *vt* desocupar.
vacation *n* vacaciones *fpl*.
vaccinate *vt* vacunar.
vaccination *n* vacunación *f*.
vaccine *n* vacuna *f*.
vacuous *adj* necio(a).
vacuum *n* vacío *m*.
vagina *n* vagina *f*.
vagrant *n* vagabundo(a) *m(f)*.
vague *adj* vago(a).
vain *adj* vano(a).
valet *n* criado *m*.
valiant *adj* valiente.
valid *adj* ayuda de cámara.
valley *n* valle *m*.
valour *n* valor *m*.
valuable *adj* valioso(a).
valuation *n* tasa *f*, tasación *f*.
value *n* valor.
valued *adj* apreciado(a).
valve *n* válvula *f*.
vampire *n* vampiro *m*.
van *n* camioneta *f*.
vandal *n* gamberro(a) *m(f)*.
vandalism *n* vandalismo *m*.
vandalise *vi* destrozar, destruir.
vanguard *n* vanguardia *f*.

vanilla *n* vainilla *f*.
vanish *vi* desaparecer, esfumarse.
vanity *n* vanidad *f*.
vanquish *vt* vencer.
vantage point *n* posición
  ventajosa *f*.
vapour *n* vapor *m*.
variable *adj* variable.
variance *n* discordia *f*.
variation *n* variación *f*.
varicose vein *n* varices *fpl*.
varied *adj* variado(a).
variety *n* variedad *f*.
varios *adj* vario(a)s.
varnish *n* barniz *m*, esmalte *m*.
vary *vt, vi* variar.
vase *n* florero *m*.
vast *adj* vasto(a).
vat *n* tina *f*.
vault *n* bóveda *f*.
veal *n* ternera *f*.
veer *vi* (marine) virar.
vegetable *adj* vegetal; * ~s *npl*
  legumbres *fpl*.
vegetable garden *n* huerta *f*.
vegetarian *n* vegetariano(a) *m(f)*.
vegetate *vi* vegetar.
vegetation *n* vegetación *f*.
vehemence *n* vehemencia *f*.
vehement *adj* vehemente.
vehicle *n* vehículo *m*.
veil *n* velo *m*.
vein *n* vena *f*.
velocity *n* velocidad *f*.
velvet *n* terciopelo *m*.
vendor *n* vendedor(a) *m(f)*.
veneer *n* chapa *f*.
venerable *adj* venerable.
venerate *vt* venerar.
veneration *n* veneración *f*.
venereal *adj* venéreo(a).
vengeance *n* venganza *f*.
venial *adj* venial.
venison *n* (carne de) venado *f*.
venom *n* veneno *m*.
venomous *adj* venenoso(a).
vent *n* respiradero *m*; obertura *f*.

ventilate *vt* ventilar.
ventilation *n* ventilación *f*.
ventilator *n* ventilador *m*.
ventriloquist *n* ventrílocuo(a) *m(f)*.
venture *n* empresa *f*;
  * *vi* aventurarse.
venue *n* lugar de reunión *m*.
veranda *n* terraza *f*.
verb *n* verbo *m*.
verbal *adj* verbal.
verdict *n* (law) veredicto *m*.
verification *n* verificación *f*.
verify *vt* verificar.
veritable *adj* verdadero.
vermin *n* bichos *mpl*.
vermouth *n* vermut *m*.
versatile *adj* versátil.
verse *n* verso *m*.
versed *adj* versado.
version *n* versión *f*.
versus *prep* contra.
vertebra *(pl vertebrae) n*
  vértebra *f*.
vertebral *adj* vertebral.
vertical *adj*; * (~ly *adv*)
  vertical(mente).
vertigo *n* vértigo *m*.
very *adj, adv* muy, mucho.
vessel *n* vasija *f*.
vest *n* chaleco *m*.
vestibule *n* vestíbulo *m*.
vestige *n* vestigio *m*.
vestry *n* sacristía *f*.
veteran *adj, n* veterano(a) *m(f)*.
veterinary *adj* veterinario(a).
veto *n* veto *m*.
vex *vt* fastidiar.
via *prep* por.
viaduct *n* viaducto *m*.
vial *n* frasco pequeño *m*, vial *m*.
vibrate *vi* vibrar.
vibration *n* vibración *f*.
vicarious *adj* indirecto(a).
vice *n* vicio *m*.
vice versa *adv* viceversa.
vicinity *n* vecindad *f*.
vicious *adj* vicioso(a).

victim *n* víctima *f*.
victimise *vt* tomar represalias contra.
victor *n* vencedor(a) *m(f)*.
victorious *adj* victorioso(a).
victory *n* victoria *f*.
video *n* vídeo *m*.
videotape *n* cinta de vídeo *f*.
vie *vi* competir.
view *n* vista *f*.
viewpoint *n* punto de vista *m*.
vigilance *n* vigilancia *f*.
vigilant *adj* vigilante.
vigorous *adj* vigoroso(a).
vigour *n* vigor *m*.
vile *adj* vil.
vilify *vt* envilecer, denigrar.
villa *n* chalet *m*, casa de campo *f*.
village *n* aldea *f*.
villain *n* malvado(a) *m(f)*.
vindicate *vt* vindicar, justificar.
vindication *n* vindicación *f*.
vindictive *adj* vengativo(a).
vine *n* vid *f*.
vinegar *n* vinagre *m*.
vineyard *n* viña *f*.
vintage *n* vendimia *f*, cosecha *f*.
vinyl *n* vinilo *m*.
viola *n* (music) viola *f*.
violate *vt* violar.
violation *n* violación *f*.
violence *n* violencia *f*.
violent *adj* violento(a).
violet *n* (botany) violeta *f*.
violin *n* (music) violín *m*.
viper *n* víbora *f*.
virgin *n* virgen *f*.
virginity *n* virginidad *f*.
Virgo *n* virgo *f*. (astrology).
virile *adj* viril.
virility *n* virilidad *f*.
virtual *adj* * (~ly *adv*) virtual(mente).
virtue *n* virtud *f*.
virtuous *adj* virtuoso(a).
virulent *adj* virulento(a).
virus *n* virus *m*.

visa *n* visado *m*, visa *f*.
vis-à-vis *prep* con respecto a.
visibility *n* visibilidad *f*.
visible *adj* visible.
vision *n* vista *f*, visión *f*.
visit *vt* visitar; * *n* visita *f*.
visitor *n* visitante *m* or *f*.
visor *n* visera *f*.
vista *n* vista *f*, perspectiva *f*.
visual *adj* visual.
visualise *vt* imaginarse.
vital *adj* vital.
vitality *n* vitalidad *f*.
vitamin *n* vitamina *f*.
vitiate *vt* viciar.
vivacious *adj* vivaz.
vivid *adj* vivo(a), intenso(a).
vivisection *n* vivisección *f*.
vocabulary *n* vocabulario *m*.
vocal *adj* vocal.
vocation *n* vocación *f*.
vociferous *adj* vociferante.
vodka *n* vodka *m*.
vogue *n* moda *f*, boga *f*.
voice *n* voz *f*; * *vt* expresar.
void *adj* nulo; * *n* vacío *m*.
volatile *adj* volatil; voluble.
volcanic *adj* volcánico(a).
volcano *n* volcán *m*.
volition *n* voluntad *f*.
volley *n* descarga *f*, lluvia *f*, rociada *f*, volea *f*.
volleyball *n* voleibol *m*.
volt *n* voltio *m*.
voltage *n* voltaje *m*.
voluble *adj* locuaz.
volume *n* volumen *m*.
voluntarily *adv* voluntariamente.
voluntary *adj* voluntario(a).
volunteer *n* voluntario(a) *m(f)*.
voluptuous *adj* voluptuoso(a).
vomit *vt*, *vi* vomitar.
vortex *n* remolino *m*.
vote *n* voto *m*.
voter *n* votante *m* or *f*.
voting *n* votación *f*.
voucher *n* vale *m*.

vow *n* voto *m*.
vowel *n* vocal *f*.
voyage *n* viaje *m*.
vulgar *adj* ordinario(a), vulgar.
vulgarity *n* grosería *f*.
vulnerable *adj* vulnerable.
vulture *n* buitre *m*.

W

wad *n* fajo *m*.
waddle *vi* andar como un pato.
wade *vi* vadear.
wafer *n* barquillo *m*, oblea *f*, hostia *f*.
waffle *n* gofre *m*.
wag *vt* menear.
wage *n* salario *m*, sueldo *m*.
waggon *n* carro *m*.
wail *n* lamento *m*, gemido *m*; * *vi* gemir.
waist *n* cintura *f*.
wait *vi* esperar.
waiter *n* camarero *m*.
waiting list *n* lista de espera *f*.
waiting room *n* sala de espera *f*.
waive *vt* suspender.
wake *vi* despertarse.
waken *vt*, (*vi*) despertar(se).
walk *vt*, *vi* pasear; andar.
walking stick *n* bastón *m*.
wall *n* pared *f*, muralla *f*, muro *m*.
wallet *n* cartera *f*.
wallflower *n* alhelí *m*.
wallpaper *n* papel pintado *m*.
walnut *n* (botany) nogal *m*; nuez *f*.
walrus *n* morsa *f*.
waltz *n* vals *m* (baile).
wan *adj* pálido(a).
wand *n* varita mágica *f*.
wane *vi* menguar.
want *vt* querer.
wanton *adj* lascivo(a).
war *n* guerra *f*.
ward *n* sala *f*.
wardrobe *n* guardarropa *f*,

armario *m*.
warehouse *n* almacén *m*, depósito *m*.
warm *adj* cálido(a); caliente.
warm-hearted *adj* afectuoso(a).
warmth *n* calor *m*.
warn *vt* avisar.
warning *n* aviso *m*.
warp *vi* combarse.
warrant *n* orden judicial *f*.
warranty *n* garantía *f*.
warren *n* madriguera *m*; laberinto *m*.
warrior *n* guerrero(a) *m(f)*.
wart *n* verruga *f*.
wary *adj* cauto(a), cauteloso(a).
wash *vt* lavar.
washbowl *n* lavabo *m*.
washing machine *n* lavadora *f*.
washing-up *n* fregado *m*.
wasp *n* avispa *f*.
waste *vi* malgastar.
watch *n* reloj *m*; vigilar.
watchdog *n* perro guardián *m*.
water *n* agua *f*.
watercolor *n* acuarela *f*.
waterfall *n* cascada *f*.
watering-can *n* regadera *f*.
waterlily *n* (botany) nenúfar *m*.
water melon *n* sandía *f*.
watertight *adj* hermético(a).
watt *n* vatio *m*.
wave *n* ola *f*, onda *f*.
waver *vi* vacilar.
wax *n* cera *f*.
way *n* camino *m*; vía *f*.
we *pron* nosotros, nosotras.
weak *adj*; * (~ly *adv*) débil(mente).
wealth *n* riqueza *f*.
wealthy *adj* rico(a).
weapon *n* arma *f*.
wear *vt* gastar, consumir; usar, llevar.
weary *adj* cansado(a).
weasel *n* comadreja *f*.
weather *n* tiempo (atmosférico) *m*.
weave *vt* tejer; trenzar.

weaving *n* tejido *m*.

web *n* telaraña *f*; red *f*.

wed *vt* (*vi*) casar(se).

wedge *n* cuna *f*.

Wednesday *n* miércoles *m*.

wee *adj* pequeñito(a).

weed *n* mala hierba *f*.

week *n* semana *f*.

weekend *n* fin de semana *m*.

weekly *adj* semanal.

weep *vt*, *vi* llorar.

weeping willow *n* (botany) sauce llorón *m*.

weigh *vt*, *vi* pesar.

weight *n* peso *m*.

welcome *adj* bienvenido(a); * *excl* ~! ¡bienvenido!.

weld soldadura *f*; * *vt* soldar.

welfare *n* prosperidad *f*, bienestar *f*.

well *n* pozo *m*; * *adv* bien.

wench *n* mozuela *f*.

west *n* oeste, occidente *m*.

wet *adj* húmedo(a), mojado(a).

whale *n* ballena *f*.

wharf *n* muelle *m*.

what *pron* ¿qué?, el que, la que, lo que, el que.

whatever *pron* cualquier o cualquiera.

wheat *n* trigo *m*.

wheel *n* rueda *f*.

wheelbarrow *n* carretilla *f*.

wheelchair *n* silla de ruedas *f*.

wheeze *vi* resollar.

when *adv* cuando; * *conj* cuándo.

whenever *adv* cuando; cada vez que.

where *adv* dónde *conj* donde.

whether *conj* si.

which *pron* que; el que, la que, el cual; cual; * *adj* qué; cuál.

while *n* rato *m*; vez *f*; * *conj* durante; mientras; aunque.

whim *n* antojo *m*, capricho *m*.

whine *vi* gemir, zumbar.

whinny *vi* relinchar.

whip *n* azote *m*; látigo *m*;

* *vt* latigar.

whirlpool *n* remolino *m*.

whirlwind *n* torbellino *m*.

whiskey *n* whisky *m*.

whisper *vi* cuchichear.

whistle *vi* silbar.

white *adj* blanco.

who *pron* ¿quién?, que.

whoever *pron* quienquiera, cualquiera.

whole *adj* todo.

wholemeal *adj* integral.

wholly *adv* enteramente.

whom *pron* ¿quién? que.

whooping cough *n* tos ferina *f*.

whore *n* puta *f*.

why? *adv* ¿por qué?

wick *n* mecha *f*.

wicked *adj* malvado(a).

wide *adj* ancho(a).

widen *vt* ensanchar.

widow *n* viuda *f*.

widower *n* viudo *m*.

width *n* anchura *f*.

wield *vt* manejar.

wife *n* esposa *f*.

wig *n* peluca *f*.

wild *adj* silvestre.

wilderness *n* desierto *m*.

wildlife *n* fauna *f*.

will *n* voluntad *f*; * *verb aux* forming future tense.

willful *adj* deliberado(a); testarudo(a).

willow *n* (botany) sauce *m*.

willpower *n* fuerza de voluntad *f*.

wilt *vi* marchitarse.

wily *adj* astuto(a).

win *vt* ganar.

wince *vi* encogerse.

winch *n* torno *m*.

wind *n* viento *m*; * *vt* enrollar, envolver, dar cuerda.

windfall *n* golpe de suerte *m*.

winding *adj* tortuoso(a).

windmill *n* molino de viento *m*.

window *n* ventana *f*.

windowbox *n* jardinera de
  ventana *f.*
windowpane *n* cristal *m.*
windowsill *n* repisa *f.*
windpipe *n* tráquea *f.*
windscreen *n* parabrisas *m invar.*
windy *adj* de mucho viento.
wine *n* vino *m.*
wine cellar *n* bodega *f.*
wine glass *n* copa *f.*
wing *n* ala *f.*
winged *adj* alado(a).
wink *vi* guiñar.
winner *n* ganador(a) *m(f).*
winter *n* invierno *m.*
wintry *adj* invernal.
wipe *vt* limpiar.
wisdom *n* sabiduría *f.*
wisdom teeth *npl* muela del
  juicio *m.*
wise *adj* sabio(a).
wisecrack *n* broma *f.*
wish *vt* querer.
wishful *adj* deseoso(a).
wit *n* ingenio *m*, gracias *f.*
witch *n* bruja *f.*
witchcraft *n* brujería *f.*
with *prep* con; por, de, a.
withdraw *vt (vi)* retirar(se).
withdrawal *n* retirada *f.*
withdrawn *adj* reservado(a),
  introvertido(a).
withhold *vt* retener, aplazar.
within *prep* dentro de.
without *prep* sin.
withstand *vt* resistir.
witless *adj* necio(a).
witness *n* testigo *m* or *f.*
witticism *n* ocurrencia *f.*
wittily *adv* ingeniosamente.
witty *adj* ingenioso(a).
wizard *n* brujo *m.*
woe *n* desgracia *f.*
woeful *adj* lamentable,
  apesumbrado(a).
wolf *n* lobo *m.*
woman *n* mujer *f.*

womb *n* útero *m.*
wonder *n* milagro *m.*
wonderful *adj* maravilloso(a).
woo *vt* cortejar.
wood *n* bosque *m*; selva *f*,
  madera *f*, leña *f.*
woodland *n* bosque *m.*
woodlouse *n* cochinilla *f.*
woodpecker *n* pájaro carpintero *m.*
woodworm *n* carcorma *f.*
wool *n* lana *f.*
woollen *adj* de lana.
word *n* palabra *f.*
wordy *adj* verboso.
work *vi* trabajar; obrar.
world *n* mundo *m.*
worm *n* gusano *m.*
worn-out *adj* gastado(a).
worried *adj* preocupado(a).
worry *vi (vt)* preocupar(se).
worse *adj*, *adv* peor.
worship *n* cuto *m*; adoración *f.*
worst *adj* el (la) peor.
worth *n* valor *m.*
worthwhile *adj* que vale la
  pena; valioso(a).
worthy *adj* digno(a).
wound *n* herida *f.*
wrangle *n* riña *f*; * *vi* reñir.
wrap *vt* envolver.
wrath *n* ira *f*, cólera *f.*
wreath *n* corona *f.*
wreck *n* naufragio *m*; ruina *f.*
wreckage *n* restos *mpl.*
wren *n* reyezuelo *m.*
wrestle *vi* luchar; disputar.
wrestling *n* lucha *f.*
wretched *adj* infeliz, miserable.
wring *vt* torcer.
wrinkle *n* arruga *f.*
wrist *n* muñeca *f.*
wristband *n* puño de camisa *m.*
wristwatch *n* reloj de pulsera *m.*
writ *n* mandato oficial *m.*
write *vt* escribir.
write-off *vt* borrar, desechar *f.*
writer *n* escritor(a), *m(f)*;

autor(a) *m(f)*.
writhe *vi* retorcerse.
writing *n* escritura *f*.
writing desk *n* escritorio *m*.
writing paper *n* papel para
  escribir *m*.
wrong *n* malo *m*, injusto *m*;
  injusticia *f*.
wrongful *adj* injusto(a).
wrongly *adv* injustamente.
wry *adj* irónico(a).

X

Xmas *n* Navidad *f*.
X-ray *n* radiografía *f*.
xylophone *n* xilófono *m*.

Y

yacht *n* yate *m*.
yachting *n* balandrismo *m*.
Yankee *n* yanqui *m*.
yard *n* corral *m*; yarda *f*.
yardstick *n* criterio *m*.
yarn cuento chino *m*; hilo de lino *m*.
yawn *vi* bostezar.
year *n* año *m*.
yearling *n* potro de un año *m*.
yearly *adj* anual.
yearn *vi* añorar.
yearning *n* añoranza *f*.
yeast *n* levadura *f*.
yell *vi* aullar.
yellow *adj* amarillo(a).
yelp *vi* aullar.
yes *adv*, *n* sí *m*.
yesterday *adv*, *n* ayer *m*.
yet *conj* sin embargo; pero;
  * *adv* todavía.
yew *n* (botany) tejo *m*.
yield *vt* dar, producir.
yoga *n* yoga *m*.
yoghurt *n* yogur *m*.
yoke *n* yugo *m*.

yolk *n* yema de huevo *f*.
yonder *adv* allá.
you *pron* vosotros, tú, usted,
  ustedes.
young *adj* joven.
youngster *n* jovencito(a) *m(f)*.
your(s) *pron* tuyo, vuestro,
  suyo: **~s sincerely** su seguro
  servidor.
yourself *pron* tú mismo, usted
  mismo, vosotros mismos,
  ustedes mismos.
youth *n* juventud *f*.
youthful *adj* juvenil.
youthfulness *n* juventud *f*.
yuppie *adj*, *n* yuppie *m* or *f*.

Z

zany *adj* estrafalario(a).
zap *vt* borrar.
zeal *n* celo *m*; entusiasmo *m*.
zealous *adj* celoso(a).
zebra *n* cebra *f*.
zenith *n* cenit *m*.
zero *n* zero, cero *m*.
zest *n* ánimo *m*, entusiasmo *m*.
zigzag *n* zigzag *m*.
zinc *n* zinc *m*.
zip *n* cremallera *f*.
zodiac *n* zodíaco *m*.
zone *n* banda, faja *f*, zona *f*.
zoo *n* zoo *m*.
zoological *adj* zoológico.
zoologist *n* zoólogo(a) *m(f)*.
zoology *n* zoología *f*.
zoom *vi* zumbar, enfocar.
zoom lens *n* zoom *m*.